Gender in Solomon's Song of Songs

Australian College of Theology Monograph Series

SERIES EDITOR GRAEME R. CHATFIELD

The ACT Monograph Series, generously supported by the Board of Directors of the Australian College of Theology, provides a forum for publishing quality research theses and studies by its graduates and affiliated college staff in the broad fields of Biblical Studies, Christian Thought and History, and Practical Theology with Wipf and Stock Publishers of Eugene, Oregon. The ACT selects the best of its doctoral and research masters theses as well as monographs that offer the academic community, scholars, church leaders and the wider community uniquely Australian and New Zealand perspectives on significant research topics and topics of current debate. The ACT also provides opportunity for contributors beyond its graduates and affiliated college staff to publish monographs which support the mission and values of the ACT.

Rev Dr Graeme Chatfield
Series Editor and Associate Dean

Gender in Solomon's Song of Songs

Discourse Analytical Abduction
to a Gynocentric Hypothesis

ALASTAIR IAN HAINES

WIPF & STOCK · Eugene, Oregon

GENDER IN SOLOMON'S SONG OF SONGS
Discourse Analytical Abduction to a Gynocentric Hypothesis

Copyright © 2016 Alastair Ian Haines. All rights reserved. Except for brief quotations in critical publications or reviews, no part of this book may be reproduced in any manner without prior written permission from the publisher. Write: Permissions, Wipf and Stock Publishers, 199 W. 8th Ave., Suite 3, Eugene, OR 97401.

Wipf & Stock
An Imprint of Wipf and Stock Publishers
199 W. 8th Ave., Suite 3
Eugene, OR 97401

www.wipfandstock.com

PAPERBACK ISBN: 978-1-4982-8845-3
HARDCOVER ISBN: 978-1-5326-0900-8
EBOOK ISBN: 978-1-4982-8872-9

Manufactured in the U.S.A.

For Flora Green
and
David Scarratt

Contents

Preface | ix
Recitative | xii

1   Introduction | 3
     §1 Allegorical or Literal? · 3
     §2 Anthology or Unity? · 10
     §3 John Callow · 14
     §4 Daphna Arbel · 20
     §5 David Clines · 24
     §6 Linguistics and Philosophy · 30
     §7 Literature and Analogy · 34

2   Literature Review | 42
     §1 Global Context · 42
     §2 Canticles Commentary · 54
     §3 Aside: The Gynocentric Hypothesis and the History of Interpretation · 70
     §4 Schematic View of Recent Scholarship · 81

3   Phillip Roberts | 90
     §1 Form and Content · 90
     §2 Cohesion and Coherence · 98
     §3 From Methodology to Conclusion · 104

4   Methodology | 118
     §1 Discourse Analysis · 118
     §2 Segmented Discourse Representation Theory · 121
     §3 Rhetorical (or Discourse) Relations · 124
     §4 Abduction · 131
     §5 Gynocentric Hypothesis · 132

5   Preludes (Song 1:2—2:7) | 134
    §1 Rightly Do the Maidens Love You (1:2–4) · 137
    §2 SDRT Analysis · 143
    §3 Remembering the Big Picture · 148
    §4 Notational Conventions · 149
    §5 Joining the Dots · 152

6   Spring (Song 2:8–17) | 156
    §1 Dramatic Narrative · 159
    §2 Excursus: Gender Archetypes · 161
    §3 Cohesion and Coherence · 167

7   Dream (Song 3:1–5) | 173

8   Bathsheba (Song 3:6–11) | 179

9   The First *Waṣf* (Song 4:1–7) | 191

10 Consummation (Song 4:8—5:1) | 200

11 Nightmare (Song 5:2-6:3) | 209

12 The Man's Second *Waṣf* (Song 6:4–10) | 217

13 Obscurities (Song 6:11–12) | 226

14 The Man's Third *Waṣf* (Song 7:1–11) | 230

15 Pivot Piece (Song 7:12—8:4) | 239

16 Love (Song 8:5–7) | 248

17 Postscript (Song 8:8–14) | 256

18 *Da Capo al Fine* | 266

19 Support: André LaCocque, Daniel Grossberg, and George Schwab | 272

20 Conclusion: Gender in Solomon's Song of Songs | 280

Bibliography | 285

Preface

BEFORE BEING REFINED INTO research questions for my doctoral dissertation, my curiosity about the Song of Songs broadly touched on two main issues. The first, its canonicity: Can a strong case be made for the canonicity of the Song, derived from the internal evidence of the text itself?

The second issue is that of apparent asymmetries between male and female voices in the text, for while there are similarities in what things each praises in the other, there are also striking differences: she praises his character as well as his appearance, but he seems stuck at only praising her appearance.

So, is there something clearly definitive and ultimate about the Song's treatment of romantic love that inclines a sympathetic reader to think, "That's profound! That's unique! That's inspired!"? Indeed, is there something about the asymmetries between male and female voices that captures the subtleties of the different roles played by men and women in courtship? Even if the Song is not unique in its insights here, does it speak within human traditions of love literature such that it intimates something that is trustworthy, beautiful, and true?

The dissertation is naturally limited in its scope by its research questions, and by requiring a specific methodology to address those questions. After wide consultation with biblical commentators and discourse linguists in the available literature, by way of methodology, I settled on wedding the purely Hebrew and linguistic work of Phillip Roberts (2007) with the Segmented Discourse Representation Theory (SDRT) of Asher and Lascerides (2003). This led to a range of conclusions that are inferences, argued in the dissertation to be pragmatically preferred interpretations of the text due to rhetorical relations between the distinctly marked poetic units of the Song. As such they arise by abduction, the best explanation of the data the text of the Song provides. Abduction is one of the three types of formal logical argument: deduction, induction, and abduction. I use the term to underline that the thesis methodology uses discourse linguistics as a science, as well as an art.

The dissertation concludes that the Song of Songs is a carefully constructed homily, strongly marked as delivered in a woman's voice. The Song contains a logically prior exhortation to men—to lifelong commitment in exclusive intimate relationships—but its major exhortation is to women: to master their own inclinations until their intimate initiatives can also be evidence-based responses. Evidence for this includes that these key lines of the Song are given in prose, and that the second exhortation is repeated three times (2:7; 3:5; 8:4). It also includes the interpretative readings: (a) that the woman turns her internal soliloquy towards (male) readers in 1:4; and (b) that the poet (in disguise) briefs his *prima donna* in 8:13.

Broader observations in the dissertation include the following. Intimate relationships are presented as inherently problematic, but worth far more than the cost. The Song presents a structured logical argument, rather than a narrative morality play. It is fictive, not historical, in its typology, and psychological, not behavioural, in its concerns. It presents an idealization of an affective psychology underlying the relations between the sexes—especially within what we would call marriage, but what the Song studiously avoids naming as anything but love and friendship. It eschews law and historical precedent to address intuition and conscience directly. It reasons without rules. Its oath, the so-called "abjuration refrain," is meaningful but playful. It portrays authentic pictures of male and female sexual appetites, recognizable in their psycho-physiology rather than their mechanical physiology, and naked of formal designations of personal status (like never married, separated, or divorced).

So much for an overview of the issues addressed in the body of the dissertation. To conclude these prefatory words, I would like to thank my supervisor, John Davies, whose long patience and encouragement was most instrumental in bringing the text of the dissertation to fruition, though there are other staff from Christ College who have also been of assistance. Likewise, Mark Harding and Graeme Chatfield have been strategic supporters of the work involved in research, in many ways and through various initiatives taken by the Australian College of Theology and implemented by the staff team. My markers—Dianne Bergant, David Cohen, and Tremper Longman—provided constructive criticism that has been included in the final version of the dissertation text. Megan du Toit has been efficient in negotiating preparation of the manuscript for publication with the Australian College of Theology monograph series, and Gina Denholm has done an outstanding job of copyediting the whole manuscript, making it ready for the publishers and a smoother experience for readers. Last, but hardly least, my family, especially my wife, her parents, and my mother, have shown tireless support towards a goal they must have sometimes despaired of ever seeing reached.

Recitative

Dich will ich auf mein Herz, auf mei- nen Arm gleich

wie ein Sie- gel set- zen, ...

auf mei- ner Lin- ken sollst du ruh'n, und mei- ne

Rech- te soll dich küs- sen.

Johann Sebastian Bach, *Wachet auf, ruft uns die Stimme!*
Bach-Werke-Verzeichnis (BWV) 140: no. 5, Dichter unbekannt.
Thomaskirche, Leipzig: 25 November, 1731.

כי שנא שלח אמר יהוה אלהי ישראל
—Malachi 2:16

ἐγὼ δὲ λέγω εἰς Χριστὸν καὶ εἰς τὴν ἐκκλησίαν
—Ephesians 5:32

Gender in Solomon's Song of Songs

discourse analytical abduction to a gynocentric hypothesis

שׂימני כחותם על־לבך	כחותם על־זרועך
כי־עזה כמות אהבה	קשה כשאול קנאה
רשפיה רשפי אש	שלהבתיה:

Stamp me like a seal on your heart	like a seal around your biceps
for love is strong like death	jealousy stubborn like Sheol
her arrows flaming arrows	the very flame of Yahweh.

I

Introduction

§1 Allegorical or Literal?

"If the *hapax legomenon šalhebetyâ* in 8:6 refers to the 'flame of Yah'—*yah* being a shortened form of the divine name—that no more makes Israel's god the subject of the poem than 'strong as death [*māwet*]' or 'flames [*rešep*] of fire' makes the Canaanite gods Mot or Resheph its subjects." — Cheryl Exum[1]

THE TRADITIONAL, ALLEGORICAL INTERPRETATION of the Song of Songs is well known.[2] Despite variations in details of how the allegory is seen to work, traditional readings were united by offering broadly the same answer to the most significant question that can be posed regarding the Song:[3] what impact is it supposed to have on those who hear it?[4] Commentators across almost two millennia of documented reflection on the Song have considered its import to lie in stimulating its audience's appreciation of a Creator's

---

1. Exum, *Song of Songs*, 64.

2. "Interpretations of the Song of Songs fall first of all into either allegorical or literal mode." Pope, *Song of Songs*, 89.

3. "It was the unanimous answer of Jewish and Christian premodern exegesis." Jenson, *Song of Songs*, 5.

4. So at least David Clines: "The question of effects on readers,... it is about time we regarded such study as part of our scholarly discipline and task." "Why is there a Song of Songs," 3–27.. And "It is the primary task of the Old Testament exegete to expound the sense intended by the author." Clines, "Image Of God," 62.

love for his particular redeemed people:[5] Israel, or Israel proleptic of its perfection in the church. What more noble theme could the Song address? What else could be its subject?

We will return to the earlier history of interpretation at a later point in this study, because of its value in establishing the ease with which traditional characterizations of femininity were found within the Song,[6] and the similar ease with which these were seen to be analogous to aspects of the relationship of creatures to their Creator.[7] However, this study—in line with much writing on the Song over the last century or so—is skeptical of any directly theological motivation for its poetic vision.[8] To borrow from the terminology of pragmatics, a case will be made that the *topic* of the Song is not God but man;[9] indeed, not merely man but woman.

This is the "gynocentric hypothesis."[10] It is not a new proposal,[11] nor yet is it out of fashion. For example, in an essay contributed for *Biblical Hebrew and Discourse Linguistics*, John Callow asserts: "The Prologue makes it clear from the start that this Song is written from the perspective of the woman, not that of the man."[12] In addition to being written *from* the woman's perspective, this study will argue that it is precisely her perspective that is the deliberate *focus* of the Song.[13] This too is not a new proposal, though what is concluded from it, say by Ginsburg or by Clines, differs markedly.

---

5. "Theologians prevailed: for twenty centuries, the Song was almost universally read as a religious or historical allegory." Bloch and Bloch, *Song of Songs*, 30.

6. E.g., Origen's "perfecta sponsa" (in Rufinus's Latin translation).

7. E.g., ". . . her humility and loveliness, and his majesty and beauty. The believer is as . . .;—Jesus is as . . ." Burrowes, *Song of Solomon*, 110.

8. "Literal modes of interpretation . . . have . . . gained wide acceptance in the last century." Pope, *Song of Songs*, 90.

9. The traditional English-language *man–God* opposition is used here to anticipate the quote from Alexander Pope.

10. Marvin Pope's terminology in summarizing views attributed to the Women's Liberation Movement: "The modern Movement has had little use for the Bible except as a provocation for protest, to be indicted as the primary document of patriarchalism. The *androcentric* Creation myth of Genesis 2–3 has been understood . . . " [emphasis added]. Pope, *Song of Songs*, 205.

11. "Let it not be said, then, that a Book which celebrates the ascendency of a virtuous woman in humble life over all the blandishments of wealth and royalty, is unworthy of a place in Holy Writ." Ginsburg, *Song of Songs*, 19.

12. Callow, 'Units and Flow," 479. For the same conclusion from different evidence see Rabin, "Song of Songs," 205–19.

13. "One way to approach the multi-level complexity of this work is to read the whole text as a woman's inner and personal discourse." Arbel, "My Vineyard," 90.

The methodology of this study, like Callow's, employs standard discourse linguistic techniques to analyze the text of the Song of Songs. In particular, it follows more recent work, like Nicholas Lunn's application of information theory to biblical Hebrew poetry. In the fifth of Lunn's suggestions for further study—dating poetic passages and "ascribing a certain style to individual authors"—the Song gets special mention because it "has only a single instance of a defamiliar verbal clause."[14] Perhaps such further study will assist with as-yet-unresolved questions regarding the provenance of the Song: is its linguistic distinctiveness evidence of the idiosyncrasies of a specific author, era, or dialect?[15] Those rather exacting questions are not, however, central to this study.

The methodology adopted is ultimately aimed at discovering objective evidence, in the received text of the Song, of a range of discourse features which, when taken together, suggest a specific most plausible explanation for the surface form of its language. As such, they contribute to an abductive—in Pierce's sense,[16] as opposed to being deductive or inductive—argument to an authorial intention to winningly present a distinctively feminine perspective on romantic intimacy.

This brings us back to the most significant question that can be posed regarding the Song: what impact is it supposed to have on those who hear it? Alexander Pope might sympathize with the answers that will be offered in what follows.

> Know then thyself, presume not God to scan,
>
> The proper study of mankind is Man.[17]

Indeed, Pope himself published *Characters of Women* (1735) only three years after the heroic couplet above. Whether or not Pope, or even the Song, can be accepted as authorities on the character of women, this study naturally abstains from attempting to be such a thing. The Song, though, does appear to presume to instruct the daughters of Jerusalem, at least in how to behave in matters of the heart—do not precipitate love! Quite plausibly, if we take the Shulamite's man as any generic masculine lover, she also

---

14. Lunn, *Word-Order Variation*, 279.

15. See Vern, *Relevance*, for dialectic variation as an alternative explanation of linguistic variation; and Noegel and Rendsburg, *Solomon's Vineyard*, for an argument to the Song attesting a *circa* 900 BC northern dialect.

16. Charles Sanders Pierce. See Paavola, "Abduction through Grammar," 245–70; and Givón, *Context*, 206–8.

17. Alexander Pope, "The Design," *Essay on Man*, Epistle 2:1. "Principles, maxims, or precepts, so written [in poetry], both strike the reader more strongly at first, and are more easily retained by him afterward."

presumes to instruct men—seal your heart! If such readings are correct, the Song explicitly, if a little enigmatically, offers romantic advice addressed *both* to women and to men,[18] as women and men, in distinction to one another.[19] The Song sings of gender and sexuality.[20] Nonetheless, whatever the Song may or may not be urging on men or women, this study presents linguistic evidence suggesting that whatever it says, it says on the basis of how a *woman* feels.

Whether the Song's advice is sound is another matter that goes beyond the scope of this study, as is the question of whether or not the Song is even accurate in its portrayal of "a woman in love."[21] Rather, the study simply proceeds on the assumption that there is a prima facie case that the surface form of much love poetry can be sufficiently explained by authorial intention to represent or elucidate personal and gender-specific romantic sentiments. For example, it will be argued that the Song explores the same emotions as those featured in romantic pop songs, just with a more fulsome explanation than their brief lyrics permit. Yet the emotions in the Song will still be seen to be more straightforward than, say, those explored by Sylvia Plath's poem in three "decades," *Daddy*, which attempted (and perhaps failed) to resolve a suicidal love–hate Electra complex.

Plath herself told us her poem was an "allegory" and about "a girl with an Electra complex. Her father died while she thought he was God." Plath's word-associations extrapolate from childhood memories, painted in black and white (and red), phonetically unified by assonance on /u:/, and playing with I–thou pronouns in two tongues ("you" and *du* and "do").

In the Song, the Shulamite's brothers and the abusive watchmen are treated strikingly less scathingly than Plath's father, Otto, is in her recollections; but the two works are alike in that the first person pronoun is not only indicative of a specifically *feminine perspective*,[22] it is also suggestive that it is the *evolution in this perspective*, over the course of each poem, that

---

18. "For [the Song] to be wisdom teaching ... It must contain insights beneficial for right living, insights that will enhance human life." Bergant, *Song of Songs*, 5.

19. "A feminist interpretation might investigate how the Song makes different claims upon female and male readers." Exum, *Song of Songs*, 82.

20. "The Song ... provides the chief biblical resource for a believing understanding of human sexuality, of the lived meaning of 'Male and female he created them.'" Jenson, *Song of Songs*, 14.

21. Segal, *Songs of Songs: A Woman in Love*.

22. As will be treated in detail later, the first person pronoun in the Song, excepting a few vocative suffixes, almost uniformly marks reactivation of a specific and feminine discourse participant—the Shulamite. The few exceptions are themselves significant in establishing the Song's stereotypical conception of gender-roles.

is intended to elicit the reader's response. This kind of analysis is well documented in the case of Plath, but is also found regarding the Song. To take a recent example, in *Flashes of fire: a literary analysis of the Song of Songs*, Elie Assis at first cautiously suggests "the possibility of an emotional and inner development in the psyche of the lovers and in the relationship between them."[23] After considerable, sober evaluation of the text, he does indeed conclude that precisely this kind of development provides the Song with a "beginning, middle and an end".[24]

Plath told us her allegory likened her father to God; she did not liken God to her father. Likewise, Song 8:6 explicitly likens the passionate jealousy of sexual love to the fire of Yahweh's zeal, not vice versa. In Richards's terminology,[25] the metaphors elevate their *referents*, without debasing their *vehicle*.[26]

It should be no surprise to find the name Yahweh (יהוה) in parallel with fire, as we do in the final colon of Song 8:6. In the context of the Hebrew Bible, fire (אש) is a conventional metaphor for God's jealousy (e.g., Deut 4:24).

כי יהוה אלהיך אש אכלה הוא אל קנא
for Yahweh your God (אלהיך) is a devouring fire
he is a jealous god (אל)

But invocation of the divine name at this particular point of the Song is even less surprising given Exodus 34:14.

כי יהוה קנא שמו אל קנא הוא
for Yahweh's very name is "Jealousy"
a jealous god is he

The two cola, plausibly epexegetical of "sealing the heart," provide us with not only one lexical parallel conventionally associated with the divine name—that of fire—but also two lexical parallels that are typically associated with each other: fire and jealousy. Metaphors, particularly conventional metaphors, imperfectly map a limited number of invariant conceptions from one conceptual domain to another (as widely discussed regarding the proposed invariance principle of metaphor).[27] They cannot be presumed to be

23. Assis, *Flashes of Fire* 25.
24. Ibid., 266.
25. Richards, *Philosophy of Rhetoric*.
26. Cf. Trible, regarding the Song generally: "At times, the standard, the figurative and the euphemistic converge so compellingly that one cannot discern where vehicle ends and tenor begins." Trible, *Rhetoric of Sexuality*, 145.
27. "George Lakoff and I first presented the Invariance Hypothesis implicitly in

anything close to reversible—metaphor does not establish an isomorphism. So this verse employs conceptions of the divine to elucidate love, rather than conceptions of love to elucidate the divine.

In fact, in this case, we are given *contrasting* images: the first passive, the second active. Sheol will not release what has fallen into its grasp—it is an immovable object (קשה). Yahweh, on the other hand, like an arrow (רשף),[28] seeks out and obtains what he wants—he is an irresistible force. The tenor of the second metaphor remains the same even if its vehicle, *resheph*, is to be understood as the consuming fire of coals (*AV*), as flames (Exum) or sparks, or as flashes (Assis), say of lightning.[29] The poetry both lays out and overlays metaphor on metaphor. The referent, love, is being described as definitive and final in character. It is not *merely* "strong"—like a strong man or strong drink—it is strong-like-death. It is definitive and final. So love is something that can be "sealed," as with an oath.

What is intended by the tightly overlapping parallel similes in this verse seems clear enough: love is a big deal (like a covenant). However, it is extremely important to note that this comment on the topic of love is not changed, even if we read *-yah* as an intensifying affix, rather than an abbreviation of the divine name. It is true, as Exum points out, that even if the divine name *is* intended, it still does not imply the Song of Songs is about Yahweh: but it is also true that if the divine name is *not* intended, *that does not imply the Song cannot still be read as being about him, canonically.* This verse is *at least* a comment on the topic of love. It does not preclude allegorical extrapolation, but neither does it demand such extrapolation. The verse is not decisive in establishing whether the Song is allegorical or not, but *neither are literal or allegorical frameworks of interpretation material to establishing the immediate sense of this verse.*

Although the following study is skeptical of divine allegory as the ultimate framework for interpreting the Song, it must be conceded that such readings can never be completely ruled out a priori. Hebrew—not only Biblical Hebrew, but also its modern counterpart—is sprinkled with lexemes with potentially theological implications: famously, in Modern Hebrew, the name of contemporary Israel's parliamentary "campus," *Mishkan haKnesset*.[30]

More than Cool Reason (1989)." Turner, "Aspects," 247–56.

28. "Darts"; Pope, *Song of Songs*, 12.

29. Marcia Falk, who did not feel bound to an impossible literalism, captures the tenor of the metaphor particularly nicely, playing on English associations, while cognizant of the Hebrew ones, and rendering *resheph* as "tongues."

30. "Let us not use the term *mishkan*. There are names in the history of the Jews that should be left untouched, because of their sanctity, or the sanctity of their uniqueness." Begin, *Knesset Record*, 2505.

Little words like *mishkan* carry big stories.³¹ Indeed, as indicated above, theological allusion guides the rendering of Song 8:6 presented here. Yet it is one thing to recognize the possibility of poetic play on extensional theological meanings (which might be the safest reading of *-yah*), but it is another to insist on a specific intentional theological meaning for the whole of the Song of Songs. A divine allegory is not an extraordinary claim, but it is still a claim that must accept a burden of proof not currently adequately borne by anything found in the literature to this date, at least not to the satisfaction of many modern scholars.

So the study below starts with an agnostic position regarding any putative divine allegory. However, allegories are not constructed ex nihilo anyway; rather, they work off at least a scaffold of more-or-less literal discourse. For example, in his famous allegory *Vor dem Gesetz* (also known as the *Türhüterparabel* ³²), Franz Kafka first activates key discourse participants, placing them within a simple narrative context:

> Vor dem Gesetz steht ein Türhüter. Zu diesem Türhüter kommt ein Mann vom Lande und bittet um Eintritt in das Gesetz.

In the case of this particularly short allegory, Kafka declines to offer the reader any key for decoding his short tale; instead, he relentlessly develops its literal and stark components. Only in delivering the final sentence does he offer an enigmatic anticlimax. Just like the man of the story, the reader who progresses to the end, seeking admission to meaning via the doorkeeper, is denied his goal—the door is shut in his face.

> Der Türhüter erkennt, daß der Mann schon an seinem Ende ist und, um sein vergehendes Gehör noch zu erreichen, brüllt er ihn an: „Hier konnte niemand sonst Einlaß erhalten, denn dieser Eingang war nur für dich bestimmt. Ich gehe jetzt und schließe ihn."

By contrast, the Song, despite being poetry, and even in our earliest records,³³ is known to have struck its *lay* audience as much more lively and forthcoming than an—admittedly dark—allegory like Kafka's. The Song offers so much at a literal level that this alone sufficed for that lay audience; but, for the sake of argument, let us allow the Song to be an allegory, understanding

---

31. "It is absolutely impossible to empty out words filled to bursting, unless one does so at the expense of language itself." Gershom Sholem, letter to Franz Rosenzweig, 26 December 1926.

32. Kafka, "Vor dem Gesetz", 2–3.

33 Tosefta, Sanhedrin 12:10; Mishnah, Taʿanith 4:8.

that allegory will still first require attention to the literal level of its discourse. If the following analysis is sound, then, it will be seen that any divine allegory readings would be better described as about "his people's response to God's love," rather than about "God's love for his people."[34] The Song of Songs appears to be the "Song of the Beloved," not the "Lover's Song." It will be argued that, in at least two significant—and objectively discernable—ways, the Song is not a song of pure mutuality, so it is not the "Lovers' Song" either.

§2 Anthology or Unity?

> It is not to be doubted, that the fire of the poem is what a translator should principally regard, as it is most likely to expire in his managing: however, it is his safest way to be content with preserving this to his utmost *in the whole*, without endeavoring to be more than he finds his author is, *in any particular place*. It is a great secret in writing, to know when to be plain, and when poetical and figurative. — Alexander Pope[35]

Allegorical readings of the Song propose a unifying principle: its diverse voices sing in harmony as they establish with concord the various themes of a spiritually resonating opus. However, with the advent of literal readings—if these additionally deny the traditional unifying principle—has come the search for some alternative to it. The Song comes to us as though it were a single work; if we abandon the allegorical tradition, how can this form of the text be explained?

Elie Assis begins his commentary with the observation that "to understand the Song of Songs, the question of whether the book is a collection of separate poems or a cohesive composition with significant continuity between the poems must first be determined."[36] He adds, "In addition to this question, the delimitation of the poems within the book is by no means an easy task."[37] Indeed, scholarly opinion on delimitation of units within the

---

34. "When we read the Song for the love between Israel and the Lord, its account of that love does not begin with the Lord's initiative, but with Israel's longing and the Lord's desirability." Jenson, *Song of Songs*, 16. For an exposition of Origen's contrary view, *vide* King, *Origen*, 269: "Origen presents the Song as nothing less than *the spirit of Scripture itself*, revealed in its essential nature as Christ the Word's eschatological song of nuptial love."

35. Pope, "Preface." Emphasis added.

36. Assis, *Flashes of Fire*, 9.

37. Ibid.

Song remains as described in Abraham Mariaselvam's dissertation: "there is no unanimity at all as to the determination of the extent of individual poetic units." Mariaselvam provides a list of twenty-one scholars offering a spectrum of counts of subunits ranging from five or six (Robert and Tourney, Exum, Shea)[38] through to thirty-one, thirty-two and fifty-two (Falk, Gerleman and Krinetzki).[39] Exum, in her more concise, but recent (2005), synoptic presentation of the views of various commentators,[40] additionally notes that Elliot and Bergant identify the same six basic units within the Song; yet Bergant asserts Song-as-anthology,[41] where Elliot argues for Song-as-unity.[42]

Of course, were the Song anthology rather than unity, it could be argued that there is not, properly speaking, any original, author-intended meaning—other than a disjunction of idiosyncratic comments on the topic of love. Rather than seeking something as precise as the author's intention, there would need to be hypotheses regarding editorial motives in selection, ordering, and possible re-workings of the component parts: either more-or-less passively, to present those parts in a felicitous manner; or more-or-less actively, for the editor to suggest something through the whole, not available in any of the individual parts alone. On the face of it, were the Song to prove to be an anthology, it could severely restrict the possibility of a satisfactorily complete answer to that most significant question regarding the Song, What impact is it supposed to have on its readers?

The distinction between original authorial or later editorial intentions, however, can be so fine as to vanish under close scrutiny: for instance, a hypothesis that proposed evidence of a great deal of deliberate editorial activity across the whole Song, especially if this were argued on the more substantial basis of semantics, rather than solely on surface features of the text. The more certainly we believe we can discern the hand of an editor, the more such an editor resembles an author utilizing sources. We know *Daddy* was written by a sole author on the 12 December 1962, only later to be incorporated into an anthology. The similarly posthumously published *Der Prozeß*, however, incorporated *Vor dem Gesetz* (narrated and interpreted by a priest in a cathedral), which we know the Prague Jewish weekly, *Selbstwehr*, had previously published as an independent work, during

---

38. Robert and Tourney, *Le Cantique des Cantiques*; Exum, "Literary and Structural Analysis," 77; Shea, " Chiastic Structure," 378.

39. Falk, *Love Lyrics*; Gerleman, *Ruth/Das Hohelied*; Krinetzki, *Das Hohe Lied*.

40. Exum, *Song of Songs*, 39.

41. Bergant, *Song of Songs*; Gordis, *Song of Songs*; and Longman, *Song of Songs*.

42. Elliot, *Literary Unity*.

Kafka's lifetime. We also know Alexander Pope published *An Essay on Man* in installments, and fell short of his original intentions regarding a more complete treatise. However, it seems a little ambitious to hope to recover with certainty any such publication details in regard to the Song. Without loss of generality, then, this study will simply speak, for convenience, of a sole author,[43] though it recognizes other historically divergent, but logically convergent, possibilities.

We should also note that there are two quite different paths to the conclusion that the Song is anthological. The gold-standard methodology would provide objective features in the surface form of the text which delineate, beyond reasonable doubt, fairly precisely where individual constituents of the anthology begin and end, concurrently demonstrating substantial semantic *independence* between those constituents. The second possible approach, however, simply devolves to proposing an anthology when no satisfactory unifying principle has been found.[44] Were the Song an anthology, that *would* explain the absence of any apparent unity; but in this second case, the conclusion arises by default rather than demonstration. Likewise, however, the conclusion that the Song is a *unity* can either: be presented via demonstration of a satisfactory unifying principle; or alternatively, be offered as an explanation for why decisive delineation of constituent portions of the Song remains elusive. Again, the former *affirmative* argument for unity is clearly much more satisfactory, and it is this that the present study attempts.

The logic that motivates the current study and shapes its questions and methodology should now be clear: Why is the Song in the canon? Does it have anything *in particular* to say? If so, what? and, How does the text succeed in communicating this? Despite considerable diversity of scholarly conclusions regarding the Song, particularly regarding arguably tangential specifics (in the case of the Song) like authorship and date of composition,[45] there is actually broad agreement about interpretative methodology. Whether or not scholars are inclined towards reading the Song as unity or anthology, almost all attempt to identify subsections and reflect on possible

---

43. "The Song's great consistency of matter and tone does suggest that one poet or closely knit group of poets is responsible for all or most of it, and the commentary will refer simply to 'the poet.'" Jenson, *Song of Songs*, 3.

44. "Many scholars claim that the book is an anthology of poems because they were unable to find an overall structure. However, as we have said, the lack of an overall structure in the book does not constitute proof that the book is not a single integrated work." Assis, *Flashes of Fire*, 18–19.

45. "Would knowing when it was written help us understand the poem? Probably not very much." Exum, *Song of Songs*, p. 67.

connections between these. Whether named by them as discourse analysis or not,[46] this is a fair appellation, understood broadly, for a good number of the approaches.[47] Biblical Hebrew poetry lends itself to such treatment: even at lower levels like cola, it is precisely the semantic associations between units that provide the artistic appeal. Lexical play on overlapping or contrasting semantic domains is a hallmark of biblical Hebrew poetry. In a very direct way, its medium is its message.[48]

Where current and future scholarship on the Song has an advantage, however, is in analysis at higher levels than bicola. Although the larger the units being compared, the more abstract the kinds of connections between them, discourse linguists over several decades have been studying the way various languages mark such relationships. For example, Biblical Hebrew is typical of a large class of languages that mark the relationship of a new clause to its prior context syntactically, via word order variation.[49] Also, although some details are still a matter of debate, it appears that languages mark "topicality" or "continuity of participant reference" according to a universal hierarchy, including null, inflectional, lexical, and syntactical devices.[50] These are empirical findings of recent times, still "finding their way" into analysis of biblical literature, but well attested nonetheless.

At the theoretical level, Kamp's Discourse Representation Theory (DRT) has given logical formalists a framework for articulating the semantics of texts, explicitly accounting for their dynamic interaction with context.[51] Of particular note is Asher and Lascarides's refinement of DRT,[52] which provides formal logical mapping of the semantics-pragmatics interface by focusing on "rhetorical relations". It might be argued that Asher and Lascarides express, in formal generalizations, the intuitions expressed ad

---

46. For example, Jenson conceives of his work as identifying *genre*; Assis presents his analysis in terms of form criticism.

47. "Going beyond the sentence level in discourse analysis and giving close attention to movements such as New Criticism, we find that the respective spheres intermingle. Terminology describing identical phenomena needs to be made compatible." Ljungberg, "Genre," 415.

48. See McLuhan, *Understanding Media*.

49. For modern language examples—Cayuga, Ngandi, and Coos—see Marianne Mithun: "Constituents appear in descending order of newsworthiness." Mithun, "Is Basic Word Order Universal?" 325. For Akkadian as an ancient semitic language example, see Agustinus Gianto: "There is a tendency to assign the first position to the information which is meant to be important." Gianto, *Word Order Variation*, 34.

50. See Givón, *Topic Continuity*.

51. Kamp, "Theory of Truth," 277–322.

52. Asher, *Abstract Objects*; Asher and Lascarides, *Logics of Conversation*.

hoc by generations of scholars of the Song: recovering its meaning requires identifying how the segments of its discourse are related to one another.

It is interesting to note that the Summer Institute of Linguistics (SIL) appears to have anticipated, in a broad sense, some of the recent linguistic work, having already advocated, for some decades, on the basis of practical translation issues, a best practice for language analysis that easily maps to several of the newer formal theoretical advances.[53] That SIL have applied their methods to biblical literature hardly needs to be said.

§3 John Callow

John Callow's essay "Units and Flow in the Song of Songs," in *Biblical Hebrew and Discourse Linguistics*, serves well to illustrate how an explicitly discourse analytical methodology approaches the Song.

> Having established the major units of the text (and inevitably some minor ones as well), I use these major units as a basis for discussing the "flow" of thought in the Cycle. Inherent in this order of presentation is the assumption that the progression of the author's thought is best seen in the light of his own grouping of the material.... Hence the importance of seeking to elucidate the major semantic units first. Not until after that do we study how the units relate to each other.[54]

Callow observes that the term *discourse analysis* may denote any of "a variety of different theoretical positions all of which operate with different assumptions and procedures."[55] He identifies his own analysis as following the "semantically or cognitively oriented theory of meaning" introduced by John Beekman.[56] One key feature of that theory is repeatedly stressed in Callow's essay: "This is a fundamental principle of the text-analysis approach that I am using ... the author of the Song wrote *to communicate*; he had a purpose which he sought to achieve by writing."[57] The principle is articulated, in the source-work cited, thus: "If it is assumed, complex though the mental processes may be, that a speaker or writer starts from the meaning which he wishes to convey and then expresses that meaning in the

---

53. E.g., Pike, *Linguistic* Concepts; Beekman et al., *Semantic Structure*; Dooley and Levinsohn, *Analyzing Discourse*.
54. Callow, "Units and Flow," 464.
55. Ibid., 462.
56. Ibid. Callow cites chapters 17–19 in Beekman and Callow, *Translating*, 267–326.
57. Callow, "Units and Flow," 473. Emphasis original.

surface forms of the language he is using, then the semantic structure is, in some sense, more fundamental."[58]

Differences of opinion between proponents of discourse analysis relevant to the current study will be discussed in more detail later, but it is interesting to note, even at this point, *similarities* between writers with different conclusions and methodology. Although differing with Mariaselvam, for example, who considered that "the SS is an anthology containing twenty-eight small poems,"[59] Callow's criteria for identifying "semantic units" are remarkably similar to Mariaselvam's criteria for "delimitation of individual poems."[60]

Mariaselvam (1987)

a. Change of speaker(s)
b. Change of listener(s)
c. Change of concrete setting or place: e.g., landscape, etc.
d. Change of moods or sentiments
e. Change of imagery or groups of images
f. Certain insights into the life-setting revealed in the poem itself.[61]

Callow (1994)

1. Continuity of speaker and addressee
2. Unity of topic
3. Stimulus and response
4. Uniformity of "conceptual domain"
5. Parallelism (but not always)
6. "Ascensiveness" (monotonicity)
7. "Tail head" linkage
8. Chiasmus[62])

---

58. Beekman and Callow, *Translating*, 271.
59. Mariaselvam, *Song of Songs*, 46.
60. Ibid.
61. Ibid.
62. Paraphrased from Callow, "Units and Flow," 463–64.

Mariaselvam tends towards literary, Callow towards linguistic analysis, as may be expected, given their respective research questions—comparative literature and discourse linguistics— however, it seems prudent to be diligent in observing their similarities, not just their differences, lest we become inclined to drive a wedge between what are, in most cases, interdependent rather than competing approaches. The current study opts to present its case essentially within a methodological framework aligned with SIL and DRT, but these guidelines are compatible with (in some cases explicitly incorporating) a wide range of other linguistic results and insights. Asher and Lascarides, for example, make a point of utilizing elements of Kripke Semantics[63] and Grice's maxims of conversational implicature,[64] both of which have their place in analyzing the text of the Song. To these can be added David Lewis's proposed formalism of truth in fiction by analogy with counterfactual propositions,[65] and John Searle's work on both fiction,[66] and speech acts in general.[67]

Callow's linguistic analysis of the text begins with "presentation of the Hebrew data."[68] Even before seeking to identify semantic units, this presentation of the data includes attention to objective and distinctive linguistic features of the text, like the syntactic functions of its words (verbs, nouns and noun phrases are mentioned). As this study will elaborate, the significance of vocatives in the text leads Callow to anticipate discussion of this feature, and already offset them in his structured presentation of the text. Likewise, parallel structures and chiasmus are marked by Callow in advance of more detailed discussion. So, Callow's presentation of the data, in keeping with his methodology, lays out surface features of the text, which are available to direct observation, before looking "behind them" for the propositional

63. Kripke, "Semantical Considerations," 83–94.

64. Grice, "Meaning," 377–88; Grice, *Studies*. See also Levinson, *Presumptive Meanings*.

65. Lewis, "Truth in Fiction," 37–46; see also *Conterfactuals*. Since the time of my pure mathematics honors dissertation, *The Subjunctive Conditional* (University of Sydney, 1987), a "mathematical translation" of the modal logic in Lewis's interdisciplinary work between linguists, philosophers, mathematicians, and computer scientists, already emergent then, has now become routine on a wide range of both theoretical and empirical questions—notably in formal semantics, but not restricted to it.

66. For example, Searle notes "the crucial role, usually underestimated, that imagination plays in human life, and the equally crucial role that shared products of the imagination play in human social life. And one aspect of the role that such products play derives from the fact that serious (i.e., nonfictional) speech acts can be conveyed by fictional texts, even though the conveyed speech act is not represented in the text. Almost any important work of fiction conveys a 'message' or 'messages' which are conveyed *by* the text but are not *in* the text." Searle, "Logical Status," 332.

67. Searle, *Speech Acts*.

68. Callow, "Units and Flow," 464.

content (broadly conceived) of the author's intended meaning, which would explain the surface forms.

Callow's attention to "units" and "flow" in the first section of the Song is actually the basis for an extended discussion of a more general theoretical translation issue: "the transfer of the discourse structure of the source language to the discourse structure of the receptor language."[69] Applying this consideration to the Song, Callow argues for the felicity of introducing headings identifying speakers, at least in English and similar languages, in which such devices are typical, and which additionally lack the gender and other discourse markings available in the original Hebrew.

This context is important for understanding why Callow picks out "units" and "flow" for attention. By demonstrating that the text is "semantically quantised," with identifiable semantic units, he establishes, in principle, that subsections can be well defined, *and* that there is semantic content available to "fill" headings for those subsections. The "units" are therefore critical to establishing that Callow's proposal for printed translations of the Song is theoretically *possible* (and on objective grounds). The "flow," on the other hand, is critical to establishing the *necessity* for some proposal like Callow's. In other words, Callow attempts to demonstrate that the discourse structure of the early part of the Song *as a whole* communicates something not available from its parts alone, or its parts in any other order, or its parts unmarked for their relationship to discourse participants.[70] Indeed, in Callow's estimation (and this study agrees with it), this first section of the Song establishes a context for comprehension of the sequel—it is a prologue (at least with a small *p*). Yet how is a reader to comprehend this, if the Hebrew-specific discourse cues are absent in her receptor language translation? It is a point very well made.

Callow's proposed "major" units are as follows.

a. 1:1–4 (31 words)

b. 1:5–6 (26 words)

c. 1:7–8 (31 words)

d. 1:9–17 (57 words)

e. 2:1–6 (46 words)

---

69. Ibid., 483–84.

70. See also Assis, *Flashes of Fire*, 266: "The Song of Songs is a unitary literary work, which has a beginning, a middle and an end. The book is a single organism, and if any of the individual poems were lacking, it would be incomplete. The order of the poems is also essential to its understanding."

Like Mariaselvam and Exum, Callow also provides a synoptic table of alternative views;[71] in his case, as befits an SIL article and the practical question it addresses, it is drawn from the work of Bible translators rather than literary commentators. The divisions indicated in the various translations support some of Callow's proposed "semantic units"; but what he is more interested in is those that appear to have either escaped the notice of translators, or been lost for want of a mandate to supply headings in lieu of source language discourse markings. Callow concludes his article, having demonstrated that there is discourse structure in the Hebrew of the Song that lacks any consistent rendition in major English translations, content to ask the question, What is to be done?

This study will largely accept Callow's detailed treatment of semantic units, extending that style of analysis to the full text of the Song. However, what is actually most pertinent to the current thesis is his discussion of a posited *flow* for the text. Callow stresses—and it is worth reiterating—that flow entails authorial (or editorial) intent. It suffices for Callow's argument to present authorial intent as an *assumption* of his methodology. In this current study, however, with the additional data of the whole Song to draw upon—like Clines, Arbel, Jenson, Exum, Assis, Noegel and Rendsburg, and other recently published scholars of the Song—it will be argued that the evidence is sufficient to establish the existence of an identifiable progression of thought, from which authorial intent follows a posteriori.

In citing the work of recent scholars, which—just maybe—might reflect an emergent consensus towards the Song-as-unity position, it seems all the more important to post a significant caveat: scholars agreeing on unity, *but for different reasons*, are not really speaking with one voice. For example, traditional allegorical readings see the Song as a unity, but for reasons this study will not accept. It would be nonsense to cite Origen in support of the current thesis, irrespective of agreement on unity of composition.[72] However, the caution is not as urgent in the case of the modern commentators: there is considerably more "common ground" (and shared skepticism, for that matter). In fact—given the typically multivalent nature of poetry—were the Song like this, with a range of related ideas to communicate, it would be unremarkable to find commentators identifying several of those ideas, while disagreeing about which were primary or "core." So be it; let the reader decide! Strictly speaking, the thesis of this study is that a woman's

---

71. Callow, "Units and Flow," 485.

72. Origen does not support the rationale this thesis will provide for discourse coherence; however, he will be offered as a voice in support of the significance for interpretation of scrutinizing the discernible engagements between the Song's drama-like, distinct, and distinctive voices.

perspective on romantic intimacy is markedly prominent in the Song, and provides a sufficient and parsimonious explanation for why the Song might have been written and canonized, as well as for how it "hangs together." It is *not* argued that the gynocentric hypothesis exhaustively explains every last feature of the received text; for example, it does not preclude the Song *additionally* serving to "encode" a political, or even a theological, allegory.[73]

So, Callow is important to the current thesis, not only for typifying the methodology, but also because the conclusions he draws via that methodology anticipate essentially the same conclusions drawn here, just based here on the data provided by the whole Song. In his analysis of "flow," Callow claims:

> It does not need to be argued that the Song is presented almost entirely as either dialogue between the Hero and Heroine (first and second person exchanges) or descriptions spoken by one of them about the other (third person material). It thus seems reasonable to assume that the author's purpose is being achieved by these exchanges. It also seems reasonable, since the Hero and the Heroine often address each other in terms of endearment, to work with the further assumption that the writer is presenting a *relationship* between these two people, the Hero and the Heroine.[74]

The detailed analysis to follow in the current study includes examination of the clearly marked distinction between first and second person discourse, as opposed to third person material, which will be seen to provide a strong line of evidence for the gynocentric hypothesis in and of itself. However, the central project is analyzing a somewhat broader range of more-or-less objective discourse linguistic features that bear on the question of just how the Song characterizes the "relationship" between Hero and Heroine (to take Callow's terms). *That* the Song provides such a characterization is not questioned in the literature, but *how* it characterizes the "relationship" remains a matter of discussion to this date. A suitable example of a scholar who recognizes the feminine perspective of the text, and views characterization of that perspective only slightly differently to what will be argued here, is (Vita) Daphna Arbel.

---

73. For arguments to political rather than theological allegory, *vide* Hug, *Das Hohe Leid* and *Schutzschrift*; Stadelmann, *Love and Politics*; Noegel and Rendsburg, *Solomon's Vineyard*; perhaps also Boer, "Keeping it Literal."

74. Callow, "Units and Flow," 473. Emphasis original.

§4 Daphna Arbel

Arbel goes a step further than Callow, by making an identification between the feminine *perspective*, apparent in the text, and the author's own perspective; hence an *actual* female author, rather than merely an "implied" one. Arbel does not argue for this position explicitly; it is advanced as a hypothesis, and indicated via consistent use of the feminine pronoun throughout the essay when referring to the author. The introduction of the feminine pronoun for the author does not cause surprise for the reader, because there is a seamless shift in the essay's third paragraph from "The woman in the Song of Songs ... she ... " to "The writer ... She ..."[75] In other words, Arbel views the Song as autobiographical—psychologically, if not historically. In fact, if a reader follows the footnote to Arbel's first statement of her proposed unifying principle for the Song—a central feminine perspective—that note introduces the possibility of female authorship via citing writers (LaCoque and Brenner)[76] who posit this on the basis of quite specific passages with observably feminine perspectives, rather than sharing Arbel's broader recognition of the gendered nature of the overall perspective of the Song. Thus Arbel concisely and gently—almost imperceptibly—guides the diligent reader to entertain her hypothesis, prior to elaborating on the considerable textual evidence there is to support its main claim: the centrality of the feminine perspective.

Arbel is making another stronger claim than that of those she cites,[77] however, by identifying the woman *in* the Song with the woman she proposes *wrote* the Song. In a minor way, this might strengthen the assumed songstress's voice; but in a major way, it weakens it. What we say about ourselves alone we can assert authoritatively; but if we speak about ourselves alone we may not engage our audience with any shared reality. So Arbel's view of the Song as "the poetic expression of the inner dreams, emotions and thoughts of one individual woman" accords with the thesis of this current

---

75. Arbel, "My Vineyard," 91.

76. LaCoque, *Romance*, 39–53, and Brenner, "Women Poets," 87–91.

77. E.g., "Such an identification (although hypothetical) would explain why a relatively large proportion of the SoS deals with feminine emotions while the male is relegated to a secondary position. Unfortunately this last assumption, which can be based on quantitative considerations, has no further evidence to support it.... To summarize: after having aired the above considerations, we still are in no position to determine with confidence which portions of the SoS express typical female attitudes with such fidelity that they can be regarded as original compositions by women." Brenner, "Women Poets," 89–90.

study,[78] except for its two posited historical reconstructions: a solipsistic woman author, writing specifically about herself. Clearly, neither of these reconstructions is actually necessary to establishing that a feminine perspective arises from the text, nor that this perspective coordinates the sense of the diverse components of the Song. In fact, even Arbel's implicit (and abductive) argument flows the other way around: the observably feminine perspective *might* be best explained by a woman poet, even one reflecting on her own specific inner world.[79]

It is probably trivial to note that most commentators consider Jane Austen, for example, to have been an astute observer of men, as well as of women, despite never having married.[80] So there should be no need to provide a long list of expert criticism of celebrated writers who have produced authentic characters of the opposite sex. More substantially, though, it should be noted that the Song, although elaborating on feminine perspectives, does include representations of masculine perspectives also.[81] So much is this the case, that many commentators have viewed the Song as antiphonal or as dialogue (including rubrics in Codex Sinaiticus),[82] not to mention Origen's view that the Song is the nuptial song of Christ himself to his bride. So to argue from the authenticity of the Song's feminine perspective to a female poet, however tempting, is tantamount to arguing for the inauthenticity of the masculine perspective(s), also expressed in the Song. That falls foul of a good deal of serious commentary, which may indeed be mistaken in various ways, but at least provides some support for the authenticity of the masculine perspectives in the Song, even if we consider such perspectives to be less significant than those commentators supposed. Ultimately, as will be explained later, it is the disappointing, but authentic, portrayal of men in the Song that proved decisive, during the course of the current study, in leading the present writer to the conclusion that the Song expresses a feminine perspective, and quite possibly with didactic purpose. In what ways are the Song's men disappointing? Men appear to be disappointing in ways in which a woman *specifically* may expect better of them.

In any case, surely, establishing the authenticity of the Song's characters (or caricatures) does not depend upon first establishing the sex of its

---

78. Arbel, "My Vineyard," 91.

79. Ibid., 91, for explicit consideration of precisely the sort of evidence needed to support such an argument.

80. "Jane Austen was an astute observer of human nature." Almond, 'Psychological Change," 307.

81. Note Brenner's *proportional* argument quoted in the earlier note.

82. Treat, *Lost Keys*.

author. Wouldn't knowing the poet's sex only be relevant if we wanted to apply gender stereotyping as part of our interpretation?[83] Perhaps gender stereotypes have something to teach us, but poets of all people are not generally received as stereotypical personalities—they "speak funny" for a start. All things considered, this study will remain "gender blind" with regard to the *actual* author (or editor) of the Song, for convenience using the masculine pronoun, but in its generic (or masculine representative) sense, as found in contemporary academic publications in formal linguistics,[84] and in Callow et al., regarding the Song.[85] However, this study agrees with Callow et al. that the *implied* author is female, and attempts to establish that beyond reasonable doubt.

In general, Arbel's elaboration of how the feminine perspective arises from the text is compelling—so compelling in fact, that it seems a pity that she is content to present it as the idiosyncratic perspective of just one specific ancient Israelite poetess. Other writers, Exum for example, see the anonymity of the woman (and the man) in the Song as pointing to a generic portrayal of a woman's (or girl's) perspective (or both): "They are identified neither by name nor by association.... The Song's lovers are archetypal lovers—composite figures, types of lovers rather than any specific lovers";[86] "the lovers are not to be confused with the poet";[87] and "the Song is not about young love only."[88]

It is worth stressing again that Arbel's reading of the Song does not really depend on establishing the sex of the Song's author, so quibbles regarding this leave its major elements untarnished. First among those elements is Arbel's proposal that the Song is expressed "in the realm of the imagination."

---

83. "The discussions of the gender of the author of the Song reveals more about us as commentators than it does about the Song. It relies on a theory of literature and of gender that believes that women and men are typecast in the way that they write." Longman, *Song of Songs*, 9.

84. Asher and Lascarides, for example, consistently use the generic masculine singular pronoun in the ordinary course of their texts, without explanation, but presumably for precision, and to avoid distraction, while articulating the logic of their analysis of language. However, a broad practice in philosophy, if we can generalize, has for some decades been to utilize generic *she*, alternating from time to time with generic *he*—to be explicitly inclusive, but also to remain clear and concise. This expedient would, however, be confusing or misleading in reference to the author of the Song.

85. "The author ... his or her" (462) and "the author ... his" (464 onwards); Callow, "Units and Flow."

86. Exum, *Song of Songs*, 8.

87. Ibid., 9.

88. Ibid.

> The writer is not simply the receiver of dreams which she reports later. Nor is she simply a recorder of real events. Instead she is an active author, describing her own experiences that are constructed on an inner level.... It is in the realm of the imagination that the writer presents her descriptions in the SoS.[89]

In support of this, Arbel offers considerable textual evidence and straightforward historical reconstruction, like: "a search by night is highly unrealistic, considering the norms of the writer's patriarchal society."[90] Whether such a search would be realistic in any contemporary society, or whether that would be due to "patriarchal" features of our own societies, are questions that need not detain us; certainly, the woman's searches in the Song have something fabulous about them, flagged in various ways in the text, and interacting with an audience's expectations of what is typical in the distinctive behaviors of men and women, pretty much anywhere.

Among other literary aspects of the Song that Arbel observes to be consistent with her reading is an apparent stream-of-consciousness progression of related ideas.

> It appears that each thought stems from a previous one in a series of associations.... This attitude, expressed in the opening scene, will color the rest of the text, in which we find free expression of the different inner fantasies and conflicting attitudes of a woman who is observing and analyzing her own feelings of love.[91]

Arbel's literary sensitivity is refreshingly engaging to read, by contrast with ponderous and clinical apportioning of "semantic units" and classification of "rhetorical relations." However, that kind of work, in the current study, is simply aimed at more formal presentation of intuitions shared with Arbel, whose "thoughts" and "associations" refer to broadly the same phenomena as Callow's "units" and "flow."

Arbel states without proof—and indeed none is needed—that the text presents by turns: "a sensual erotic woman, a hesitant young girl, a protected virgin, an admired lover, a seductive dancer ... It seems that the writer presents the contents of her imagination freely and openly."[92] Though, given that this particular list of *dramatis personae* is drawn from well-known stereotypes of the feminine, it is a struggle to follow Arbel to her conclusion that,

---

89. Arbel, "My Vineyard," 92.
90. Ibid.
91. Ibid., 93.
92. Ibid., 92–93.

"She takes the liberty of avoiding fixed gender roles and attitudes, allowing for multidimensional female characters to surface."[93] It would seem that even stereotypical characterizations of femininity, like those Arbel lists, are actually multi-various anyway.

However, it is the second part of Arbel's conclusion—and what this study will also argue is engagingly present in the text of the Song—that goes to the heart of the matter: *because* it is expressed in the language of the imagination, a synchronicity of otherwise mutually exclusive roles— "sensual erotic woman" and "protected virgin", or "hesitant young girl" and "seductive dancer"—are possible. More profoundly, entertaining mutually exclusive possibilities in the imagination is the prelude to making a choice. Whether constrained by our desires to retain the approbation of our peers, or constrained by cherishing our own personal idealistic hopes of romantic intimacy, such abstractions are radically perturbed when confronted by the precipitation of a concrete instance of a real, or even imminent, sexual encounter. If Arbel is right, as what follows hopes to show she is, the Song is effective in evoking the drama of decision-making in the course of court-ship, *from the perspective of a woman*.

Arbel's reading of the Song is outstanding in capturing the authenticity of passions expressed in the Shulamite's speeches. Arbel's hermeneutical key—that the language is the language of the imagination, specifically a woman's imagination—just as she claims, seems to provide a plausible unifying principle for the Song. The man in Arbel's reading (and more-or-less in this study too), is little more than the Shulamite's *perception* of him—he (almost) doesn't exist,[94] unless he is present to the senses of her imagination. But he *is* the catalyst for her Song. Well may we ask, who rouses whom in the Song of Songs? This study will agree with Arbel that the Song expresses a female fantasy; but it will also agree with David Clines, that it expresses a male fantasy also.

§5 David Clines

David Clines's essay, "Why is there a Song of Songs and What does it do to you if you read it?" is a rather challenging paper in many ways, and one that demands consideration. Although not originally published in a feminist journal or series, it roundly condemns the Song along moral lines drawn from feminist ethics and in line with feminist theories of gender and culture:

93. Ibid., 93.

94. See below for explanation of the qualifying "almost": the chorus is *essential* to anchoring the man in reality.

"[It] is a dangerous text, not a gross one. A more blatantly sexist text would do less damage than one that beguiles."[95] More precisely, Clines appears to apply some pertinent elements of Althusserian Marxist hermeneutics to the Song,[96] which lead him to a striking, if unsettling, reading.

Clines provides an introduction typical of his distinctive and urbane pedagogical style: laying foundations on the best of authorities, raising original and excellent questions, setting out his methodology plainly, all the while personably dropping gems of insight. In this particular case, Clines first leads his audience (his text was originally delivered as an address) to consider a question of implied authorship: What might we infer from the text of the Song about the psychological motivations of its author? This question is framed with skillful economy, reflecting a sophisticated appreciation of scholarly discussion of related issues—both that which has been unquestionably valuable, and that which many would consider to have been less fruitful, yet sparing his listeners the details of the latter.

In setting out to answer his question, Clines starts by raising another easily overlooked but essential question: Why was the Song documented? Why was it committed to written form as text? He suggests: "Whatever else the Song of Songs is, it is not a song."[97] He means, of course, that the text we have is not sheet music for a popular ditty, which he then shows is just as significant as it is demonstrably true. Texts have all sorts of characteristics that folk songs (or *Volkdichtung*; Clines quotes Murphy) do not.[98] A text is a rather particular kind of publication, and one that is typically received (by readers) in private. Clines stands out from the last century or so of biblical scholarship here, in being willing to contemplate a biblical text with relatively little or no history of redaction prior to it coming into the received form in which it has survived. As his argument unfolds, it becomes apparent that such a premise can be at least as helpful to accurate interpretation, if not more helpful, than many more speculative reconstructions.

Of course, we do have evidence that the Song was, in fact, performed in public; but the Song as text already existed at that point.[99] Furthermore, there seems to be something artificial about performances of the Song as

---

95. Clines, *Interested Parties*, 121. By contrast, Falk, in the "translator's note" to the gift edition of her translation of the Song of Songs, recollects begging to differ with one of her professors because, "the Song of Songs was not the sexist text that he apparently took it to be." Falk, *Song of Songs*, xi.

96. Clines utilizes conceptions drawn from Althusser, Lacan, and Jameson, whom he acknowledges in footnotes.

97. Clines, *Interested Parties*, 98.

98. Murphy, *Song of Songs*.

99. Clines quotes Tosefta, Sanhedrin 12.10 in a footnote.

Aqiba describes them, even after accounting for his personal disapproval. Aqiba speaks of the "tremulous" (trilling or sing-song) voice of a singular singer: no duality of lovers, no plurality of chorus. So Clines raises and examines a very significant possibility: that of the Song originating as a literary "contrivance" (Clines's term). He also drops one of his gems into a footnote: "The 'tremulous voice,' by the way, couldn't be of a male impersonating a female, could it?"[100] If the Song's implied author is feminine, as claimed in this current study, Clines's lateral thinking, regarding the evidence from Aqiba, recovers a possible historical source to support the thesis presented here.

Another gem comes while Clines is attempting to reconstruct a social setting for the composition of the Song (or to "historicize" it, *à la* Marxist hermeneutics). Some of the, perhaps slightly playful, reconstruction might stretch a little too far into stereotypes of *machismo* to remain credible for some readers, but in at least one particular it has the sober backing of the behavioral sciences, and suggests a plausible understanding of the Song's superscription. Stereotyping men as quintessentially competitive may seem like sexism, but both ethology and ethnology have demonstrated that it is accurate sexism: naturally high levels of androgens correlate with female spotted hyenas (*Crocuta crocuta*) behaving competitively (and also growing phalluses).[101] *Homo sapiens* with Y-chromosomes do not generally escape the potent effects of these androgens either; indeed, they are not male when they don't (see Androgen Insensitivity Syndrome in medical literature). Conceding to Clines that masculine competitiveness may be accepted as a generalization regarding our species, perhaps the superlative of the Song's superscription is indeed evidence of a masculine hand at work, just as he proposes. In fact, although Clines is satisfied to answer his own question of who judged the Song to be the best of Songs *generically*—a man—perhaps the superscription, even if only in the fiction of the Song, confirms Clines explicitly and *specifically*—yes, a man, King Solomon. *Shir haShirim asher liShlomo* could be taken in the sense "the greatest of Songs, according to Solomon," which harmonizes with the proposal of many other scholars that the superscription reflects a bid, at some stage, to establish the Song's canonicity by association with Solomon.

There is much that overlaps between social milieu and politics (perhaps the personal has always been political) and this is reflected in Clines's

---

100. Clines, *Interested Parties*, 100, n.8.

101. "One such extreme example of the role of androgens in the development of masculine phenotypes can be found in the spotted hyena (*Crocuta crocuta*)." Hotchkiss et al., "Of Mice," 1037–50.

reconstructions of the ancient Israelite setting of the Song as he moves from what he terms the "social matrix" to the "political matrix."

> The social reality in ancient Israel, as in most societies known to us, is [that of] men having power over women, of women as a class having no power to speak of outside the domestic setting, and of a system in which *women are regarded and treated as effectively the property of men*.[102].

Indeed, Clines's first proposition—regarding women at best constituting only a minority in representative roles of public responsibility—is generally regarded by cultural anthropology to be a human universal, but is nonetheless particularly well documented in the case of ancient Israel: both in the scrolls of the Hebrew Bible themselves and in contemporary criticism of them. However, it is the second proposition—regarding possession—that is key to the minor premise of the syllogism at the heart of Clines's paper. The major premise of the syllogism is attributed to Jameson: that all texts aim to maintain social equilibrium by obfuscating various forms of injustice.[103]

Major

All texts obfuscate injustices, doing so in order to maintain the *status quo*.

Minor

The Song is a text that presents a *mutual* possession refrain rather than a faithful picture of the injustice of men possessing women in Israel.

Conclusion

The Song's function is to pacify by presenting a fantasy of romantic egalitarianism.

In Clines's words, this conclusion reads: "The patriarchal social system not only created the Song of Songs; it needed it."[104]

The syllogism above is, of course, valid; but the important question is whether or not it is sound. That is, is the truth of the premises sufficiently

---

102. Clines, *Interested Parties*, 101–2. Emphasis added.

103. Jameson, *Political Unconscious*.

104. Clines, *Interested Parties*, 100. Again, Falk provides an explicit voice in contrast: she believes the women of the Song speak "in words that do not seem filtered through the lens of patriarchal consciousness." Falk, *Song of Songs*, xv.

well established that the conclusion must be accepted? Longman takes issue with Clines, on the basis that his argument relies on the "supposition that no woman would [be interested] in the kind of love that the beloved articulates."[105] However, Longman seems to have missed that Clines's argument actually rests on Jameson's theorem, which would affirm that women do indeed find beguiling the kind of love articulated in the Song. In fact, Clines's argument actually relies on *the very supposition* Longman mistakenly believes Clines to deny. The Song, according to Clines's application of Jameson, is constructed by a man (or men) psychologically motivated to reconcile both their own consciences, and those of any protestant women, to the gender injustices described in detail in the Hebrew Bible. Although, as quoted by Longman, Clines *does* assert "the need of a male public for erotic literature,"[106] Longman does not quote the subject of Clines's sentence: "The material cause of the Song of Songs is, then, [this] need." Clines, quite explicitly—as per Jameson et al.—wants to look deeper than the material cause to the "political unconscious", the "psychological motivations of [the Song's] author". So, Clines's argument runs deeper than Longman's criticism recognizes.

However, looking beyond the author's intention to his (or their) psychological, unconscious and political motivations pushes the boundaries of what this study will be able to demonstrate from objective features of the discourse structure of the Song alone. Communicative intentions, unless hopelessly incompetent, largely make themselves explicit; they are the *raison d'être* of language, the material cause for its surface forms—lexical, syntagmatic, and pragmatic. Psychological motivations, though, real enough as they are, can be quite opaque to observation via the medium of text alone, especially highly contrived text like poetry. So, although the current study concurs with Arbel's assessment of the Song as being expressed "in the realm of the imagination,"[107] and so accedes to the suitability of Clines's methodology—"My route into this question is to regard the text as a dream, its author's dream"[108]—it will attempt to avoid reading modern gender-stereotyped psychological profiling into the characters of poet, audience, and discourse participants, in order to reconstruct any gender stereotypes explicit or implied by the author of the Song. Whether any such ancient stereotypes may be more or less appealing than modern ones is a matter of great contemporary interest; but this study will only attempt to describe,

---

105. Longman, *Song of Songs*, 9.
106. Clines, *Interested Parties*, 102.
107. Ibid.
108. Ibid., 104.

rather than evaluate, whatever the text of the Song may, or may not, articulate for us regarding gender stereotypes.

So Callow, Arbel, and Clines illustrate what appears to have become something of a theme in scholarly analysis of the Song over the course of several recent decades. However, contemporary interest in gender dynamics may best be considered a new tangent on an old trajectory, making more explicit, and sharpening focus on, the importance for responsibly interpreting the Song of the research question: What is the *character* of this gendered relationship between the Shulamite and her love? Even the traditional allegorical commentators, theocentric and androcentric as their readings were, had their principal concern in this relationship. Recent commentators—both conservative and progressive—have divided (not entirely along "party lines") when offering simple summaries of how Shulamite and lover interact: Brenner, Longman, Noegel, and Rendsburg et al. see Shulamite as dominant; Clines sees a deception, Trible and Falk see a real ideal of gender egalitarianism in the Song; Exum sees plenty of evidence of a hard reality, behind the hype, of the Shulamite ultimately being submissive; Arbel sees independence and autonomy for the Shulamite, at least in her imagination.

Given the luxury the current study has of addressing this question in detail, however, it can attempt to draw its conclusions without being constrained by a simplistic dipolar scale like "relative dominance," which is intuitive and highly evocative, but only rarely objective or even well-defined. Most recently, Assis, but also others before him, have presented more nuanced analyses of the relational dynamics between the Shulamite and her love. Assis and others, it will be argued here, offer a more comprehensive picture of the text of the Song, that does indeed articulate various forms of influence—women upon men, and men upon women—some of which might be termed as dominance, but yet others of which are at best only unnaturally so classified.

The Song depicts interactions that are quite diverse, as well as flowing sometimes one way, sometimes the other, and yet other times being genuinely reciprocal.[109] So, if this understanding is correct, the current thesis will

---

109. See Ancona and Greene, *Gendered Dynamics*, for a number of essays that explore multifaceted perceptions of gender relations in Latin love poetry, including critical reflection on Roman social expectations. "Latin love elegy is a deeply self-conscious literary genre. Not only do elegiac poets constantly allude to the conventions within which they are writing and to their debt to and/or difference from earlier authors, but the subject of their poems (ostensibly, the poet's love for his mistress) often serves a metaphorical function. Elegy is poetry about poetry." Valladares, "Lover as a Model Viewer," 206.

be objecting to little of what other scholars have affirmed, only to what some have denied.[110]

§6 Linguistics and Philosophy

> What I shall have to say here is neither difficult nor contentious; the only merit I should like to claim for it is that of being true, at least in parts. The phenomenon to be discussed is very widespread and obvious, and it cannot fail to have been already noticed, at least here and there, by others. Yet I have not found attention paid to it specifically. — John Austin[111]

As already noted, advances in linguistics—especially in discourse analysis and pragmatics—have brought fresh insights to literary studies, though it needs to be acknowledged that, in many cases, these advances have simply confirmed or formalized intuitions that had already found various kinds of expression within traditional literary criticism. Discussion above also shows, however, that even literary analyses, informed by—and sensitive to—linguistic advances, nonetheless sometimes differ in the conclusions they draw from the "data" the text of the Song provides.

There is, of course, something naturally preferable about broadly literary rather than narrowly linguistic approaches to textual artifacts, especially in regard to poetry: the full range of readerly skills can be brought to bear by experienced literary critics. Linguistic evidence in isolation can be ambiguous, and linguistic evidence always needs prudent weighting to keep it in line with higher-level literary contextual cues. Some features of communication, advances in pragmatic analysis notwithstanding, operate at subtle levels of abstraction, not crudely marked phonologically, lexically, or syntactically. If such features of communication have any accessible explanation, they have it in the rich world of human cognition, and the developing fields of psycholinguistics and cognitive poetics.[112] Indeed, modern linguistics shares many research questions in common with the traditional purview of literary analysis.

---

110. Strictly speaking, of course, *both* affirmations and denials simply express propositions. Often however, and in this case, "affirmations" are quantified existentially— $xÎX . P(x)$ —whereas the corresponding "denials" are universals— $\sim xÎX . P(x) Û "xÎX . \sim P(x)$.

111. Austin, *How*, 1. John Austin's lecture notes for the 1955 William James Lectures, published as *How to Do Things with Words*.

112. For cognitive poetics, see Reuven Tsur and the Routledge guides by Peter Stockwell, and by Joanna Gavins and Gerard Steen.

Insights into the Song, like those of Arbel and Clines, where they disagree, reflect realities about ambiguities in human communication. Texts are written to be received, as Clines so pointedly reminds us.[113] Texts are, in a sense, most real at the point of their reception, but that is also precisely where there is the most diversity in their character. Readers can and do reconstruct texts to suit their own prejudices. This study, however, attempts to constrain itself to discerning, if possible, the more mundane matter of how the author (or editor) of the Song intended readers to respond, rather than the more challenging issues associated with the many logically possible alternative readings that might have been, or could potentially be, offered. As such, the study is a contribution only to establishing some first principles regarding the text it examines, and so falls at the opposite end of the spectrum to more comprehensive works that can aim to provide the "last word" on interpreting the Song.

There are some simple questions that can be asked of the text of the Song, which could easily be overlooked just because they are simple. Linguistic methodology exists to address a number of such questions. For example, some word order variation appears to be a deliberate feature of biblical Hebrew poetry, gratuitously and artfully introduced by poets in various contexts, to defamiliarize the "cadences" of their purposeful expression. Yet, according to Nicholas Lunn's analysis, this device is utilized but once in the Song (4:8b):

אתי מלבנון כלה אתי מלבנון תבאי

With me from Lebanon, my bride

with me from Lebanon, come!

The text above is particularly interesting because it is an example of retrograde gapping, where "invariably the verb" is absent from the first colon, line, or hemistich, only being supplied as the last element of the parallel construction.[114] It is "a much rarer feature of parallelism" (Lunn's data contained only five examples).[115] One of the other examples of the structure is Psalm 70:2, the opening verse of the Psalm leading Lunn to note that Song 4:8 is also frequently read as providing an aperture: after a series of verbless clauses describing the woman, the invitation introduces a new section.[116] Likewise, the opening of Psalm 94 attests the same device; whereas Psalms

---

113. "A text implies, for its realization, only a reader." Clines, *Interested Parties*, 98.

114. Lunn, *Word-Order Variation*, 188.

115. Ibid.

116. Longman, *Song of Songs*, 148; Murphy, *The Song of Songs*, 158–59.

92:10 and 94:3—with "marked" word order—are taken by several commentators as *closing* sections.[117] So, Lunn's division of non-canonical word order into variations marked with pragmatic intent, and those marked for poetic defamiliarization, may be significant in understanding the oppositions appreciated by poet and audience, and how they were utilized to signal transitions in biblical Hebrew poetry.

Lunn's work is self-consciously an application of information theory to word order variation in Biblical Hebrew. Although this study can only benefit from Lunn's identification of defamiliarization in a solitary verse of the Song, Lunn also identifies marked word order in many other verses. Word order variation is a feature of surface form, and like other surface form features provides objective data for interpreting language. Information theory correlates such surface features with the underlying focus structure of intended communication.[118] The focus structure of communication is a first-order representation of the flow of information from originator to recipient. Information theoretical analysis involves identification of: communicative participants, referents, activation states of referents, topic-comment relationships, degree of prominence or focus, and old–new or presupposed–asserted propositional content. Anaphoric pronouns frequently carry a good deal of this information, all the more so in Biblical Hebrew and in the Song of Songs, because Hebrew marks second person verb forms for gender, and the Song juxtaposes female-to-male and male-to-female speeches.[119]

The current study utilizes more than just information theory. A number of the key theoreticians, whose work shapes the methodology, have already been noted in the text or footnotes above. Detailed treatment of how their theoretical understanding is relevant to elucidating the Song is deferred to later chapters, where the value of the theories stands out more sharply in the context provided by concrete examples from the text of the Song. At this point, however, it is worth making the general observation that the theoretical work used in the analysis below is, in general, the product of two well-known, late-twentieth-century developments: dynamic semantics and cognitive science. The change from static, truth-functional semantics to the current understanding of meaning as context change potential (CCP) is normally considered to date, approximately, from the publication of Hans Kamp's discourse representation theory in 1981; though the literature shows, unsurprisingly, that Kamp was addressing existing questions, and

---

117. Lunn, *Word-Order Variation*, 189.

118. See Lambrecht, *Information Structure*.

119. See the published version of Katsuomi Shimasaki's PhD thesis. Shimasaki, *Focus Structure*.

interacting with the results of other semanticists. The rise of cognitive science as an independent discipline, however, traces the history of an even more eclectic interest across many disciplines in related phenomena that can be broadly termed "cognitive."

Although these general tendencies in current research programs are now widely applied, the methodological grounding for the present study remains conservative, being drawn from only a handful of well-regarded results within these large movements in contemporary linguistics and literary studies. It also bears repeating that, although expressed in the terminology of contemporary interdisciplinary academic discussion, the conclusions drawn here are not so very different from insights already published by distinguished commentators in the history of literary interpretation of the Song, *mutatis mutandis* with regard to the terminology.[120]

The research questions of the present study address high-level abstractions regarding the text of the Song. That is to say, they are more concerned with the pragmatics and semantics of the Song than with its tropes—syntagmatic or phonological.[121] As such, the study takes its lead from theoretical linguists working at or above the semantics–pragmatics interface. A measure of scientific objectivity, in seeking methodical answers to the research questions, is sought by employing linguistic analyses that have proved to be repeatable: typologically (across a range of languages), and by linguists working with a spectrum of complementary approaches (viz., "functional" linguistics). In particular, these include: Dik,[122] Givón,[123] Halliday,[124] Lakoff,[125] Pike,[126] van Valin,[127] and the Prague and St Petersburg schools.[128] It is a striking feature of the complementary approaches of "linguistic functionalism" that they are marked by strong currents of interdisciplinary investigation, as noted by Givón:

120. E.g., the "voices" in the Song, here often termed "discourse participants,", Origen calls πρόσωπα. Of course, many commentators, modern and medieval, while recognizing the Song's voices, make no usage of any specific technical terms when referring to them.

121. See Berlin, *Dynamics*; and extensively applied to the Song by Bergant, *Song of Songs*.

122. Functional Grammar: see Dik, *Functional Grammar*.

123. Givón, *Syntax*.

124. Systemic Functional Grammar: Halliday and Matthiessen, *Introduction to Functional Grammar*.

125. Cognitive Grammar: see Lakoff, *Women, Fire*.

126. Tagmemics per SIL: see Pike, *Linguistic Concepts*.

127. Role and Reference Grammar: see Valin, "Synopsis."

128. E.g., Sgall et al., *Meaning of the Sentence*.

> The antecedence of functionalism in linguistics should not be sought primarily in the work of linguists, but rather in the work of anthropologists, psychologists, and biologists. And long before them, in the work of philosophers.[129]

Givón recognizes the contribution to theoretical linguistics by philosophers as far back as the Greeks, and especially their contribution to the linguistic field of pragmatics. For example; Charles Sanders Pierce, Givón observes, "is generally considered the Godfather of modern pragmatism, with insights ranging all over the pragmatic agenda."[130] First among the contributions Givón attributes to Pierce is his revitalization of Aristotle's third class of logical argument type, termed ἀπαγωγή ("reduction") by Aristotle,[131] but "rechristened *abduction*" by Pierce.[132] In Givón's estimation, abductive inference is a "pragmatic mode *par excellence*."[133]

The work of theoretical linguists and philosophers of language, however, although of great interest in and of itself, is ultimately aimed at serving practical issues in language comprehension. In this current thesis, language theory is being applied as a means to an end—a literary-critical end.

§7 Literature and Analogy

> The nationality of a worthwhile writer is of secondary importance. The more distinctive an insect's aspect, the less apt is the taxonomist to glance first of all at the locality label under the pinned specimen in order to decide which of several vaguely described races it should be assigned to. The writer's art is his real passport. His identity should be immediately recognized by a special patter or unique coloration.[134] — Vladimir Nabokov

The formal presentation that follows works "bottom up," as an abductive argument to a hypothesis: it works from what is best known and understood, towards clarifying what is less clear and debatable. Such a presentation is typically limited in its appeal to rather particular forums, like the current one—of academic discussion. Perhaps this is because the cognitive

---

129. Ibid., 1.

130. Givón, *Context*, 26.

131. εἰ οὖν ὁμοίως ἢ μᾶλλον πιστὸν τὸ ΒΓ τοῦ ΑΓ ἀπαγωγή ἐστιν· Aristotle, *Prior Analytics* 69a (2:25:26–27).

132. Givón, *Context*, 26.

133. Ibid.

134. Appel and Nabokov, "Interview," 127–52.

processes responsible for language comprehension may indeed operate in some analogously detailed fashion, but for native speakers at least, the minutiae of discourse features in language normally fall below the threshold of conscious thought. It can be an effort to articulate explicitly what a *therefore* is there for, when language competence in most cases appreciates its significance via something approaching a reflex. Yet when interpretations of a piece of language disagree, we are thrown back on first principles to resolve our differences. The following study is offered as a contribution to such discussion of the Song.

However, some more informal arguments may also be presented in support of the gynocentric hypothesis for the Song, "top down," as "intuitions"—more literary than linguistic. For example, on the basis of observable literary characteristics, attempts have been made to classify the Song (or parts of it) as like to other works of similar genre (or form). If the species *Shir hashirim* can be demonstrated to be typical of some identifiable literary genus on the basis of some of its uncontroversial characteristics, then other characteristics of that genus might be inferred to apply to the Song and aid in its interpretation. Clearly the Song is poetry, but is it also reasonably classified as drama? John Milton, seeking "Dramatick conſtitutions . . . doctrinal and exemplary to a Nation," considers after Sophocles and Euripides, but before the "Apocalyps of Saint *Iohn*," that "the Scripture alſo affords us a divine paſtoral Drama in the Song of *Salomon* conſiſting of two perſons and a double *Chorus*, as *Origen* rightly judges."[135] Even if the Song is not drama proper, is it sufficiently dramatic that some results from literary analysis of drama might be applicable, at least to the research questions of the current thesis?[136]

An analogy between biological classification and literary classification is, of course, rather approximate only, since literary inheritance has considerably more degrees of freedom than genetic inheritance. "Interbreeding" constrains biological classification to a tree-like structure, whereas "cross-pollination" has accelerated over the course of literary history. Literary genres frequently involve deliberate innovations and departures from any merely simplistic reproduction of "canonical literary forms." So, resisting the temptation to categorize the Song too precisely can leave us free to compare and contrast it with documented human thought and art *one degree of freedom at a time*: as reflection on the topic of love (content); as poetry

---

135. Milton, *Reason*, preface to book 2.

136. "Even though the Song is not structurally a drama, [the] recapitulated theme of seeking and finding does impart to it a certain dramatic quality." Kline, "Bible Book of the Month," : 22–23, 39.

(form); as a work from the classical era (date); as an opus drawn from the corpus of Afro-Asiatic or Semitic dialects (language);[137] as a Palestinian, Levantine, or Oriental work (place, culture);[138] and, not least, as a sacred text—Aqiba's (and Origen's) *most* sacred of sacred texts (religion).[139]

The Song might also be a maverick among texts,[140] like de Laclos's and Lewis's (*inter alia*) "epistolary" novels, *Les Liaisons dangereuses* and *The Screwtape letters*, or like Alexandre Pushkin's love story *Eugene Onegin*,[141] for example. Just as the Song has often been thought to be an allegory, so many critics have followed Vissarion Belinsky's famous appraisal of Pushkin's "novel in verse" (роман в стихах) as "an encyclopedia of Russian life."[142] Likewise, just as there is a good case for the Song reflecting some familiarity with other ancient Near Eastern literature, so Pushkin explicitly quotes— and otherwise alludes to—earlier European literature, being considered to have been especially strongly influenced by the writers of seventeenth-century France,[143] and by Byron's *Don Juan*. *Eugene Onegin* was composed as a long sequence of sonnet-stanzas, with an unconventional rhyme scheme, which also alternated "masculine" (oxytonic) and "feminine" (paroxytonic) rhymes.[144] While this marks the work as exceedingly, deliberately poetic, it

137. See Fox, *Song of Songs*.

138. See Leick, *Sex and Eroticism*.

139. Comparisons and contrasts between *independent* literary traditions—which are *unlikely* to have had any historical interaction—are of particular scientific value. Cultures of oral poetry antedate not only classical civic literature, but also literacy itself, cross-culturally. Biology tells us sexual reproduction evolved independently in different branches of the tree of life. Was poetry (and love poetry) integral to the earliest human societies? Did regional differences lead to different trajectories of development, or do we have evidence of independent *origins* for poetry? Sadly, there is a paucity of scholarly treatment of *contrasts* between the Song and the famous Sanskrit love story of mortal man and immortal woman in the Purūravas–Urvaśī tradition. This extends from hymn 95 of the tenth *mandala* of the Ṛg Veda, through the Śatapatha Brāhmaṇa, on to the Bhāgavata Purāṇa (9:14), thence to Kālidāsa's *Vikramōrvaśīyam*.

140. Cf. "Art—the arts generally—are always unpredictable, maverick, and tend to be, at their best, uncomfortable." Lessing, "Political Correctness."

141. *Eugene Onegin* was subtitled *A novel in verse*. Serial instalments (1823–1831) preceded publication of the first full-text edition (1833) and a second and final edition (1837).

142. Belinsky, "*Eugene Onegin*"

143. "Pushkin was less interested in the prose which he considered the strength of the French than in the poetry which he considered their weakness.... [He] always insisted that there was no real poetry in France before the seventeenth century." Maguire, "Pushkin," 101–9.

144. Hofstadter, author of Pulitzer prize-winning *Gödel, Escher, Bach* (1979), later published his own version of *Eugene Onegin* (subtitled *A Novel Versification*). Prior

is just as evidently couched as a narrative by its author, who describes his creative process in its penultimate stanza. Here, Pushkin describes his unusual opus as a novel, but a "free" one (свободного романа). That *Eugene Onegin* is a multi-genre opus is sufficiently obvious to inspection that such a classification does not even need its author's imprimatur, in title and in text; however, it may well be that the Song of Songs is a somewhat similarly "trans-genred" work. Codex Sinaiticus's version of the Song offers rubrics with "scene-setting stage directions" and specifies the speakers (starting simply with ἡ νύμφη),[145] since the Song's second person verbs, marked for gender in the Hebrew, require some other device to communicate this deictic information in Greek (and English, as per Callow above). Likewise, Origen did not simply see the Song as merely to be appreciated allegorically; he based this on a primary literary analysis of the Song, in which he makes much of its noticeably dramatized presentation.[146] To be sure, the Song is dramatic poetry, not drama in verse, as in Indo-European traditions;[147] however, this widely recognized literary feature, of dramatic voices and *personae* in the Song, helps motivate the linguistic analysis of discourse participants in the body of this study.

In its received form, the Song may be analyzed as having up to almost a dozen potentially significant discourse participants. It is the purpose of this study: firstly, to establish that the Shulamite is indisputably the central figure among these discourse participants—the gynocentric hypothesis; but also, secondly, to examine closely the way gender is portrayed in the relationships between the Song's characters—is it patriarchal, as Exum, Clines *et al.* propose, or does it rescue the Bible from patriarchalism, as Trible, Falk, et al., propose? Focusing on the discourse participants of the Song, and their explicit or implied relationships, provides a clear framework within which both these research questions can be addressed. Detailed evidence (predominantly linguistic) occupies the bulk of this current study, but the overall picture may be sketched in outline, in a more literary way, relatively briefly, here.

---

to publishing his own version of Pushkin's novel, he sounded a striking note of praise for translations that carry rhyme from source text to receptor language, because "at a higher level of abstraction, all the key relationships among sounds are preserved isomorphically." Hofstader, "What's Gained," 47–48.

145. See CodexSinaiticus.org: the color of the rubrics stands out clearly.

146. King, *Origen*.

147. Perhaps including the "dialogue hymn" Pururavas and Urvashi (RV 10:95), in the Vedic form of the archaic *triṣṭubh* meter—four *pada* (feet) of eleven syllables each, with a caesura and regular cadence.

Whether the Song was written to be performed (or, as per Clines, only ever to be read), and whether or not it was compiled from earlier material; in the form we have it now, *the Song presumes an audience*. For all its celebrated freedom of metaphor and compellingly authentic portrayal of intimate—even private—emotions, and despite some relatively opaque motivations for transitions from speaker to speaker and section to section, the Song retains a distinctive and literary, deliberate and formal character as a text. Such is the stuff of published poetry. Poets may write verses for their own private consumption only: as exercises, as drafts, or for personal reasons. Even so, even without any intention to publish, there is still an implied audience, even if this audience may never have been intended to be wider than the poet herself. Plath's *Daddy*, for example, does not easily generalize to just any reader sharing Plath's experiences as described in the poem. In the case of the Song, however, the anonymity of the protagonists, the genericness and plurality of the characters of the chorus and other "extras," and the very subject of romantic love itself, suggest it is likely that the poet (or compiler) so constructed the Song that it would address a wide, general (and gendered) audience. That is not true of all genres of literature, nor of all poetry, not even in the Bible, if we can accept the standard view that poetic passages in apocalyptic are couched in baroque language, at least in part, to communicate they are intended for an audience of "initiates only."

The Song, in stark contrast to apocalyptic, appears to be a "public domain" work. Not only that, but the Song is also "interactive"—it self-consciously engages with its audience. The Song is no crude morality play,[148] but when the Shulamite calls on her friends to stop glancing at her dark skin, surely we sympathize with her, position ourselves among her friends, and accede—in our imagination—to her request, as we are drawn into the fiction of the poem. When she places her friends on oath not to arouse or awaken love, we ourselves feel challenged. When the Shulamite soliloquizes, without response from her love or her friends, we do not conclude she is really talking to herself alone or only to the air. We know, and the poet knows we know, that she is talking to us, the audience. Indeed, by the end of the Song, we know the Shulamite sufficiently well to distinguish between the genuine hyperbole of her exulting about the size of her breasts, and her perfectly sincere declaration regarding the life-or-death nature of the ideal of love she (and the poet) are presenting *to the audience*.

---

148. "Only in such children's stories as contain the concluding 'and the moral of the story is . . .' or in tiresomely didactic authors such as Tolstoy do we get an explicit representation of the serious speech acts which it is the point (or the main point) of the fictional text to convey." Searle, "Logical Status," 332.

Strictly speaking, neither poet nor audience are literal discourse participants (or "voices") within the Song, yet the burden of proof must still fall on those who would deny that the Song reflects a deliberate message from poet to audience. Counterintuitively, this is all the more so, since the poet is so deliberate in refraining from activating his persona. Shelley offers us a concise and simpler example of the same phenomenon in his sonnet, *Ozymandias*.[149] Although the very first word of that short poem is "I," and the second discourse participant is an anonymous "traveller from an antique land," the topic of the discourse is clearly the Ozymandias of its title, and it is only he that is named: "My name is Ozymandias, King of Kings: Look on my works, ye mighty, and despair!" Of course, the irony is that it is not Ozymandias's works we see, but the brilliant work of the remaining, "silent" discourse participant, the royal mason: "its sculptor well those passions read / Which yet survive." Shelley's poem provides a simple linear progression of participants regarding one another: reader looking on Shelley, looking on traveller, looking on sculptor, looking on Ozymandias, looking on the world. By contrast, the Song has the daughters of Jerusalem regarding the Shulamite regarding her love regarding her, and other complexities. Yet, just as with Shelley, the poet of the Song makes his points through the words of the characters he constructs.

We can press the analogy between *Ozymandias* and the Song a little further. The "I" of *Ozymandias* is no more Shelley than Ozymandias, in the poem, is actually Ramses II. They are types, made concrete to suspend reader disbelief, and to avoid confusing multiple layers of abstraction. Rather nicely, Shelley's opening line orients the reader to the discourse, economically and effectively. At the same time he provides a variant on the "once upon a time" formula, and yet—in British empiricist tradition—he also provides an "audit trail" of fictive eyewitnesses. He is saying, "this may not quite be a true story, but it might as well be." The "I" of *Ozymandias* functions like the daughters of Jerusalem in the Song; they confirm or "second" the testimony of the main speaker. In both cases, these participants are provided by the poets to orient readers to the discourse, and to suspend disbelief—they model reader response (as in Umberto Eco's *lettore modello*).[150] Shelley suggests, "I was struck by this, and so shall you be." The poet (or compositor) behind the Song suggests, via the daughters of Jerusalem, "We are listening to you, O Shulamite; we ourselves have seen the truth of what you say."

---

149. Shelley, "Ozymandias," 24. The autograph, from a leaf of a notebook, is held in the Bodleian Library, with a draft of the poem on the reverse.

150. See Eco, *Lector in Fabula*.

In the case of *Ozymandias*, the sculptor is held up, if I may phrase it thus, as prophetic, having enduringly carved his understanding of the vanity of ambition in the face of time and space. There is a positive irony here, with the sculptor ultimately being heard "far away" from his "antique land." It is the truth of humility that endures, not the vanity of ambition: those with ears, may they hear.[151] It is interesting to contrast Shelley's poem with Horace Smith's poem of the same name, published in *The Examiner* three weeks later, where Smith speaks directly of Egypt and London. Although Smith uses no first person pronoun, it is Smith's poem, not Shelley's, that comes across more directly as poet preaching to reader;[152] it also reveals that Smith is an Englishman, writing for an English audience. Pushkin, even more explicitly, injects himself into *Eugene Onegin*, speaking as a Russian to Russians,[153] and addressing readers directly (о мой читатель), even acknowledging foes (недруг) as well as friends (друг).[154] Among all these sonnets, Shelley's *Ozymandias* is the most elliptic; the main point of his poem is fictively attributed to the sculptor. But in Smith's, it can only be attributed to the poet himself. Shelley's "I" in Ozymandias does not, in fact, introduce the poet to the reader, but rather invites the reader into the narrative, via identifying with the poet: "I can imagine *myself* listening to a traveller's tales, such as these" (see Eco's *lector in fabula*).[155]

Yet, returning to the Song, it is not the Shulamite's "I" the reader is, at first, invited to identify with—her intimations are too specific, personal, and intense for that. At first, the reader identifies most closely with the daughters of Jerusalem.[156] Yet this seems to work as a "hook" as the Shulamite's exhortations to the daughters give way to implications, then assertions, of gener-

---

151. "Tyrants will come and go, [Shelley's] poem confidently implies, but civilisation outlasts them. (Shelley was writing only two years after the Battle of Waterloo and the defeat of Napoleon.)" Barlow, *World and Time*, 117.

152. "Shelley doesn't spell out how we should react: he lets the ruined statue dwarfed by the endless desert speak for itself." Ibid., 115.

153. "That most Russian of Russian poets," according to Hofstadter, "What's Gained," 47.

154. Pushkin, *Eugene Onegin*, 8:XLIX.

155. Eco, *Lector in Fabula*.

156. "The women's presence is always a reminder that what seems to be a closed dialogue between two perpetually desiring lovers is addressed to us, for our pleasure and possibly our enlightenment." Exum, *Song of Songs*, 7. This is not just a modern "reader response" literary analysis; Aristotle preferred Sophocles to Euripides on the grounds that "it is necessary the chorus be understood as one of the actors, to be part of the whole, to be participating (συναγωνίζομαι)." Καὶ τὸν χορὸν δὲ ἕνα δεῖ ὑπολαμβάνειν τῶν ὑποκριτῶν, καὶ μόριον εἶναι τοῦ ὅλου καὶ συναγωνίζεσθαι μὴ ὥσπερ Εὐριπίδῃ ἀλλ' ὥσπερ Σοφοκλεῖ. Aristotle, *Poetics*, d 1456a.

alities regarding her vision of love. By the end of the Song, it is impossible to discern just whom the Shulamite is addressing. Quite plausibly, she addresses all: daughters, brothers, Solomon (real or fictive), *and the audience.*

As the sculptor is Shelley's prophet, so the Shulamite is the Song's prophetess.[157]

At least, that is the gynocentric hypothesis this study aims to place on a foundation of objective linguistic evidence: in the first place, in regard to the pragmatic "flow" of the Song, variously activating its discourse participants; and secondly, in regard to the semantic "units," in particular the gendered "macroroles" (and other collocations) apparent in the surface form of the text.[158]

---

157. "The woman audaciously declares, on behalf of the poet . . ." Exum, *Song of Songs*, 253.

158. *Macrorole* is borrowed from the language of Valin's (et al.) Role and Reference Grammar (RRG); and the relevant collocations are language-specific lexical choices identified by Critical Discourse Analysis (CDA) as reinforcing gender typology: *e.g.,* "beautiful woman" *vis-à-vis* "handsome man."

2

Literature Review

> No composition of comparable size in world literature has provoked and inspired such a volume and variety of comment and interpretation as the biblical Song of Songs. — Marvin Pope[1]

§1. Global Context

GIVEN THE RESEARCH AIM of investigating the illocutionary force of Solomon's Song of Songs in regard to gender, and the methodology of using discourse analysis, an early step was exploring ancient Near Eastern "world knowledge" and literary conventions broadly pertinent to love poetry.[2] Oxford University's Electronic Text Corpus of Sumerian Literature (ETCSL) provides access to a substantial fraction of the primary source material, and Dietz Otto Edzard's *Sumerian Grammar* an accessible introduction to the language.[3]

---

1. Pope, *Song of Songs*, 17.

2. For an excellent overview, see the published version of her doctoral thesis—Leick, *Sex and Eroticism*; an anthology of essays on the broader theme of gender across ancient cultures beyond the Near East, but with a focus on religion, is Penner and van der Stichele, *Mapping Gender*; and one of several classic more specific studies of the Song in ancient Near Eastern context is Fox, *Song of Songs*.

3. Edzard, *Sumerian Grammar*; the Society of Biblical Literature published a paperback version, and the *Review of Biblical Literature* an index to works cited in the *Grammar*; a classic text on Sumerian culture and history is Kramer, *Sumerians*, available in several editions, and with open access online at Chicago University.

Egyptological resources are numerous; but ultimately the Song of Songs is very similar indeed to the Ramesside love songs, with their thematic treatment of love, broadly associated with the culture of the eighteenth and nineteenth dynasties of Egypt, late second millennium BCE, just prior to the Eastern Mediterranean Bronze Age collapse. However, just as the Song was first transmitted within local and regional contexts, as Pope's observation above highlights, this local phenomenon also has a context in world literature. Indeed, the Song is not just embedded in literature and history, but also in preliterate oral traditions and even in vast contemporary markets for love songs. (Both poetry in lines and sexual jealousy are believed to be human universals.)[4] The biblical song itself continues to inspire musical settings, not just commentary. There are hundreds of these, though a personal favorite is Palestrina's 29 motets, progressively covering the Vulgate of Canticles 1:2-7:12, a few lines per motet.[5]

Reflecting on the canon of world literature, we might want to start with the Chinese anthology of generally short poems, known as *Shijing* (詩經, *Classic of Poetry*)—rather longer than the Song—which has also generated both enduring and extensive commentary.[6] Likewise, the Rigvedic hymnic love story of a marriage between heaven and earth,[7] in the persons of the heavenly nymph (*apsarah*) Urvashi and earthly king Pururavas—rather shorter than the Song—has also generated much commentary, mainly vicariously through Kalidasa's creative and popular retelling of the love affair, in the classical meters of his Sanskrit drama and its versions.[8] However, far more profoundly influential has been the metrical Ramayana narrating the love story of Rama and Sita, though—like *Shijing*—it is much longer than the Song.

In his extensive prefatory contextualization of the Song,[9] Pope does consider the influential twelfth-century CE Indian Gita Govinda regarding divine Krishna and mortal Radha as loosely comparable with the biblical Song,[10] and he additionally quotes a lengthy section from one of Kalidasa's several candid but tasteful passages regarding sexual desire, though Pope—probably fairly—makes no comment regarding the older Asian works due to clear contrasts in length, and probably genre as well: the Song is neither

4. Brown, *Human Universals*.
5. Palestrina, *Motettorum*; see also Dahlenburg, *The Motet c. 1580-1630*.
6. Riegel, "Eros," 143-177.
7. RV 10:95, commentary in ŚB 11.5.1, and several puranas.
8. Kalidasa, *Urvashi*.
9. Pope, *Song of Songs*, 17-288.
10. Ibid., 85-89.

a lengthy anthology like *Shijing* nor a lengthy narrative like the seven volume Ramayana. Even the Gita Govinda is longer than the Song, and has an unambiguous plot.

Like Pope, this study will also pass up on any attempt to offer detailed treatment of romantic love in world literature by comparison and contrast with the Song. Even restricting consideration to gender and sexuality as attributed to supernatural beings in world mythologies would be a huge task, valuable in itself, but extending well beyond what is necessary to address the aim of discerning the illocutionary force of the Song. What is unwieldy given so much concrete data in world love lyrics, however, is more tractable in the abstract, namely concerning language typology and conventions of discourse structure—recently developed and still expanding disciplines, with a literature of their own to be briefly reviewed here below (in chapter four).

What is also more tractable is consideration of typologies of social and cultural settings that canonize poems: for ritual use, for education, or for entertainment (though the distinctions between these functions for literature are not always clear). I have found immersing myself in the historical and contemporary poetry of one particular setting quite fruitful for providing independent evidence regarding questions about the *Sitz im Leben* of the Song. This is not a matter of establishing historical particularities of the ancient Near East, but a matter of obtaining "control" data, human "default" life-settings that provide the "market" for love songs, however that might be realized in particular cultures at various times.[11] It is an aid to realism, objectivity, and clarity, via familiarity with at least one concrete cultural setting for love poetry, other than my own, as well as that setting being distinct from the host culture of the Song itself. It is the "triangulation" methodology recommended in social and cultural anthropology.[12] The significance of certain theoretical claims about abstract discourse generalities (and how they may apply to love poetry) stand out more sharply to be verified or falsified when testing them against scholarly commentaries outside both discourse analysis and ancient Near Eastern specializations.

It is the slowly shifting Javanese culture that I have found consistently provides confirmation or counterexample for many cross-cultural claims. Javanese culture attests to multiple strata of obvious cultural borrowing over

---

11. For a contemporary classic regarding sociological context for romance, see Giddens, *Transformation of Intimacy*; there is also extensive literature in regard to so-called "lipstick" feminism by its advocates, critics and observers, Naomi Wolf and Katie Roiphe being key writers in the field; David Clines wrote two articles on the Song of Songs into this context and addressing some of its key issues directly.

12. Kleine, "Beyond Triangulation," 117-25; Denzin, *Research Act*; Geertz, *Local Knowledge*; Malinowski, *Diary*.

more than two millennia, most of these influences still being clearly present in one way or another among the rural tenant farming peasantry of the island,[13] and even in its largest urban centers, including the national capital of Indonesia, Jakarta. Javanese rather than, say, Japanese or Aztec (formally, classical Nahuatl) culture as a control study, is a somewhat arbitrary choice, based on personal opportunities and tastes, though some of the considerations of other alternatives are worth mentioning. Perhaps Javanese culture would have been the preferred choice, even without it having the advantage of being accessible to me personally.

Ethnomusicologists, especially several prominent figures associated with the University of Sydney, have studied traditional Australian Aboriginal songs, including those that feature relations between the sexes.[14] Several things make these non-ideal for comparison with the Song of Songs, however. Amorous relations are not frequently attested in Aboriginal lyrics,[15] and the dating of the content of Aboriginal song cycles is subject to many uncertainties, including influences introduced since European co-settlement. There are ethnographic accounts of Papuan societies that also provide lyrics of traditional songs, but these suffer from similar issues to those of Aboriginal Australia: little focus on amorous relationships and uncertainties regarding the history of transmission and cultural contact.

Much better documented are ethnographies from India, like those associated with the Muria Gonds, who additionally had a much-discussed social institution of compulsory premarital cohabitation and sexual experimentation for peripubescent youths.[16] Young lads in early adolescence were fined if they did not change the girl they were sleeping with on a regular basis, even according to a strict and imposed timetable. Later marriage involved payment of bride-service of a year or two in the household of the

13. Koentjaraningrat, *Javanese Culture*.

14. Among others: Berndt, *Love Songs of Arnhem Land*; Keogh, *Nurulu*; for song-poems since European co-settlement see Dixon, *Little Eva*.

15. Nineteenth-century European writers were not uniformly convinced that Aboriginal men actually loved their wives, and the matter is discussed by Durkheim, Westermarck, and Malinowski. Well prior to the advent of "political correctness," however, the older (and possibly never majority) view was debunked and abandoned. Traditional Aboriginal society was neither primitively promiscuous nor casually brutal, despite it clearly admitting to a reluctant acceptance of occasional marriage by capture, sometimes termed "rape marriage," though it appears more often to have been a matter of non-consenting elders or parents and willing brides—elopement then, rather than rape.

16. Classic ethnographies are: Elwin, *Muria*; and Grigson, *Maria Gonds*; for more recent commentary see Lyons and Lyons, *Irregular Connections*; see also Craig Scott, *Pagan Sex*.

prospective father-in-law. Different villages had different practices, but so long as a lad was up to date with his household chores during his years of domestic service, sexual access to his fiancée was not unusual. Muria practices are exceptional in several ways to various human social near-universals regarding pre-marital sexuality (they appear to be very unrealistic about pregnancy), but ultimately their marriage patterns fall well within the known range of variation in strategies for family formation.

At the other extreme to preliterate societies that have survived into the contemporary global world are traditions of "courtly love" poetry from literate societies with highly complex economies and polities. Sumerian, Akkadian, Egyptian, and other ancient Near Eastern literary traditions fall into this category, and are necessarily part of our considerations in the current study because of many known points of cultural contact with ancient Israel; but for that very reason they cannot provide us with independent perspectives on the attested range of variation in human, poetically-expressed reflection on gender and sexuality. In South Asia, neither northern Indo-Iranian nor southern Dravidian poetry is in principle sharply independent from Semitic poetry and culture. Indo-Iranian contact was possibly being mediated along the Silk Road (or, more accurately, roads) via Old Avestan and Bactria by the latter part of the second millennium BCE, and certainly via Persia by the mid-first millennium. Dravidian contact is probably even older, being mediated along the Persian Gulf sea trade between Harappa and Sumer (also Elam) via Mohenjo Daro during the third millennium, and continuing via Arabia after the collapse of the Indus Valley civilization.[17]

In sum, archeologists outside the Near East continue to find material evidence of cross-cultural contacts all over the Old World antedating the advent of literacy. Contemporary ancient history is redefining the boundaries of the discipline to include, alongside traditional documentary evidence, ever more material evidence—as would be expected—but also increasingly sophisticated genetic evidence (including the genetics of domesticated flora and fauna), and a certain degree of linguistic reconstruction (although this last element is particularly prone to controversy). Those three strands in particular are much discussed: archaeology, genetics, and linguistics.[18] Writing no longer delineates a sharp boundary between history and prehistory, except in a functional way relative to specific locations or people groups. This also suits the aim of studying *human* and *world* history without privi-

---

17. For comparisons and contrasts between the Song of Songs and the Tamil (Dravidian) love poems in the Sangam literature, see Mariaselvam, *Song of Songs*; see also Rabbin, "Song of Songs," 205-219.

18. For an up-to-date Australian archaeologist's perspective, see Bellwood, *First Migrants*.

leging branches of the family on the grounds of specific technologies (like writing), nor assuming a Mediterranean (read Eurocentric or Abrahamic religious) narrative perspective.

The world history of human expansion reached an important turning point when, like Ouroboros, it finally "ate its own tail" with European "discovery," conquest, and co-settlement in the New World. Mesoamerican civilization offers a kind of independent witness to Old World variation in literary culture, with Aztec poetry—in their classical Nahuatl language—having being popularized to the English speaking academy by the anthropologist Daniel Brinton via his late nineteenth-century diglot anthology of twenty-seven poems.[19] Three of these "ancient" songs, however, are Christian hymns, naming Jesus as Messiah and using Spanish theological terms. Considerable English language study of classical Nahuatl was conducted over the course of the twentieth century, with two fine scholarly editions of manuscripts of poetry being published by John Bierhorst: Cantares Mexicanos,[20] and Codex Romances.[21] At least in the literary register of classical Nahuatl, not just in poetry, pairs of hendiadic conventional metaphors were used so regularly that for many common nouns no single lemma is attested, only compounds, including word pairs for "city" and "king" and "poetry," the last of which was known as "flower-song." Nahuatl poetry is beyond the scope of this thesis to document, but furnishes another clear example of the value of control variables in scientific study. The Azetec poets are undoubtedly writing according to traditions completely unrelated to ancient Near Eastern conventions, yet there are similarities as well as differences in their topics and manners of expression, and indeed similarities and differences in the questions that scholars of Aztec culture and literature address by comparison with scholars of the ancient Near East. Brinton may well have had the Song of Songs in mind when he wrote the following:

> Perhaps [the 60 songs of Nezahualcoyotl (d. 1472), poet-king of Tezcuco] were framed on themes which he furnished, or were selected by him from those sung at his court by various bards. The history of the works by royal authors everywhere must not be too minutely scanned if we wish to leave them their reputation for originality.[22]

19. Brinton, *Ancient Nahuatl Poetry*.
20. Bierhorst, *Cantares Mexicanos*.
21. Bierhorst, *Ballads of the Lords.*.
22. Brinton, *Ancient Nahuatl Poetry*, 36.

His list of features of Nahuatl poetry, although dated, demonstrates well how different it was to Hebrew poetry, and yet clearly the Song of Songs does make frequent use of metaphor, very richly; more so than most psalms. Brinton found Aztec poetry to be characterized by the following:

1. Extreme frequency and richness of metaphor. Birds, flowers, precious stones and brilliant objects are constantly introduced in a figurative sense, often to the point of obscuring the meaning of the sentence.

2. Words are compounded to a much greater extent than in ordinary prose writing.

3. Both words and grammatical forms unknown to the tongue of daily life occur. These may be archaic, or manufactured capriciously by the poet.

4. Vowels are inordinately lengthened and syllables reduplicated, either for the purpose of emphasis or of meter.

5. Meaningless interjections are inserted for metrical effect, while others are thrown in and repeated in order to express emotion.

6. The rhetorical figure known as aposiopesis, where a sentence is left unfinished and in an interjectional condition, in consequence of some emotion of the mind, is not rare and adds to the obscurity of the wording.[23]

The independence of the Nahuatl tradition of poetry is attractive as a source of control data, but there is insufficient published love poetry to really make this possible, and there is even less information regarding its own patterns of borrowing. On the other hand, well-documented imperial China—from a very early stage—and Japan—from somewhat later—definitely offer tales of sexual jealousy, which is believed to be a human universal,[24] and they offer strong traditions of poetry as well. What makes Java preferable, though, is the layers of linguistic and religious influence—Hindu, Buddhist, Muslim, and finally Christian, all overlaid on an Austronesian and south-east Asian, metal-working, gong culture substratum.[25] And there is the distinctively

---

23. Ibid., 30.

24. Symons, *Evolution of Human Sexuality*; Brown, *Human Universals* quoted in Pinker, *The Blank Slate*; and Buss, *Evolution of Desire*.

25. Jaap Kunst is known for coining the term "ethnomusicology," though his personal focus was traditional Indonesian performing arts. A substantial collection of his journal publications was translated into English, see Kunst, *Indonesian Music and Dance*.

prominent place of songs at Javanese weddings—weddings that still come to close to involving whole villages dancing and singing.

Love songs in Indonesia, and especially those in Javanese, frequently refer to God explicitly, chiefly—but not exclusively—due to Islamic influence;[26] but it was not always that way. Indian literature was extensively appropriated in Java over the course of the first millennium CE, so much so that the whole lexicon of Old Javanese was heavily Sanskritized. The surviving "capital city" of Javanese culture—Ngayogyakarta (Javanese, officially Yogyakarta)—is named after Ayodhya, thanks to the influence of the Ramayana. Sanskrit metrical systems were adopted in committing local mythology to writing. Old Javanese is locally called Kawi, which refers specifically to its role as the vehicle of transmission for the classical poetic works, the *kakawin*.[27] Some of these are still recited in the original language by professional performers, particularly in Bali. There is even a contemporary Javanese term, *kumawi-kawi*, for pretending to have such skill with the Kawi language, due to its ongoing prestige when genuine.

Modern Javanese popular love songs, on the other hand, have lyrics called *syair* (from Arabic, so cognate by borrowing to Šir haŠširim, the Song of Songs).[28] Frequently, such lyrics are written to be performed as duets,[29] but often involving the *gamelan*, *keroncong*, or fusion musicians (or even the crowd) as a chorus. There is a centuries-old tradition of female vocalists (*sindhen*) in traditional Javanese music (*gendhing*),[30] and it may partly explain the frequency of the contemporary duet: historically, professional soloists appear to have been predominantly women (who work in teams). What is particularly captivating about Javanese performance traditions, however, is how integral they are to village life. Drama, with musical accompaniment, including modern political satires, but also with classical love stories and classical poetry, is still popular culture among tenant farmers in Java; it is not simply a matter of the high culture of the palace (*keraton*). On

---

26. For more recent scholarly commentary on twenty-first-century Indonesian popular music, written for a broad readership, see Weintraub, *Dangdut Stories*.

27. For the classic overview of the *belles-lettres* of Old Javanese, see Zoetmulder, *Kalangwan*.

28. Three popular lyricist-performers with distinctive styles are Manthous, Didi Kempot, and the group Catur Arum.

29. A few popular examples are: *Tresna sudra, Jambu alas, Rondo peng lima, Janda baru*, and *Rondo kempling*.

30. For an ethnomusicologist who actually trained as a *sindhen*, and also comments on the social issues related to the profession from a feminist perspective, see Walton: *Sindèn and Patet*; *Mode in Javanese Music*; and *Heavenly Nymphs*.

Bali this does often now interact with tourism,[31] but on Java it remains integrated within society, without much support from international tourism, even within the youth culture of the smaller cities, and even if older people may view some modern fusions of Indian, Arabic, and Western musical and performance traditions with local ones as more or less of a debasement.

Following Geertz, many scholars of diverse disciplines have agreed with one another that the performing arts are so integrated with the core of popular discourse in Javanese (and wider Indonesian) society, that such a society can be viewed as a "performance culture."[32] Anecdotally, expatriate workers have warned me against "giving an Indonesian a microphone," which suggests they have observed the same thing as the scholars. During the writing of the current thesis, I married my Jakarta-born wife, so have come to understand intimately what the scholars and expatriate community are talking about. Yes, within Indonesian cultural expectations, extended family and community social life can feel like participating in a permanent wedding reception; but I have come to delight in participating by frequently auditing others sharing the load of entertaining and encouraging one another by passing around microphones. It is especially refreshing because it typically involves a lot of honest expression of emotions (*rasa*, from Sanskrit), with more personal detail than Westerners expect (or north-east Asians for that matter), in regards to the trials of life (*pacobaning urip*), and it expresses the very high value they place on teamwork (*gotong royong*) in addressing these trials.[33] These are cultural values regularly articulated in pop songs, but also in the official political ideology of the nation, the five principles known as Pancasila (from Sanskrit for "five principles"). Indonesian performance art is still in touch with village life, and so—in some respects—is even the official public culture of this very populous modern nation.

All these fortuitous features of contemporary Javanese culture raise questions for me in regards to the *Sitz im Leben* of the Song of Songs. Were ancient Israelite villagers influenced by Egypt and Aram, and even ancient (to them as well) Sumer? Did they entertain one another with songs when it was too dark to work in the fields? Did villagers have a good-natured, healthy cynicism about Jerusalem and national politics? Is a good love song one so stylized that it makes it easy for the hearer to read herself into its fifty shades of grey? Is the biblical Song of Songs not a folk song, but a literary work of some other kind?

---

31. Yamashita, *Bali and Beyond*.
32. Geertz, *Negara*.
33. Koentjaraningrat, *Some Social-Anthropological Observations*.

There is a real sense in which there is a cultural ideal of the Javanese woman and the Javanese man often expressed in cultural distinctives of both symbolisms in performance and ideology underlying texts.[34] Some of this will be associated with natural human adaptations to pregnancy, nursing, and child-rearing on the slopes of active volcanoes, where I have seen girls about the age of ten liberating their mothers to harvest in the rice fields (*sawah padi*) by providing the childcare, carrying babies' milk bottles and their infant siblings in slings called *cukin*. If it sounds harsh that nursing mothers are doing hard labor in the fields on the slopes of these volcanoes (and one sees it regularly), it needs to be remembered also that the fathers are sometimes invisible because they are harvesting sulfur *inside* those volcanoes![35] Various other cultural ideals related to gender in Java, and specificities of divisions of labor, are undoubtedly more arbitrary, less realistic, or more amenable to change with changing economic circumstances. Princesses, and daughters of the educated elite (*priyayi*), for example, have long had comforts and opportunities unavailable to farmers (*tani*) and their sons.[36] A rapidly swelling new middle class is making millions of youths, male and female, modern equivalents of *priyayi*. As these young people negotiate romantic relationships, and we hear them thinking aloud in love songs, for the most part their thoughts are immediately recognizable, though there are certainly patterns of thought that are also obscure or foreign, sometimes charming or quaint, other times unsettling. It is a culture familiar with polygamy, concubinage, and easy divorce. The last is particularly commonly referred to, *Janda Baru* (literally, "Recently Divorced") being one extremely popular upbeat cheeky duet based on that setting. The twice-shy young woman of the song has the last word, a guarded invitation to her duet partner: "Do not treat me cheaply on account of me being recently divorced."[37]

From the perspective of the Judaeo-Christian legacy in the West (or vestiges of Victorianism), the Song of Songs appears to be less foreign than some of these Javanese realities, yet the Song is also closer to Javanese culture in its intimate knowledge of and reference to polygamy, concubinage, and even rape![38] Here lies the value of triangulation: Is any one of the three cultures—ancient Israel, contemporary West, or traditional Java—somehow

---

34. Williams, *Javanese Lives*.
35. Mount Ijen near Banyuwangi in East Java is famous for its sulfur industry.
36. Sears, *Fantasizing the Feminine*.
37. *Aja sembrana nadyan aku janda baru.*
38. For a recent cross-cultural study in Asia and the Pacific, see Fulu et al., "Why do Some Men Use Violence?"

normative? How do they look pairwise to each other?[39] What cultural specifics or universals does the Song assume or address? To use Laurie Sears's terminology,[40] some aspects of Javanese culture express *fantastic* (in the literal sense) ideals of the feminine; but to use Fiona Black's term,[41] although the Song of Songs is clearly *artificial* (again in the literal sense), are the issues related to the feminine in the Song artificial or perennial? One cannot answer those questions without engaging with history and culture *beyond* the literary traditions of the Mediterranean world and the Abrahamic religions. It is beyond the scope of this study to write that up in any detail, but the survey above aims to show that what is written below is not written without extensive consideration of the context of the Song as a literary work addressing unquestionably universal human issues in the joys and challenges arising from the intimate relations between the sexes. Cultures certainly encountered them universally, or they could not have continued reproducing.

Before turning to literature directly dependent on the Song of Songs, it is worth mentioning that I have taken the opportunity of this study to retrace some of my own teen reading, including—in translation—*Eugene Onegin* and *Dangerous Liaisons*:[42] an "anthology" of sonnets that comprise a novel about love, and a novel that is an "anthology" of love letters, and both of which have been adapted for dramatic performance.[43] Both works obviously mix genres as part of searching social criticisms of inhumanity in affairs of the heart. Perhaps we can allow the biblical Song some license to play with genre as well.

Additionally, it seems noteworthy, although history may well pass over it, but during this time, I also found I could not help tapping my own hooves along to a new "horse dance"; not the famous *jaranan* horse dance of Java, nor due to a *jaran goyang* (lit. "swaying horse"), the famous Javanese love

---

39. A recent Indonesian commentary on the Song is Anand Krishna, *Kidung Agung* (Jakarta: Gramedia, 2007).

40. Sears, *Fantasizing the Feminine*.

41. Black, *Artifice of Love*.

42. Pushkin, *Eugen Onegin*.

43. *Eugene Onegin* was adapted: as a film-opera, Konstantin Shilovsky (libretto), Alexander Ivanovsky, and Roman Tikhomirov, *Eugene Onegin*, directed by Roman Tikhomirov (St Petersburg [Leningrad]: Lenfilm Studio, 1958); and as a film Peter Ettedgui and Michael Ignatieff, *Onegin*, directed by Martha Fiennes (New York: Samuel Goldwyn Films, 1999). *Les Liaisons Dangereuses* has been adapted into several different cultural settings, languages, and mediums of performing arts.

spell,[44] nor a newly rediscovered Scythian routine,[45] but a Korean pop-song that clocked up more than one billion YouTube hits in about six months: *Gangnam Style* (강남스타일).[46] A huge proportion of the world population heard and enjoyed this song, even without translation, though ironically its name is a fusion of syllables from the two most widely-spoken world languages, Mandarin and English.[47] Love poems and linguistic and cultural borrowings are not quite human universals, but once they start there seems to be no stopping them.

The current section, presenting as it does an overview of a vast body of literature, has necessarily been fairly cursory. It took its lead from Marvin Pope, whose large commentary on the Song included a substantial treatment of "world literature" in an attempt to understand the Song in a literary context. In an attempt to be both original and even broader than Pope, the section has looked beyond the ancient Near East and South Asia for clues about "world knowledge" and literary conventions regarding love poetry—things that are pertinent to discourse analysis. World knowledge involves presuppositions held by writers and readers that are part of the interpretative process. Literary conventions regarding poetry include that, as a cross-cultural universal, poetry is based on lines of text, though these lines are not always metrical, and certainly do not always rhyme. Love poems are typically short, but not always. They rarely, but sometimes, involve duets. The Song is a little unusual in both these regards, something we can only know by the sort of comparison with world literature undertaken above. Love poetry is very rarely allegorical or anthological. These are key concerns in the Song and its interpretation, by discourse analysis or by any other methodology. Although it has not been spelled out in detail in every instance, the quick survey of world literature above has been aimed at providing evidence of cultural universals and counterexamples to some theories related

---

44. Groenendael, *Jaranan*.

45. Prior to domestication, a native of the Eurasian steppe, see Anthony, *Horse, Wheel, and Language*.

46. Park Jae-Sang and Yoo Gun-hyung, *Gangnam style*, Seoul: Y.G., Entertainment, 2012.

47. Gangnam is a fashionable suburb of Seoul, south of the Hangang river, which is precisely what the syllables *gang* and *nam* mean in Chinese. *Gang* is the Korean pronunciation of *jiang* (江, "river") as in Zhang-jiang (長江, the *Yang*-tze, lit. "long river"). Similarly, *nam* is local pronunciation of *nan* (南, "south"), as in Nan-yueh (南越, Viet-*nam*, lit. "southern Yueh = Viet people"), and the character engraved on the mahjong tile for the south wind. Jiang-nan (江南) in Chinese refers to the broad geographical region south of the lower course of the Yangtze river, and includes both the cities Shanghai and Nanjing (南京, lit. "south capital"; cf. Beijing, 北京, lit. "north capital").

to the Song. It is assumed that individual readers will have informed their own conceptions of love poetry in global context in the course of engaging with the section, adding or subtracting presuppositions depending on their own prior world knowledge. With something of a common foundation of presuppositions about love poetry, we can now progress discussion by narrowing focus to the Song itself, and to consideration of the divergent views held by scholars concerning its structure and interpretation.

§2. Canticles Commentary

There are many published bibliographies for the Song of Songs. Marvin Pope is most often cited in commentaries that have been published since his very extensive 1977 listing (55 pages, still in print) of scholarly works addressing the Song of Songs.[48] Pope's list is not annotated; on the other hand, just under half of Ginsburg's 1857 commentary is devoted to summary, quotation, and translation of earlier commentaries. He achieves a close approximation to being comprehensive as regards the extant history of "exegesis" of the book—as Ginsburg himself terms it—up to publication of his own translation with extensive front matter and interpretative footnotes.[49] A messianic Jewish scholar, Ginsburg's rather rabbinic-style commentary follows through the history of interpretation of the Song by dividing it into two logically distinct Jewish (39 pages) and Christian (42 pages) scholarly legacies. This is particularly useful given that until the Enlightenment, the ubiquity of allegorical readings meant that the Song was interpreted in ways presumed to harmonize with the different biblical canons and doctrinal systematics of the two faith communities. Since Ginsburg, the rise of literal readings to all but a consensus among scholars of all faiths or no faith, has led to a new dichotomy, however, between those seeking to identify numbers of distinct poems within an anthology, and those seeking to propose a unifying macro-structure.

It is impossible to comment adequately on the entire history of Song scholarship in a thesis concerned more particularly with introducing a new methodology for deriving interpretation. However, it will soon be evident that it is still worth summarizing the celebrated work of others, particularly Ginsburg; the question is how to summarize all that work. Below I take as a rough basis for inclusion, in a very compressed summary, that included works had proposed readings bearing on discourse analysis or gender issues, or that they are still somewhat commonly cited. I have limited myself

48. Pope, *Song of Songs*, 233-88.
49. Ginsburg, *Song of Songs*, 20-102.

to a short section for commentators prior to Ginsburg, allocating that evenly between Jewish and Christian scholars as he did. Very terse quotations are provided in some cases, either from the original sources, or from Ginsburg's translations. I also make an attempt to provide entries in these summary tables so that there is a genuinely representative sampling of the more conspicuous examples of general trends in interpretation. This is more than a little subjective, and should only be taken as a way of showing that discourse analytical and gender concerns are attested within a broader history of Song interpretation, certainly at the dates specified, and approximately or accidentally within a relatively slow evolution of thought, which a reader might speculate about from the limited data presented. Attempts to explain the historical trajectories of Song interpretation are not among the research goals of this thesis, which rather attempts an independent and new interpretation via direct application to the received text of a twenty-first-century style of formal semantic discourse analysis, believed to be both language-independent and consistent with intuition.

Commentary prior to Ginsburg is presented below. It is notable that various allegorical approaches to the Song attempted to demonstrate internal structure. In other words, the interplay of unity and substructure is not an altogether new feature of scholarly analysis of the Song. In a second short table, I present a bibliographical list of prominent anthologists. These scholars reflect work subsequent to Ginsburg, which coincided roughly with the rise of source criticism. The body of this thesis interacts with the anthologists via Phillip Roberts, who adopts their "bottom-up" methodology but derives a different conclusion from them; which is to say Roberts considered that exacting micro-analysis actually supports the unity of the Song, but a unity without any elaborate macro-structure. A careful consideration of Roberts, his methodology, and how the current thesis complements his work is provided in the next chapter (chapter three). The list of anthologists below is, like the summary from Ginsburg, again only an attempt to give the reader a broad feel for names and dates representative of a strong current within the history of interpretation, this time from mainly twentieth-century scholarship of the Song: those scholars most cited, and those with whom Roberts interacts, and hence with whom this thesis also interacts, though more indirectly. Mariaselvam and others also provide lists of scholarly commentators on the Song who adopt anthological approaches, mainly by way of explaining why they will not themselves follow any of the (other) anthologists, almost no two of whom agree (in detail) on the number of independent poems they posit to make up the anthology.[50]

A further short segment below is devoted to the last three decades of scholarship on the Song, from Carr (1984) to Assis (2009), restricted to those who read the Song as more-or-less a unity comprised of various macro-units, typically subdivided, and have published their perceived structure in explicit detail. These tables are laid out such that the first two tables show comparative subdivisions for the first half of the Song (to 5:1), and the next two tables show the comparisons between scholars for the second half of the Song. More than half of the analyses have been published since the turn of the millennium, a trend of increased interest in the Song noted among more recent commentators, and also seen in an increasing relative frequency of unpublished dissertations on the Song documented at WorldCat (there are several dozens of these from diverse disciplines).

Given that outline of the structure of the approach taken in this literature review, let us now turn to its first component, the summary from Ginsburg, beginning with an additional reason for choosing Ginsburg as model. Ginsburg is most commonly cited by scholars of *biblical* literature, but Elizabeth Clarke (2011) and Noam Flinker (2000) are representative of a different scholarly line of interest in the Song,[51] drawn to surveying the impact of the text within more popular and relatively secular literature.

In early modern protestant England, sex and politics and sexual politics were addressed in sermons and in public tracts and writing, often drawing on traditional or ad hoc allegorical appropriations of texts or themes from the Song of Songs, notably among the Ranters, but also stalwart orthodox Puritans like Calvinists, whose allegorizing was turned towards "proper social order" rather than Ranter libertinism. Flinker draws attention to Richard Littledale's (1869) survey of scholarly commentary on the Song,[52] which fills in the obvious early lacunae in Ginsburg (1857), but is essentially far more compressed, selecting only fifty-three writers overall, presented in only nineteen pages, and omitting writers of the eighteenth and nineteenth centuries, since Littledale considered his readers could locate works from recent centuries readily enough for themselves. Littledale's annotations are also generally more concise than those of Ginsburg, but his selection criteria for later writers appear to reflect an explicitly sectarian and confessional stance in his analysis.

---

50. Mariaselvam, *Song of Songs*, 45.
51. Flinker, *Song of Songs*; Clarke, *Politics, Religion*.
52. Littledale, *Commentary*, xxxii-xl.

Having turned from global context of the Song within a world of songs about love, across cultures and through ages, to a similar high level survey of scholarly attempts to understand the structure and significance of the Song itself, and having explained the rationale for presenting the three simplified tables reproduced below, let us now look at a limited number of ideas in all that context that are most pertinent to the current investigation. First among these is Rashi's objection to earlier commentaries, that "they are compatible neither with the language of Scripture, nor with the **connexion of the verses**" (Ginsburg's translation, my bold typeface, also added in the table below).

Rashi is sensitive to constraints implicit in natural language regarding what logically possible relationships might obtain between verses (sentences or clauses). In modern parlance, this is a principle of text linguistics or discourse analysis. Part of everyday language competence is recognizing that certain interpretative options are less pragmatically felicitous than others, or altogether impossible. For example, in answer to *Would you like tea or coffee?* the reply *Yes, please!* is correctly articulated, grammatically well formed, returned in the appropriate politeness register, and it is even strictly logically consistent; however, it breaches Grice's maxims of conversation. The offer of tea or coffee requests an answer with sufficient information to allow the host to fulfill the offer being made. One good conversational turn of speech act deserves another. The guest in our example has not adequately responded to the unarticulated presupposed elaboration of the request for information: *I will make you a cup of tea, a cup of coffee, something else if you want it and I have it, or nothing at all if you are not inclined for a drink at the moment; please tell me which of those four options is your preference.*

Rashi's reference to "the connexion of the verses" suggests he had an intuitive appreciation of the importance of context in interpretation, pragmatics, and correctly attributed this to an unarticulated and frequently unmarked element of natural language lying "between the lines." Rashi's insight is not peculiarly applicable to biblical literature, nor to Hebrew and Aramaic alone, but also to French, German, Yiddish, and English; indeed, to all natural languages (and the rigid syntax of many computer languages too). This current thesis is precisely an attempt to utilize that feature of natural language, "the connexion of the verses," now called dynamic semantics, in an attempt to refine understanding of the structure and significance of the Song of Songs. The formalism of dynamic semantics is new;[53] its study

---

53. Formally introduced by Hans Kamp, but also independently proposed by Irene Heim in a logically equivalent but more metaphorical manner as "file change semantics," both in the early 1980s.

over a growing number of natural languages is new; simulations in computerized technology are new; but the basic insight about needing to "read between the lines" is obviously at least as old as that phrase, at least as old as Rashi, at least as old as Aristotle, and—even in formalisms—as old as Pāṇini and his Sanskrit grammar. Though the key thing is that the formalisms only describe what competent native language speakers do instinctively in interpreting speech and conversations, even when, or especially when, we are only overhearing half of a conversation between two other people, as—in a sense—the poet causes us so to overhear the Shulamite, her love, and her friends in the Song in a very selective, and necessarily selective, way. This thesis uses contemporary technical language for essentially intuitive observations.

Among the Jewish commentaries, one also finds—in a few cases at least—division of the Song into three macro-sections, each of two subsections (Immanuel ben-Solomon, 1272-1350, citing earlier works). The latter two macro-sections are claimed to be divided such that each second subdivision is epexegetical of the first; not only that, but the lines of division between macro-sections and subsections, according to ben-Solomon, match those of many modern scholars, as we shall shortly see. Ben-Solomon, like Rashi, appeals to a reader's sense of what contemporary text linguistic (and biblical) scholarship calls Rhetorical Structure Theory (RST): spans of text—nucleus and satellite—falling into a taxonomy of types of pairwise constraints on nucleus and satellite, which set of constraints seems to account for close to the full range of possible relations between spans within natural language texts.[54] So-called "elaboration" is one well-known relation, or one class of well known rhetorical relations, encompassing the literary category of epexegetical expression.

Summary of Ginsburg
Jewish interpretation to Rashbam

date (per G)	interpreter	quotes and notes	p
323-246	Septuagint	"If the authors of the Septuagint had understood this book in any other than its obvious sense, they would have betrayed it in the translation."	21
180 BCE	Sirach 47:14-17	G contra Keil: Sirach does *not* imply allegory.	21

---

54. For example, Mann and Thompson, *Discourse Description*.

date (per G)	interpreter	quotes and notes	p
120 BCE	Wisdom 8	"Peruse ... Wisdom in the chapter quoted, and the bride in the Song of Songs ... there is no intentional resemblance whatever."	22
37–95 CE	Josephus *C. Ap.* 1:8	"It is far more likely that [Josephus] placed it among the four books which he describes as consisting of hymns to God and precepts for the life of men." [i.e. Ps., Prov., Eccl., & Cant. v. Job prophetic-historical]	23
100–500	Yadaim 3:5	R. Akiba, 1st c.: Song is holy of holies within scripture.	25
	Abodah Sarah 2	G paraphrases R. Dimi: "The beloved is taken to be *God*, and the loved one the *Congregation of Israel*."	26
	Talmud (in general)	"Most of this interpretation has been obtained, either by the separation of words, the transposition and change of letters, or by substituting in the commentary words, similar in sound to those in the Scriptures. . . . The hermeneutic rules laid down by R. Hillel, and augmented by R. Ishmael".	27
550	Targum	"The Targum takes the Song of Songs as an allegory, describing prophetically the history of the Jewish nation".	28
892–942	R. Saadias "Gaon"	"Arabic ... original Constantinople edition in the British Museum"; Hebrew translation in the Rabbinic Bible (Amsterdam, 1724).	34
1000–1040	R. Solomon ben-Judah "ha-Babli"	Liturgy "used in a poetical paraphrase on the first and second morning services of the Passover feast, ... designed to celebrate the Exodus from Egypt as the commencement of the conjugal relation between God and his people."	38

date (per G)	interpreter	quotes and notes	p
1040-1105	R. Solomon ben-Isaac "Rashi"	Rashi (on the Song): "My opinion is that Solomon foresaw, by the aid of the Holy Spirit, that Israel would be carried into sundry captivities, and undergo sundry dissolutions; that they would lament in their captivity over their former glory, and recall the former-love, which God manifested for them above all other nations; that they would say, 'I will go and return to my first husband, for then was it better with me than now' (Hos. 2:9); that they would acknowledge His kindness and their own rebellion, [and the good things which He promised] to give them in the latter days. This book is written by inspiration, and represents a wife forsaken by her husband, and shut up, longing for him, recalling to her mind her love in youth to her beloved, and confessing her guilt; her beloved sympathising with her affection, and remembering the kindness of her youth, the charms of her beauty, and her good works, which had tied him to her with an everlasting love. The design of this book is to show to Israel that God has not afflicted her (i.e., Israel) willingly; that though He did send her away, He has not cast her off; that she is still His wife, and He her husband, and that He will again be united to her." Rashi (on interpretations): "[There are] a number of other commentaries on this Song; some containing an exposition of the whole Book, and others of separate passages, but they are compatible neither with the language of Scripture, nor with the connexion of the verses."	39
1085-1155	R. Samuel ben-Meier "Rashbam"	Rashbam: "Foreseeing the Israelites in their captivity sighing after the Holy One who went away from them, as a bridegroom separates himself from his beloved, Solomon sings this song in the name of the congregation of Israel, who is like a bride to Him (God)."	42

Summary of Ginsburg
Jewish interpretation after Rashbam

date	interpreter	quotes and notes	p
1093–1168	R. ibn-Ezra ben-Meier "Rabba"	Ibn-Ezra: "This book is allegorical, and describes the history of Israel; commencing with the days of our Father, Abraham, and coming down to the days of the Messiah ... [it] is suppositious, because such an actual manifestation, in so public a manner as here recorded, would be regarded as highly improper." Nonetheless, Ibn-Ezra finds a plot involving "a damsel who kept a vineyard, and a shepherd" [G paraphrase] and "that *the king* is a *separate* and *distinct* person from the beloved shepherd." Ibn-Ezra: "The philosophers explain this book to refer to the mysterious harmony of the universe, and to the union of the divine soul with the earthly body; and that others, again, explain it literally."	44
1200–1250	Joseph ibn-Caspe	Ibn-Caspe: "This book represents the union between the active intellect (*intellectus agens*) and the receptive material intellect (*intellectus meterialis*)." "[This] is not my discovery; [Maimonedes] has enlightened our eyes ..., especially in 3:51 (of *More Nebochim*)".	46
1272–1350	Immanuel ben-Solomon of Rome	Ben-Solomon: "I submit that all truly wise men who commented upon this book philosophically, saw clearly that it is divisible into three principal sections. [1:2–2:17; 3:1–5:1; 5:2–8:14]" "The first section is again subdivided into two parts. The first part [1:2–2:7] represents one who fears God and shuns evil; but his knowledge of God is derived from tradition, and has no wisdom of his own. The second part (2:8–2:17) represents one who has studied mathematics and physics." "[The] second section is also subdivided into two parts; [3:1–3:5; 3:6–5:1]; the second part is epexegetical of the first." "[The third] section is subdivided into two parts: [5:2–8:4; 8:5–14]; the second part being epexegetical of the first."	49
1288–1370	Levi ben Gershon	One of several medieval scholars in the Rabbinic Bible (Amsterdam, 1724). [1:1–8; 1:9–2:7; 2:8–2:17; 3:1–4:7; 4:8–8:4; 8:5–8:14]	56

date	interpreter	quotes and notes	p
-1300	unknown	Unpublished anonymous French commentary ms of 12th or 13th c. Bodleian Oppenheim Collection #625. Literal reading, "celebrating the virtuous love contracted between a humble shepherd and shepherdess". Solomon is a third party.	56
1350	Isaac Sehula	"This book represents the love of the people of Israel to their God."	57
1360-1730	various	Meier Arma (b. 1475) philosophical commentary published along with competing views in the Rabbinic Bible (1724); his father, Isaac, had published a different view; Obadiah Sforno (1475?-1550) published in the 1724 Bible; Moses Cordovero (1522-1570) mentioned but never printed; Abraham Levi and Ibn-Shoeb printed together in Sabionetta, 1558; Elisha Galicho in Venice, 1587; Moses Alshech in Venice 1591; Isaac ben Judah Abravanel (1437-1508).	57
1729-1786	Moses Mendelssohn	Löwe and Wolfssohn (Berlin, 1788) commented on Mendelssohn's translation, finding a compendium of many literal songs.	58
1798-1821	Löwisohn	G: "The first who recognised and elucidated the true design of this book." "[The Song] celebrates the victory of true and virtuous love in humble life over the temptations of royalty". *Melizat Jeshurun* (Vienna, 1816)	59
1832	Zunz	The Song is an epithalmium.	59
1848	R. Dr. Salomon Herxheimer	"The Shulamite, a rustic maiden warmly attracted to a young shepherd, is taken against her will to the court of King Solomon." (4:367)	59
1854	R. Dr. Phillipson	"Love is invincible, and is not to be bought, but is a flame of God".	60

Summary of Ginsburg
Christian interpretation to Luther[55]

date	interpreter	quotes and notes	p
185-254	Origen	"[Origen] admits an historical sense as an epithalmium on the marriage of Solomon with Pharaoh's daughter, but in him we meet with a full exhibition of the allegorical allusion to the marriage union of Christ and his Church, which has been adopted by the majority of expositors to the present day [1857]." Bridegroom = Christ; bride = church; male chorus = angels and saints; female chorus = believers.	61
296-373	Athanasius	"The whole book is an allegory, and is to be understood enigmatically from the beginning to the end. ... The book is full of dialogues between the Son of God and the human race; sometimes between men in general and Christ, sometimes between Him and his ancient people; sometimes between Him and the Gentile Church, sometimes between the Gentiles and Jerusalem; and sometimes between ministering angels and men."	62
331-396	Gregory of Nyssa	Gregory: "*Let him kiss me*, etc., is the language of the soul to God, which has become worthy to speak to God face to face."	64
331-420	Jerome	"[Jerome] seems to have embraced almost entirely the theory of Origen."	64
354-430	Augustine	On the adjuration refrain (2:7): "The church in these words addresses her own daughters. She is a field of God, fruitful in graces, to which by loving Christ the martyrs come, whom he wishes to lay down their lives as lovingly as he laid down his life for them."	65
360-429	Theodore of Mopsuestia	Bishop, expositor, author of *Against the Allegorists*. G: "Pity that his commentary is lost".	65

---

55. Ginsburg does not claim to be comprehensive. Some omissions: Hippolytus of Rome (170-235), *In Canticum Canticorum*; Ambrose of Milan (340-397), *Commentarius in Canticum Canticorum*; Gregory of Elvira (d. 392), *Tractatus de epithalmio (In Cantica Canticorum libri quinque)*; Isodore of Seville (560?-636), *In libros veteris ac novi testamenti prooemia De libris Salomonis*. For Hippolytus see Smith, *Mystery of Anointing*; for Latin commentary to 1200 see Matter, *Voice of My Beloved*.

date	interpreter	quotes and notes	p
386-457	Theodoret	"There are some who do not admit that the Song of Songs has a spiritual sense, and make of it such a texture of fables, which is unbecoming even to the insane. Some maintain that Solomon is here celebrating himself and the daughter of Pharaoh; others take the Shulamite, not as Pharaoh's daughter, but as Abishag; and others, again, considering the thing with a little more reverence, call this book a Royal address, and take 'the bride,' to be the people of Israel, and 'the bridegroom,' the king."	65
390-444	Cyril of Alexandria	Palanquin = cross; silver legs = 30 silver pieces; purple cushion = purple garment; nuptial crown = crown of thorns.	67
650 [?]	Aponius	Allegory of history of God's people up to the return of the Messiah.	67
673-735	Venerable Bede & Gregory the Great	"Bede . . . wrote seven books on the Song of Songs, one being merely a copy from Gregory the Great [540?-604], in which he defends the doctrine of grace against the Pelagians."	67
1091-1153	Bernard of Clairvaux	Bernard: "The unction and experience can alone teach the understanding of such a Song. It is not to be heard outside [. . . in the street]." G: "Bernard delivered 86 sermons upon . . . the first two chapters only."	68
1270-1340	Nicholas de Lyrs	Messianic Jewish commentator, historical allegory, church enters at 8:1.	68
1538	Martin Luther	"The bride is the happy and peaceful State under the dominion of Solomon, in which Solomon thanks God for the obedience rendered unto him as a divine gift: for where the Lord does not direct and rule there is neither obedience nor happy dominion, but where there is obedience or a happy dominion there the Lord lives and kisses and embraces his bride with his word, and that is the kisses of his mouth."	69

Summary of Ginsburg
Christian interpretation after Luther to Wesley[56]

date	interpreter	quotes and notes	p
1542	John Brentius	followed Luther's political interpretation.	69
1544	Sebastian Castellio	followed Luther in rejecting other allegorical views, but also rejected Luther's political interpretation, hence viewed text as secular not sacred.	69
1585	Thomas Wilcocks	"Love of bridegroom to his spouse, which is never removed, but always abideth constant, how oftsoever she fall away."	69
1600	Thomas Brightman	Historical allegory, two major epochs—legal and evangelical church—each subdivided into three matching eras of obedience, followed by alienation, and culminating in restoration. Each era is further subdivided into specific historical periods. (A) Legal church (Song 1:1-4:6). (A1) David to exile (1:1-2:2): (a) David (1:1-2); (b) Solomon (1:3); (c) Rehoboam (1:4-9); et cetera. (A2) during exile (2:3-14): (a) remnant preserved in land (3); (b) captives preserved abroad (4-7); (c) promise of liberty (8-9); (d) approach (10-13); (e) arrival (14). (A3) exile to cross (2:15-4:6): (a) Antiochus Epiphanes (3:1-3); (b) recovery (3:4-5); (c) incarnation (3:6-11); (d) earthly ministry and preaching of Jesus (4:1-6). (B) Evangelical church (4:7-8:5). (B1) ad 34-334 (4:7-11): (a) 40 days resurrection to ascension (4:7); (b) pentecost (4:8); (c) Antioch (4:9); Nero (4:10-11); et cetera. (B2) ad 334-1510 (4:12-5:16): (a) Diocletian and Arius (4:12); (b) Constantine (4:13-14); (c) Nicea; etc. (B3) 1517 to parousia (6:1-7:14): (a) Luther (6:1); (b) Melancthon (6:2); et cetera.	70

---

56. Ginsburg does not claim to be comprehensive. For works to 1600, see Engammare, *Cantique*. For seventeenth-century English writers (including some from the late sixteenth century), see Elizabeth Clarke, *Politics, Religion*.

date	interpreter	quotes and notes	p
1583-1645	Hugo Grotius	First the Song is literal, "Solomon with Pharaoh's daughter", next "God to the Israelites, and then the love of Christ to the Church."	75
1609-1699	John Cocceius	Historical allegory, seven consecutive eras: 1:1-2:17; 3:1-4:16; 5:1-6:8; 6:9-7:10; 7:11-8:3; 8:4-6; 8:7-14.	76
1648	John Cotton	Historical allegory, eight eras, matching the chapter divisions.	77
1650	John Trapp	"parable of a marriage", "dramatical and dialogistical"	78
1688	Hennischius	Historical allegory, seven eras, matching seven churches in Revelation.	78
1693	Bishop Bossuet	Epithalamium for Solomon with seven sections for seven day feast: 1:1-2:6; 2:7-17; 3:1-5:1; 5:2-6:9; 6:10-7:11; 7:12-8:3; 8:4-14.	79
1700	Bishop Patrick	Song 7:2 chalice of wine + belly like wheat = eucharistic bread & wine	79
1710	Mathew Henry	"This book is a Divine allegory, which represents the love between Christ and his church of true believers, under figures taken from the relation and affection that subsist between a bridegroom and his espoused bride."	80
1723	James Durham	"[The Song] holdeth out the Church's case, and Christ's care of her".	80
1723	William Whiston	"folly, vanity, and looseness," "it was written by Solomon when he was wicked and foolish, and lascivious and idolatrous"	82
1728	John Gill	"mutual love . . . Christ and his Church; also . . . suited to . . . experience."	83
1753	Bishop Lowth	"marriage-feast of Solomon" G: "dramatic form . . . seven parts"	83
1764	Thomas Percy	Literal reading should ground and constrain allegorical suppositions.	84
1765	John Wesley	"Could not with decency be used or meant concerning Solomon and Pharaoh's daughter; . . . absurd and monstrous; . . . to be understood allegorically, . . . spiritual love . . . between Christ and his Church."	85

A third simple observation from the history of Jewish interpretation is that of Isaac Sehula (1350), whose allegorical reading drew out a conclusion analogous to the conclusion of this current thesis. Like Rashi, Sehula expressed some impatience regarding earlier commentaries: he did not so much hear a duet in the Song as he heard an elaboration of Israel's love towards her God. In other words, like this thesis, he observed at a literal level a gynocentric exploration of an idealization of love, which he then extrapolated allegorically and intertextually to harmonize with the canon of the Hebrew Bible, where Yahweh is not infrequently portrayed as husband to Israel. Sehula read the Song allegorically, but with a focus on the bride rather than on the groom.

Taking these three insights from Jewish commentary together, we get something rather similar to the current thesis. In a very real sense, this thesis does not present any entirely new insights at a macro level, it simply utilizes very late twentieth- and very early twenty-first-century text linguistics to place on a more formal, objective, and reproducible footing—in the language of science as it were—literary insights previously available even to scholars familiar only with medieval grammars, though those grammars were—of course—very much part of a famous flourishing in the late medieval period that ultimately tapered into the flowering of the Renaissance. At least, so the vast bulk of standard narratives of European history suggest.[57] The methodology of contemporary discourse analysis is just a more comprehensive version of literary precursors, one still suited to demonstrating why, of two reasonable interpretations, one might be more preferable, or each correct the other in places.

So, let us now see what the traditions of Christian interpretation offer. Again I have selected only three key points that interact with observations the current thesis will go on to make. Following Gregory (the Great) explicitly, but broadly Origen and Hippolytus as well, Bede's eighth-century commentary on the Song,[58] as Christian commentaries were wont to do, substituted for Yahweh and Israel, Christ and Church. Yahweh as husband is a figure of graciousness in the Hebrew Bible, and grace is a core theme in Christian doctrine and exhortation; indeed, Christ as bridegroom is a figure of graciousness in the New Testament, deliberately in imitation of Yahweh in the original Hebrew Bible. So, one might imagine that Jewish allegoriza-

---

57. Standard narratives of European history are not infrequently suitable to being criticized in the same way as the Hebrew Bible can be criticized—as an "official" version of history. Even where historicity can be demonstrated, the significance of the story in histories involves more intangible things, like explanations of intentions, criteria for ideological or ethical evaluation.

58. Bede, *On the Song*.

tion would translate smoothly into Christian allegorization. However, it is rather more problematic than that. At least Jewish interpretation allegorized within the tradition in which the Song had first been canonized.

It is not difficult for Jewish commentators to feel a focus on the bride and her response, more than on the groom and any details of his emotions, since that matches much of the Hebrew Bible—Law, Former Prophets, and Psalms—though Yahweh is hardly shy about expressing emotion when he chooses to do so, especially in the Latter Prophets. Indeed the lover in the Song articulates emotions too. However, it does need to be said that although Yahweh is the foundation for interpreting the history of Israel in the Hebrew Bible, the history of Israel is its focus. Yahweh is the interpretative key that unlocks the meaning in Israel's history. That is the genius of the Hebrew Bible. It is the literature of a people who used monotheism to make sense of their own lived experience (or as many contemporary scholars would propose, to anchor construction of a unifying but invented national history). Is it not rather trite to say either *It is all about Yahweh*, or *It is all about Israel*? Either assertion can have helpful and accurate rhetorical impact, but the full story is actually that the Hebrew Bible relates the (traditional) history of Israel to Yahweh, and vice versa, according to very specific conceptions of the nature of that relationship. Likewise, matrimony is not "all about the bride" nor is it "all about 'patriarchy.'" On the other hand, this thesis argues that the Song actually *is* all about the bride. The Song is not the final word on marriage, since it does not really address the masculine perspective. Or if the Song does address this, it does so implicitly rather than explicitly. That is what this thesis is written to propose.

Christian commentators, with some degree of contrast to Jewish commentators, show a distinct bias in attending to "the one the Shulamite's soul loves," gleaning for hints of the character of the glorious gracious love of the Messiah; the *sine qua non* of the Christian gospel, the passion of the Christ. This creates a strong and dangerous impetus for the Christian interpreter, towards overloading interpretation with presuppositions alien to the intentions and expression of the text. It is right and proper for Christian scholarship to seek to derive the character of the Messiah from the Hebrew Bible, but not to read the assumed character of Jesus of Nazareth back into it. However, grace is arguably there in the text of the Song of Songs. If the adjuration refrain ("Arouse only after!" though more precisely an *abjuration* refrain, "Do *not* arouse until!") counsels patience to young women towards their suitors, so they see and feel a suitor's commitment prior to committing themselves, then there is indeed a strong semantic note of grace in the Song of Songs, expected of suitors, though this is not *textually* where the early Christian commentators were looking for the semantics of grace.

Misdirected by gender expectations, they looked everywhere *except* where it may be found, reading it into rather than reading it out of the text. The explicit prevenient grace in the Song is actually that of daughters, obedient to the Shulamite's abjuration, who make a certain type of consummation possible by waiting for their lovers to come to them. In a sense it is the daughters who love first and their suitors who respond to that love. Again, this is the interpretation advanced by this thesis, not the settled consensus of the traditions within scholarship, though as I have noted the insight—if such it is—is foreshadowed there in various writers with gynocentric interpretations, bride in focus.

In deference to the Christian tradition of interpretation, however, I would offer that there is indeed a second sense of grace evident in the Song, though my slowly maturing meditation suggests this might be better viewed as mutual grace, distorted to look like male-towards-female grace because it is viewed from the female perspective I have mentioned. This is right at the heart of the current thesis. A Puritan, Thomas Wilcox believed himself to be reading a Hebrew poem encoding a Calvinist "perseverance of the saints," via the ever-sleep-walking bride and ever-bounding-back-home groom [59] Wilcox reads a messianic groom forever rescuing his bride from wandering astray. I happen to personally share Wilcox's confessional theological position, but I cannot find it in the Song, unless it is in the "unconditional election" of the adjuration (abjuration) refrain.[60] In fact, I would argue the opposite of Wilcox's reading obtains, in that the Shulamite departs on her nocturnal forays precisely because she is insecure about her love's return. She is actually moving towards him; it is he that is failing to move towards her, at least in her fears. Also, at the end of the Song, the Shulamite charges her love to seal her on his heart—in other words, to vouch to be faithful until death—because she fears he may not prove to be forever faithful, in the same way she must already be so committed to exclusivity, or she would not ask to be requited in an irrevocable emotional contract to which she was not also offering to be party herself. The Shulamite's lasting faithfulness is not in doubt, or rather it is assiduously elaborated, and presented as all but dangerously involuntary. The Song is full of diverse articulations of her heartfelt and enduring longing for union. This is grace too. This is her gift to the one her soul loves: she feels compelled to keep giving her soul, even when he is

---

59. The fifth of the five main points regarding doctrine in dispute in the Netherlands, decided at the 136th session of the synod of Dordt (1618-1619), on the afternoon of Tuesday 23 April 1619. *Acta Synodi Nationalis* (Dordtrecht: Elzevir, 1620), 1:240.

60. The second of the five main points regarding doctrine in dispute in the Netherlands, ibid.

absent. The Song articulates the Shulamite's struggle to wait, patiently, for he whom her soul loves. By waiting, she gives him room to manoeuver. It is an active gift, yet a passive one too. Circumstances may be beyond her control, but her response to the circumstances is within her power such that she can adjure others to follow the example.

Bede and Wilcox home in on perceived echoes of christocentric grace in the Song, which overlooks the Shulamite and her soul as the real subject of the Song's exposition, and her own compulsive graciousness. They expect grace to be masculine, and the masculine to be gracious. They miss that brothers and watchmen, Solomon and his guards, are not gracious. They miss that the Shulamite is actually attempting to describe to her friends the mystery of her own discovery of her own compulsive graciousness (*that* is the perseverance of the saints). They miss that masculine graciousness is actually in doubt; so it is adjured of a male lover in the final chapter, and would-be female lovers are abjured from love until such graciousness, as so adjured, be first evidenced by their suitors. Wilcox has the matter precisely the wrong way around. It is the Shulamite's faithfulness that is not in doubt (as constructed by the poet, for the sake of his argument), but rather there is a fear of her lover straying. The bridegroom of the Song stands in *contrast* to Christ as bridegroom, looking backwards, from a Christian perspective. There is a sense of a perpetual seeking for the perfect bridegroom, not a once-and-for-all finding of one. A Christian reading of the Song might better view human marriage as being as imperfect a sacrament of grace as the sacrificial system when viewed through the lens of the epistle to the Hebrews.

§3. Aside: The Gynocentric Hypothesis and the History of Interpretation

The current thesis has the modest aim of demonstrating that the whole Song may be interpreted as disclosure of a woman's heart in support of advice regarding the formation of intimate partnerships. This is inferred via a methodology that works cumulatively through progressive examination of the text. It is rather dry and formal unless the significance of the question being addressed is understood.[61] The research question and methodology do not arise in a vacuum, and then proceed to a conclusion isolated from other concerns. Rather, the interpretation of the Song as womanly disclosure in

---

61. "Literary criteria are more elusive than philological data, but far more valuable, since they introduce us directly to the cultural issues." Landy, *Paradoxes of Paradise*, 10.

support of advice to unmarried girls is addressed to the history of interpretation being presented in this literature review; hence this aside "brings forward" conclusions the rest of the thesis attempts to demonstrate, in order to show how those conclusions assist in answering dilemmas posed by the commentaries being discussed in the present chapter, but not returned to in any detail later. This aside is located here, since the contrast between Jewish and Christian interpretations providentially helps clarify the meta-narrative of what motivates the whole thesis: the practical Why? of the thesis, not just the What? and How? The meta-question of the thesis is, What does the Song claim to know about gender?

If the Song addresses romantic love rather than religious devotion, are all men and all women correctly typed in the Song? I am not sure that this is true. What lover is not, like the Shulamite, jealous to retain his beloved's affections? To a male reader, it is the men of the Song that seem foreign to him—they are figures from the dreams and nightmares of *women*; on the other hand, the heart of the Shulamite is not so foreign to a man that he cannot recognize a reflection of his own passions in hers, at least as one who desires him as he would like to be desired. However, the Song does not present this mutuality in reality; it presents one side of it in fiction. Perhaps the Song is gendered as it is so that the publication of a pattern of generic female desire in a fiction encourages the distribution of a pattern, in private reality, of what the Shulamite exhorts: lads declaring lifelong devotion to lasses, eager to receive this without themselves demanding it first.

Furthermore, were the Shulamite's man to express a perfectly symmetrical consistency in compulsive longing, her own doubts would no longer be rational, in the fictive world of the Song. The men of the Song are less than ideal. Even the one her soul loves is *not* the ideal lover. What is he doing away on those hills all the time? All his talk of her beauty is all very well, but will it last? She knows the only beauties he ever refers to will not. At least we readers understand that. Surely the poet would not think we could be ignorant of that. The Shulamite is not only the soul of passion in the Song; she is the soul of wisdom. She loves a man who is less than perfect, and she can speak to this because she admits herself she is less than perfect. The Song is full of themes suited to Christianity, but that is because Christianity is full of healthy Judaism, not because New Testament themes are being deliberately anticipated in some supernatural way.

There is much mutuality in the interpretation I have sketched above, but there is still an asymmetrical gendered element to it. First the mutuality: the adjuration to lifelong fidelity can only be reciprocal. Over time, it becomes irrelevant who initiated the contract: the parties must both remain equally committed to its terms; there can be no gender distinction.

A faithful party calls to a tempted party, from out of the shared space of their covenant, not to stray from it. There is only faithful and unfaithful, not masculine and feminine. Although each sex has been known throughout history to accuse the other of being characteristically unfaithful, the truth is that both sexes are often unfaithful, but far more typically faithful. In pair bonding, it takes two to tango. Infidelity must, mathematically, always be strictly equally apportioned by sex. The *adjuration* to fidelity is an *abjuration* against terminating what must not be terminated, but this mutual possession must first be made to exist. That is where the Song suggests asymmetry: in establishing the partnership in the first place.[62]

To some extent, the Song appears to presume the hearer will already view romance as a relationship characterized by fidelity in mutual possession. To some extent, the Song appears to elaborate via description rather than prescription in regards to such relationships. Although it reaches a climax in calling for fidelity, it has been playing with the theme all along. Why is the Shulamite in her bed alone? Why does she leave it? Who might be going astray from the covenant? Who seeks to confirm it? These questions arise quite naturally if asking the questions discourse analysis asks to explain transitions from one span of text to another: clauses, sentences, paragraphs, stanzas in poetry. In the language of pragmatics, faithfulness in romantic relationships, particularly *the desirability to a woman of a man's faithfulness*, is the topic of the Song. The key observation about the Song at a global level—if it is indeed a unity—may lie in the part that the threefold adjuration refrain plays (or, as I shall term it as much as felicity permits, the abjuration refrain, to distinguish it from the actual adjuration of the man by the Shulamite). The threefold nature of this refrain suggests

---

62. Arguably, were the typology of Proverbs to intentionally be part of the cultural background of the Song, and beyond that the Hebrew Bible as a whole, there may be a biblical gendering of faithfulness: the sons of Yahweh call his daughters into lifelong covenants from youth; unfaithful women call men away from this pattern, to consume men for themselves. Such a pattern does fit the cultural specificities of ancient Israel and the theological metaphors of the Hebrew Bible. However, there is a strong theme in the New Testament of false teachers as seducing Christian believers, where the gendering is of male predators devouring believers typed as feminine. Once again, Jewish and Christian perceptions, where based on their different canons, will produce different emphases regarding gender imagery: Israel is Yahweh's son, unless daughters are specified; the Church is Christ's bride, unless metaphors focus on continuity between covenants to present salvation as an eschatological inheritance, and believers as epicene sons. It is possible that the difference between noun-class systems in Semitic and Indo-European influence such imagery. The coincidence of masculine and feminine with personal and impersonal in Semitic gives way to inclusion of the personal feminine when that option is systematically available courtesy of a providential feature of grammar.

to me that—again in the terminology of pragmatics—we are dealing with new information being placed in focus, or foregrounded. We are not dealing with something like fidelity that can be assumed, and form part of the presuppositional background. An enduring and faithful romantic coupling is the topic of the Song, but getting into such a relationship is its focus. The advice offered—let him come of his own free will—is absolutely counter to instinct (which is why so many of a certain type of single woman will seek out self-help books by agony aunts), and that provides a perfect motivation for offering such advice, and doing so in an elaborate and persuasive way (for those who need such persuasion, the daughters of Jerusalem). It is hard to tell whether the Song is written to encourage lads to man up and launch themselves at lasses, or whether it is written to encourage the lasses to keep their composure as they enter the names of lads in their *programmes du bal*.

At a literal level, the Song is addressed to virgins.[63] It is about establishing a permanent romance, not maintaining one in any detail. It introduces, presupposes, assumes, describes, implies, illustrates, elaborates, and exhorts permanent romance, but none of the poetry exploring that conceptual do-

---

63. They are termed *adulescentulae* by the Shulamite in the Vulgate. It is a fair rendering of the Hebrew עלמות, which literally suggests exclusivity, exclusion from the regular world of married-hence-adult-and-solely-licit sexuality, and exclusion typically on the grounds of age. In Hebrew, it is a predominantly sociological rather than a physiological term. Adolescence is cross-culturally associated with the season of life involving courtship, betrothal, and marriage, the logically prior goal of the other two institutions. The institutional terms are descriptions of aspects of sociological management of sexuality. Adolescence is a term of socially managed début, not of asexuality. Girl children are not secluded, as are maidens. It is precisely the sexuality that gives rise to the managed sociality. Adolescence is an age at which lasses become aware of their own desirability, *and* their own desires. The one is exchanged to meet the other. The same is true of the lads, perhaps with desires more prominent than desirability. Why are the lads not also secluded? I think the Song provides two answers: (1) the culturally-kept door that separates lad from lass also separates lass from lad, so they *are* both secluded, each from the other; and (2) the imagery—historically a concrete reality in many, but far from all societies—of lass within and lad without, accords with her not arousing until he so desires. It is the manning of a lad to find his way to a maid, and her security to monitor his progress. Female vulnerability and male aggression are stereotypes with basis in reality; but mainly lasses are more robust and adventurous than we give them credit for, and mainly lads are more gentle and unsure of themselves than we care to admit needs us to invest in encouraging them. Dainty teen girls and macho teen boys are actors. His macho is his make-up; her tears are her swagger. It is *Homo sapiens's* courtship dance, a way of forming families, not of managing families. Families retain integrity through fidelity. So this writer understands the issues anyway. The literature on related topics is very extensive; there are various principled schools of thought, and empirical and theoretical writers of various temperaments and political colors in several disciplines remain in vigorous dialogue regarding many aspects of the issues.

main is attempting to present anything contrary to expectation; quite the opposite, it presents baroque wedding cakes and adds fairies on top, such that any six-year-old girl could certify it for accurate representation of what marriage should be like. However, it also unmistakably hints at sex in such a way as the recently-post- or peri-pubescent virgins it purports to address can giggle and blush and sense a welcome adventure not at all out of step with wedding-cake dreams, but clearly very grown up, and a sharing of the very secret of secrets (and perhaps some compensation from the cosmos for suffering menstrual cramps).[64]

These elements of the Song, into which falls the lover *when he is present*, are the fantasy background of the Song, concordant with intuition, and hopefully happy domestic experience modeled by parents. They are sustained in a way that keeps the Song upbeat throughout. They are so pervasive that the Song has a reputation for being an idyllic portrayal of romantic love. But the Song actually addresses isolation and heartache. It forewarns and forearms. It protects. Just maybe, it heals; I cannot pronounce regarding healing. The methodology used in this thesis can only identify participants and focus and flow. Those suggest the protective message is: to wait, and to accept only a man who will start as one would like him to intend to go on. It may be that, in the way the Song invents its quasi-typological romance, evidence of his compulsive attraction is sufficient for romance formation, but needs some follow-up in explicitly clarifying the permanence of the relationship.

By "romance formation" I do not mean coitarche; the Song it seems is graciously evasive, neither licentious nor legalistic. Betrothal was the cultural category prior to marriage, and had legal protections regarding sexual exclusivity. The womanly voice of the Song, without drawing much attention to formal status, speaks out of her personal experience of marriage, betrothal, and courtship to virgins eager to be courted (those not eager can spend their time reading something more profitable for them). Courtship simply *is* sexy, with or without coitus. In a sense, sexuality is simply a biological imperative for courtship, one that does not cease with the social provision for it in marriage. The text of the Song is not chronological (except within subunits), so no conclusions for or against sex during courtship or betrothal can be reliably deduced or inferred. I suspect this was deliberate. The potential for non-monogamous sex is explicitly recognized in Song, but it also runs counter to the Shulamite's agenda. It is presented as a contrast

---

64. "They asserted that adolescents need guidance more than any other stage because the adolescent stage is so vulnerable and filled with secrets." Kelefang, *Sexuality Education*, 23.

between dream and nightmare,[65] and between aloof despot and intimate shepherd. The poet did not want to mar a natural law exposition of marriage, protective of typical sensitivities, by reducing a voluntary adventure into a mechanical, legally prescribed cultural norm with a regimented chronological timetable. In the Song, marriage is made for women in love; women are not made for marriage. The woman in love is mistress of marriage. This does not contradict Genesis 2; it suggests the poet of the Song imagined Eve felt the same way about Adam as he felt about her. Surely we would rather hope so. If Genesis foregrounds Adam, the Song foregrounds Eve. Discourse analysis reads between the lines, and perhaps the poet of the Song read between some lines too. It is controversial to suggest it, but perhaps the power of fiction to crystalize profound, timeless and universal, infallible and inerrant, *observational* anthropological truths, inspired the poet of the Song while reading Genesis (all of it; it is a sexy book, tragically so). Marriage and family are viewed by the anthropological academy and Genesis alike as first principles of sociology, though historically the empirical fieldworkers did have to disabuse the moralist theoreticians of the notion that it was religion that first brought marriage to *Homo sapiens* and civilized our species. Hunter-gatherer marriage is ample evidence, but ethology is also suggestive that pair bonding would have been the universal norm throughout the Paleolithic.

The Song may have been written (but only in small part) to demolish widely attested (but very far from universal) prudish stereotypes about female sexuality. It is not a "lock up your daughters" poem,[66] it is the rational alternative to that: educate your daughters to be their own gatekeepers. Perhaps it is suggesting that women ought better to be viewed as not merely *assenting* to the sexual dimension of marriage, but preferably responsibly

---

65. The "rape passage" in the Song is nightmare, not the so-called "rape fantasy" of the psychological literature, interpreted by some as a subconscious way of reconciling healthy female sexuality in social contexts that restrain its expression. So the theory has it, that if it was not by her consent, she could not be to blame. In other words, so-called "rape fantasy" is a misnomer. If the theory is correct, what some women actually fantasize is fulfilled desire without dishonor; never do they fantasize unwanted sexual contact. Other conceptualizations are possible: sexual fulfillment as a welcome surprise (a healthy attitude prior to coitarche, consistent with the Song); having sexual desires met without having to negotiate them (male romantic initiative, consistent with the Song); being so powerfully desirable to a man he cannot restrain himself (consistent with the Song). Such healthy forms of the fantasy do not involve violence, debasement, or even abandonment (not consistent with the ideals of the Song).

66. The Song is not a cautionary tale, although it may hint that "bad things happen to sexually active, forward women"; Exum, "Ten Things," 30.

consenting to its sexual dimension. This is possibly concordant with Jesus speaking with the Samaritan woman,[67] and with various things Paul says.[68] If I may coin a term, *memetic criticism*, by analogy with textual criticism, and using *meme* in Dawkins's sense of the word,[69] it is rather hard to tell if bachelors like Jesus and Paul derived insight into female sexuality from indirect observation, or partly assisted by reading the Song of Songs, though at least Paul tends to be explicit about when he is influenced by Jesus.[70] I do not mean to deny the logical possibility of direct divine revelation, but rather to affirm that it is still meaningful to attribute inspiration to texts that reliably transmit trustworthy insights into human nature, even when that can be adequately explained in empirical and naturalistic terms, without metaphysical commitment either way regarding existence of a personal Providence. In fact, attributing each word of the New Testament text exclusively to an otherwise inexplicable miracle shortcuts the possibility of establishing the submission of New Testament writers to the canon of the Hebrew Bible.[71] On the other hand, if the historical bachelor Jesus had read the Song of Songs and, partly instructed by that, sympathized with yet challenged the Samaritan woman,[72] the semantic content of memes in the Song of Songs may be traceable in the logic of his conversation: its propositions, assumptions, presuppositions, or implications. This thesis does not have

---

67. Λέγει αὐτῇ Ὕπαγε φώνησον τὸν ἄνδρα σου καὶ ἐλθὲ ἐνθάδε (Jn 4:16). He said to her, "Go call your husband and come here."

68. Νεωτέρας δὲ χήρας παραιτοῦ· ὅταν γὰρ καταστρηνιάσωσιν τοῦ χριστοῦ, γαμεῖν θέλουσιν (1 Tim 5:11). "But with younger widows, deny their request, for where they become impassioned counter to Christ, they will want to marry." I read this as what is standardly typed as a third class conditional: with the *form* of a subjunctive protasis (καταστρηνιάσωσιν) and present apodosis (θέλουσιν); and the *function* of asserting a future, more probable modality (rather than less probable, which would be fourth class, using the optative) for the proposition in the apodosis. In short, the sense is that sometimes some younger widows have been impassioned as described, and when this is so, more often than not, they end up wanting to marry—a pattern that is believed to be ongoing. This is asserted as part of justifying prioritizing other charities ahead of younger widows.

69. Richard Dawkins, *The Selfish Gene*, 1976.

70. Τοῖς δὲ γεγαμηκόσιν παραγγέλλω, οὐκ ἐγὼ ἀλλὰ ὁ Κύριος, γυναῖκα ἀπὸ ἀνδρὸς μὴ χωρισθῆναι (1 Cor 7:10). "Now to those who have married I command, not I but the Lord, a woman is not to be separated from a man."

71. Μὴ νομίσητε ὅτι ἦλθον καταλῦσαι τὸν νόμον ἢ τοὺς προφήτας· οὐκ ἦλθον καταλῦσαι ἀλλὰ πληρῶσαι (Matt 5:17). "Do not any of you think that I came to revoke the law or the prophets; I did not come to revoke but to fulfill."

72. Πέντε γὰρ ἄνδρας ἔσχες, καὶ νῦν ὃν ἔχεις οὐκ ἔστιν σου ἀνήρ· τοῦτο ἀληθὲς εἴρηκας (John 4:18). "For you have had five men, and the one you have now is not your man; what you have said is true."

scope to address that question in detail, however one simple but important example will make the point more concrete.

Jesus asserts singleness is preferable for the Christian man who can accept it.[73] Paul asserts the same, citing Jesus, but extends precisely the same principle to women.[74] Again, this is just the two-to-tango mathematical logic. On average, there will be as many unpaired women as there are unpaired men. However, numerical economics is insufficient rationale for communitarian ethics, humanitarian or theological. Were few men but no women suited to singleness, we would have a conflict of interest and moral dilemma requiring prioritization of needs. As bachelors, by definition, Jesus and Paul were qualified to testify to personal ability to find contentment in celibacy. Could the Song have convinced them that at least virgins can find a contentment in waiting (perhaps even in waiting in vain),[75] since the Shulamite adjures it? Could the Song have convinced Paul that the issue may be more problematic for younger *widows*,[76] but not all of them?[77] Could the Song have underscored for Paul that marriage will be felt as having trials?[78] There are other texts that could have given Paul confidence. His own observations could do the same. We need not appeal to a supernatural insight, though strict application of logic cannot deny that either. On the other hand, where advice about romance is offered in texts deemed canonical, whatever their origin, the proof of a pudding is in its eating. If one dares, one may personally verify or falsify the material reality of the value or otherwise of practical

---

73. Καὶ εἰσὶν εὐνοῦχοι οἵτινες εὐνούχισαν ἑαυτοὺς διὰ τὴν βασιλείαν τῶν οὐρανῶν. Ὁ δυνάμενος χωρεῖν χωρείτω (Matt 19:12). "And there are eunuchs such that they made themselves so on account of the kingdom of the heavens. He who is able to accept this, let him accept this."

74. Λέγω δὲ τοῖς ἀγάμοις καὶ ταῖς χήραις, καλὸν αὐτοῖς ἐὰν μείνωσιν ὡς κἀγώ (1 Cor 7:8). "So I say to the unmarried and to the widows, it is good for them if they remain [single] as I am too."

75. Ὥστε καὶ ὁ γαμίζων τὴν ἑαυτοῦ παρθένον καλῶς ποιεῖ καὶ ὁ μὴ γαμίζων κρεῖσσον ποιήσει (1 Cor 7:38). "So both he who gives his virgin in marriage does well and he who does not does even better." Is the implied audience for the Song of Songs the Shulamite's father? Or is it just addressed to daughters in the hearing of their fathers?

76. Βούλομαι οὖν νεωτέρας γαμεῖν, τεκνογονεῖν, οἰκοδεσποτεῖν (1 Tim 5:14). "Therefore I want the younger [widows] to marry, to have children, to manage their households."

77. 1 Cor 7:8, as above, n. 71.

78. Ἐὰν δὲ καὶ γαμήσῃς, οὐχ ἥμαρτες, καὶ ἐὰν γήμῃ ἡ παρθένος, οὐχ ἥμαρτεν· θλῖψιν δὲ τῇ σαρκὶ ἕξουσιν οἱ τοιοῦτοι, ἐγὼ δὲ ὑμῶν φείδομαι (1 Cor 7:28). "So if you would marry, you do not sin, and if the virgin would marry, she does not sin; but such as do so will face the trials of life, and I am sparing you from them."

advice. If one does not dare, one may still study the testimony of others, and of nature itself, to see if that evidence is consistent with the claims of any celebrated advice deemed inspired. However, one must do one or the other; one cannot have one's pudding and eat it too. Marry in haste, repent at leisure?

Advice in regards to romance is much sought after and much discussed. It is sometimes taboo, sometimes policed, sometimes dogmatic, but is always a subject of folk wisdom. For more than a century now, it has been a subject for intense academic theoretical speculation and empirical study.[79] This thesis only attempts to recover what the Song seeks to articulate about romance, not to provide empirical evidence for or against its claim to offer infallible wisdom. However, it is written deliberately to address what Cheryl Exum calls "metacommentary" by seeking to "investigate how the Song makes different claims upon female and male readers."[80] Exum sees that as a project for a feminist interpretation, which would make this thesis a contribution to feminist analysis of the Song. Intriguingly she asks, "Are female readers asked to adopt a male point of view that requires reading against their interests?"[81] The mechanics of establishing the case for the gynocentric hypothesis of this thesis are so dispassionately philological, this "metacommentary" aside—buried within a review of two millennia of other commentaries—is deemed necessary to establish the important humane motivation for the work at hand. It should be apparent already that the informal reading, sketched above and based on data explored below, views the Song not as a matter of female readers being asked to adopt a male point of view at all, but rather male readers being asked to adopt a distinctively female point of view, and one explicitly claiming to be in the interests of *both* parties, but especially the female party. Not only that, but the bilateral exchanges of desire and desirability between woman and man in the Song—so intense they cry out for enduring fidelity—although that cry is articulated as a legitimate claim of a bride on a groom in the Song, would not sound ill were groom to testify to the same sentiments under oath in public, as indeed is customary cross-culturally at weddings, and presumably since before there was writing. The wedding was invented before the *ketubah*. As noted by so many recent scholars, mutuality is a prominent feature of the Song. The only strikingly gendered theme in the Song is that of male romantic initiative and

---

79. For example, Josef Breuer and Sigmund Freud, *Studien über Hysterie*, Vienna: Franz Deuticke, 1895; and Sigmund Freud, "Über die weibliche Sexualität," *Internationale Zeitschrift für Psychoanalyse* 17 (1931) 317-32.

80. Cheryl Exum, *Song of Songs*, p. 82.

81. Ibid.

female romantic circumspection. Were the waiting adjured upon the lasses to be "equally" adjured upon the lads, they would never come together to perpetuate the Song's refrains.

> והשבתי
> מערי יהודה ומחצות ירושלם
> קול ששון וקול שמחה
> קול חתן וקול כלה
> כי לחרבה תהיה הארץ

> I will bring to a stop
> in the cities of Judah and the streets of Jerusalem
> to the voice of jubilation and the voice of joy
> the voice of bridegroom and the voice of bride
> for the land will have become desolate.[82]

So, it is she who gazes, outwards, with a sense of barely-contained legitimate expectation that he should arrive. The Song is a Song of self-mastery in invitation, bordering on command: Let him kiss me! To whom does she appeal? Not to him—too direct. She will accept no other man than one willing and able to find her for himself. So, who would deprive her of one her soul would love? Could she be talking to us? What *is* the poet saying?

If the Song of Songs ultimately has the Shulamite speaking on behalf of the "teeny boppers" she is addressing, I can imagine few things more anathema to the establishments of moral righteousness, cloistered or secular, in the age in which I am writing.[83] Yet the Shulamite does not expect the mouth kiss she is given, to be given without a ring to go with it. And that ring is anathema to the temporal legislature.[84] There appears to be a separation between church and state, though they may be united in seeing the Shulamite as a bad influence, whichever way you take her. That is, of course, an excellent reason for a humble researcher to stick to philological issues

---

82. Jer 7:34.

83. "This study examined sexual coercion and psychosocial correlates among 284 diverse adolescent and emerging adult *males* in high school and college. Over 4 in 10 participants (43%) experienced sexual coercion: more specifically, the participants reported: verbal coercion (31%, n = 86), seduction coercion (26%, n = 73), physical coercion (18% n = 52), and substance coercion (7%, n = 19). Rates were comparable across high school and college students." French et al., *Psychology of Men & Masculinity*. Emphasis on the word *males* is added.

84. This is another highly controversial issue in contemporary society. Marriage is not officially "for life" in many jurisdictions, but only *entered* into on the expectation of it being for life. We can only imagine what words the Shulamite might share with those officiating within such regimes. My fancy is they might not be poetic.

he hopes he has a chance of comprehending, while leaving the literary and cultural issues to those with braver souls than his.[85] To paraphrase Exum: in the world around us, whose voice speaks to girls such that hearing those voices is not for those girls to listen against their interests?

To bring this aside to a close, and link back into the systematic review, a concise summary of the logic involved in the discourse move of providing the aside may both aid the reader, and—at the same time—provide another worked example of text linguistics, discourse analysis, rhetorical structure, or whatever we may prefer to call it. Ancient and medieval Jewish and Christian commentators on the Song allegorized in slightly different ways, driven by theological presuppositions; in particular, Christian scholars were inclined to seek the notion of grace as hallmark of an inspired text, and to expect it to have male embodiment. Christians were somewhat more inclined to gender the Song against the grain in ways the Jewish scholars were noticeably less inclined to do. Most contemporary scholars view the ancient and medieval commentaries as having been injured by presuming things about some ultimate theological message of the Song in advance, and by presuming things about gender also. This has been demonstrated in the aside above by "carrying forward" an overview of key elements of the interpretation of the current thesis by way of contrast with the early extant commentaries. Among the points made has been that logic demands that if lasses are to exercise restraint, then lads who have a view to lifelong follow-through need encouragement to act, lest the lads and lasses never meet in the middle. A single powerful word to this effect is the very first word of the song: *yiššaqeni*, "Let him kiss me!" This may be the distinctive gendered message of the Song. It may be an accident of the adaptation of *Homo sapiens*, or of *H. sapiens* as mediated by an artifice of ancient Israelite culture. It may be created by culture, or it may drive culture; or both, as the circular structure of the Song might suggest. It may be providentially or divinely instituted and inspired, or it may be all of the things listed here. What the ancient and medieval commentaries share with the current thesis is a view of the Song as a unified and gendered typology of some kind. The difference lies in the two-centuries-old move to viewing sex, gender, and marriage as proper topics in their own right, without them needing to be extrapolated to theological conclusions. However, if religions do not own marriage, then again, nor do states. Luther proposed a political allegory somewhat reminiscent of Confucius; however, not many commentators have followed him in viewing the Shulamite as a prophetess of the personal being political.

---

85. Paraphrase of Landy, *Paradoxes of paradise*, p. 10.

> 大昏既至，冕而親迎，親之也。
> 親之也者，親之也。
> 是故，君子興敬為親；
> 舍敬，是遺親也。
> 弗愛不親；弗敬不正。
> 愛與敬，其政之本與。

> Yes, in the great (rite of) marriage there is the extreme manifestation of respect;
> and when one took place, the bridegroom in his square-topped cap
> went in person to meet the bride;—thus showing his affection for her.
> It was his doing this himself that was the demonstration of his affection.
> Thus it is that the superior man commences with respect as the basis of love.
> To neglect respect is to leave affection unprovided for.
> Without loving there can be no (real) union;
> and without respect the love will not be correct.
> Yes, love and respect lie at the foundation of government.[86]

> 禮，其政之本與。

> Yes, (this) ceremony (of marriage) lies at the foundation of government.[87]

§4. Schematic View of Recent Scholarship

The next two (overlapping) phases of scholarly interpretation summarized in this literature review each address errors in the assumptions of so much of the earlier commentary. Firstly, the anthologists attempt to establish the sense of the Song step-by-step without importing and presuming a unifying intended message in advance, including eschewing a default narrative structure to the Song, connecting its distinct components (the "dramatic" interpretations). Secondly, scholars who have felt a non-narrative unity in the Song have attempted to find formal and structural evidence to explain their perception of unity. There are some other classes of interpretation I

---

86. Confucius's reply to Duke Ai in the Book of Rituals (禮記, Li Ji), Questions of Duke Ai (哀公問, Ai Gong Wen) §6. English translation from Legge *Li Ki*.
87. Ibid., §8.

am omitting, which are particularly nicely categorized in Longman's commentary.[88] There was a strong tradition of Jewish philosophical and mystical allegorical reading of the Song, which does speculate about the nature of gendered humanity. Also, early "literal" readings are often viewed as "dramatic," which does connect spans of speeches by rhetorical relations. So such readings do resonate in their own ways with the reading advanced in the current thesis. However, since these approaches make assumptions about gender or narrative that this thesis avoids, and the approaches are well classified, described, and evaluated elsewhere, they will not be elaborated here. The Jewish mystics correctly recognized the Song addresses the relations between the sexes, but they molded that to fit their own presuppositions. The dramatists correctly recognized the Song is rhetorically structured in segments, but again they tweaked this to fit their expectations of a genre evoked by the Song, but to which it does not properly belong. What is important to observe for the sake of the current thesis is only the ubiquitous element of a need among all commentators to find significance in the gendered nature of the Song, and the tendency to connect the sections of the Song together in a chronological narrative manner, with more or less attention paid to the integrity of its sub-sections, and enough has been said about that already from the main stream of commentaries.

We now turn to the anthologists, more as a phenomenon as a school of thought than as authors of any decisive proposed reading of the Song, who nonetheless made (and still make) a major and decisive contribution to progressing scholarship along the lines of scientific interpretation. Instead of seeking continuity over the whole Song, the anthologists attempt to break down a difficult problem into component pieces, by delineating portions of the text that appear to have self-sufficient coherence. That methodology produces results, and a theory that the Song is no more than the sum of its parts, and need not be more than the sum of its parts. A difficulty arises with this methodology, however, because coherent text can often be further subdivided, depending on various criteria. Should units look like chapters? Should they look like sections? Paragraphs? Sentences? Legal texts can be enumerated even by clauses. If some of the anthologists are laid out as Roberts lays them out, we see how imprecise the results of the basic broad methodology can look when repeated by many different researchers.

---

88. Longman, *Song of Songs*, 20–47.

songs	anthologist	reference
12	Haupt	*AJSL* 18 (1901-02): 193-241
16	Lamparter	Die Botschaft des Alten Testaments 16 (1962)
18	Bettan	The Jewish Commentary for Bible Readers (1950)
20-21	Snaith	NCB (1993)
23	Jastrow	*The Song of Songs* (1921)
~25	Eissfeldt	*The Old Testament* (1965) [1936]; [pp. 489-90 "about 25"]
28	Gordis	*Song of Songs* (1954)
28	Mariaselvam	Analecta Biblica 118 (1988)
~30	Würthwein	*Die fünf Megilloth* (1969); ["etwa 30" (Hohelied, p. 25)]
30	Loretz	*Studien zur althebräischen Poesie* (1971)
30	Rudolph	*Das Buch Ruth, Das Buch Hohe Lied* (1962)
31	Falk	*Love Lyrics* (1981)
31	Gerleman	*Ruth, Das Hohelied* (1965)
32	Segert	in *Charisteria orientalia praecipue ad Persiam pertinentia* (1956)
42	Keel	ConC (1994) [1986]
52	Krinetzki	*Kommentar zum Hohenlied* (1980)
>>25	Landsberger	*JBL* 73 (1954): 203-16 ["many, many more"]

As inconclusive as this list may look, though, the numbers are not so very different to the proposals of scholars who started with literary *unity* as their intuition, seeking formal sub-structure that might support that proposal. For example Carr (1984) reported 28 units within 5 major sections and supported unity (see below). The main difference between anthologists, and what I shall treat as essentially an early twenty-first-century emergent consensus towards unity, lies only with the anthologists' denial of connections between sub-units and hence no overall unity of flow, direction, or purpose. By contrast with the anthologists, when the structures proposed by commentators who find unity in the Song are laid out side by side in the synoptic table below, it can be seen that all see new sections starting in the Song at 2:8 and at 5:2, and that all but Dorsey (and Tanner) see a new section starting at 6:4. Also popular as section apertures are 3:1, 3:6, 4:1,

7:1, and 8:5. All these proposed text boundaries are marked in the table with a shaded background. The section division between the verses 5:1 and 5:2 is particularly notable because it divides the Song essentially into two remarkably equal halves, whereas all other divisions are rather irregular in regards to the length of text by words or cola that are included within spans. What is also notable about the approach of commentators perceiving unity over the Song is the view of many that the sections of the Song are arranged in a hierarchy, such that within a larger section various subsections can be detected, operating at a more intimate level of distinction between textual units. Roberts takes this hierarchical organization further than other commentators, working bottom-up rather than top-down as he does, and hence providing a limiting case. Roberts starts with the smallest units that can be called units and groups them together to produce his overall structure for the Song. What Roberts does explicitly, however, we should read others as doing at least implicitly, and that is clearly the case with the commentators who have published two levels of structure. These are marked in the table with outlined boundaries for alternating sections (first macro-section outlined, second unmarked, third outlined, etc.). More recent (twenty-first-century) commentators appear to have made more appeal to tiers of structure uniting the Song, whereas earlier (twentieth-century) commentators were more focused on identifying macro- rather than sub-units.

Late twentieth-century structural analysis of first half of Song

Carr 1984	Goulder 1986	Elliot 1989	Dorsey 1990	Murphy 1990	Wendland 1995	Longman 2000	Bergant 2001
28 (5)	14	6	7	10	8	23	20 (6)
1:2-4	1:1-8	1:2-2:7	1:2-2:7	1:2-6	1:2-2:7	1:2-4	1:2-6
1:5-7						1:5-6	
				1:7-2:7		1:7-8	1:7-2:7
1:8-11							
	1:9-2:7					1:9-11	
1:12-14						1:12-14	
1:15-2:2						1:15-17	
						2:1-7	
2:3-7							
2:8-9	2:8-17	2:8-3:5	2:8-17	2:8-17	2:8-17	2:8-17	2:8-17
2:10-13							
2:14-15							
2:16-17							
3:1-5	3:1-5		3:1-5	3:1-5	3:1-5	3:1-5	3:1-5
3:6-11	3:6-11	3:6-5:1	3:6-5:1	3:6-11	3:6-5:1	3:6-11	3:6-11
4:1-15	4:1-7			4:1-5:1		4:1-7	4:1-7
	4:8-5:1					4:8-9	4:8-5:1
						4:10-5:1	
4:16-5:1							

86　GENDER IN SOLOMON'S SONG OF SONGS

Early twenty-first century structural analysis of first half of Song

Roberts 2007 [2001]	Davidson 2003	Garrett 2004 [1993]	Barbiero 2011 [2004]	Exum 2005	Hess 2005	Jenson 2005	Assis 2009
>50 (13)	14	17	26 (4)	9	35 (6)	30	24 (5)
1:2-4	1:2-2:7	1:2-4	1:2-4	1:2-4	1:2-7	1:2-4	1:2-4
1:5-6		1:5-6	1:5-6	1:5-2:7		1:5-6	1:5-6
1:7-8		1:7-8	1:7-8			1:7-8	1:7-8
					1:8-11		
1:9-11		1:9-2:7	1:9-14			1:9-17	1:9-11
1:12-14					1:12-14		1:12-14
1:15-17			1:15-17		1:15		1:15-2:3
					1:16-2:1		
2:1-3			2:1-3			2:1-7	
					2:2		
					2:3-7		
2:4-7			2:4-7				2:4-7
2:8-9	2:8-17	2:8-17	2:8-17	2:8-3:5	2:8-9	2:8-17	2:8-17
2:10-14					2:10-14		
2:15-17					2:15		
					2:16-17		
3:1-2	3:1-5	3:1-5	3:1-5		3:1-5	3:1-5	3:1-5
3:3-4							
3:5							
3:6	3:6-11	3:6-11	3:6	3:6-11	3:6-11	3:6-11	3:6
3:7-8			3:7-8				3:7-11
3:9-10			3:9-10				
3:11			3:11				
4:1a-1b	4:1-7	4:1-15	4:1-7	4:1-5:1	4:1-8	4:1-7	4:1-7
4:1c-3							
4:4-6b							
4:6c-6d							
4:7							
4:8	4:8-15		4:8-5:1			4:8	4:8-5:1
4:9					4:9-15	4:9-5:1	
4:10-11							
4:12-15							
4:16	4:16	4:16-5:1			4:16		
5:1a-d	5:1				5:1a		
5:1e-f					5:1b		

LITERATURE REVIEW 87

Late twentieth-century structural analysis of second half of Song

Carr TOTC 19	Goulder JSOTSup 36	Elliot EHST 371	Dorsey *JSOT* 46	Murphy Herm	Wendland JOTT 7	Longman NICOT	Bergant BerOl
28 (5)	**14**	**6**	**7**	**10**	**8**	**23**	**20 (6)**
5:2–8	5:2–9	5:2–6:3	5:2–7:10	5:2–6:3	5:2–6:3	5:2–6:3	5:2–8
5:9							5:9–6:3
5:10–16	5:10–6:3						
6:1							
6:2–3							
6:4–10	6:4–12	6:4–8:4		6:4–12	6:4–7:10	6:4–10	6:4–10
6:11–12						6:11–12	6:11–12
7:1–6	7:1–10			7:1–8:4		7:1–11	7:1–6
7:7–10a							7:7–10a
7:10b–8:4							7:10b–14
	7:11–8:4		7:11–8:4		7:11–8:4		
						7:12–14	
						8:1–4	8:1–4
8:5	8:5–10	8:5–14	8:5–14	8:5–14	8:5–14	8:5–7	8:5a
							8:5b–7
8:6–7							
8:8–10						8:8–10	8:8–10
8:11–14	8:11–14					8:11–12	8:11–12
						8:13–14	8:13–14

88 GENDER IN SOLOMON'S SONG OF SONGS

Early twenty-first century structural analysis
of second half of Song[89]

Roberts SiJ	Davidson JATS 14	Garrett WBC 23b	Barbiero VTSup 144	Exum OTL	Hess BCOTWP	Jenson Interp	Assis JSOTSup 503
>50 (13)	14	17	26 (4)	9	35 (6)	30	24 (5)
5:2-8	5:2-8	5:2-8	5:2-8	5:2-6:3	5:2-8	5:2-8	5:2-8
5:9-16	5:9-6:3	5:9-6:3	5:9-16		5:9	5:9-16	5:9-16
					5:10-16		
6:1			6:1-3		6:1	6:1-3	6:1-3
6:2-3					6:2-3		
6:4	6:4-12	6:4-10	6:4-12	6:4-7:10	6:4-10	6:4-9	6:4-10
6:5-7							
6:8-9							
6:10						6:10	
6:11-12		6:11-7:1			6:11-12	6:11-12	6:11-12
7:1-7	7:1-10		7:1-11		7:1	7:1	7:1-10
		7:2-8:4			7:2-10a	7:2-6	
						7:7-10	
7:8-11							
					7:10b-8:4		
	7:11-8:2			7:11-14		7:11-14	7:11-8:5
7:12-14			7:12-14				
8:1-4	8:3-14		8:1-4	8:1-14		8:1-2	
						8:3-4	
8:5a-b		8:5-7	8:5-7		8:5a	8:5a	
8:5c-e					8:5b-7	8:5b-c	
8:6						8:6-7	8:6-7
8:7							
8:8-10		8:8-12	8:8-10		8:8-9	8:8-10	8:8-10
					8:10		
8:11-12			8:11-12		8:11-12	8:11-12	8:11-12
8:13-14		8:13-14	8:13-14		8:13	8:13	8:13-14
					8:14	8:14	

Each author's division of the Song is summarized in the table above, by analogy with the anthologists, by designating the number of sub-sections the author proposes. Where a higher level of macro-sections is also proposed by an author, this follows the first number and is placed in parentheses. It

89. The table above is not exhaustive. Other proposed structures have been published, e.g., Tanner, "Message," 142-61: 1:2—2:7; 2:8-17; 3:1-5; 3:6—5:1; 5:2-8; 5:9—6:13; 7:1—8:4; 8:5-14.

will be seen that there are similarities between authors who see unity and the anthologists at a basic numerical level. Specific boundaries can also correspond between the two types of author. By working bottom up, and by seeking connections between units, Roberts provides close scrutiny comparing and contrasting the commentators who preceded him, as we shall see in a later chapter, and throughout this current thesis. Roberts's work has the potential to explain the divisions perceived by other commentators. Others seem to see boundaries where they do because of the micro-units and connections between them working as Roberts attempts to show them to be working, on the basis of poetic form alone. Like describing a castle built of children's blocks, commentators report the patterns cast by uniformity of colors between blocks, but Roberts looks at each block in turn, its boundaries and color, and how it connects with other blocks. More apposite might be the analogy of an aerial photograph of rural terrain, fields clearly demarcated by the signature pattern of the crops with which they have been seeded. Anthologists are content to explain the Song as though it were a matter of locating field by field. Unified views of the Song attempt to see some order across cropping patterns over wide distances. Roberts seeks to connect fields with crops to bridge the gap between the two competing perspectives on the text of the Song of Songs.

Roberts is unique in his methodology, bringing together the two schools of twentieth-century thought regarding Song as anthology or unity, and his work provides a framework for the current thesis, so I will turn now to an overview of Roberts's work and how it informs the current study in a new chapter.

3

Phillip Roberts

§1. Form and Content

PHILLIP ROBERTS'S DOCTORAL DISSERTATION—PUBLISHED as *Let Me See Your Form*—noted that, since the demise of the allegorical approaches to the Song of Songs, not only has no widely accepted overall *interpretation* of the Song been established, no proposed overall *structure* for the Song has gained such acceptance either.[1] Those observations are not controversial, but the additional observation that Roberts makes is particularly helpful, and also readily confirmed:

> Works that have argued for some sort of unity ... have argued from the top down. ... Conversely, it is only the anthologists, ... who have started at the bottom and focused on the microstructural elements.[2]

In other words, scholars of either camp—Song as unity or Song as anthology—unsurprisingly concentrate on offering evidence in support of their own reading, either of unity or of anthology. Assuming the work is a unity, then we expect to find global correspondences across the text of the

---

1. "This work represents, almost without change, my 2001 dissertation." Preface to Roberts, *Let Me See Your Form*, xvi. The original dissertation was through Westminster Theological Seminary, 2001. "In sum, the specific issue of the structure of the Song is as unresolved as the correlative issue of its overall interpretation, and this is true on both the macro- and the micro-levels." Ibid., 13.

2. Ibid., 13.

Song—and we do find them. Assuming the work is an anthology, then we expect to find both substructure and discontinuities—and we do find them. Both groups find sufficient evidence in support of their own theory that they are left with little need to explore the alternative position. Yet neither approach is finally convincing on its own, because global correspondences are not only possible but likely, under the hand of a redactor creatively composing an anthology; and substructure, and even some discontinuity, is also not only possible but even more likely within the mind of a unique original poet deliberately presenting his own material. Scholars of both camps are making observations that can, by and large, all be confirmed: many potentially global correspondences on the one hand, and many discernibly self-contained passages on the other. So, it is finding a compelling macro-structure in support of reading the Song as essentially a unity that remains elusive,[3] as does explaining away the many global correspondences across the Song, if it is indeed essentially an anthology.

The very fact that two schools of thought continue to be advanced suggests that the best explanation of observed features of the Song is yet to be offered. It could be that there is simply not enough evidence to ever decide the matter one way or the other, or it could be that there is more to be observed, and that a superior explanation, which accommodated such additional evidence, might still arise. However, there is also another option, simple to state, but with a significance better appreciated if the logic of Roberts's methodology for his own study is understood first.

The key point in Roberts's summary evaluation of scholarly literature on the Song concerns this methodological issue, and drives his whole study. It is only natural that writers have adopted two distinctively different methodologies for reading the Song—top down or bottom up—since those methodologies are consistent with their views of the Song being either unity or anthology respectively. What is missing, according to Roberts, is more "bottom up" work from those who view the Song as a unity. He calls this "swapping methodologies."[4]

Roberts does not actually elaborate on a possibility of more "top down" work from the "anthologists" (Roberts's term), perhaps because Roberts's own leaning is towards unity and readers who share his inclination, or perhaps because it is not as clear that a "swap" of methodology would actually make sense viewed from the other perspective, that of the anthologists. Why would a scholar pursue study of global themes, if the verifiable

---

3. Ibid.: "In the particular case of the Song,. . . any possible macro-structure is so elusive that many deny its very presence."

4. Ibid.

existence of substructure and discontinuities has already persuaded her that such broader themes would be either illusory or superficially imposed on otherwise essentially disconnected material? Well, the latter may provide evidence of the hand of a redactor, if the superficiality could be objectively determined; and the former may have polemical value, if such illusions could also be objectively deconstructed. Such objectivity, however, does not come easily with matters as abstract as global themes in poetry, especially when the putative anthology would be one of poems collected on the basis of addressing the common theme of romantic love, perhaps even more specifically a collection of epithalamia of similar provenance. So potentially, a considerable amount of genuine organic commonality might indeed be expected, without being either imagined or artificial, and yet still—in accordance with the hypothesis of anthology—also without being indicative of any authentic authorial intention such as the hypothesis of unity requires.

Roberts, personally inclined to expect scrutiny of the Song to reveal unity, instead of assuming what he wants to demonstrate (which, he irenically notes, is not always bad methodology),[5] chooses to adopt a principled analytical approach: seeking objective markers of substructure ("segments"), and collating evidence of similarly objective relationships between those segments ("connections"). Under this theoretically rigorous methodology, it is the potential consistency of any connections between segments that might demonstrate overall unity across the Song. So his main concern is what he calls "cohesion": the degree of connectivity that can be found between subunits.[6]

In the next chapters of this thesis, in partial contrast, my main concern will be what I will call "coherence." The two are alike, however, in being descriptions of types of textual unity, both involving observations regarding how various objective *features* of objectively delimited *parts* of a text objectively *relate* to one another. At least these observations are to be theoretically objective in principle, even though many of the features, delimitations, and relationships involve a certain degree of inherent and unavoidable subjectivity in practice. In other words, there is an inevitable element of uncertainty

---

5. Ibid.: "It is not necessarily bad methodology to start with the macro-structure of a work . . . especially if the macro-structure is reasonably clear."

6. See Dionysius of Halicarnassus on the exemplary quality of Sappho's (now only surviving song, her) hymn to Aphrodite, where he attributes the felicity of the lyrics to phonetic cohesion—συνέχεια—using a range of related metaphors to reinforce the idea (ἁρμονία, λειότης, παράκειμαι, συνυφαίνω, οἰκειότης, συζύγιος). ταύτης τῆς λέξεως ἡ εὐέπεια καὶ ἡ χάρις ἐν τῇ συνεχείᾳ καὶ λειότητι γέγονε τῶν ἁρμονιῶν· παράκειται γὰρ ἀλλήλοις τὰ ὀνόματα καὶ συνύφανται κατά τινας οἰκειότητας καὶ συζυγίας φυσικὰς τῶν γραμμάτων. Dionysius, *On Literary Composition* 116.

associated with the data to be collected, arising from the possibility of "experimental errors" due to limitations of the observational equipment (the human mind) and the nature of the object being studied (natural language). Throughout his study, Roberts regularly makes sober assessments of the potential for subjective divergence of opinion regarding certain observations concerning features of the text, its delimitation and putative relationships between those delimited units. However, the patiently accumulated data, largely freed from presuppositions and speculations, ends up being able to bear the weight of some careful concluding generalizations.

Roberts concludes,

> We are inclined to view the structure of the Song as paratactic, i.e., as consisting of a series of related, but largely self-contained vignettes. Nevertheless, this paratactic structure consists of a much higher order of structural units than is typically recognized by anthologists. Moreover, it evinces a high level of compositional unity that makes it essentially one Song and not many.[7]

If this description by Roberts is correct—that the Song is a paratactic compositional unity, a concatenation of self-contained but related scenes—it still does not provide us with an interpretation of the Song, nor explain why the poet gave this particular form to his work; but those were not Roberts's research questions! Roberts only wanted to observe, describe, and summarize the formal structure of the Song, as comprehensively and objectively as possible.

However, the limited conclusions that Roberts was able to draw do, in fact, end up explaining the dichotomy of scholarly perceptions regarding the Song. The Song does indeed appear to be an anthology of relatively self-contained cameos, but they also appear to be united by paratactic relationships. Although parataxis provides more ephemeral kinds of relationships between components of text than temporal narrative or logical hortatory relationships would provide between segments, it is still a genuine and deliberately imposed cohesive structuring, whereby its parts work together to convey a unified holistic conception constituted of more than the aggregate sum of those parts alone. So, if parataxis is a fair description of the Song's structure, then it is *both* unity *and* anthology, and the intuitions and supporting insights of scholars of both schools of thought are vindicated. Moreover, they are vindicated in the same sorts of terms as they have been argued by those scholars themselves. This was the third option I delayed mentioning earlier. It is such an obvious possibility in hindsight; it would

---

7. Roberts, *Let Me See Your Form*, 396.

have undermined appreciation of its significance to have stated it explicitly prior to giving an overview of Roberts's study. Why are there two schools of thought? Because both are right! A dichotomy between anthology and unity is a false dichotomy in the case of a paratactically structured text.

The discussion in the paragraph above is somewhat abstract, dealing in the logic of meta-analysis, but its value lies in stepping back from entrenched scholarly theses and antitheses to re-examine hidden assumptions. Texts, even highly artificial formal texts, need not be structured according to chronology as in narrative discourse, nor according to axiomatic-deductive logic as in hortatory discourse; art can also imitate life—including cognitive or psychological life—presenting a brainstorm, a stream-of-consciousness text, one in which fragments of incidents—both real and imagined, both leading to and following from a core motivating concern—contribute to construction of a voice more personally recognizable to an audience than a narrator or lecturer. An audience can readily—perhaps even more readily—identify with a poet's presumed underlying sea of chaotic emotions, upon which are tossed a flotsam of memories, cherished or painful, and dreams as well as nightmares. The biblical Song fits the broad, diverse genre of lyric poetry, but it is not a ballad, nor a hymn, nor an anthem. Discourse type and genre aside, though, is this Song merely entertainment? Why does it present what it presents, and why does it do so in the way that it does so? Perhaps the form is driven by the content, and the author's intentions for reader response, as we would expect.

Roberts's study, if we accept it, also explains the failure of the top-down methodology: the Song does not appear to have been conceived by the poet—or adapted by a redactor—to offer such a macro-structure to the reader; instead he achieves cohesion via a range of other devices. That range of other devices is also what explains the failure of the purist anthological readings to win the balance of scholarship to their school of thought: the global correspondences across the Song are indeed organic to the text, not overlaid upon pre-existing material.

Explanatory power is one measure of a good theory, but despite its modest aims and cautious conclusions, Roberts's study also provides a foundation for further research, which was Roberts's stated motivation for his own research questions. A paratactic anthology by a single author is no longer the kind of anthology that threatens to invalidate any attempts to present an overall interpretation of the Song; to the contrary, it invites such an interpretation, and even suggests some appropriate lines of inquiry (like examining rhetorical relationships between minimal textual components), while warning against other investigations (like seeking global macro-structure that simply seems unlikely to actually exist).

Roberts's observations lead us to see a poet who appears to expect his audience to grasp his intentions via a linear, accumulative reading of the Song, part by part, drawing readers in and leading them along in a sustained intimate exploration, rather than by him using distancing devices, for example, to propel readers into a "big picture" perspective of the topic he is addressing (as in Genesis 1-3, Job 1-2, psalms of ascent, apocalyptic, and so on). If we accept Roberts's analysis of the Song, again with hindsight, we see the form suits the content. Isn't romantic love often reflected in literature, as it is felt in life, as an accretion of intimate vignettes? Isn't it often claimed that romantic love is "blind," a notion that actually works both ways: romantic love is too involved to see itself clearly, but by the same argument, it can *only* be understood from the "inside" (the eye of the beholder), rather than dispassionately from the outside?

So a paratactic structure could also suggest that the "hermeneutical key" or "bottom line" for interpreting the Song might lie towards its end (allowing that Roberts agrees with scholarly consensus that the Song does not actually have an end), rather than towards its center, and rather than being strongly anticipated towards its beginning; either of which options are sometimes ideal to facilitate communication from authorial intent to reader reception in, for example, theologized narrative (say the structuring of the story of the deluge or the book of Judges), wisdom literature (Proverbs), or even prophetic poetry (Amos)—but would such other structures suit the subject of romantic love? With hindsight once more, Roberts's analysis resonates with expectations that form suit content.

However, it is one thing to observe the intuitive appeal of Roberts's conclusions in explanatory value and in their potential utility as part of attempting an overall interpretation of the Song, but we cannot responsibly accept those conclusions as valid, simply because they seem to work. Providentially, given advances in discourse analysis in the decade since Roberts's dissertation (2001) was accepted, we can now attempt to independently reproduce his results, looking at semantic structure (coherence) rather than formal structure (cohesion), but in an equally objective way: the same bottom-up methodological logic, with the tools of a different technology, viz., Segmented Discourse Representation Theory [SDRT] (2003-). In fact, although Roberts minimized addressing content (semantic) questions to safeguard the objectivity of conclusions about formal structure, it might be argued that to a certain extent that methodology itself makes it difficult to justify any meaningful, intended macro-structure, which is why Roberts found himself seriously restricted in what he could conclude. To some extent it is his methodology that returned the verdict of paratactic structure: how could cohesion be much more comprehensive than that, when only formal connections were included and content connections were excluded? Content provides various aspects of cohesion to texts, not simply limited to semantic coherence. If the Song were to be a unity, with something to actually say that united it, we would be dealing with content and semantics, not just with form. Roberts implies in several places that he is aware of this. He was looking to establish a lower bound on cohesion: What is the most reliable evidence? What does it establish regarding a *minimum* level of cohesion in the Song?

Roberts explicitly distanced himself from both semantics and discourse analysis, but for different reasons. Although Roberts's distancing provides scope for independent investigation of features of the Song, and the possibility of confirming or contradicting his results, entering this territory—that Roberts himself proscribed for his own analysis—comes with caveats. While Roberts notes that "The present writer is, in fact, sympathetic to the view that poetic form and content are ultimately inseparable,"[8] his overriding concern is that "formal devices can be evaluated with minimal interference from overall theories about the Song and its meaning."[9] Roberts wanted the firmest foundation possible, one that did not depend on his own or any other subjective opinion, nor on importing assumptions or appealing to speculations. Micro- and macro-structure are interdependent contexts in semantic analysis, but macro-structure is built upon micro-structure when it comes to formal devices (for example, a macro-structural *inclusio* depends on recognition of the formal correspondences between micro-structural elements of the opening and closing markers of the *inclusio*). Formal devices, because of this unidirectional nature, safeguard independence of analysis. In Roberts's words:

> We will conduct this investigation by describing and analyzing the structuring function of the various formal devices that are characteristic of Hebrew poetry, with a view to defining the micro-structural building blocks of the Song that any macro-structural interpretation must account for.[10]

Emboldened by the results of 400 pages of analysis, he reaffirms and strengthens this assessment: "Any plausible explanation of the structure of the Song must incorporate this type of analysis at least as one of its major components, if not its actual foundation."[11] (Longman echoes this in his

---

8. Ibid., 15, n. 1.
9. Ibid., 15.
10. Ibid.
11. Ibid., 395.

endorsement of *Let Me See Your Form*: "Future study of the Song will be required to interact and appropriate Roberts' insights.")[12]

So the first caveat, according to Roberts, is the complexity of semantic analysis, the circularity of hermeneutics. However, SDRT is designed quite specifically to provide a theoretically satisfying systematic way of drawing together contributions to interpretation of discourse, analyzing different types of contribution in distinctively different types of formal logic, as we shall see in the next chapter. Roberts's second caveat relevant to this thesis is in respect to discourse analysis, or rather the discourse analysis available at the time of his study, where he noted that, "To date, the tools of discourse analysis have been much better honed for working with narrative texts rather than poetic texts."[13] SDRT is designed to work with dialogue, not just narrative; but it is not a poetic or literary tool, so we must grant it still falls under Roberts's caution. However, I will be using it rather like Roberts used his focus on form to avoid interference from theories of interpretation of the Song, only in reverse. We will seek semantic coherence without being distracted by scholarly disagreements about formal delineation of text boundaries according to poetic devices, as if we were draining the Song of its poetry to get at the evolution of its meaning. At least, in principle that could appear to be what we are doing, though in practice what is done is to broadly accept Roberts's formal structural analysis; independently verifying pure semantic coherence works in parallel with and confirms it.

Roberts describes his own study as being "very much a product of the structuralist movement that followed the New Criticism in the nineteen-sixties and seventies."[14] However, he disambiguates the sense of "structuralism" in the context of biblical studies to exclude both the "esoteric semiotic theories derived from the French structuralists" and "the simple rhetorical analysis associated with the New Criticism" itself.[15] Instead he means to associate his own study with "Russian formalism and its descendants in the Prague school of linguistics,"[16] identifying Roman Jakobson,[17] from within this movement, as having been particularly influential on studies of biblical Hebrew poetry like "the recent introductory works of Alter, Berlin, and

---

12. Ibid., back cover.
13. Ibid., 12, n. 60.
14. Ibid., 16.
15. Ibid.
16. Ibid.
17. Jakobson, "Linguistics and Poetics," 350–77.

Watson."[18] Among "the more focused studies,"[19] O'Connor (*Hebrew Verse Structure*) is seen by Roberts as the most explicitly influenced by Jakobson, though he lists a number of other major studies that also adopt linguistic approaches to Hebrew poetics, colometry, and parallelism (Kurylowicz, Cooper, Collins, and Geller).[20]

Before we look in detail at Roberts's results, it is worth making one specific distinction about what those results demonstrate and what they leave open for future research like the current thesis.

§2. Cohesion and Coherence

Colorless green ideas sleep furiously. – Noam Chomsky

Cohesion and coherence both articulate that most human textual artifacts (even many anthologies) are more than arbitrarily delimited sets of words, merely the sum of their parts. In fact, they are not only more than amorphous combinations of words (as in a crossword puzzle), they are also more than even ordered permutations of words (as in a dictionary). Often the terms reflect that the unity of many partitioned texts in some sense logically precedes the partition of such texts (cohesive and coherent texts), and so characteristics of the partition reflect the relationships between the parts and the unity towards which they contribute something (overall cohesion, or coherence, or both). At a very simple level, the unity of a sentence logically precedes the classification of its partition and arrangement of words according to parts of speech as nouns and verbs and so on, depending on how those words contribute as parts of the unit of coherent speech we call a sentence.

In this current thesis, the ultimate concern is a matter of content rather than form—the semantics rather than the shape or style of the text—interpreting and understanding the text at an abstract level, rather than describing the surface form at a physical level. Our ultimate concern is therefore semantic *coherence* (which is mainly a matter of *content*) rather than stylistic *cohesion* (which is mainly a matter of *form*), or at least so shall I intend the distinction between the terms for the purpose of the current study, though

---

18. Roberts, *Let Me See Your Form*, 16; Alter, *Art of Biblical Poetry*, 37; Berlin, *Dynamics*, 7-17; Watson, *Classical Hebrew Poetry*, 121.

19. Roberts, *Let Me See Your Form*, 16.

20. O'Connor, *Hebrew Verse Structure*, 9-20; Kurylowicz, *Studies in Semitic Grammar*; Cooper, *Biblical Poetics*; Collins, *Line-Forms*; Geller, *Parallelism*.

similar distinctions are made by many authorities.[21] I am driven to the usage to be faithful to our main authorities, being Roberts who speaks mainly of cohesion, and Asher and Lascerides who speak mainly of coherence. Some reflection on what may prompt their usage is therefore in order, as well as clarifying the usage I will myself be adopting.

The arrangements of words in crossword puzzles and lemmas as dictionary headwords have a type of formal stylistic cohesion, *organizing* many diverse words: into a *united* puzzle by indexing rows and columns; or into a *united* lexicon or glossary indexed according to alphabetical order. Even a shopping list has a cohesion based on denotations all corresponding to items available at a shopping center, though the irrelevance of sequencing the items may mean the list has a kind of *cohesion* without being strictly a *coherent* text. "Sun, moon, and stars" or "red, white, and blue" or "good, bad, and ugly" are phrases with a feel of cohesion about them, though without further context they are suggestive of potential coordinated meaning rather than being precisely meaningful in advance of what they will denote given a logically prior context to aid interpretation. The phrase "first, second, and third" provides cohesive "shape" into which coherent meaning can be "poured." The Chomsky sentence above provides an example of grammatical cohesion, but with essentially insuperable difficulties in resolving meaning or coherent sense from the sentence, despite it being well formed around its subject plus complement including a finite verb. The form of the Chomsky sentence is fine; difficulty lies in the content. Semantic coherence is "derailed" en route from the lexicon as oxymoronic adjectives and incompatible modifiers and headwords are forced together by the tight cohesion of the sentence structure.

Cohesion and coherence are alike in relating parts to a united whole, but different in the manner in which they do it and in the type of whole under which parts are being organized. Cohesive text "sticks together" in a single discourse unit; coherent text "works together" towards a single discourse purpose; or at least, some such simplified usage will suffice for the

---

21. Martin views discourse cohesion as an "aspect" of discourse texture which is itself an aspect of discourse coherence: "Cohesion can be defined as the set of resources for constructing relations in discourse which transcend grammatical structure (Halliday 1994: 309)." Martin, "Cohesion and Texture," 35-53. Martin's perspective and terminology are influenced by Halliday- (1964) and Hasan- (1968) inspired Australian Systemic Functional Linguistics (SFL), canonically expressed in Halliday and Hasan (1976, according to Martin), and in dialogue with Gleason (1968) and Hartford-based stratificational linguistics, canonically expressed in Gutwinski (1976). Indeed, Roberts observes, "As far as cohesion is concerned, both Halliday and Hasan and Gutwinski distinguish between grammatical and lexical features." Ibid., 25.

purpose of distinguishing Roberts's formal-devices-only approach to the Song from the dynamic semantic discourse analysis applied in this thesis.

With regular prose or poetic texts there are many relationships between the form and content of texts that are essential parts of the process of inferring content, often recursively, from the surface form of the text being considered. That hallmark of Hebrew poetry, semantic parallelism, is a perfect illustration of the point. Content is so much part of the form of Semitic poetry that etymology often argues from parallel lexeme usage to the probable meaning of many specific ancient words: consideration of form is especially helpful in constraining the domain of possible interpretations of content in the case of Semitic poetry.

That definitive identification of formal structuring in the Song has proved problematic under analysis is an important consideration. It appears to many that its degree of formal cohesion is relatively weak. However, it is an even more important issue that the semantic coherence of the Song is also problematic under analysis. To suggest coherence is weak is to suggest the Song does not really quite make sense, or at least that it does not offer any single simple clear sense overall, whatever ideas it does present failing to cohere together in such a way that we feel confident we have been purposefully addressed. If this were true, at least three out of four Gricean maxims—quantity, relevance, and manner—would be violated: the Song including more (or less) than necessary to make a point; that surplus being irrelevant to whatever point it is aiming to make (or deficit falling short of making a point); and hence the Song becoming unclear, irrespective of how genuine an attempt to communicate the Song might have been in its author's own imagination.

The decisive importance of coherence over cohesion becomes clear if, for the sake of argument, we presume the Song to have an identifiably strong formal cohesion, just so happening to have escaped scholarly scrutiny until we now—according to our counterfactual hypothesis—discover it, and this formal cohesion is sufficient to at last place beyond scholarly doubt the unity of the final form of the Song as we have it in our received text. Yet now let us permit the semantic coherence to be just as indisputably weak as its formal cohesion is strong, and we now have a demonstrably incoherent author!

In the next chapter, I will use the term *coherence* both narrowly according to SDRT usage, and more broadly to refer to semantic relationships between segments of text. Semantic coherence is itself a form of text (or speech) cohesion. Typically, discourse connectives mark natural language so a speaker can signal to a hearer how a new utterance relates to prior context, if this is not otherwise obvious from discourse context on its own, or from communicative conventions, or from world knowledge, or whatever else might be relevant. A rough analogy is found in syntagmatic cues within single sentences. Conventions of word order, vocal or typographic stress, intonation, word morphology, and clitic particles all contribute to encoding and decoding information packaged to pass from speaker to hearer. In a natural language sentence, discrete lexemes are enriched by markers signifying their relationships to one another, in order that they cohere to express a thought.

The pre-theoretical notion that a sentence expresses a "complete thought" is essentially a semantic description of sentence coherence. What defines a sentence as a self-contained unit is the thought that it expresses, whatever the conventions of lexicon and syntax that are used to package it. That translation is possible proves the point. Without being too particular about details, the same thought can be expressed in English, French, or German according to different lexicons and rules of syntax; the unity of the complete thought of a sentence precedes the manner of expressing the sentence in one dialect or another.

Likewise, it is the underlying semantic *content* that drives the typographical *form* of a sentence—beginning with a capital letter and ending with a full stop—or vocal analogues, like providing a caesura between sentences, which each end with intonational variations. So, even without punctuation or audible cues, the internal sentence structures of a written paragraph can usually be reconstructed by identifying complete thought units. However, there are challenging cases, like those provided by dead languages, textual fragments with lacunae, genres like poetry, or direct speech dialogues without explicit markers of change of speaker. In such cases, recovery of the sense of the text involves inference from observations of both whatever content is unambiguously present, and various formal conventions of text structuring that may apply.

The point of this sentence illustration is to connect with basic intuitions about language use. In examining the structure of the Song of Songs, as laboriously convoluted as the analysis may sometimes appear, it is essentially based on the same kinds of logical relationships we are more familiar with assuming when we parse text, as a subconscious reflex, while interpreting the syntax of natural language sentences in our native languages. The primary conception underlying coherence and cohesion is that of interrelatedness leading to a perception of unity, the "completeness" of a sentence under my analogy. What I am striving for with the Song of Songs is to grasp just what it is that constitutes the completion of its sense. To what logically prior whole do its component parts contribute?

Even as part of a paragraph, a sentence contributes a *single* complete thought to a narrative, description, argument, commentary, or such like—it is a basic unit, whole, integer. Multivalency of a sentence (or colon) is still possible, of course—and that will be noticeable in places within the Song—but each of however many senses a multivalent sentence may contribute to its context exists in parallel with the others, they are still part of a unit, which is precisely part of the intended effect of multivalency, distinguishing it from the expression of the same or similar senses in a non-unitary, canonical sequential manner.

This unity of the sentence is also discernible despite being itself comprised of words and phrases that have lexical meanings independent of one another. The sentence is a natural, rather than artificial, level of packaging information. Cohesion and coherence both assume a hierarchy of textual groupings. The idea is that a span of text at a higher level of text organization is meaningfully and naturally considered to be a unity due to the close relationships between its elements at a lower level of text organization. Ultimately, in linguistics, this process reaches a limit with phonetics, where relationships between discrete sounds combine to form discrete words. Language, like discrete mathematics, works with whole building blocks rather than a flux of infinitesimal gradients. The essence of discrete objects being discrete lies in them having boundaries; in the case of spheres, a surface; in the case of words or text, a beginning and an end.

In a stand-alone poem, aperture and closure do not require formal devices to mark them.[22] That a poem begins and that it ends are each sufficient on their own (and can be used as such to deliberately give prominence to chosen content). On the other hand, the formal convention of marking sentences with capitals and full stops exists to segregate them in contexts where they are expected to have neighbors. Hence, the fact that the Song has observable gratuitous poetic devices marking aperture and closure of subsections is suggestive that these sections were composed with broader context in mind—that they were intended to contribute to a greater, whole conception. A redactor putting together an anthology, by simple juxtaposition of independent compositions of similar style and theme (and identical dialect), would not—in all likelihood—produce a text with such formally and poetically marked subdivisions.

Counterintuitively, the more definitively the Song is perceived to be segmented by deliberate poetic devices, the less likely it is to be an anthology of independent poems. The strongest case in support of reading the Song as an anthology would be made by demonstrating that semantic segmentation exists without there being corresponding formal poetic devices of aperture

---

22. "Of course, the very first words of a work do not need any formal mark of opening, at least for the purpose of segmentation, since nothing precedes." Ibid., 50.

and closure at the semantic boundaries. Conversely, the strongest case in support of a unified reading of the Song would be made either by identifying semantic boundaries, then finding formal poetic devices marking those same boundaries, or vice versa: identifying structural boundaries, then demonstrating semantic coherence within those structural boundaries. This thesis adopts the second strategy, broadly accepting Roberts's carefully objective analysis of poetic substructure.

It is particularly striking that Roberts's predisposition was towards viewing the Song as a unity, yet ultimately his conclusion found against definitive top-down literary macro-structure in the Song. However, Roberts makes explicit that he is refraining from pronouncing on semantic issues, particularly those with scope over the whole of the Song, like global themes and overall interpretation. How this thesis views macro-structure with additional input from semantics will arise in the body of the text. For now it is simply worth noting that Roberts finds cues suggestive of the opening of the Song being marked for opening, redundant as such marking is: "the hortatory force of the jussive ישקני has an opening effect";[23] "the striking alliterative sequence in ישקני מנשיקות strengthens the opening";[24] "The use of the longer form of the third person masculine suffix in פיהו is very rare in the Song, and occurs only in opening cola."[25] Roberts offers other evidence of markers of aperture as well. What opens must close, and with the closure we have a discrete unit. This is primary evidence of cohesion.

The question is whether the Song closes where it finishes, as it opens where it starts, forming one complete thought comprising the whole Song. This thesis, like Roberts, believes the answer to that question is Yes to the complete thought, but No to a simple beginning, middle, and end structure to the Song. I shall go one step further than Roberts in seeing a semantic pointer from the final lines of the Song back to the opening lines. In other words, coherent closure of the Song is achieved by implying circularity. This actually suits the material in the body of the Song and common intuition about the nature of romantic love. It also would explain the euphony of marking the opening for aperture, so it could be repeated following on from the last lines in an actual reading or singing of the Song. The Song is written down in A–B form, but may have been performed as A–B–A, where A is Song 1:2—5:1 and B is Song 5:2—8:14.

---

23. Roberts, *Let Me See Your Form*, 50.
24. Ibid.
25. Ibid.

The contrast between this thesis and Roberts is that Roberts finds a linear formal cohesion across the Song, whereas this thesis finds a circular semantic coherence.

§3. From Methodology to Conclusions

Roberts's study sought "minimal structural units *above* the level of the bicolon," which he called strophes.[26] He uses the term strictly in this sense of a level in a hierarchy of structure, without any theoretical implications for norms of Hebrew poetry outside the Song (in regard to the putative existence of strophes as a deliberate feature of Hebrew poetry, or in regard to historical expectations about such putative units of Hebrew poetry). His usage thus accords with Raabe (*Psalm structures*),[27] Wahl (*Strophic structure*),[28] and Lugt (*Strofische structuren*),[29] rather than the more specific usage of Watson (*Classical Hebrew poetry*),[30] or the more general usage of Exum ("Literary and structural analysis").[31]

Within the Song, Roberts's study ultimately found such strophic units to be "pervasive."[32] Roberts does find occasional bi- and tricola in the Song to lack formal cohesion with neighboring text, and sometimes counts these as though they are free-standing strophes. What "binds" bi- and tricola together into strophes in Roberts's analysis are poetic structuring devices, "'schemes' as opposed to 'figures' or 'tropes.'"[33] He lists some of these as "mechanical devices of presentation in Hebrew poetry, including, but not exhausted by, refrains, inclusio, chiasmus, and parallelism in all its variations, many of which incorporate classical rhetorical schemes of ellipsis, anadiplosis, anaphora, etc."[34] What also stands out is Roberts's attention to marks of opening and closing, which demarcate boundaries between strophes and reveal a cohesive paratactic progression throughout the Song. The Song is ubiquitously punctuated, as it were, by such devices, irrespective of how

---

26. Ibid., p. 39.
27. Raabe, *Psalm Structures*.
28. Wahl, *Strophic Structure*.
29. Lugt, *Strofische Structuren*, 518.
30. Watson, *Classical Hebrew Poetry*.
31. Exum, "Literary and Structural Analysis," 47–79.
32. Roberts, *Let Me See Your Form*, 41.
33. Ibid.
34. Ibid.

such punctuation may mesh with subtle semantic themes. Obvious refrains, however, are part of the punctuation by Roberts's accounting, as cited above.

Roberts sees "formal structuring devices . . . contributing to the establishment of either cohesion or segmentation."[35] The dichotomy here is that of cohesion as against segmentation; precisely the same question leveled at the whole Song with regard to unity or anthology, but just as apt when closely considering poetic form. Whether aperture or closure is marked, a boundary or segmentation is implied that interrupts cohesion. Cohesion relates, formally speaking, to the text that lies within marked boundaries. Cohesion primarily extends (or fails to extend) over a segment or span of text. Roberts is able to find cohesion between neighboring spans of segmented text by looking upwards one level of hierarchy in structure. This is why bottom-up methodology is so effective at showing unity across the Song. A bicolon opens and closes and has cohesion via parallelism perhaps, and so does a following bicolon, but what "binds" the two bicola together? It must be some text feature that resides at a "higher level." Roberts finds, very plausibly, a pervasive structure of strophes that open and close with cohesion evident at a higher level of abstraction than parallelism, for example, in a single bicolon. The ten opening lines of the Song illustrate the point. Poetically and semantically, these lines are not only coherent but also cohesive. They work as two strophes of five lines each. Line ten echoes line five. That echo simultaneously closes each five-line strophe while connecting them to one another at a higher level of abstraction. Once this hierarchical structuring of text is appreciated, in principle it can extend via segmentations all the way up to the entirety of the Song.

Roberts presents his work methodically bottom up, but he does arrive at a global paratactic structure, which was outlined in the synoptic table of proposed Song structures offered by recent commentators in the literature review above. As with several other scholarly analyses, the proposed hierarchical arrangement of the text was presented as macro-sections segmented into subsections. What was not made evident in the case of Roberts was that his subsections are further subdivided in the course of application of his methodology. The fine-grained segmentation provided by Roberts helps explain how other scholars arrive at alternative delineations within the structuring of the Song. This could not easily be shown in the table above, but will be covered in the body of the thesis below.

In his final "Summaries and Conclusions" chapter, Roberts lists features that his study had found to achieve three main poetic functions: opening, closure, and sustaining cohesion. He also distinguishes between

---

35. Ibid.

such features as they apply at the level of "minimal structural segments" as opposed to "higher structural levels."

In regard to opening devices, Roberts notes that these are not always "distinctly poetic in nature,"[36] and that some are features of text "that tend to occur near the beginning of a sentence in any circumstance (vocatives, interjections, imperatives, interrogatives)."[37] In other words, some opening devices are intuitively obvious as opening features that could have been expected even prior to the painstaking analysis of the study. Part of their value, however, lies in being a reliable objective indicator of opening, after the fact of which other opening devices can be seen to co-occur with them. First among such devices Roberts lists are deictic particles and demonstratives: "Though less frequent than vocatives in the Song, the deictic particle הנה and the demonstrative pronouns זה and זאת, which also have a deictic force, are also consistent markers of opening."[38]

Volitional (imperative, jussive, cohortative) verbs are also associated with effecting opening of strophes in the Song according to Roberts, and in sources he cites regarding Hebrew poetry in general. The most immediate examples are found in the first two strophes of the Song: ישקני and משכני at 1:2 and 1:4 respectively. Although exceptions are "numerous" according to Roberts, "Only in 8:13c (לקולך השמיעיני) does an imperative occur in a closing position in a strophe, and there as a transition to the following dialogue."[39] Likewise, despite exceptions (like 1:7c–e, 7:1c, and 8:8c), interrogatives frequently effect opening in the Song: "All three instances of מי זאת have a strong opening function (3:6a, 6:10, and 8:5a)."[40] So too מה is opening at 4:10a, 7:2a, and 7:7a. In the Song, "opening interrogatives are frequently doubled"[41] as at 5:9, 4:10a–b, 6:2, and 7:7.

Independent first- and second-person personal pronouns are also typical of features associated with opening. "Of eleven total instances of אני, all but two occur in the first colon of a segment . . . and most occur as the first word."[42] Of particular importance for the current thesis, but at a global interpretative level, "Only the woman uses the independent first person pronoun to refer to herself; never the man."[43] An interesting contrast is that

---

36. Ibid., 370.
37. Ibid.
38. Ibid., 371.
39. Ibid.
40. Ibid.
41. Ibid.
42. Ibid., 372.
43. Ibid.

the only independent second-person pronoun is addressed by the man to the woman. Roberts notes in passing that independent third-person forms work differently, probably because they involve anaphoric references necessary to maintain textual coherence, the first- and second-person forms being used, on the other hand, for exophoric deictic reference to the woman.

So far, the features we have considered are not particular to poetry; they are just grammatical features that are easy to observe objectively. Roberts also finds a good deal of evidence of poetic features being used to effect opening across the Song. He observes: long four-stress cola, phonological intensity, parallelism, "semantic expressions of beginning," dialogical changes, and a catch-all category of "any type of change." Regarding long four-stress cola, Roberts goes further, noting that these are often monocola, and often have a clear middle caesura.[44] Although there are four-stress cola that do not open sections, these only occur in four short sections of the Song where longer cola are the general pattern of the text (2:11–13b, 3:1–4, 4:10–11, and 8:11–12).[45] Here we have the potential for a poet to be deliberately shaping his text to have opening and closing contours with intervening cohesion. Words are being chosen carefully, according to a design native to Hebrew, but not to English. At least, so the evidence of the Song may indicate, though Roberts does offer caveats regarding how Hebrew stress was counted and if it was genuinely important to the original poets.[46]

Regarding phonological intensity, Roberts has in mind things like assonance and alliteration, or both. He gives an impressive non-exhaustive list of examples: 1:2a, 1:15a, 2:9a, 2:15a, 2:16a, 3:6a, 3:11a, 4:5a, 4:7a, 4:11a, 4:15a, 5:2b, 5:2c, 5:10a, 6:3a, 6:4a, 6:9a, 7:1a, 7:2c, 7:8a, 8:1a, 8:2a, 8:5a, 8:5c, and 8:8a.[47] Again, however, Roberts has to issue caveats. He is not certain that phonological intensity alone effects opening without additional features that typically mark opening. It is also the case that phonological intensity is not restricted to marking opening cola alone. "Yet it is still clear that the opening of strophes is often supported by some attention-arresting pattern of assonance and/or alliteration."[48]

Roberts started out expecting he might find patterns of parallelism that were preferred as structural markers in the Song, for opening, closure or cohesion.[49] As a general rule, he did not find such a preference, however;

---

44. Ibid., 373.
45. Ibid.
46. Ibid., 372.
47. Ibid., 374 and n. 13.
48. Ibid., 374.
49. Ibid.

"staircase" parallelism is an exception, though, in that it does consistently occur at the beginning of a strophe when it does occur. By contrast, where Roberts had been looking for patterns of parallelism and did not generally find them, he had not been looking for semantic features, but was forced to recognize some. "Though semantic and thematic features are not, strictly speaking, part of this study, they are often intertwined with and combined with more mechanical features in effecting opening in strophes."⁵⁰ For example, "Words meaning 'to arise' (קום), 'to awake' (עור), 'to open' (פתח), and the like, are ideally suited to opening cola."⁵¹

Perhaps the most distinctive feature of the Song, even in translation, is the pattern of shifts of voice from one speaker to another. Clearly, where there is a change of speaker or voice there is a kind of opening at a level higher than that of a bicolon or even of a strophe. This is not a grammatical feature; more a poetic or semantic feature that structures the overall text of the Song. One simple way of segmenting the Song is to do so according to who is speaking. One may ask how strongly marked each speech is for opening and closure and how cohesive are the bodies of such segmented speeches. One may also ask how related to each other are the speeches. Even if the cohesive quality of the speeches is granted, much of the perception of the Song as problematic in regard to unity has to do with the difficulty of ascertaining how (or if) the speeches coordinate with one another.

There are some difficulties with even changes of speaker as a mark of opening. Roberts shows his rigor in noting that in 4:16, "it is not immediately clear that a change of speaker has taken place . . . until we reach the fifth colon of the strophe."⁵² Roberts is not looking to oversimplify the Song, but to be realistic about its challenges. In the end, changes of speaker alone prove the value of Roberts's analysis: we cannot simply look to speech segments for poetic boundaries; they are an aid, not the final word. Changes of speaker are part of the poet's technique in the Song, not the essence of it. Roberts notes that changes of speaker are not the only changes being rung by the poet, and that any change signals opening in a very direct way. One example he gives is the change from noun clauses to verb clauses at 4:16a. Another is the sudden reappearance of the brothers at 8:8a.⁵³

Such are the features effecting opening of minimal structural units (strophes) according to Roberts. However, although Roberts has a corresponding list of different features effecting closure of minimal units, his

50. Ibid., 375.
51. Ibid.
52. Ibid.
53. Ibid., 376.

work is not done simply by offering a sequence of discrete segments of text. He needs to "join the dots," as it were. He needs some evidence that minimal units are themselves bound together into higher-level structural units. But what he looks for is essentially the same kind of evidence he has already looked for at the lower (lowest) level: features of opening, closure, and cohesion. How are these marked in the Song for higher-level structures? Although Roberts does not find a wide range of new devices that signal such higher-order opening, he does note that the more markers of opening that obtain in opening a strophe, the more likely it is that such a strophe also opens higher levels of cohesive text. Roberts does also think that monocola offer some degree of marking of opening for the longer, more narrative sections of the Song at 2:8–17 and 5:2—6:3.[54]

Before looking at features Roberts identified as effecting closure of minimal structural segments, armed as we now are with at least the examples of such devices as regards opening, a diagram may help crystallize the way Roberts's methodology produced the conclusions we are considering. In the diagram below, the text of the Song at any arbitrary point is schematically represented in the right hand column. It is shaded or plain in alternation to reflect the scope of individual strophes, identified by their opening and closing features and by features effecting cohesion between aperture and closure. Tying the second and third strophe together in the diagram is a higher-level unit with its own opening and closing devices and features effecting cohesion. This unit is called Section 2 in the diagram, to distinguish it from the sections that precede and follow it. As will be seen in the body of the thesis below, Roberts typically identifies more than one higher level of text organization above the level of the strophe. These extend the same rationale as the diagram outwards to the left of the diagram and will often be represented that way in this thesis, where graphical presentation is considered to be a helpful aid to grasping the structures Roberts outlines mainly in words alone.

Higher level		Strophe level
Final strophe		Cohesive text
Section 1	**Closing colon**	Closing colon
First strophe	**Opening colon**	Opening colon
Section 2	**Cohesive text**	Cohesive text
	Cohesive text	Cohesive text
	Cohesive text	Closing colon

54. Ibid., 376–77.

	Higher level	Strophe level
Second strophe	**Cohesive text**	Opening colon
Section 2	**Cohesive text**	Cohesive text
	Cohesive text	Cohesive text
	Closing colon	Closing colon
First strophe	**Opening colon**	Opening colon
Section 3		Cohesive text

The first marker of closure that Roberts notes is the ו-initial final colon. As is typical of many of the markers Roberts considers, the relationship of feature to function is not a one-to-one relationship such that every ו-initial colon closes a strophe, nor that all cola closing strophes are ו-initial. Rather, ו-initial cola—when they are present—tend to confirm that a colon is final when other features also suggest it is final. An obvious analogy exists in English with lists that conclude prefixed by *and*: north, south, east, *and* west. Not every use of *and* in English closes a list, nor do all lists close with *and* (some close with *or* or have no marker), but *and* is nonetheless genuinely a marker of closure of lists in English.

Having noted that sometimes longer cola were used to open strophes (in longer quasi-narrative passages of the Song), Roberts explored the possibility that shorter cola might be used to close strophes, and they do in 1:4e (מישרים אהבוך) and 8:6f (שלהבתיה). However, he could not find that this was a general pattern. Likewise, although longer cola do close some strophes in the Song, they do so at places like 2:11b, 2:12c, 2:13b, 4:11c, and 8:11c, where longer cola are typical of the sections they close anyway. So Roberts rejects length of cola as a primary indicator of authorial intention to mark closure.[55]

Following Alter, Roberts notes that "compared to many other parts of the OT, strong synonymous parallelism is relatively infrequent in the Song."[56] However, where such parallelism does exist in the Song it tends to be found in the last two bicola of strophes, so Roberts proposes it as among the poetic closing devices in the Song. The first example of this is in 1:5c-d (כאהלי קדר / כיריעות שלמה). Chiastic parallelism is also infrequent in the Song, and also associated with closure when it does exist. The first example of this is in 1:6d–e (שמני נטרה את הכרמים / כרמי שלי לא נטרתי).

As with features effecting opening, phonological intensity can also be part of effecting closure. Roberts notes in particular that colon-initial

---

55. Ibid., 378.
56. Ibid., 379; compare Alter, *Art of Biblical Poetry*, 186.

alliteration and end rhyme tend to lead into closing cola across the Song. These are more specific types of phonological intensity than the opening devices, and they draw more attention to the segmentation of the Song line by line. After all, each line begins and closes and has cohesion, and so does each word, at the absolutely lowest levels of analysis of the poetry of the Song.

Naturally, *inclusio*—where it is used—effects closure (and—after being identified—also reveals aperture). The two main types of *inclusio* in the Song, according to Roberts, are semantic and phonological *inclusio*. Interestingly, the only two instances of a first person pronoun outside opening cola (2:4–5 and 5:8) look to be cases of semantic *inclusio*, where they close after an opening first-person singular pronominal suffix verb form at the beginning of the strophe.[57]

Again, as with features effecting opening in the Song, Roberts notes that some very direct semantic cues are part of the poet's repertoire. With closure he finds these to be very numerous and simply provides two classes as broad summaries of how these work. The two classes are (1) abstract value judgments and (2) narrative goal attainments. Concerning value judgments, the words "all" (כל) and "none" (אין) are commonly found in closing cola; concerning goal attainment, the sense resides at a higher level of semantics than individual words, hence Roberts lists phrases rather than words as examples: 2:17a–b, 4:6a–b, 4:16f, 5:6b, 5:6c, 7:13e, and 8:8d.[58] These are precisely the sorts of features dynamic semantic discourse analysis is aimed at observing, and they provide a crossover between Roberts's methodology and the self-consciously complementary semantic methodology of the current thesis.

Roberts notes miscellaneous other features effecting closure in minimal structural units, but what is more notable is what he finds regarding closure at higher structural levels. He finds more markers here than he does with higher order opening markers. First among these is again the ו-initial final colon, which can operate at any level to close a segment.[59] Secondly he notes that in the Song, the refrains are normally associated with closure, not opening.[60] *Inclusios*, like ו-initial final cola, can operate at any level to close segments.[61] Monocola twice close sections (though they more often

---

57. Roberts, *Let Me See Your Form*, 381.
58. Ibid., 382.
59. Ibid.
60. Ibid., 383.
61. Ibid., 384.

open sections in the longer narrative portions of the Song).[62] Finally, there is thematic closure, though Roberts repeats his distancing of his study from assessment of semantic and thematic issues: "Thematic closure is not really the primary subject of this study. But it is difficult to ignore the role that strong thematic closure can play."[63] As with features effecting opening at higher structural levels, Roberts again notes that a multiplicity of closing devices is typical of higher level closure. He adds, however, that there can be multiple "layers" of closure also, though he appears to mean by this a closure of semantic themes over several consecutive cola or strophes, giving the example of triple closure at the midpoint of the Song: the woman invites the man into his garden; he declares he has gone into his garden; and the friends urge on the lovers in eating and drinking.[64] This very strong closure, particularly given that it is located right in the middle of the Song, is so remarkable that I shall have more to say about it later.

So far, Roberts has proven good to his promise of adopting the methodology of the anthologists, stressing the segmentation of the Song; albeit that his admission of higher levels of structure anticipates his ultimate finding of both segment-wise and overall cohesion for the Song. Roberts's findings regarding cohesion in minimal and higher-level structural segments form the penultimate section of the conclusions of his study, and bear a good deal of the weight of his argument as it diverges from that of the anthologists. To a large extent, Roberts's thesis convinces a reader to the extent that the reader finds plausible its identification of features that effect cohesion, especially at higher levels of structure in the Song. First, however, Roberts lists features that effect cohesion in minimal structural units: first among these are grammatical features, and first among grammatical features is that cohesion is effected when a strophe is also a single sentence.[65] Also of particular interest for the discourse analyst, but with intuitive appeal as well: pronominal anaphora are singled out as a grammatical feature effecting cohesion.[66]

Coreference of anaphoric pronouns ties text together in an indisputable way. The issue of anthology versus unity is equivalently the question of whether the personal pronouns referring to male and female protagonists across the Song corefer or only seem to do so, because none of the subsections of the Song strictly identifies who its protagonists actually are. Are there many "hes"s and "she"s, or just one of each? Coreference to other

62. Ibid., 385.
63. Ibid.
64. Ibid., 386.
65. Ibid.
66. Ibid., 386–87.

abstractions, entities, and persons denoted in the Song helps provide an independent line of evidence towards coreference by indicating cohesion. Where SDRT in particular is helpful is in its highly developed analysis of pronoun coreference at levels *higher* than the sentence. In SDRT, if a text is not just cohesive but coherent, all pronoun references need to be resolved, and the theory shows how that works in a way that satisfies natural language intuitions. Roberts does not go into great details about anaphora, just noting they are a feature that effects cohesion in a grammatical fashion in minimal structural units. In the body of the thesis, I will go further than Roberts in pursuing this line of evidence from not only pronominal anaphora, but propositional anaphora as well (see Asher 1993).[67]

Roberts proposes that "the most recognizable, and perhaps the most efficient cohesive device employed within single strophes is lexical repetition."[68] The first example of this in the Song is in 1:2–3 with repetition on טובים. Other examples are "abundant," according to Roberts.[69] The Song also provides several examples of prepositions and pronominal suffixes being repeated in ways that effect cohesion. Within a strophe, especially a sentence-strophe, repetition of such small words is not surprising, nor so much poetic as grammatical—equivalent to pronominal coreference and maintaining parallel "case endings." However, they are still objectively observable real choices, made by the poet, that communicate cohesion.

More subtly than lexical repetition, grammatical repetition also marks cohesion, especially in long descriptive lists.[70] This is so in the Hebrew, but an English translation would naturally follow the same pattern in most cases. The longer the list, the more some device of cohesion is needed to signal that attention is resting on the same thing being described. In speech one might alter tone to initiate listing items, then maintain the same tone until list items are exhausted, changing tone again to indicate having reached the end of the list. In shorter strophes, grammatical parallelism effects cohesion in the Song as in other biblical Hebrew poetry.[71] One might consider some cases of grammatical parallelism to reflect a similar logic to listing items pairwise. In any case, where grammatical forms are repeated over neighboring cola within strophes of the Song they generally effect cohesion—and fairly unambiguously.

67. Asher, *Abstract Objects*.
68. Roberts, *Let Me See Your Form*, 387.
69. Ibid.
70. Ibid.
71. Ibid.

Still on the theme of repetition effecting cohesion, phonological repetition is advanced by Roberts as a poetic device effecting cohesion within strophes. He finds that such phonological repetition is "pervasive" in the Song. Alliteration, assonance and end rhyme are the main devices used by the poet in the Song according to Roberts.[72] Finally, he lists bivalent cola as effecting cohesion. Bivalent cola, by Roberts's definition both close a preceding bi- or tricolon and open a following bi- or tricolon. Roberts considers such bivalent cola to be an "important" technique in the Song effecting cohesion within strophes, and lists examples at: 1:16–17, 4:16, and 8:6.[73]

Roberts's evidence of cohesion within strophes is important to establish his thesis that the Song is ultimately comprised of a "pervasive" structure of such minimal units above the level of the bi- or tricolon. After looking at the text in detail, I find his evidence to be compelling. However, to establish his claim for the Song being a paratactic unity, it is actually the establishment of cohesion over higher-order structural levels that needs to be suitably grounded on sufficient evidence. To that end, Roberts offers: narratological features, dialogical features, grammatical features, *inclusio*, chiasmus, lexical repetition, similar opening and closing cola, grammatical repetitions, phonological features, and superimposed features.[74]

With both narratological and dialogical features, Roberts notes that his methodology is poetic rather than semantic, and thus cannot evaluate the contributions of such structures in detail. This is something the current thesis seeks to address. However, Roberts cannot help noticing that sections like 2:8–17 (and 3:1–4, and 5:2—6:3) come across as narrative in such a way that the whole text is apparently cohesive in some sense.[75] Likewise, the turns of speech across the Song bind components of the speeches together as whole speeches.[76]

Also of interest for the current discourse-focused thesis: the grammatical features that effect cohesion at higher structural levels are seen by Roberts as "infrequent," but "established … by conjunctions and pronominal anaphora."[77] Two examples he gives (though this thesis will offer far more) are: from 2:11a, where "The core of the man's invitation to the woman … is tied to the opening component … by the conjunction כי";[78]

72. Ibid., 388–89
73. Ibid., 389–90.
74. Ibid., 390–93.
75. Ibid., 390.
76. Ibid.
77. Ibid.
78. Ibid.

and from 4:1–7, the first *waṣf*, where "the entire list of body features is tied to the opening component of the *inclusio* by the anaphoric ב."[79] Roberts considers such grammatical features to be "infrequent" for at least a couple of reasons that do not rule out the kind of work done in the body of the current thesis, but in fact invite such work. Firstly, much grammatical cohesion effected by conjunctions and anaphora falls "below Roberts's radar" because it operates between sentences or between cola, and so at structural levels beneath the strophe level that forms Roberts's main focus of attention. What they do provide though is a way of demonstrating coherence across strophic boundaries. This contributes to showing the unity of the Song, though it does not contribute to showing how poetry segments the Song. Secondly, Roberts is looking at cues that demonstrably exist in the text of the Song, not at semantics that lies "between the lines" of the Song, often with no lexical items to mark the implied connections between cola, strophes, and higher-order structures across their boundaries. Considered independently of Roberts's poetic analysis, there is a case for semantic coherence via dynamic semantics across the whole text of the Song; but only rarely does Roberts's analysis interact with such features of the text. That there is "infrequent" interaction is actually ideal, since the interaction provides a genuine connection, but the lack of frequency shows the general independence of the two methodologies.

Roberts lists *inclusio* and chiasmus as features effecting high-level cohesion. He observes that although *inclusio* is only apparent to a first time reader at the point of closure, with a formal poem, it is read repeatedly and its features are remembered, with *inclusio* binding together the text it encloses.[80] Unlike several other scholars of the Song, Roberts finds very limited evidence for use of chiasmus at higher levels in the Song. He prefers to speak of "chiastic-*like*" features. He only offers various parts of chapter 2 of the Song as evidence of either chiasm or chiastic-*like* features.[81]

Where cohesion is most evidently marked in the Song is in lexical repetition, according to Roberts: "lexical repetition is the most fundamental and widely employed device for effecting cohesion in the higher structural levels of the Song."[82] Roberts offers examples from all over the Song to make his point—too many to repeat here. This is the heart of his evidence for the unity of the Song: poetic evidence, a hallmark of Semitic poetry in repetitions, all seemingly evoking cohesion across various passages of the Song,

79. Ibid.
80. Ibid., 391.
81. Ibid.
82. Ibid.

many working to form a regular pattern of *inclusios*, "one of the primary high-level structuring devices in the Song."[83]

Patterns of similar opening and closing cola also draw Roberts's attention. Found in "strophic pairs [they] are one of the most common structural patterns in the Song."[84] They dominate both the first and last long sections of the Song (1:2—2:7 and 8:8–14).[85] The first example Roberts lists is the matching pair of 1:3c (על כן עלמות אהבוך) and 1:4e (מישרים אהבוך).

Pervasive across the other forms listed, Roberts observes grammatical repetitions. However, he does not find grammatical repetition plays much of a role independent of its integration along with such other devices. It appears to work mainly at effecting cohesion at lower levels in the Song, unless it is part of accompanying one of the patterns above.[86] Likewise, phonological features only rarely feature effecting cohesion at high-level structural units, as may be expected; however, assonance on *ḥolem* in 3:6–11 counts, in Roberts's opinion, as a genuine case of phonologically reinforced cohesion.[87] Few would question that 3:6–11 forms a cohesive unit within the Song, purely on semantic grounds; but we are reminded that Roberts is disciplined about seeking to establish cohesion on formal and poetic grounds alone.

Roberts finally mentions a handful of exotic cases where different kinds of structural cohesion apply to parts of the Song simultaneously, such that there is a superimposition of structures that effect cohesion. In particular he notes: the two strophes at 2:1–3, four at 3:6–11, and six at 7:12—8:4. The details of how these work as superimpositions are different in each case.

To summarize all his findings, Roberts notes: "That segmentation should be effected by variation, and cohesion by repetition seems, in hindsight, like a simplistic observation that should need no demonstration. But the great variety of ways in which change and repetition are presented easily obscures the underlying principle." He also observes that opening is more often effected by non-poetic methods than are closure and cohesion, and that closure is typically more marked than opening in any case.[88]

Thus we have Roberts's presentation of poetic evidence for the unity of the Song of Songs. From an essentially purely formal perspective, there is a *prima facie* case to take the Song as a cohesive unity, quite apart from the many semantic and thematic cues normally advanced towards the same

83. Ibid.
84. Ibid.
85. Ibid.
86. Ibid., 392.
87. Ibid., 393.
88. Ibid., 393–94.

conclusion. If we accept Roberts's conclusion, and go just one step further in allowing that to inform our resolution of pronoun reference, so that one unique sister of brothers, who addresses daughters of Jerusalem, about the one her soul loves, is consistently speaking and being addressed, then we have the basic framework for a coherent discourse that can be examined in detail for its dynamic semantic structure according to SDRT. So we shall turn next to a brief introductory overview of that theory; and this as the last step in preparing ourselves to apply it as a methodology to investigate the coherent unity of the Song, especially such that the female protagonist is actually the character around whom the whole discourse turns.

4

Methodology

> Over the past twenty years, discourse level phenomena have received ever increasing attention from sociolinguists and linguistic anthropologists, functional linguists and structural linguists, as well as from text linguists and literary theorists. But among generative grammarians, even those who occasionally use examples which consist of two sentences instead of only one, there appears to be widespread agreement that discourse is too complex, too messy, too ill defined to be treated in a rigorous manner. — Livia Polanyi.[1]

§1. Discourse Analysis

DISCOURSE ANALYSIS AND TEXT linguistics—its closely allied discipline—are often loosely defined as fields that study communicative structure above the level of the sentence boundary. As the quote from Polanyi indicates, the field is both relatively new and interdisciplinary. Additionally, practitioners of text linguistics offer different, overlapping methodologies rather than a standard uniform approach to addressing the questions that arise in analyzing discourse.[2] Also as indicated by Polanyi, the results of discourse analysis are not always embraced by scholars in neighboring disciplines. We have

---

1. Polanyi, "Linguistic Structure of Discourse," 265–6.
2. "The term *discourse analysis*, may be used for a variety of different theoretical positions which operate with different assumptions and procedures." Callow, "Units and Flow," 462.

already seen that Phillip Roberts is one scholar who falls into that camp, at least regarding the analysis of poetry and the Song of Songs: "Unless the concept of discourse analysis is expanded, at least for poetic texts, to absorb the related method of rhetorical analysis . . . it still plays a subsidiary role in the structural analysis of Hebrew poetry."[3] The work in the body of this thesis is only aimed at being subsidiary to work like that of Roberts; though it is precisely the rhetorical analysis involved in our chosen theory of discourse (SDRT) that suits it to extending Roberts's own work.

In the 2010 published version of her dissertation,[4] Miriam Urgelles-Coll analyzes English language usage of the word *anyway* as a discourse marker, and considers four different alternative approaches to discourse analysis, choosing as guide for her own study Nicholas Asher and Alexandra Lascerides's Segmented Discourse Representation Theory (SDRT, 2003)[5] ahead of William Mann and Sandra Thompson's Rhetorical Structure Theory (RST, 1987),[6] Jerry Hobbs's approach (1990),[7] and the Inten-

3. Roberts, *Let Me See Your Form*, 27.
4. Urgelles-Coll, *Syntax and Semantics*.
5. Ibid, 78– 92; Asher and Lascarides, *Logics of Conversation*.
6. Urgelles-Coll, *Syntax and Semantics*, 92–93; Mann and Thompson, "Rhetorical Structure Theory," 243–81.
7. Urgelles-Coll, *Syntax and Semantics*, 94-98; Hobbs, *Literature and Cognition*; see also Hobbs et al., "Interpretation as Abduction," 69–142. Of particular note for the current thesis, Hobbs is happy to apply his style of discourse analysis to poetry and to coherence, see in particular, "Lawrence of virtuous father virtuous son: A coherence analysis," chapter 6 in *Literature and Cognition*, which begins: "A sonnet is brief enough that we can examine it in detail in the framework presented in this book, with something approaching completeness. The one we shall examine is John Milton's 20th sonnet, given below. Jakobsen and Jones (1970) displayed a similarly close reading of a sonnet in their brilliant analysis of Shakespeare's 129th sonnet. The difference between that analysis and this is instructive. They focused on oppositions and correspondences between various divisions of the poem as revealed by phonological, lexical, and syntactic features. At the time their analysis was written, linguistics had very little to say about how the meaning of texts was composed out of the meaning of its constituents, and in their analysis the meaning of the poem is taken for granted. Indeed, it is very nearly ignored. The oppositions that are pointed out are rarely related to meaning; they are left rather as a stunningly dense but ultimately irrelevant texture of decoration. In the past two decades substantial progress has been made in our understanding of how the meaning of texts can be represented and computed, and in the analysis below, the focus is on how this happens. No attention is given to phonological features, and lexical and syntactic features are examined only insofar as they relate to the reader's construction of the meaning of the poem. It is an account of how the ordinary meaning of the poem is accomplished, both by the writer and by the reader—an account of how the reader creates the meaning and what the writer has done to enable the reader to create it." Hobbs, *Literature and Cognition*, 115–16.

tional Approach of Barbara Grosz and Candace Sidner (1986).[8] Grosz and Sidner saw their own work arising from cognitive science and especially the artificial intelligence work within computational processing of natural language:

> More research has been done in the cognitive sciences than could be reported in this chapter, we focus on work that has taken computational or processing questions to be central. We begin with a survey of early approaches to discourse within artificial intelligence.[9]

However, the issues Grosz and Sidner consider are not restricted to computational nor cognitive science, but interact with mainstream studies of language: "The utterances a discourse comprises are not random sequences, but rather have structure much in the way that the words in an individual sentence have structure."[10] In their 1993 review of literature that gave rise to their own work, they start with basic pronoun and intention recognition in Woods's computational LUNAR system (1972 and 1978) and Winograd's SHRDLU dialogue system (1971, 1972).[11] They go on to note that "analysis of a variety of types of discourse has established that discourses divide into discourse segments, and that these segments may bear different kinds of relations to one another."[12] Among the types of discourse listed in the review by Grosz et al. are dialogues (as investigated by Grosz 1978, and Mann et al.), and narratives (as investigated by Polanyi, 1985).

I will not attempt to retrace the historical development of schools of thought within formal academic study of discourse in detail, beyond noting as I have a handful of key names and theories that recur in the literature. More apposite for my purposes are researchers like Urgelles-Coll, selecting from among relatively popular approaches to discourse that are still current into the second decade of the twenty-first century. Like her, I will avail myself of elements of SDRT ahead of RST and other options: elements suited to reinforcing Roberts's presentation of formal and poetic cohesion across the text of the Song of Songs with a presentation of coherence of semantic content across the Song as well.

---

8. Urgelles-Coll, *Syntax and Semantics*, 98–102; Grosz and Sidner, "Attention, Intentions," 175–204.

9. Grosz et al., "Discourse," 437.

10. Ibid., 439.

11. Ibid., 438.

12. Ibid., 439.

§2. Segmented Discourse Representation Theory

Segmented Discourse Representation Theory (SDRT) focuses on what it calls the rhetorical relations between atomic discourse units (ADUs), normally clauses. The theory considers a range of much broader issues, but the core questions it developed to answer are addressed principally by its approach to rhetorical relations. SDRT is a dynamic semantic theory, in that the semantic content of a new utterance appended to a discourse is viewed in terms of how it changes or updates the semantic content of the prior context, a feature called context change potential (CCP). A new utterance is a speech act of a certain type depending on the way it relates to prior context. These speech-act types are called rhetorical relations. Several writers have commented—and Asher and Lascarides acknowledge—that SDRT is an extension of Hans Kamp's dynamic semantics in Discourse Representation Theory (DRT),[13] wedded with a typology of rhetorical relations more simplified than those of Mann and Thompson's Rhetorical Structure Theory (RST).[14]

A strength of SDRT is the way the theory explicates how rhetorical relations are integral to the pragmatics of natural language in an unavoidable way. RST, on the other hand, recognizes a considerable collection of rhetorical relations, but simply observes them rather than explaining why they arise. Much of the distinctive work in the current thesis will be a matter of identifying rhetorical relations that obtain between cola (and strophes) in the Song. What is needed to show the value of the methodology at this point is not simply listing the available options for rhetorical relations—the names of these speech act types—(though I shall do that); what is most needed is a sense of the way the Song, if coherent, is necessarily a sequence of speech acts, before classifying those into types. The identification of types is subsidiary to the fact that the Song has a unified coherence based on an essentially unbroken sequence of related speech acts. How can the pragmatics of such speech acts be recovered from the text? This is a question Asher and Lascarides address in motivating their own work, connecting with a reader's intuition about natural language to prepare the way for the more involved issues of their full theory.

The first example Asher and Lascarides offer in their monograph introducing SDRT is aimed at showing how natural language usage expects interpreters to infer various semantic issues rather than making all implications explicit.

---

13. Kamp and Reyle, *From Discourse to Logic*.
14. Ibid.

a. John arrived in Edinburgh by train.

b. Max met him at the station.

c. ??Max met him at the shop.[15]

The sentence sequence (a)–(b) leads to the inference that *the station* is the station where John's train arrived, viz., Edinburgh. Thus the two sentences cohere in some sense. On the other hand, there is nothing wrong with the sequence (a)–(b'), but *the shop* enters the discourse somewhat "out of the blue," as Asher and Lascarides describe it. There is an element of pragmatic infelicity, or a lower level of coherence on some kind of scale of coherence. We are not looking at complete incoherence here, after all, there is still the inference that the *him* of (b') is the John of (a).

Rhetorical structure has implications for resolving the semantics of temporal sequence. Asher and Lascarides present this as "perhaps the most straightforward" effect of rhetorical structure. Their first example is from French:

> Pierre entra dans le salon. Il s'assist sur la banquette. Il s'endormit.[16]

They note that if the sequence of propositions is true, then all occurred in the past, and in the order in which they are introduced in the discourse. This basic example is then extended to a more challenging case, to show how rhetorical structure can constrain resolution of temporal sequence more subtly.

a. Max fell. John helped him up.

b. Max fell. John pushed him.[17]

In the first pair of sentences (a), the rhetorical structure is temporally sequential, whereas in the second pair of sentences (b) a reverse chronology obtains. Although both pairs of sentences use the same simple past tense verbs, a reader infers a different chronological order: why? It has to do with semantic content and rhetorical structure. The speaker's intention in the first pair of sentences is best explained by the semantics of the verb "to help up" chronologically following an event of someone falling. On the other hand, the intention in the second pair of sentences is best explained by the semantics of pushing leading to falling. The rhetorical "voice" in the first

---

15. Asher and Lascarides, *Logics of Conversation*, 1.

16. Ibid., 6.

17. Ibid.

METHODOLOGY 123

pair of sentences is narrative, whereas in the second pair it is explanatory. These are two different types of speech act—narrating and explaining—and they induce different rhetorical structure on contexts where they obtain. Correct inference of truth conditional compositional semantics depends on recognizing this rhetorical structure. There is an interaction between syntax and pragmatics at their interface in natural language.

Still in the earliest stages of their introduction to SDRT, Asher and Lascarides provide what is the most widely cited illustration of their theory.

a. Max had a lovely evening.

b. He had a great meal.

c. He ate salmon.

d. He devoured cheese.

e. He won a dancing competition.[18]

To this is often added:

f'. ??It had been a beautiful pink.[19]

The point of the addition is to show that there are constraints on rhetorical structure. Presumably, the beautiful pink refers to the salmon, in which case standard usage requires sentence (f) to be interposed between sentences (c) and (d), where the salmon of sentence (c) has scope to be picked up by the anaphoric pronoun *it*. This matter of scope is associated with a hierarchy of structure where elaborations subordinate text to the mainstream of the flow of the discourse while narrations coordinate with one another sequentially and chronologically. The sentences above are structured as suggested by the following diagram, where subordination is indicated by vertical lines and coordination by horizontal lines.

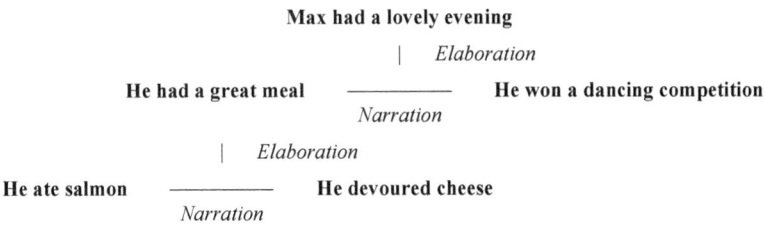

18. Ibid., 8.
19. Ibid., 158.

§3. Rhetorical (or Discourse) Relations

Several writers during the 1980s, most notably Mann and Thompson, provided descriptions of a range of rhetorical relations observable in natural language discourse. Asher and Lascarides opt for a shorter list of rhetorical relations than most authors, although some writers see subordination and coordination alone as sufficient to describe the rhetorical structure of texts. In SDRT the aim of distinguishing the rhetorical relations bears directly on the effects such relations have on interpretation of the semantics of units of discourse connected by the relations. As such, various fine-grained distinctions are not materially significant for the theory. So, for example, various types of *Contrast* relation are distinguished in RST, but these have no impact within SDRT, so just one *Contrast* relation suffices for Asher and Lascarides. On the other hand, in presenting the relations that *are* used in SDRT, several of these are introduced pairwise to *highlight* the distinctions between them. For example, *Elaboration* and *Explanation* are introduced first and distinguished from one another.[20] Both relations rhetorically subordinate the new discourse unit to its prior context, but there are key differences. Urgelles-Coll follows the same procedure of pairwise introductions in her summary review of SDRT,[21] and so shall I do here also.

Elaboration and Explanation

1a. Max fell. John pushed him.

1b. Alexis did really well in school this year.
She got As in every subject.[22]

2a. Jane answered the phone.
It had been ringing for an hour.

2b. Jane was laughing.
She was nearly crying with laughter.[23]

The first of the sentence pairs (a) in each of the above—(1) Asher and Lascarides, (2) Urgelles-Coll—expresses an *Explanation*, where the second of the pairs (b) in each expresses an *Elaboration*. There is a temporal difference

20. Ibid., 159.
21. Urgelles-Coll, *Syntax and Semantics*, 82–92.
22. Asher and Lascarides, *Logics of Conversation*, 159.
23. Urgelles-Coll, *Syntax and Semantics*, 83.

between the ways the sentences are related. *Explanation* involves the second sentence necessarily temporally preceding the first sentence, whereas *Elaboration* involves the second sentence necessarily being temporally included within the temporal boundaries of the event to which the first sentence refers.

There are other semantic consequences that follow when clauses are related by *Elaboration*. One of these is transitivity. If a second clause (π_2) is related to a first clause (π_1) by *Elaboration*, and a third clause (π_3) is also related to the second clause by *Elaboration*, then *Elaboration* also holds between the third clause and the first clause.[24]

(*Elaboration*(π_1,π_2) and *Elaboration*(π_2,π_3)) $\rightarrow$ *Elaboration*(π_1,π_3)

Distributivity also holds, since if a longer span of text comprising several clauses elaborates some earlier clause, then the events denoted in the clauses that make up the longer span of text will also be part of the event in the earlier clause they are elaborating. Urgelles-Coll describes this as "any element attached to a constituent of an elaboration should be part of the same elaboration."[25]

A simple diagnostic for *Explanation*(α,β) obtaining between two clauses (α and β) is that the content of the second clause (Kβ) should help to answer the question *Why Kα?* where Kα is the content of the first clause.[26] A clear example of *Explanation* in the Song of Songs comes from the first two lines.

α ישקני מנשיקות פיהו

I want him to kiss me with the kisses of his mouth.

β כי טובים דדיך מיין

[Why?] Because your caresses are better than wine.

Explanation(α,β)

---

24. Asher and Lascarides, *Logics of Conversation*, 161.
25. Urgelles-Coll, *Syntax and Semantics*, 83.
26. Asher and Lascarides, *Logics of Conversation*, 162.

Narration

a. Max fell. John helped him up.[27]

b. Jane answered the phone.

She received bad news.[28]

Narration is the default relation between clauses in coherent text; however, it is scalar in the sense that there is a scale of relatively greater or lesser coherence depending on various constraints. For *Narration* to hold, there is a temporal constraint such that there should be overlap between the temporal settings of the two clauses. In the first (Asher and Lascarides) example above, Max *being in the fallen state*, John helps him up from being within that state. In the second (Urgelles-Coll) example, Jane *being in the answering state*, she receives bad news while within that state. Where Asher and Lascarides speak of "overlap," Urgelles-Coll asserts, "The temporal structure of *Narration* means that the following proposition will start when the first proposition ends."[29] In her own reading of her own example, Jane's answering of the phone is completed as she receives bad news. This distinction between Asher and Lascarides and Urgelles-Coll is not sharp, but fits with the scalar nature of *Narration*: the greater a spatiotemporal gap between the clauses, the less coherent the discourse is as narrative; though it is still narrative: the sequencing of related events over elapsing time.

A common topic, or multiple common features of a topic, is also part of what constrains a rhetorical relation to be identifiable as *Narration*. Additionally, the event of the first proposition must occasion the event of the second topic. An early example of *Narration* in the Song of Songs comes from 1:4a–b.

α משכני אחריך נרוצה

Draw me after you. Let us run.

β הביאני המלך חדריו

The king has brought me into his chambers.

Narration(α,β)

---

27. Ibid.
28. Urgelles-Coll, *Syntax and Semantics*, 83.
29. Urgelles-Coll, *Syntax and Semantics*, 83.

One needs to read 1:4a as being a *Result* (see below) of 1:2a, so that the intent of the drawing and running is to find a place to kiss with the mouth, and thus 1:4b narrates the consummation of that intent. There is spatiotemporal overlap—the desire of 1:2a remains until it finds consummation—and there is commonality of topic at various levels driven by world knowledge implications of the lexical content of the early lines of the poem. Thus, at least the first seven lines of the Song form a tightly coherent rhetorical structure, based on their semantics alone, irrespective of formal and poetic features. The prior context of 1:4b occasions our interpretation of the line as denoting the fulfillment of the opening desire of the Song.

Narration can be marked in English by the phrase *and then*. In Hebrew, it is often marked by *vav*-consecutive forms in narratives.

Explanation and Result

a. I went to the supermarket.

I didn't have any food.

b. I didn't have any food.

So I went to the supermarket.[30]

Urgelles-Coll illustrates *Result* by its relationship to *Explanation*. They are "mirror image" relations. A second clause is related to a prior clause by *Result* if the first clause expresses the *cause* for the eventuality expressed in the second clause. The order of the clauses, as to which answers the diagnostic *Why?* question, is reversed between *Result* and *Explanation*. We have already seen *Explanation* connecting the second line of the Song to the first line, *Result* connects the fifth line to preceding lines, as marked by על כן (on account of which).

α שמן תורק שמך

Your name is poured oil.

β על כן עלמות אהבוך

That is why maidens love you.

Result(α,β)

---

30. Ibid., 85.

This is a case of propositional anaphora: maidens (עלמות) love you (אהבוך) on account of (על) something (X). The X is a proposition that must be supplied from context that has scope over the text of the line; in this case it is the man's reputation, his name—a good reputation, like a fine scent, suited to being presented in public, like being poured out. In the rhetorical structure of the early lines of the Song, the goodness of the man's reputation is both a reason for and cause of the woman's desire for his kisses, and for the love of other young women. It is related by *Explanation* to the woman's desire, and the maidens' love for him is related by *Result*.

Result is often marked in English by the word *so*. In Hebrew, על כן and other forms can be used.

Result and Background

a. Kim entered the room. It was pitch black.

b. Kim turned out the light. It was pitch black.[31]

The second pair of sentences (b) illustrate the *Result* relation from above, and the first pair (a) illustrate a new *Background* relation. Like *Narration*, *Background* involves temporal overlap between the clauses it relates: *while* Kim was entering the room, it was *already* pitch black; as opposed to *because* Kim had turned out the light, it *became* pitch black. *Backgound* elaborates states and events other than the main line of narration, hence it is different to *Flashback*, which reverses the order of the narrative. It expands where *Elaboration* narrows the semantic content that is in focus. A relatively complicated example from the early part of the Song comes with the introduction of the second major section, where the Shulumite requests that her hearers do not gaze on her dark skin. She is dark but lovely, she asserts. This serves as background to the earlier text, and changes the focus of attention in the coherent unfolding of the content of the Song.

Consequence and Alternation

a. (π1:) If it rains, (π2:) we won't play football.

b. (π1:) Either it is raining (π2:) or she took a shower before coming.[32]

---

31. Asher and Lascerides, *Logics of Conversation*, 208.
32. Urgelles-Coll, *Syntax and Semantics*, 86.

The relations in the sentences above are *Consequence* (a) and *Alternation* (b). These relations are different to the other relations we have considered due to a feature Asher and Lascarides refer to as veridical or non-veridical relations. Most rhetorical relations are veridical in the sense that both propositions they connect assert truths. *Alternation* and *Consequence* do not assert truth in both propositions; rather, they assert it more complexly. In the examples above, each sentence asserts truth, but the individual components need not be true for the overall sentence to be true. For example, if there is no rain, π1 in both sentences (a) and (b) is false; however both sentences can still be true, so long is they do not play football in sentence (a), or so long as she took a shower before coming in sentence (b). The two relations are actually closely related in propositional logic.

Parallel and Contrast

1a. Did you buy the apartment?

1b. Yes, but we rented it.[33]

2a. (π1:) John likes Eastenders (π2:) and his wife enjoys Coronation Street.

2b. (π1:) John likes Eastenders (π2:) but his wife hates it.[34]

The first two sentences and the last sentence illustrate *Contrast*, often signaled in English by the word *but*. The remaining sentence, due to Ugelles-Coll, illustrates *Parallel*. They are similar relations, constrained by dealing with similar material—a common topic—and are very much like synonymous and antithetical parallelism in biblical Hebrew poetry. As with *Narration*, they are scalar in that a greater or lesser degree of shared thematic content is considered more or less coherence in discourse comprehension. An early example of *Parallel* in the Song of Songs is found at 1:5c–d.

α כאהלי קדר

Like the tents of the Kedarites.

β כיריעות שלמה

Like the curtains of Solomon.

Parallel(α,β)

---

33. Asher and Lascarides, *Logics of Conversation*, 209.
34. Urgelles-Coll, *Syntax and Semantics*, 87.

Scholarly consensus sees an example of *Contrast* earlier in the same verse at 1:5a.

שחורה אני α

I am dark.

ונאוה β

But [I am] lovely.

Contrast(α,β)

As we have noted, the whole verse may be understood as being attached by *Background* to the opening verse of the Song. This dynamic semantic attachment "crosses the boundary" of the poetic break between 1:2–4 and 1:5–6, hence is suggestive of semantic coherence uniting the text of the Song, over and above the formal and poetic devices that segment and "punctuate" it, and "color" it with features effecting cohesion, as we have seen described by Phillip Roberts.

As *Contrast* can be marked in English with *but*, so *Parallel* can be marked with *also* or *too*. The ways Hebrew uses *Contrast* and *Parallel* are very widely recognized in the standard literature on biblical Hebrew poetry.

Continuation and other relations

Similar to *Narration* but without the temporal constraints, *Continuation* is a looser rhetorical relation that is quite common. Asher and Lascarides also mention *Evidence* in their monograph,[35] and a range of more exotic relations tailored to precisely formulating their theory. In other works, *Precondition, Commentary, Source,* and *Attribution* among others are mentioned as rhetorical relations with semantic effects suited to SDRT analysis. There is a good deal more to SDRT than a list of discourse relations and our other brief comments here can cover. However, for the purposes of considering the rhetorical structure of the Song of Songs at an essentially intuitive level, we have sufficient exposition of the types of rhetorical relation available to us from SDRT in the sections above.

---

35. Asher and Lascarides, *Logics of Conversation*, 162.

§4. Abduction

Abduction is argument to the best explanation. It is the essence of the scientific method according to Charles Pierce, who reckoned that the argument form was recognized by Aristotle. Jerry Hobbs has applied it as a method of discourse analysis.[36] In the current thesis, abduction is relevant in more than one way, but at a meta-level; it is the shape of the overall argument of the whole work. Abduction draws an inferred hypothesis from available data. One quality of a better hypothesis is that it will account for more of the data; another is that it will explain the data more simply: Okham's razor, *lex parsimoniae*, the rule of economy.

What interpretation of the Song accounts for its text in detail, and in larger structure, such that little remains obscure; and what interpretation does so most economically? How does one find such an interpretation from scratch? Abduction is not like deduction that it can be pursued and an answer be derived automatically; nor is it like induction where an evident existing answer is extrapolated—though it is closer to induction than deduction. Were there a deductive method available to interpret the Song of Songs, it would have brought consensus among scholars by now. Were consensus to already have been achieved, we could further confirm that consensus after the fashion of induction. But there is no consensus regarding an overall interpretation of the Song of Songs. We are all left in the situation of making educated guesses and checking how well they work at explaining the data the text of the Song provides.

Abduction is not a new argument form original to this thesis. It is the standard argument form among interpreters of the Song; all advance evidence supporting various hypotheses. What this thesis attempts is to be clear about its interpretative hypothesis up front, and to test that hypothesis, bottom up and top down, as it works through the text of the Song, confirming its coherent unity. After all, there can be no overall parsimonious interpretation of the Song if it is not a unity but a loose anthology of distinct poems. On the other hand, if the right unifying themes are picked "up front," then the coherence of the text should be more readily apparent, as the text rests on assuming that the reader is roughly on board with its main thrust.

What the current thesis attempts to do is to demonstrate that a particular hypothesis works well to explain most of the data the Song provides—and to do so with marked simplicity. That is its primary focus. However, it can also be understood as a close reading of the Song, where the hypothesis

---

36. Hobbs et al., "Interpretation as Abduction," 69–142.

suggests itself, little by little, gaining momentum through the cycle of the text. The thesis is a defense of a hypothesis, but it is also means of showing how this reader came to entertain that hypothesis.

§5. Gynocentric Hypothesis

The hypothesis proposed in this thesis has three parts: (1) the Song is a unity; (2) it is concerned with the woman's state of mind, rather than the man's; and (3) what the woman herself is concerned with is *rewarded patience*. All three parts are subsumed by the term *gynocentric*: (1) for the Song to have a center, it must be a unity; (2) the woman is the center rather than the man; and (3) the Song presents patience and reward as a positive cyclical fact of life in affairs of the heart, devolving upon the woman.

The Song starts with the woman longing for a kiss, and "ends" with her invitation as well. Throughout the Song, there are repeated cameos of separation and longing followed by reunion and consummation. These are nearly all described from the woman's perspective. There is just enough evidence to ascertain that the man behaves and speaks as though he is moved reciprocally, but this largely needs to be inferred. The man does not wax philosophical about his longing. When they are separated, he is invisible and silent, whereas she is at her most loquacious (and sometimes audacious). The implied audience of the Song stands in the vicinity of the Shulamite, not of her roaming lover. There is a pattern, one that feels like repetition, of separation followed by reunion, and in that order. The Song sustains tension by repeatedly re-invoking separation, only to have the tension dissolve yet again at some new reunion. Although there is talk of the two going out and away together, they never take us with them, though they are quite candid about cuddles together at home.

The Shulamite is dark-skinned due to her patient suffering under her harsh brothers. She is tempted to run off after the shepherds to find her love. There are hardships involved with waiting, and dangers involved with not waiting. When she seeks her love at night, the watchmen mistreat her. What can she do but wait? She can imagine the time of consummation, while she seeks patience waiting for it. She can endure certain hardships, while avoiding dangers. Even when love is found, it has its seasons and separations. It is the nature of romantic (or erotic) love that it brings with it frustration when it cannot be continuously indulged. For the Shulamite to counsel patience to the daughters of Jerusalem is only to urge them to accept the nature of love as it will be when it comes anyway. It does not come such that couples live happily ever after in uninterrupted bliss, but rather in such a way as patience will be rewarded. The words to the man at the end of the Song, that he honor love as a matter of life and death, are a call to a promise of guaranteeing a lifelong rewarding of patience.

Such is the shape of the gynocentric hypothesis proposed in this thesis. We have already seen that Phillip Roberts's work provides evidence supporting the first element of the hypothesis: a unified Song, hence one that may in principle have some sort of center to it. But it needs a close reading of the Song to confirm that the implied audience resides in the hearing of the woman, rather than of the man, and thus that the Shulamite is effectively the implied author of the Song. This close reading will avail itself of discourse analysis by way of rhetorical relations to "close the gaps" in Roberts's work—where this genuinely adds insight—and will provide some "detailed cross-checking" of Exum's work on how gender plays out in the Song,[37] since this is actually the main subject of scrutiny for the thesis—gender in the Song.

---

37. Uehlinger, "Review," 202–11.

5

Preludes (Song 1:2—2:7)

May he kiss me with the kisses of his mouth,	ישקני מנשיקות פיהו a	1.2
For your caresses are better than wine.	כי טובים דדיך מיין b	
The fragrance of your oils is good;	לריח שמניך טובים a	1.3
Your name is poured oil:	שמן תורק שמך b	
Therefore the maidens love you.	על כן עלמות אהבוך c	

Draw me after you. Let us run.	משכני אחריך נרוצה a	1.4
The king has brought me into his chambers.	הביאני המלך חדריו b	
Let us rejoice and be glad about you.	נגילה ונשמחה בך c	
Let us remember your caresses better than wine.	נזכירה דדיך מיין d	
Justly have they loved you.	מישרים אהבוך e	

I am dark but lovely,	שחורה אני ונאוה a	1.5
Daughters of Jerusalem,	בנות ירושלם b	
Like the tents of the Kedarites,	כאהלי קדר c	
Like the curtains of Solomon.	כיריעות שלמה d	

Do not look at me because I am dark,	אל תראוני שאני שחרחרת a	1.6
Because the sun has stared at me.	ששזפתני השמש b	
The sons of my mother were angry with me;	בני אמי נחרו בי c	
They set me to watch the vineyards.	שמני נטרה את הכרמים d	
My own vineyard, I have not watched.	כרמי שלי לא נטרתי e	

Tell me, you who my soul loves,	הגידה לי שאהבה נפשי a	1.7

PRELUDES (SONG 1:2—2:7)

Where do you pasture?	איכה תרעה	b	
Where do you recline at noon?	איכה תרביץ בצהרים	c	
Why should I become like a veiled woman,	שלמה אהיה כעטיה	d	
By the flocks of your companions?	על עדרי חבריך	e	
If you do not know,	אם לא תדעי לך	a	1.8
Most beautiful of women,	היפה בנשים	b	
Follow the tracks of the sheep,	צאי לך בעקבי הצאן	c	
And pasture your goats	ורעי את גדיתיך	d	
By the tents of the shepherds.	על משכנות הרעים	e	

To a mare in the chariotry of Pharaoh	לססתי ברכבי פרעה	a	1.9
I compare you, my friend.	דמיתיך רעיתי	b	
Your cheeks are lovely with ringlets,	נאוו לחייך בתרים	a	1.10
Your neck with its necklace.	צוארך בחרוזים	b	
We will make ringlets of gold for you,	תורי זהב נעשה לך	a	1.11
With pointings in silver.	עם נקדות הכסף	b	
While the king is on his couch,	עד שהמלך במסבו	a	1.12
My nard gives its fragrance.	נרדי נתן ריחו	b	
My love is a sachet of myrrh to me,	צרור המר דודי לי	a	1.13
Lodging the night between my breasts.	בין שדי ילין	b	
My love is a cluster of henna to me,	אשכל הכפר דודי לי	a	1.14
In the vineyards of En-gedi.	בכרמי עין גדי	b	

Look at you, so beautiful, my friend.	הנך יפה רעיתי	a	1.15
Look at you, so beautiful.	הנך יפה	b	
Your eyes are doves.	עיניך יונים	c	
Look at you, so handsome, my love,	הנך יפה דודי	a	1.16
And so pleasing;	אף נעים	b	
And our couch is luxuriant.	אף ערשנו רעננה	c	
The beams of our house are cedars,	קרות בתינו ארזים	a	1.17
Its rafters juniper.	רהיטנו ברותים	b	

I am the Lotus of Sharon,	אני חבצלת השרון	a	2.1
A lily of the valleys.	שושנת העמקים	b	
Like a lily between thorns,	כשושנה בין החוחים	a	2.2
So is my friend among the daughters.	כן רעיתי בין הבנות	b	

Like an apple tree in the woods,	כתפוח בעצי היער a	2.3
So is my love among the sons.	כן דודי בין הבנים b	
In his shade I delight, and I sit,	בצלו חמדתי וישבתי c	
And his fruit is sweet to my palate.	ופריו מתוק לחכי d	

He has brought me into the house of wine,	הביאני אל בית היין a	2.4
And his banner over me is love.	ודגלו עלי אהבה b	
Sustain me with raisin cakes,	סמכוני באשישות a	2.5
Refresh me with apples,	רפדוני בתפוחים b	
For I am weak with love.	כי חולת אהבה אני c	

His left hand is under my head,	שמאלו תחת לראשי a	2.6
And his right hand embraces me.	וימינו תחבקני b	

I put you under oath,	השבעתי אתכם a	2.7
Daughters of Jerusalem,	בנות ירושלם b	
By the she-gazelles and the does of the field,	בצבאות או באילות השדה c	
Do not arouse nor awaken Love,	אם תעירו ואם תעוררו את האהבה d	
Until it so desires.	עד שתחפץ e	

ROBERTS ANALYZES THIS MACRO-SECTION as six two-strophe pairs and a two-strophe unit where the strophes are separated by a bicolon. He names these: Rightly Do the Maidens Love You (1:2–4), Dark But Lovely (1:5–6), Where Do You Pasture Your Flocks? (1:7–8), The Ornaments and Fragrances of Love (1:9–14), Look at You (1:15–17), The Narcissus of Sharon (2:1–3), and His Banner Over Me Is Love (2:4–7).[1] He is explicit about organizing this section as a unit, not because it is self-evident that it is cohesive, but because the question of its cohesion must be addressed.[2] He sees the section as a "microcosm" of the issue of addressing cohesion across the Song as a whole.[3] He is neither convinced by the arguments of scholars who see unity for this section within macro-structure for the Song, nor by anthologists who divide this early section, though he appreciates the evidence advanced by both groups. Although he does not share "their level of certainty,"

---

1. Roberts, *Let Me See Your Form*, 47–101.
2. Ibid., 98.
3. Ibid.

Roberts says he is ultimately most influenced by Elliot and Heinevetter in cautiously considering the section to be a cohesive macro-unit.[4]

As evidence in favor of cohesion, Roberts offers first that the closing force of the adjuration refrain "seems much too strong for 2:4–7 alone,"[5] a view shared with Heinevetter.[6] Secondly, there are semantic motifs that seem to serve as *inclusios* in Roberts's opinion: the man brings the woman inside (הביאני, in 1:4b and 2:4a); and, in both cases, there is also an association with wine (יין, in 1:2b and 2:4a). To these can be added the reference to a king in an indoor setting (המלך, in 1:4b and 1:12a). Roberts offers more detailed evidence, and concludes with Heinevetter's proposal that the structure of repeated "matching strophic pairs" is itself suggestive of a formal and poetic form of cohesion. Roberts observes: "many have claimed a development from separation and longing at the beginning of the segment, to union and fulfillment at the end."[7] However, he personally rejects this reading on the basis of the consummation found in the king's chambers in 1:4b. In this I disagree with Roberts and follow the majority, as we shall discuss more below.

§1 Rightly Do the Maidens Love You (1:2–4)

Callow (1995) cites Delitzsch regarding the initial unit of the Song (1:2–4).[8] In his original 1851 monograph, Delitzsch identified these verses as a specific unit of the Song, interpreting it as a Chorus: "Das Drama beginnt mit einem Chorgesang der בנות ירושלם.... Der Chorgesang (1, 2–4),... besteht aus zwei fünfzeiligen Strophen."[9] His terminology, but not interpretation, is slightly different in his 1875 contribution on the Song to the celebrated Keil and Delitzsch commentary: "Die zwei pentastichischen Strophen v.2–4 sind ein Skolion, das Tischlied der Frauen."[10] Callow accepts Delitzsch's two-by-five line structure for the unit, though he follows most recent commentators (and Ginsburg, 1857)[11] in attributing the bulk of the lines to the Shulamite.

---

4. Elliot, *Song of Songs*; Heinevetter, *Komm Nun, Mein Liebster*.
5. Roberts, *Let Me See Your Form*, 99.
6. See Heinevetter, *Komm Nun, Mein Liebster*, 95.
7. Roberts, *Let Me See Your Form*, 100.
8. Callow, "Units and Flow," 477.
9. Delitzsch, *Das Hohelied*, 90.
10. Delitzsch, *Hoheslied und Koheleth*, 21.
11. "The Shulamite began with invoking her absent beloved in the *third* person; but no sooner had she expressed her desire to be with him, than he is, as it were, present to her mind, and she forthwith, dropping the third person, addresses him in the *second*, and so continues to speak to him throughout the third verse. She begins

The strength of the two-by-five analysis lies in the parallel between the jussive first line and imperative followed by cohortative sixth line, and in the identical final word of both putative subunits: *'ahebuka* ("they love you").

Here I shall take a slightly different view. From a dynamic semantic point of view, the more highly marked subdivision within the first subunit of the Song seems to comprise seven lines of three words each, before there is a change of speaker. It is explicitly marked by the linguistic forms of the words of Song 1:2a and Song 1:4b, which suggest they stand in a relationship of grammatical parallelism. According to Berlin, "There is almost always some degree of grammatical correspondence between parallel lines, and in many cases it is the basic structuring device of the parallelism—the feature that creates the perception of parallelism."[12]

ישקני מנשיקות פיהו

. . .

הביאני המלך חדריו

<3ms-VERB-1cs> <prefix-NOUN> <NOUN-3ms>

may-*he*-kiss-*me* with-kisses of-*his*-mouth

. . .

he-has-brought-*me* the-king to-*his*-chamber

The most distinctive elements of the parallelism are the suffixed first person object pronoun and the particularly striking third person forms of the

---

the fourth verse in the same way, imploring her beloved, in the *second* person, to take her away, telling him that "*the king*, 'he,' has brought her into his apartments" (mark the change from the *second* to the *third* person)." Ginsburg, *Song of Songs*, 132. Ginsburg's typography.

12. Berlin, *Dynamics*, 31.

masculine pronouns. These stand out so sharply because of the intervening second-person forms, presumably denoting the same referent, which dominate the body of this unit, nested within its *inclusio*. The enallage—third person to second person *and back again*—smoothes transition between the internal structures of the local unit of discourse and the broader and global discourse structures. In addition to marking *inclusio*, Song 1:4b provides a climactic terminus for the long sequence of unresolved masculine pronouns (both second and third person) with its explicitly definite referent—*hammelek* ("the king").

כי־טובים דדיך מיין

לריח שמניך טובים

שמן תורק שמך

על־כן עלמות אהבוך

משכני אחריך נרוצה

BECAUSE-better *your*-loving [is] than-wine

regarding-fragrance *your*-scent [is] good

poured scent [is] *your*-name

THEREFORE maidens love-*you*

draw-me after-*you* let-us-hurry

*SMALL CAPITALS indicate lexical markers of discourse relations

While the sense of *hammelek* is generally understood by contemporary scholars to be metaphorical, given the broader context of the Song, it is instructive to ask why the poet did not make the metaphor more explicit by using a simple alternative expression like *malki* ("my king"). Such an expression would have given a more precise definiteness: relating the "king" directly to the speaker, rather than simply indicating some "king" unambiguously available as a discourse referent to all recipients. The loss of a syllable may have been perceived as injurious to prosody, but it seems to me to be more likely that the constraint felt by the poet was associated with avoiding dilution of focus on the masculine singular referent, and securing completion of a more robust formal grammatical parallel with 1:2a. So, both parallel and focus are marked in the text, even without the term *hammelek*, but evidence for the popular metaphorical interpretation is strengthened by a discourse analytical explanation for why the actual terminology of the text is what it is at this point.

The grammatical *contrasts* (morphological and syntagmatic) between 1:2a and 1:4b apparently underscore closure: the plural *minnešiqot* ("with kisses") intensifies the verb, whereas *hammelek* at last provides a unique explicit subject; and the jussive *yiššaqeni* ("may he kiss me") seems to find its fulfillment in the completion suggested by the hiphal-perfect *hebi'ani* ("he has caused me to come").

The definite masculine singular referent, *hammelek*, whatever its poetics, is also significant in the light of contemporary discourse theories regarding resolution of anaphora, in this case the cataphoric masculine singular pronouns of the preceding verses. While it is absolutely appropriate to interpret the pronouns as deictic, unambiguously denoting some man known well enough to the daughters of Jerusalem—the audience within the fictive internal world of the Song—the poet also knows well enough that his real-world audience have no such advantage. The elevated, even hyperbolic, nature of what the poet has the Shulamite predicating, regarding the masculine singular topic of her lyrical phrases, short-circuits any reader surprise at her ultimately designating this man to be her "king." The poet so constructs the discourse that it both plausibly reflects the intimacy of deictic reference within the fictive world he is constructing, and concurrently satisfies the necessities of communication with a real audience. Direct speech in any television show or airport novel does the same: we only observe dialogue in the fictive worlds insofar as such dialogue intelligibly advances plot or character development for the audience or readers.

Further marking of the initial unit of the Song comes with 1:4c, where we have a second, minor aperture, with the likely entry of a new voice into the discourse. The question is, to whom do the first person plural forms refer? Do they denote the *alamot* ("maidens") voicing a plural exclusive *we*, or the Shulamite voicing a dual inclusive *we* on behalf of the lovers?[13]

---

13. Another option is that "In some very rare instances in Mesopotamian and biblical love poetry, there exists an unexpected shift from singular to plural that is occasioned by the passionate outburst of a female lover." Paul, "The Plural of Ecstasy," 597. Yet another option is that the young woman is speaking on behalf of all the young women; see Keel, *Hoheleid*, 45. However, Longman finds this option to be "stretched

Both discourse referents have already been introduced—in 1:3c and 1:4a respectively. In either case, however, we have a closely linked new subunit, since: just as in 1:2b-4a, in each of 1:4c-e there is a second-person masculine suffix-pronoun: *-ka*; additionally, 1:4d echoes the very words of 1:2b exactly: *dodeka miyyayin* ("your caresses better than wine"); and, as noted above, the final word parallels the final word of 1:3c: *'ahebuka*.

נגילה ונשמחה בך

נזכירה דדיך מיין

מישרים אהבוך

we-rejoice and-**we**'re-glad about-*you*

we-remember *your*-loving beyond-wine

rightly they-love-*you*

There is at least one twenty-first-century commentator who has followed Delitzsch in reading this initial unit of the Song as table-talk,[14] a sequence of separate contributions from distinct voices; however, although that will not be the reading offered here, it doesn't actually change the SDRT rhetorical relations that obtain between the utterances in this instance.[15] In other

---

and unnecessary." Longman, *Song of Songs*, 94.

14. Berichto, *Song of Songs*.

15. Asher and Lascarides quote an example from Harvey Sacks, *Lectures on Conversation* (Oxford: Blackwell, 1992).

a. Joe: We were having an automobile discussion . . .

b. Henry: discussing the psychological motives for

c. Mel: drag racing in the streets.

It is readily apparent to intuition that the conversational turns do not change the rhetorical relation of Elaboration that obtains across the boundaries between voices. Three speakers simply articulate in sequence what presumably any one of the speakers could have articulated alone. All three speakers were participants in the conversation that they are co-operating to describe to a hearer or hearers who were not present. Sacks was working with text from a corpus. Asher and Lascarides also offer a constructed example, *Logics of Communication*, 297.

words, Delitzsch could be right and the reading I am presenting could be wrong, yet the discourse structure under either reading not only remains coherent, but in this case both actually conform to precisely the same structure. At other places in the Song, the diversity of readings among commentators will pose more of a challenge, because they will suggest distinctively different discourse structures; still, it will be seen that even so, those alternative structures are still coherent structures, which is ultimately the essential point of this thesis—the surface form of the text of the Song can be adequately explained as resulting from a coherent discourse structure. That the Song can potentially be explained by several permutations of possible structures bolsters the current thesis rather than challenging it, since it is the *coherence* of the discourse, not any specific discourse structure in itself, that is foundational to an argument for an authorial intention.

Indeed, it is typically a tacit assumption of arguments offered by commentators for any particular reading (of any text, not just biblical texts) that it ought to provide a coherent interpretation of the author's intention. Readings are presented as being constrained by various features of the text, like lexical semantics, or grammar (morphology or compositional semantics), but the pragmatic semantics or discourse logic tends to be mentioned only when default assumptions about that logic are problematic in some way.

It tends to be the option of last resort for a commentator or translator to have to dismiss text as incoherent or corrupt, when it remains possible instead to accept the more likely explanation that the author(s) or editors of a text have assumed presuppositional common ground with those to whom they envisage themselves to be communicating. Such background can be lost to those of us coming to a text well-removed from its original setting. The more removed we are from original author and audience, the more likely it is that apparent incoherence has precisely this explanation. Corrupt texts are not rare, and incoherent ones are not unknown. However, the most reasonable scholarly approach is to presume author and text to be innocent until proven guilty. I encountered an example of this scholarly ideal expressed irenically by Kate O'Brien in the introduction to her translation of a major Old Javanese poetic saga. O'Brien expressed it gently, but it was resoundingly endorsed by a reviewer.

> If we do not understand something, the fault lies not in the text but in our lack of understanding, or, in her words: "Therefore, I would venture to say that if anything still exists within the tale that seems without purpose, it is because we do not yet understand what the poet intended by its inclusion" (p. 1).[16] For me

---

16. O'Brien, *Sutasoma*, 1.

she need not tentatively "venture to say" this; she is absolutely right![17]

§2 SDRT Analysis

Early in *Logics of Conversation*, Asher and Lascarides provide discussions of two sample discourse fragments, each of which is providentially similar in structure to the initial cola of the Song of Songs. The first is a constructed example, originally from Asher:

a. One plaintiff was passed over for promotion three times.

b. Another didn't get a raise for five years.

c. A third plaintiff was given a lower wage compared to males who were doing the same work.

d. But the jury didn't believe this.[18]

The point of the example is to provide evidence for a right-frontier constraint in anaphora resolution by considering the possible antecedents for the anaphoric propositional pronoun *this* in (d). What precisely was it that the jury did not believe? The jury could have doubted the claim of the third plaintiff, which would provide the antecedent for the pronoun from the immediately preceding sentence (c). However, there is another option. The jury could have doubted the truth of a generic topic, an assertion common to all three plaintiff claims, each of which elaborates that topic: viz., that there was a management "culture" of acting unfairly, or that it was typical of management so to act, or some such generalization expressing unjust management practice, the claims exemplified by the three plaintiffs being put forwards *together* as evidence to establish it. Indeed, given only the discourse structure of this constructed example, it may be that the second reading is preferable in such an instance. That is not Asher and Lascarides's point, however. The point is merely that the anaphoric propositional pronoun, placed where it is, cannot refer to the claim (a) of the first plaintiff alone, nor to that (b) of the second plaintiff alone. The claims of those first plaintiffs cannot be reactivated in the discourse by the simple expedient of a pronoun, because the claims of subsequent plaintiffs have been activated more recently, and only the most recent is available or accessible to a pronoun in an immediately subsequent clause. That is the concept of the right frontier. It is nuanced

17. Meij, "Kakawin Sutasoma," 330-31.
18. Asher and Lascarides, *Logics of Conversation*, 3, 15.

by hierarchy in discourse structure, however, since propositional pronouns may still refer to concepts associated with a dominant node, which remain topical throughout discourse subordinate to it, and hence still topical at the right frontier. In the case above, the purported injustice of management remains topical throughout the three clauses that provide continuation of the elaboration of evidence regarding that topic at hand.

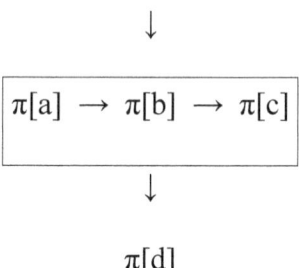

The terms π[a] etc. are labels for the text of sentences (a) etc. in the example. The arrows represent rhetorical relations. The names of the actual types of relation are not pertinent to the discussion in this case. Asher and Lascarides also offer a second example, from the British National Corpus (BNC):

> Lansbury resigned from the parliamentary leadership (π1). His support for pacifism received only 102,000 votes (π2) and he was personally attacked by Ernest Bevin (π3). He was replaced by Clement Attlee, the party's first public-school educated middle-class leader (π4).[19]

$$\pi_1 \rightarrow \pi_4$$
$$\downarrow$$
$$\boxed{\pi_2 \rightarrow \pi_3}$$

---

19. Ibid., 32.

From an SDRT perspective, the key to unlocking the discourse structure of the first five lines of the Song lies in the first word of the fifth line, the idiomatic discourse marker *'al-ken* (עַל־כֵּן), frequently glossed as "therefore,"[20] which can be expanded to suit compositional semantics and discourse analysis as "[resultant]-upon such[?]-[as has just been said]."[21] Here the idiom denotes that the clause that follows it, "maidens have loved you" (עלמות אהבוך), articulates a *fact* (hence truth-valued assertion, viz., proposition) the speaker is marking as being a *result* of some other proposition already articulated, so already activated in the discourse context, and available to be the referent of the propositional anaphora implicit in this particular usage of *ken* (etymologically an indexical), and rendered as a subscript question mark in the expanded gloss above.

Analyzed so, it now provides, quite literally, a textbook case of using SDRT for one of the purposes for which it was specifically designed—explaining pragmatic preferences for resolution of anaphora in coherent discourse. It matches the example of the plaintiffs above, which was constructed to illustrate how resolution of anaphora appears to be subject to a right frontier constraint, arising from the hierarchy of discourse structure, the example explicitly utilizing *propositional* anaphora to illustrate the point. In the constructed example, the jury disbelieved some proposition carried forwards from prior context by the demonstrative *this*; in just the same way, the speaker in the Song asserts that the girls' love is based upon some proposition carried forwards from prior context by the idiom *'al-ken*. Since our purpose is literary-critical rather than theorizing about natural language processing (NLP), at this point we shall reason in longhand, instead of providing the complete condensed formal symbolism of underspecified logical form (ULF) utilized in SDRT, as indeed do Asher and Lascarides while introducing their methodology.

Since *'al-ken* means "on account of that[?]", we need to ask "on account of what?" The answer to the question supplies the unknown proposition, to which *ken* refers, represented by the subscript question mark. The right frontier constraint gives us two options: either the proposition is (1) provided by the immediately preceding clause (1:3b);[22] or it is (2) provided by a dominant topic, to which that clause is subordinated. Option (1), in this

---

20. BDB 485-86 II. כֵּן adv. so 3. With prepositions:—f. [145] עַל־כֵּן *upon ground of such conditions, therefore* (introducing the statement of a *fact*, rather than a declaration), Ct 1:3 [typography original, ellipsis unmarked].

21. Holladay 159 II כֵּן adv.: — 1. so, thus (= as has just been said) (120×) [typography original, ellipsis unmarked].

22. See below for discussion and specification of alphanumeric clause reference designators.

case, gives us a proposition with a positive predication in regard to the man's name (שמן תורק שמך), which certainly grounds a putative cause for the girls' love, but is it the only basis, or even the pragmatically preferable basis for their love?

Option (2) needs a little more work to evaluate: firstly, to check if the clause we have just considered is subordinate to some dominant topic or not. Looking back one additional clause (1:3a) gives us a proposition with a positive predication in regard to the man's olfactory presence (לריח שמניך טובים), which also grounds a putative cause for the girls' love. Because this one-step-removed second-clause-backwards expresses a proposition still relevant as a potential cause for the girls' love, it is evidence that both clauses may well be subordinate to a dominant topic previously introduced, to which *'al-ken* may refer, and thus potentially provide preferable grounds for the girls' love to that of the goodness of his name alone. And indeed that is precisely what we find, when we look still further back, and observe the relationship between the first two clauses of the Song (ignoring the superscription).

Not only do we find that the second clause of the Song provides yet another positive predication in regard to the man (טובים דדיך מיין), but it opens with a discourse marker (כי, *ki*, etymologically cognate with *ken*) relating it to the first clause of the Song: the Shulamite is wanting her lad to kiss her on the mouth *because* his caresses (דודים) feel so good (at least in her imagination). Yet is that the only reason she wants to taste his kiss? No. In *Continuation*, one after another, three clauses each predicate perceptions of the man that exemplify generic attractiveness, offering both an *Explanation* for the first speaker's desire for a kiss, and a plausible cause for the *Result* of girls in general loving him as well.

Futhermore, there is a familiar-to-the-point-of-cliché implicit *Contrast* between one young woman wanting the (exclusive) attention of a lad, *but* all the other girls wanting him too (and all alike wanting him for the same reasons). The pragmatics, however we might analyze it, works in such a way as we are *not* being presented with the valid but trivial logic of universal instantiation—every woman loves a certain man; so also, woman that I am, I love him too—in which there is a *Parallel* relation between protasis and apodosis, arising from structural similarity and similarity of theme. Rather, we are being presented with a relation of *Contrast*. By presenting the propositions in reverse order to the standard syllogism, and with the speaker's love being presented in the strikingly intimate terms of kissing deeply with the mouth, and being drunk on caresses, a defeasible conversational implicature is first created, in which the speaker is associated with the object of her affections in a one-on-one, assumed-to-be-sexually-exclusive way. This expected implication is then modestly challenged by the subsequent assertion of others fantasizing about him in the same way.[23] Indeed, that the language we are dealing with is the language of the imagination, suggested by the first word of the Song in its jussive inflection, can now be appreciated as an underlying theme in this prologue to the Song.

Not that the matter is in doubt among commentators, but these lines can be seen to be cohesive text, not just as a matter of important but ad hoc literary appreciation of idiosyncratic poetics, but as an outcome of a demonstrably principled semantic methodology, and with a precise description of semantic relationships that actually constitute the substance of the discourse coherence.

However, at least two literary questions arise spontaneously out of the analysis at this point. Firstly, is it deliberate or fortuitous (or perhaps in between, partly a result of subconscious elements of human cognition), that the caresses of the second clause suit themselves better to a rationale for a one-to-one relation of sexual intimacy, whereas the "refined-but-broken-loose fragrance" of the sound of the name of an attractive person suits itself better to being a rationale for, or even to being a description of, the one-to-many relation of popularity? As regards intimacy, if there is a progression through the first five lines, it is a relaxation away from the intensity of the first line, where one mouth meets one single other mouth.[24]

Secondly, is it significant that the sensuousness of the language covers all the senses save one?[25] Clause by clause we have the taste of kissing with the mouth, the feel of being touched by caresses, the smell of being close to a man, and the sound of hearing his name, but we do not actually see this man, as we encounter him step by step at greater distance and with more objectivity. Again we could ask if this is deliberate or fortuitous in regard to authorial intent, and again the absence of the author precludes a definitive answer. However, as readers we can weigh in the balance for ourselves how much the force of third- to-second-person enallage, the absence of mascu-

---

23. One typical characterization of the *Contrast* relation has this pattern of violation of expectation: a default consequence of one component of a *Contrast* relation (here sexual exclusivity) is contradicted by a default consequence of the other component (here the man's ongoing attractiveness to young women other than the Shulamite). The classic example in Asher and Lascarides is: John hates sport. But he loves football. Ibid., 168, 296.

24. "In the last stage the man is far away from her, she does not sense his touch, nor his smell, and she cannot even see him . . . it is the opposite of a real loving encounter between two people, where intimacy gradually grows." Assis, *Flashes of Fire*, 38.

25. "The one theme that does run through vv. 2-4 is the appeal to every one of the senses." Hess, *Song of Songs*, 47.

line response, and the absence of appeal to sight, each contribute to mitigating the force of the second person forms of the subsequent pronouns, deflecting them away from prototypical "literal" personal-address usage, towards a counterfactual modality in keeping with the jussive opening of the Song, an "imaginary mood" for the evocation of intimacy in advance or retreat. The illocutionary force of this irrealis mood marks the discourse as intending to convey assertions about the speaker's disposition towards potential eventualities, rather than making assertions about any putative eventualities themselves.

§3 Remembering the Big Picture

Before exploring the text further, enough has already been observed to be worth recording it in a simplified way that can be reviewed conveniently when generalizing about the Song in later analysis. The current thesis is attempting to explore gender as a theme in the Song, but wants to establish whether such a theme is merely incidental, or perhaps inevitable given the prior topic of romantic love. For it to be a deliberate theme, either the Song would have to be an anthology of poems, all of which were deliberately selected because they were exploring the theme (akin to the book of Proverbs exploring wisdom), or the Song would have to be a unified composition that set out for itself to explore the theme (akin to the book of Ecclesiastes exploring wisdom). The latter would be ideal, since we would then expect a specific, consistent presentation and development of the theme; but to assume unity where it did not exist would invalidate certain arguments regarding themes, even were various conclusions about such themes to indeed prove to be consistent with what can be observed in the Song.

A substantial number of arguments for the unity of the Song have already been published, and any or all of these could be rehearsed in this thesis to back an assumption of unity in the exploration of the theme of gender. However, the existing arguments, whether broadly literary or narrowly linguistic, point to evidence strongly suggestive of unity, like evident character continuity in the main female voice, or the pervasive use of the relative particle -שׁ, but do not actually constitute a detailed demonstration of the Song's unity. Unified readings have been provided, traditionally under the umbrella of a divine allegory, but the subjectivity of that approach is borne out by the sheer diversity of such readings. Contemporary readings are not as expansively diverse; but even now, no two major commentators answer the same basic questions of date, authorship, structure, or purpose the same way. From a scientific point of view, the findings of the major commentators reporting on their research of the Song are simply not replicated.

This is where the value of SDRT analysis lies. It is really only since the later decades of the twentieth century that research and development towards formal and structured theories of discourse continuity have been flourishing (1985-1995 providing a particularly fruitful period for the publication of foundational papers). What has not been widely available previously is now possible—formal presentations of discourse structure based on more or less objective constraints. SDRT is far from the only theory of discourse structure, but its explicit concern for coherence, together with its eclectic grounding in other major theoretical work, suits it to answering this current thesis's research question regarding the Song's coherence; and in an ideal way, in that it allows for demonstrating this coherence by identifying the rhetorical relations that bind the Song together, and so actually *constitute* its coherence.

§4 Notational Conventions

The longhand discussion above refers to "lines" of the Song—the identification of which is not generally in doubt—throughout the text of the Song, and across the various alternative readings of scholars. These lines, however, are related to standard biblical verse numbering in a many-to-one relation, so I adopt the usual convention of appending lower case Roman letters (a to f) in alphabetical order to designate specific lines within verses. The line-within-verse divisions follow Roberts's colometry; originality is not attempted. Because the atomic segments of SDRT are clauses, not lines, and clauses sometimes relate to lines of the Song in a many-to-one relation also (e.g., [1:4a]: נרוצה / משכני אחריך), I adopt the convention of further adding Greek letters in alphabetical order (α then β then γ) to designate specific clauses within lines, where necessary (hence [1:4aα]: משכני אחריך). This subdivision of lines does involve a degree of subjectivity (including Song 1:4a), and so commentary in justification is sometimes provided in the course of analysis. Additionally, very commonly, there is clear substructure in lines of Hebrew poetry, so for convenience, the same expedient of recourse to Greek letters is adopted on occasion to specify sub-components of lines.

In SDRT, individual clauses are given simple names, called labels. By convention these labels are comprised of the Greek letter π, together with a subscript to distinguish one clause from another, for example: π^1, π^2, and π^3; or π^a, π^b, and π^c. The π symbol does not mean anything special in itself;

it is just a visual cue that one is dealing with a label. The same notational convention is extended in order to also label representations of (contiguous) segments of discourse, which comprise the prior context of new clauses as each in turn is analyzed to identify its relationship to earlier discourse. So, in general, the π symbol signals a label for a segmented discourse representation structure (SDRS) rather than just simply a label for a clause.

In the following analysis of the Song, I blend the conventions of SDRT and biblical scholarship in the following way. The "atomic" clauses of the Song are given SDRT-style labels using the Greek letter π, but instead of a subscript, the actual standard verse reference is used, augmented by the Roman (and sometimes additional Greek) letters described above, and enclosed in square brackets. So the label for the clause that constitutes the first line of the Song is π[1:2a].

The main feature of SDRT that will concern us is the vocabulary of rhetorical relations it proposes as adequate to describe the primary intersegmental substructure of coherent discourse. In SDRT these relations are typographically marked by italics and capitalization of the first letter of the name, for example: *Explanation, Continuation, Result, Contrast*. Rhetorical relations always describe the nature of the association between two and only two discourse segments, technically called the *arguments* of the relation, the relations themselves being described as *dyadic*, because they associate precisely two arguments. In discussion above, we noted that Song 1:2b is related to Song 1:2a by providing an explanation for it. We will write this in our modified SDRT-style as *Explanation*(π[1:2a], π[1:2b]). The label for the earlier discourse segment usually precedes the label for the later discourse segment within the parentheses. In cases where rhetorical relations obtain that include an argument constituted of a (contiguous) discourse segment of more than one clause, we label it by specifying the first clause designator (e.g., 1:2b), followed by an en dash, and closed by the second clause designator (e.g., 1:3b), but without the chapter number and colon unless the segment crosses a chapter division. So, if three clauses, say Song 1:2b, 1:3a, and 1:3b, continue an explanation of Song 1:2a, we will write this as *Explanation*(π[1:2a], π[1:2b–3b]).

For the first five lines of the Song we can concisely represent much of our analysis as follows. The female (♀) and male (♂) symbols are used to indicate speaker and as a subscript to specify pronominal coreference. The letter *X* is used to indicate a posited female chorus of daughters of Jerusalem. The letter *Y* is used for the male chorus of brothers.

[1:2a]: ישקני מנשיקות פיהו

♀: [I♀] Would that he♂ kiss me♀ with the kisses of his♂ mouth.

[1:2b]: כי טובים דדיך מיין

♀: How much better your♂ caresses than wine!

[1:3a]: לריח שמניך טובים

♀: As for fragrance your♂ scents are good,

[1:3b]: שמן תורק שמך

♀: your♂ name is spilt scent;

[1:3c]: על־כן עלמות אהבוך

♀: that's$_{[1:2b-1:3b]}$ why the girls$_X$ have loved you♂.

Analysis:

Explanation(π[1:2a], π[1:2b-3b])

Continuation(π[1:2b], π[1:3a])

Continuation(π[1:3a], π[1:3b])

Result(π[1:2b-3b], π[1:3c])

Contrast(π[1:2a], π[1:3c])

There is room to debate these relations, especially *Contrast*, but the main point is that something like this can be offered as a description of how the text coheres, irrespective of formal and poetic "coloring" on top of the basic semantic structure. The *Continuation* relations are supported by commentators like Hess, who sees that "the sense created is the (paratactic) piling on of one descriptive phrase after another."[26]

---

26. Hess, *Song of Songs*, 47.

§5 Joining the Dots

It requires no new methodology to establish that the first five lines of the Song work together as a unity; all I am showing is an alternative route to a common destination. It takes a little more work to show that the whole first two-strophe unit coheres. Key to this is showing how dynamic semantic coherence "crosses the boundary" between the two strophes. This is where the *Contrast* relation becomes useful: *because of* the conflict of interest between the speaker and the (other) young women,[27] *that is why* she expresses her love to her lover in an urgent appeal to enjoy love together in private. In other words, the first line of the second strophe updates the context such that it stands in a *Result* relation to that context. Given our notational conventions we can write: $Result(\pi[1:2-3],\pi[1:4a])$.[28] What is important, however, is that there is a continuous rationale underlying the semantic content as we cross a strophe boundary. The poetic "coloring" changes, but the trajectory of the discourse logic continues along an unbroken course. That the king takes the woman into his chamber is likewise part of this ongoing discourse trajectory, this time a $Narration(\pi[1:4a],\pi[1:4b])$. Hess notes, "At this point the perspective shifts from desire to narrative."[29]

What this means is that it is ascertaining the semantic coherence of the text of the Song over strophic and higher level boundaries that is critical to establishing the overall cohesion of the Song, without needing to demonstrate it in detail where cohesion is already admitted. Roberts's paratactic structure can be accepted, and the "shape" of transitions in that parataxis can be the focus of our attention. In the first macro-section he posits seven subunits; what we need to do is identify six dynamic semantic transitions "joining these dots." We can do that in a similar way to how we have looked in minute detail at just the cola of the first strophe—our lowest level of analysis—and at the strophe boundary between the first two strophes, the next level above bi- and tricola. When we look one level higher again, at the boundary between the first two subunits Roberts and others posit, we see that the key rhetorical relation that connects the second unit to the first is $Background(\pi[1:2-4],\pi[1:5-6])$. In fact, this is anticipated in the final clause of the first unit, where the maiden's upright love for the man is asserted by the Shulamite also as $Background(\pi[1:4c-d],\pi[1:4e])$. Their love and her

---

27. So Assis, *Flashes of Fire*, 38: "The woman is not describing her longings on the basis of an experience she has had, but rather that this is an initial longing for a man who is far from her, who is desired by many girls, just as she describes him."

28. More precisely, there is a rhetorical relation specific to imperatives, $Result_r$, in SDRT, but we do not need this level of precision for our purposes.

29. Hess, *Song of Songs*, p. 53.

dark complexion extend backwards and forward in a spatio-temporal way that makes the main semantic thread of the love between Shulamite and lover a line of focus offset against these background features of the universe of the discourse. All that is predicated of the intimate love affair falls within a broader conception of a state of affairs where she is dark-complexioned and he is attractive to the young women.

Within the presentation of this *Background*(π[1:2-4],π[1:5-6]), the Shulamite also offers a *Flashback*(π[1:6b],π[1:6c-d]), that serves as an *Explanation*(π[1:6a],π[1:6b]), for why the *Background*(π[1:6c-d],π[1:6e]) for the discourse is as it is regarding her complexion: she has not watched over her own vineyard. This is the story of her brothers and the vineyard, though as Exum notes, "everything in these verses resists narrativization."[30] What Exum is pointing to is the radically underspecified nature of the text, were it to be approached as a sequence of *Narrative* relations. Important aspects of "plot" go undeveloped: "Why are the brothers angry? What is the relationship of the vineyards they made her tend to her own vineyard, which she has not tended."[31] These factors also make SDRT analysis difficult, because there is considerably more scope to interpret text according to different rhetorical structures, depending on how the multivalency of the text is resolved. On the other hand, this is just the kind of context that can make SDRT analysis useful, because inferences regarding rhetorical structure help with making other inferences about pragmatically preferred interpretations of otherwise ambiguous text.[32]

So, if we accept what most commentators recognize in the separate cohesion of 1:2-4 and 1:5-6, and for that matter of 1:7-8, recognizing a rhetorical structure that makes 1:5-6 subordinate to 1:2-4 as *Background* to it, allows us to view 1:7-8 as being related narratively to either 1:2-4 or to 1:5-6 according to SDRT's Right Frontier Constraint (RFC).[33] This is precisely how many commentators appear to take the text, even though not arguing from SDRT. In literary rather than technical language, the interplay between the woman and her shepherd lover in 1:7-8 can be read either as following on from the incident with the brothers—so past with respect to

---

30. Exum, *Song of Songs*, p. 103.

31. Ibid.

32. "Recognizing . . . rhetorical relations is important for understanding [a] dialogue, because, just as with monologues, their truth conditional entailments capture some intuitive aspects of the dialogue's meaning." Asher and Lascarides, *Logics of Conversation*, 297.

33. The RFC requires coordinating relations like *Narration* to "attach" to labels for text that either immediately precedes them or to labels for text to which the preceding text is attached to by subordination.

entering the "king's" chambers—or it can be read as a return to focus on the thread of the narrative introduced in the early verses—and so as future to entering the king's chambers. Is the dialogue with the shepherd to be understood as coming before or after the lovers resorting to the king's chambers? Are we seeing loosely connected cameos where tight discourse coherence should not be assumed? Or may even the characters be entirely different in two completely unrelated scenarios? It seems to be impossible to tell for certain, but what is possible is a coherent reading with some flexibility as to timing. This is all the current thesis attempts to find—possible coherent readings—so that the hypothesis of unity can be supported, and hence a further hypothesis of authorial intent to convey an essentially unified message regarding gender dynamics in romantic relationships.

Regarding internal dynamic semantic coherence in addition to formal and poetic cohesion for 1:7–8, these verses exemplify an SDRT rhetorical relation called Question–Answer Pair (*QAP*). There is even more rhetorical structure internal to these verses; however, since they are normally considered by commentators as a unit anyway, there is no point making more complex technical arguments for what is widely accepted on the basis of intuition. What is more to the point is examining the difference between scholars like Roberts, Garrett, Longman, and Barbiero, who dissociate 1:7–8 from the rest of 1:2—2:7, and Murphy, Bergant, and Exum, who do not. Landy asserts: "1.9—2.7 is the only sustained dialogue of the Song, introducing the lovers to each other, and admitting us to their discourse together.... Each of these units suggests the possibility of elaboration, rapidly cut short, a pattern of expectation and frustration."[34] Exum finds a chiasm in 1:5–11. She sees descriptions of the woman by the man in 1:9–11 (A') answering to those given by herself in 1:5–6 (A), as the shepherd (1:8, B') literally answers to the shepherdess (1:7, B).[35]

Although the matter cannot be settled simply, and not by any simple appeal to SDRT, there is certainly scope to view the dialogue section to 2:3 as a continuation of 1:2–6 as described above. At 2:4 the female voice reverts to third person pronominal reference to the man, and we need to reconsider how to "join the dots" between the dialogue and the return of the Shulamite to addressing the female chorus. As I read it, there is a conceptual *inclusio* from one remembered consummation in 1:4 to a second remembered consummation in 1:13, where the post consummation ambiance is then elaborated afterwards, first in dialogue between the lovers, and then as a prelude to the cautionary adjuration refrain. It is on the basis of how overwhelming

34. Landy, *Paradoxes of Paradise*, 46.
35. Exum, *Song of Songs*, 102.

is consummated love that the Shulamite adjures her peers, or abjures them from bringing it on themselves precipitously. Love is like strong wine, needing a degree of circumspection to be enjoyed smoothly, if indeed the course of true love can ever be enjoyed smoothly. The Song appears to anticipate Shakespeare.

In the case of 1:2—2:7, we do not need to join each strophic pair to show a possible coherent reading because there are strong signals of both cohesion and coherence that are covered by commentators already. This is not a denial of the existence of substructure as per the analysis of Roberts et al.; it is the non-denial that there is higher-level structure over the section, something Roberts is at pains to demonstrate himself. Where I am differing with Roberts is in viewing a level of structure that ties the "dots" of the four dialogue strophes (1:7-8, 1:9-14, 1:15-17, and 2:1-3) together as a dialogue about love, as Exum and others take it. It is possible to view these as a more intimate and extended view of the same consummation of 1:2-3, just couched in different imagery. In fact, we may not be dealing with any implied historical incidents, but rather poetically imagined stylizations of the nature of lovemaking. Even in the fiction of the Song, the references to lovemaking need not be historically specific, albeit that the nature of language is such that readers will default to assuming narrative without cues to do otherwise. The hyperbolic nature of the imagery is suggestive that we *are* dealing with idyllic fabrications rather than sober descriptions, so readers *do* have cues not to assume references are to actual occasions of lovemaking but rather to ideals of lovemaking.

Regarding even higher-level structure, it needs to be mentioned that the adjuration refrain is possibly not just a closing device, but sets up the striking section that follows it. The refrain counsels waiting, but the very next line of the Song has a lover full of ardor bounding his way home. Those are not unrelated ideas, as we shall consider while examining the next macro-section of the Song.

6

Spring (Song 2:8-17)

> As for what she—(my) sister—did to me,
> should I keep silent to her?
> She left me standing at the door of her house
> while she went inside,
> and did not say to me "Welcome!"
> but blocked her ears in *my* night.[1]

The sound of my lover!	קול דודי	a	2.8
Look there he comes!	הנה זה בא	b	
Leaping on the mountains,	מדלג על ההרים	c	
Lunging on the hills.	מקפץ על הגבעות	d	
My lover is like a gazelle,	דומה דודי לצבי	a	2.9
Or young buck of the deer.	או לעפר האילים	b	
Look there he stops!	הנה זה עומד	c	
Behind our wall,	אחר כתלנו	d	
Peering through the windows,	משגיח מן החלנות	e	
Peeking through the shutters.	מציץ מן החרכים	f	
My lover responds, and says to me:	ענה דודי ואמר לי	a	2.10
"Get yourself up—	קומי לך	b	
My friend, my beauty—	רעיתי יפתי	c	
And get yourself going!	ולכי־לך	d	

---

1. Papyrus Chester Beatty I, group C, no. 46, tr. Fox, *The Song of Songs*, p. 75; παρακλαυσίθυρον, Plutarch, *Amatorius* 753b.

For look! Winter has passed,	כי הנה הסתיו עבר	a 2.11
The rain moved along. It's gone!	הגשם חלף הלך לו	b
The blossoms are seen in the Land.	הנצנים נראו בארץ	a 2.12
The time of singing has arrived.	עת הזמיר הגיע	b
And the sound of the turtle dove is heard in our Land.	וקול התור נשמע בארצנו	c
The fig tree sweetens figs,	התאנה חנטה פגיה	a 2.13
And the vines in bud give scent.	והגפנים סמדר נתנו ריח	b
Get yourself up—	קומי לכי	c
My friend, my beauty—	רעיתי יפתי	d
And get yourself going!	ולכי לך	e
My dove in the crevices of the cliff,	יונתי בחגוי הסלע	a 2.14
In the cloister of the crag,	בסתר המדרגה	b
Let me see your look,	הראיני את־מראיך	c
Let me hear your voice,	השמיעיני את קולך	d
Because your voice is pleasant	כי קולך ערב	e
And your look is agreeable.	ומראיך נאוה	f
Catch foxes for us,	אחזו לנו שועלים	a 2.15
Little foxes,	שועלים קטנים	b
Ruining vineyards;	מחבלים כרמים	c
And our vineyards are in bud!"	וכרמינו סמדר	d
My lover is mine and I am his,	דודי לי ואני לו	a 2.16
Grazing among the lilies,	הרעה בשושנים	b
Until the day breathes	עד שיפוח היום	a 2.17
And the shadows flee.	ונסו הצללים	b
Return! Liken yourself, my lover, to a gazelle	סב דמה לך דודי לצבי	c
Or young buck of the deer	או לעפר האילים	d
On the mountains of Bether.	על הרי בתר	e

Roberts divides this macro-section into three subsections, each of which is further divided: The Arrival of the Man (2:8-9); The Man's Invitations to the Woman (2:10-14); and The Woman's Response (2:15-17).[2]

He analyzes the first subsection as an opening monocolon followed by two strophes enclosing a bicolon: the first strophe of three lines, the second of four. He names these four components: The Sound of My Beloved (2:8a); Coming Over the Mountains (2:8b-d); Like a Gazelle (2:9a-b); and Standing at the Window (2:9c-d).

The second subsection is also seen as introduced by an opening monocolon followed by two invitation panels, the first a three-part *inclusio*—with the central strophe comprised of three units forming an ABA chiasm—and the second invitation panel consisting of a single strophe. He names the

---

2. Roberts, *Let Me See Your Form*, 102-30.

three parts within the *inclusio* of the first panel: My Beloved Answered (2:10a); The Invitation to Springtime (2:10b-13); and The Invitation to a Secluded Dove (2:14). The repeated tricolon that forms the *inclusio* for the first panel is called Come My Dear One (2:10b-d; 2:13c-e); and the chiastic central strophe is called Spring is Here (2:11-13b). (It is difficult to represent this depth of hierarchy in levels of analysis in a one-dimensional form as above, so a two-dimensional representation is given below.)

Roberts analyzes the third and final subsection as comprised of three strophes, the first two of four lines each and the last being three lines long. These he names: Foxes and Vineyards (2:15); Mutual Belonging (2:16-17b); and A Gazelle on the Mountains (17c-e).

Two-dimensional representation of text structure in Song 2:10–13 per Roberts

panel or unit tier	strophe tier	multi-colon & parallelism tier	line tier	ref.
My Beloved Answered (10a)		monocolon	ענה דודי ואמר לי	10a
Invitation to Springtime (10b–13)	Come My Dear One (2:10b–d)	tricolon (or bicolon) inclusio	קומי לך	10b
			רעיתי יפתי	10c
			ולכי־לך	10d
	Spring is Here (2:11–13b) 7 line, 3 unit strophe (?) with ABA chiasm	bicolon	כי־הנה הסתיו עבר	11a
			הגשם חלף הלך לו	11b
		tricolon ABA chiasm	הנצנים נראו בארץ	12a
			עת הזמיר הגיע	12b
			וקול התור נשמע בארצנו	12c
		bicolon	התאנה חנטה פגיה	13a
			והגפנים סמדר נתנו ריח	13b
	Come My Dear One (2:13c–e)	tricolon (or bicolon) inclusio	קומי לכי	13c
			רעיתי יפתי	13d
			ולכי־לך	13e
Invitation to a Secluded Dove (14)	6 line, 3 unit strophe	parallel bicolon	יונתי בחגוי הסלע	14a
			בסתר המדרגה	14b
		parallel bicolon	הראיני את־מראיך	14c
			השמיעיני את־קולך	14d
		parallel bicolon	כי־קולך ערב	14e
			ומראיך נאוה	14f

Roberts notes his second designated macro-unit, Song 2:8-17, is "widely recognized" as a "unity."[3] True to his principle of eschewing content and interpretation in favor of form, he lays aside the perceived internal "narrative cohesion" that "largely" motivates other critical commentators' findings of a unity over this section, even from those within the anthological school.[4] In this present study, however, semantic coherence is precisely the concern, so we will first turn to a couple of major commentaries published since Roberts submitted his dissertation.

§1 Dramatic Narrative

In her 2005 commentary, Exum goes so far as to say that this section is "extraordinary," in that "the woman tells a story . . . with narrative movement and a sense of closure, . . . in other words, with a plot . . . more of a plot line than any other part of the Song."[5] Assis (2009) presents the same section as the fourth poem of his second of five units for the whole Song, stating what is unquestionably explicit in this section (and the current thesis argues is implicit everywhere): "The entire poem is seen from the woman's perspective."[6] Assis speaks of the section as "dialogue" and "dramatic" rather than as narrative, whereas Exum speaks not only of narrative but of a narrator: "For the first time, the Song of Songs acknowledges the presence of a narrator."[7]

Surely, both observations—that of Exum and that of Assis—are correct, though that ought to surprise us. We are not surprised at first, because with Song 2:8-17 in front of us, we see a natural example of narrated dramatic dialogue. We know that narrated dialogue "genre" from everyday reported speech, "he said-she said" speech, though Plato narrating Socratic dialogues also jumps to mind as a more literary form of the same type of discourse; the book of Job provides an extended biblical example of text with broadly similar features. However, although drama and narrative typically have in common that they present plots, they are just as typically significantly distinct

---

3. Phillip Roberts, *Let Me See Your Form*, 103.

4. Roberts draws special attention to Roland E. Murphy, "Cant 2:8-17—a Unified Poem?" in *Mélange bibliques et orientaux en l'honneur de m. Mathias Delcor*, edited by A. Caquot, S. Légasse, and M. Tardien, AOAT, vol. 215 (Kevelaer: Butzon & Bercker, 1985), pp. 305-10. He also cites Landy (1983), Heinevetter (1988), Dorsey (1999), and Rudolph (1962), Gerleman (1965), Würthwein (1969) among the anthologists.

5. Cheryl Exum, *Song of Songs*, p. 123.

6. Assis, *Flashes of fire*, p. 77.

7. Cheryl Exum, *Song of Songs*, p. 123.

in regards to the *methods* of their presentation. Drama typically involves the interplay of the multiple voices of performers addressing direct speech to one another, mostly effacing the audience. Narrative, on the other hand, is typically univocal, only sometimes involving direct speech, but even then essentially being reported to an audience addressed by the narrator directly. Where drama often recreates events, featuring voices interpreting their own experience from "inside" those events, narrative often interprets events and speech from the "outside": the so-called omniscient narrator.

With stream-of-consciousness first-person narration we get a privileged look at the inner world of the narrator, at the expense of some decontextualization of the wider world. The first-person narrator's grasp of the facts is simultaneously privileged and limited. It is incomplete, as indeed the Shulamite's grasp of her love seems—in some senses—to be incomplete, from the very first word of the Song, right through until its last exhortations. Yet the adjuration refrain might be part of leading us to view this positively: it is simply the nature of passionate romantic friendship that its satisfactions are never lastingly complete. The Song may not present a simplistic happily-ever-after picture, nor a permanently frustrated-ever-after picture, but rather a picture of wellings up and quellings down, by turns, forever after. Romantic love has its cons as well as pros. Realistically it is a somewhat destabilized lifestyle (so also Jesus and Paul according to the canonical literature),[8] with a characteristic pattern of welling and quelling.

Gérard Genette observed: "In the narrative mode, the poet speaks in his own name, in the dramatic it is the characters themselves who speak, or, more accurately, it is the poet who speaks in the clothes of the various characters."[9] In a similar way, turning our focus from speaker (or Genette's poet) to hearer (or audience): in the narrative mode, a hearer is addressed by name, whereas in the dramatic it is the characters who are addressed by one another, or, more accurately, it is the audience that is addressed through the *performance* of dialogue between third parties, rather than by the words of a playwright directly.

Here, potentially, is a key to interpretation of the Song. In the first section, Song 1:2—2:7, right from the beginning, the poet introduced the daughters of Jerusalem into the text, essentially gratuitously. From then on, we are never certain as to whether they have left the "stage" (except in 1:4e as we shall discuss later) such that we can be sure the Shulamite has turned

---

8. Both Jesus and Paul recommended singleness over marriage (and practised what they preached), but rather enigmatically suggested that their own path was not viable for all. Classic proof texts are Matthew 19:12 and 1 Corinthians 7:7.

9. Gérard Genette, *Narrative Discourse: An essay in method* (Oxford: Blackwell, 1986 [1980]), pp. 98, 150; quoted in Barbiero, op. cit., p. 15.

her attention to addressing us, the audience, directly. And what would it mean if she did? A fictional character addressing readers she cannot know and who cannot know her? But by this device of supplying both a narrator and an audience *internal* to the text, the poet gives the *actual* audience an uncomfortable privacy. Just how far are we expected to remain aloof, observing Shulamite and daughters from a distance? And how far are we to feel drawn in as though we are members of that chorus of young women, or bystanders the Shulamite is aware of, but only addresses elliptically? This is all the more uncomfortable because the text probably intends to move us somewhat differently in different places, and differently dependent on who we are: single, engaged, married, widowed or divorced, young or old, child or parent, male or female. That the Shulamite addresses both the daughters and the man, with equal ease and without preliminaries—again from the enallage of the Song's very first strophe—and that they all speak up from time to time, suggests they are continuously available as discourse referents and as participants.

Brothers and others might be part of an implied audience, but they are certainly marginalized. Although poet and those responsible for canonization, transmission, and public presentation of the text can reasonably be assumed to have been almost entirely exclusively men, the text itself really only admits one man, in one particular role, and only to articulate little more than stylized phrases of praise, desire, and invitation for the Shulamite to come out, and come again. He is not quite the perfect boyfriend Ken doll, suited to attending tea parties on demand and on time, with no unwanted genitals to intrude. The Shulamite's dream man is anatomically correct and she is unashamed of embracing that reality firmly and enthusiastically; indeed, it stimulates her to bemoan his absences, which appear to be beyond her control. We never are told just precisely what it is that keeps taking him away from her. Does it matter? Of course not. This is all about her. She is secluded in his absence, and he returns to call her *out* of that seclusion.

§2 Excursus: Gender Archetypes

There is an asymmetry yet a mutuality about the relationship presented to us in this section. Her love calls the Shulamite *outwards* to freely enjoy (in his exclusive company) an external physical and psychological reality where his bounding over mountains (or "tall buildings in a single stride") seems to suggest his mastery. Yet she meets this with an equal and opposite calling him *inwards* to freely enjoy (in her exclusive company) an internal physical and psychological reality, the key to the door of which she adamantly insists she is rightly mistress of, to use as she sees fit. In this passage a male and female meet at the door; each opens for the other to enter his or her world. It is an image of perichoresis: mutual indwelling, mutual invitation, mutual sovereignty. Fathers tend to love their children by hugging them close but face outwards towards the world. Mothers tend to love their children by hugging them close but face-to-face with smiles and kisses. Not always. (Do I really need to say that?) What we label in culture as *yin* (陰) and *yang* (陽) appear to be evolved differences in brain neurology, preferences adaptive for reproduction and survival, in dialogue with cultural expression. And we encounter such gender archetypes here in 2:8–17 (and elsewhere) in the Song.

Which of two vitally essential complementary things is inferior or superior, or disposable or preferable? Do we make a law that babies be held face-to-face, or that they be held face outwards? Or do we dynamically adapt, a negotiation between intimate partners, conflicting instincts by constraining them according to reason, as we assess changing contexts and progressive development of our offspring? The fruit of your reproduction, and the fruit of my reproduction. Must we vote for thesis or antithesis? Or is it not rather our duty to seek synthesis? How might a rational scientific couple raise their children? By empowering one partner's instincts over the other's? Or by empowering the minor under our duty of care through drawing on complementary evolved insights bequeathed to us through a legacy of genetic recombination and sexual dimorphism? And of course, cultures of families of origin. The reader will understand these questions are leading questions in regard to various contentious issues in gender studies. Answers to such questions are not the aim of this thesis—that is well beyond its scope; its modest goal is to draw attention to evidence that the Song does speak to modern issues because they are perennial issues, evolutionary psychological issues; and it speaks from an insightful, authentic, and distinctively feminine (read womanly) perspective.

I personally prefer the tropics to the poles, but temperate climates with summer and winter are preferred by many. The Song seems to prefer spring. Yet it also seems to prefer a woman's perspective. She speaks of day and of night, and of good and evil both, each under the sun and each also by night. If the Song provides us with a classical paraclausithyron, I would argue the woman is calling for her lover to open a door from the outside, while he calls for her to open it from the inside. She goes out with him and he goes in with her. In mathematics this relationship is called antisymmetry: neither mirror image symmetry, nor unrelated apples-and-oranges asymmetry. It is more like Newtonian equal and opposite, complementary reactions. It matters more to the lovers that a door stands between them, than it matters to them who is on the inside and who is on the outside. In the sequel, both parties pass through that door at the invitation of the other to enjoy consummation on the other side.

The inside world is not more tame in the Song, but a place where the woman is abused or frustrated without her lover. The outside world is a place where even Solomon needs guards against the terrors he faces during night marches. Solomon retreats from conflicts to find peace and contentment and joy in his wedding at the city gates, greeted by the daughters of Jerusalem. The Shulamite escapes from conflicts with brothers and watchmen to find peace and contentment and joy in her lover's arms, whether inside or outside. Both male and female retreat from the harshness of their regular lives as they find their place of rest in each other. Each is locus of the other's contentment. Each is "home" to the other. Is the Shulamite at home when she is home without the one her soul loves? Is she away from home when she is away with him? Their strengths and courages are different, their weaknesses and failures are different; indeed, their joys are different, since each finds joy in bringing joy to the other.

The inside and outside imagery resonates with masculine and feminine associations from a time in history prior to women entering factories during the industrial revolution. But holding babies face-to-face, internal looking rather than external looking, may be preferable over the masculine, outward-facing default, up to a certain age. Love also may be preferably made face-to-face. These do not seem like matters suited to being the basis of legislation; but a modern world passionately pursuing making factories more friendly for women working on the assembly lines, while men are bullied working online from home, may see metaphors of inside and outside at a place of residence inverted. Such an inversion may not change the way men and women make love face-to-face and cuddle their babies in complementary ways. Far be it from me to comment on such things, though I do think the Shulamite speaks to them, and not in any stuffy Victorian way at all. That is our speciality, not hers. Quite possibly it is our public discourse that is antiquated. Youthful labor on computers enriched Mark Zuckerberg. The issues of the nineteenth century are not those of the twenty-first. Do we liberate teenage lads from workplace exploitation through formal education, or deprive them of making fortunes? Are we really doing young women favors if we forbid them from getting in at the ground floor, as muses and partners to hackers at the top of their game, locking in an equal share (whatever that means) for themselves through a lifelong contract, formerly known as marriage? Are we really egalitarian if we baulk at the idea of a youthful female genius entrepreneur locking in, by a promise of an equal share (whatever that means) of the fruit of her genius, some lad her soul loves and she takes as husband of her youth? The Shulamite's Song seems to place fewer constraints on young *marriage-oriented* love than early twenty-first-century social expectations.

The challenge of hearing the Song speaking to the topic of gender is akin to the difficulties apparent when interpreting some parables of Jesus. The chief priests and Pharisees "knew he was talking about them" (Matt 21:45),[10] but just what does that imply about speech acts of fictive dialogue and divergent hearer responses? As readers, we may struggle when reading the Song because the Shulamite does not fit communicative conventions. Sometimes she speaks as a first-person narrator from outside events she narrates that describe herself; other times she speaks from within those events as she recreates them by performing them. English speakers can misunderstand this as tense, and we grope to sequence events and form a plot. However, if the aspectual understanding of the two conjugations of the Hebrew verbal system has been correctly reconstructed, the "inside-outside" aspectual distinction between these two perspectives on events, as related within narrative discourse, may well have been simple matters of reflex interpretation for native speakers, even at a "meta-talk" level of comprehension. Cognitive- and psycho-linguistics, and linguistic typology, may prove to be able to demonstrate something like this empirically with reader response to literature in living languages that have high degrees of aspectual marking on verbs.

In this second section, Song 2:8-17, just as the actual audience have already been effaced by the expedient of an explicit *internal* audience, so too the actual poet is now effaced by the expedient of an explicit *internal* narrator. All texts communicate from author to audience. A business letter may start by making those two key things explicit, as well as the intention of the communication. But if our business is presenting a general perspective on romance, does it matter who we are or who our audience is? With the very first word of the Song, *yiššaqeni* ("would that he kiss me"), one imagines that the topic of this poetically expressed treatise on love is made instantly unambiguous, and the following lines establish implied author and audience, while elaborating on the topic. Is it not something of a cliché for open discussion of romantic issues to include presentation of real scenarios via the privatizing expedient: "I have a friend who . . . "? Perhaps the Song is an example of a poet using a similar anonymizing method of addressing "everything you wanted to know . . . but were too afraid to ask." Rather than arguing from a presumption of personal or institutional authority, in the tradition of anonymous literature, a case is presented where the "facts" and

---

10. καὶ ἀκούσαντες οἱ ἀρχιερεῖς καὶ οἱ Φαρισαῖοι τὰς παραβολὰς αὐτοῦ ἔγνωσαν ὅτι περὶ αὐτῶν λέγει

the logic are thought to argue sufficiently for themselves. The name of Solomon may have been given to the Song later, to secure its canonicity through such a claim to external authority, but its real authority lies in the voice of the woman whose fictively expressed vision for romantic intimacy is actually diametrically opposed to the historically realized practice of Solomon. The authority of her voice actually lies in our own hearts: she is giving voice to our own dreams and aspirations and assumptions. To contradict the Shulamite is to deny our own selves. Or at least this is so for most readers, even perhaps homoerotic readers,[11] confirmed bachelors, or survivors of abuse struggling with bitterness.

The Shulamite is not telling us what to feel or what to do, for the most part anyway, but rather summoning from the "collective unconscious" things survivors of abuse would label as those things violated by abuse, things the homoerotic testify to seeking in same-sex partners rather than other sex partners, things that underlie the psychology of people seeking to identify with the social stance and erotic preferences of the sex complementary to their own genital sex rather than those of people who share the same genital physiology. In theory, at least, what the Shulamite evokes as her erotic inclination towards the man her soul loves, could be "owned" by survivors exploring reconstructing assertion of their own sexuality, all the more so since the Shulamite herself, on plain reading of the text, seems to be a survivor too. Perhaps so-called "femme" partners of self-styled "butch" women in lesbian relationships could gloss the man of the Song as portrayal of a "butch" role, or at least of elements of their idealization of such roles.

The historicity of Solomonic traditions is of less importance here than the consistency of those traditions themselves. Even if the Solomon of the Hebrew Bible is larger than the life of some eastern potentate who once ruled Israel, or simply an invented and idealized ruler injected into a fabricated chronology and king list; the Song interacts with a Solomon recognizably consistent with what has survived of that tradition, at least of the Hebrew canonical tradition. Ethiopian, Arabic, and Islamic traditions regarding Solomon introduce additional questions. However we receive the Song in terms of canonical traditions, or whether it is approached independently of such issues, the point at which it engages our interest is a point related to matters of romance, sex, and gender. As Exum notes, it presents a traditional perspective on these topics,[12] but just precisely what is that perspective and how does the Song succeed in presenting it?

11. Johnson, *Song of Songs*.

12. "The subjectivity conferred upon the woman by the poet inevitably reflects a patriarchal worldview; how could it not?" Exum, *Song of Songs*, p. 82.

In 2:8–17, it appears that poetic hyperbole is used regarding external and internal worlds, either side of a door, to evoke a sense of two psychological spaces in contact with one another at that door. The door might be construed as the locus of negotiation: the place of a kiss of greeting leading to further kissing later, on the outside or on the inside. The language of consummation in this section is that of the outside world—"grazing among the lilies" and "on the mountains of Bether"—but it is equally that of the inside world—"until the day breathes" and "Return!"—unless we view the lovers as spending the night in the open, which is not necessary given the text is poetic rather than literally narrative.

The text works with a stereotype of woman on the inside and man on the outside, but this is not the substance of what the Song is seeking to hold up as an ideal. It is simply convenient that the woman's longing be portrayed as though it is stretching for something at a distance. The same effect could be produced, and is produced in other love poems, by having a male lover express longing for a distant female counterpart. Nor is the Song suggesting that woman longs awaiting less committed man, though that is closer to the point. The man's ardor is explicit in this section,[13] but it is true that the woman is waiting upon his distant choice to return. Like the word *return* itself, there is a sense of circularity in this passage of the Song.[14] It opens with the lover returning without explicit reference to having heard a call for his return. He feels such a calling within himself. His own ardor rouses him. He is *both* responding to an open invitation, *and* expressing his own unprompted desire. The lovers do not act to constrain one another to conform to particular desires; rather, they are being depicted as free with respect to each other while constrained by external forces. The most powerful of those is a regular rhythm of seeking consummation of passion, though various other forces are present as obstacles to finding satisfaction. These are devices, like the distance in 2:8–17, that make the Song more realistic about the trials of love, rather than forever dwelling on unbroken fulfillment.

The Song's reflection of gender archetypes is full of cycles, reflections, mutualities; but there are repeated cameos expressed from the woman's point of view of her waiting for the coming of her lover that find only a muted echo in the words of the man as to what we can assume of his experience of waiting. He does not wait without doing something about it. Whether she does or does not do something while waiting is not a settled issue in the

---

13. "The recurring structure presents the man as acting ardently and swiftly in coming to the woman. The transition between the two poems strengthens this feeling." Assis, *Flashes of fire*, p. 79.

14. "V. 17 points back to v. 9 and closes off the unit." Fox, *The Song of Songs*, p. 112.

Song; rather, sometimes she does something and sometimes she just waits, with different results depending on the strategy she adopts. Immediately abutting as it does the abjuration refrain, the feel of 2:8–17 in this context is that waiting is counseled on the basis that waiting will not be so very long if a man requites—of his own independent initiative—a woman's romantic inclination towards him. He will do something about it, and quickly.

§3 Cohesion and Coherence

Since the present section, 2:8–17, is largely considered to be a unity by scholars of all schools of thought, demonstrating in detail what is already accepted need not detain us as we push beyond the question of the unity of the Song to what it says about gender; however, there is room to make a little use of our SDRT methodology in dialogue with the poetics of the text by way of maintaining something of a voice of independently verifying the work of earlier scholars.

Poetics and semantics of Song 2:8–9

In the diagram above, arrows mark semantic rhetorical relations: those pointing downwards are subordinating elaborations; horizontally, they are coordinating continuations. The similes regarding gazelle and young deer buck are explicitly given as alternative perceptions in the Hebrew via the word "or" (או); but here the usage is semantically inclusive rather than logically exclusive, so it is not strictly speaking intended in the sense Asher and Lascarides call the rhetorical relation of *Alternation*. On the other hand, the coordinating continuation from the lover's approach to his arrival includes a very strongly marked sense of temporal progression, so the appropriate classification of the relation in SDRT is *Narration*.

The semantic structure and rhetorical relations are language independent, based on the content of the text rather than its form. However, in the Hebrew—and the terse English phrases I have supplied—there are also grammatical parallelisms in the surface form of the poetry, which are naturally language dependent. The body of the text also involves six cola in three pairs of semantically parallel lines (the bottom rows of the diagram). Two of these pairs also feature identical grammatical form (on mountain, on hill; from window, from lattice). This is a semantically gratuitous feature of the text; in other words, it embellishes the form of the text without changing its meaning. Or to put it in scientific terminology: the form of the text is better explained by aesthetics rather than informatics.

However, we can actually reliably infer far more than this. Although strictly semantically gratuitous, the poetic features of the text convey meaning at the pragmatic level by subtly refining the illocutionary force of the utterance in various ways: they communicate the implied author's disposition to what is being related, and also to how she expects it to be received. At the highest order of abstracted meta-talk, by utilizing the conventions of Hebrew poetry, the poet suggests his claim to be presenting something of public significance. At a lower—but still elevated—order of abstracted meta-talk, internal to the text, the narrator (or implied author) suggests her claim to be presenting something of *personal* significance.

We might well ask how we would punctuate this span of text were it prose. There are three finite verbs in these verses: two intransitive—בא ('come'), עמד ('stand' or 'stop'); and one stative דמה ('be like'). One punctuation strategy might minimize sentence length, satisfied the relations between clauses suggest themselves. Another might seek to show the unity of the verses by setting them in a complex compound sentence, with explicit coordinations and subordinations. An intermediate approach might capture something of the mutually reinforcing semantic and poetic structures by using two parallel sentences with simple matrix clauses predicating approach and arrival on the lover, with additional adverbial slots for time, place, and manner: he comes across the mountains like a gazelle, then stands at the wall peering in. But these two clauses are not just parallel to one another; they are subordinate to a topic expressed in Hebrew poetry in a way that is not immediately amenable to expression in English. Should the noun phrase expressed as a construct chain, "the sound of my lover" (קול דודי), be construed as an existential matrix clause—*there is the sound of my lover*—to which the clauses describing his actions are subordinated? Should we make the first person narrator more explicit—*I hear the sound of my lover*—or should this introductory colon be read as a subtitle?

To help with these questions, there are three contextual clues that SDRT-style discourse analysis suggests we scrutinize, those are: the clauses that immediately precede ("do not arouse love until it desires"); and follow it ("look here he comes"); and the clause that attaches to it once the subordinate elaboration comes to closure ("my lover responds"). If the gendered expression of the adjuration refrain—literally addressed to women rather than men—is taken at face value, it may be advocating two courtship constraints that are not mutually exclusive: do not unilaterally inflame your own unrequited romantic sensitivities; nor attempt to secure a suitor by inflaming his passions. Neither interpretation might be implied by the refrain, but if the second *were* intended as part of its sense, then I can hardly imagine a more positive encouragement to trust its advice than the following received text of the Song: "here he comes . . . my lover responds."

I think it is important to feel the weight of the *non sequitur*, "my lover *answered*" (ענה דודי). Her lover answered what? And to whom? And how? The speech and/or action of answering or responding necessarily assumes something that precedes it, logically even if not chronologically. The predication on a discourse referent of speech or action that answers or responds requires—by virtue of its fundamental semantics—at least three additional places in the predication other than the subject, though pragmatics typically permits such direct or indirect objects of the verb as can be assumed from context to remain implicit. Assuming a temporal context for the sake of illustration, some trigger is presupposed in the past, the answer or response is delivered to someone at the point of inception of the answering or responding, and the answer or response evolves as words or actions into time that is future to the point of inception of the answering or responding. These observations would ideally be nuanced in various ways, and consider similar verbs and metaphorical usages as well, but the basic idea of the simple illustration is robust, and suited to showing both what is *not* missing in Song 2:10a and what appears to be missing. The colon is very clear about the person to whom the lover is responding: he is responding to the speaker. It is also clear about how he responds; indeed, the text that follows is precisely an elaboration (or narration) of that. The verb is used here because it suggests speech, having very common usage in Hebrew to introduce direct or indirect speech. However, what is missing is the speaker's speech *to the lover* that the lover is answering! She has been speaking non-stop for some time in the poetic world of the discourse as we have it, but there has been no indication that the lover is present, not since his couplet about a rose between thorns at the top of the chapter. Indeed, far more prominently, even and especially in the immediate *narrative* context, the whole point has been that the lover is crossing mountains to close the—perhaps multivalent and metaphorical—distance between the lovers, only to arrive and not be able to see what he is looking for.

Perhaps we are being invited to assume that on arrival he cannot see his friend, but he can hear her. The door is locked but he hears her calling out, and in his eagerness to see her tries to get a glimpse of her even on her way to unlock the door. Perhaps the verb is used simply to imply that when she saw him looking in, she called out a greeting as she rushed to the door, a greeting not worth repeating in detail. Both these proposals are reasonable; they are plausible interpretations of the explicitly represented communicative intention of the voice within the text. The thing to note, however, is that they depend on the semantics of the verb, and the way that forces the formation of a pragmatic presupposition. It is also important to note that both interpretations above not only logically form a presupposition on the basis of the semantics of verb "to answer or respond," but they also assume that the presupposition they should form is one that contributes to a narrative description. However, I believe we also need to recall that there are two levels of actual addressees in this case: the daughters of Jerusalem, internal to the text; and the reader, addressed by the poet. Each of these levels contributes additional pragmatic context that permits inference of what I believe to be a more satisfactory interpretation than one that finds its resolution in narrative detail. Firstly, the daughters of Jerusalem have just been told, in no uncertain terms, that they should forswear from stirring up love. In fact, this abjuration itself carries a pragmatic presupposition, along with any form of language of prohibition, that those so exhorted are inclined to want to do what they are being asked not to do. The same is true of adjurations to conduct that one might have some natural resistance towards. In the terminology of pragmatics and speech act theory, commands and prohibitions are infelicitous if issued to those whose compliance can be assumed. Hence, it is actually perceived as rude to tell someone not to be rude. Famously, the politely expressed *Have you stopped beating your wife yet?* is an insult, because it creates the presupposition that not only has the addressee been a monster in the past, but it is also considered possible that his ongoing disposition remains monstrous. Although there are monstrous men in the Song of Songs, with some of whom the Shulamite is intimately acquainted, it is precisely the point in 2:10, that some men are not monsters, that is here being made by the Shulamite: my lover responded. It is not so much a matter of character broadly conceived, but a matter of romantic sensitivity—and that probably fairly narrowly conceived.

On my reading, the Song itself provides substantial caveats and constraints on what it is claiming, yet it appears to come out boldly in favor of urging women to time their own amorous initiatives carefully. It is just when you want to arouse love that you need to be exhorted not to, but if you exercise restraint, your restraint will not be in vain; your lover will feel and answer your desire. When the mistress is ready, the lover appears. Of course it is not that simple, and the Shulamite has not finished her argument. Despite the Shulamite's positivity and poetry, the poet appears to be a man of the world, and so the sage voice of the woman of the Song addresses domestic violence, rape, arranged marriage, workplace relations, restrictive social expectations, and patriarchy, but all in good time. As we hear her voice, the Shulamite breaks the silence, disclosing her soul, without bitterness, showing us how, without losing either personal integrity or personal satisfaction in her love life, and despite some "dark" passages that transpire in the course of her romantic adventures, she has navigated her journey. Contrary to popular belief, it is *not* always springtime in the Song; it is summer as the sun scorches the Shulamite under the abuse of her brothers. The nightmare scene of rape is as chilling as winter, and the night in the Song is as full of dread and shadows outdoors as it is of love indoors. It may be conceded, though, that it is never autumn and never twilight in the Song, perhaps because the Song, like love, never ends. The Song of Songs is not an anthology, but it is—literally—a cycle of poems.

It is striking that although "the voice of my lover" (קול דודי) captions the ensuing panel of text (2:8-9), it is not actually the male lover who speaks, but the female beloved. At first he is too far away to be literally heard, of course, but even after he arrives, he does not speak, he observes. However, to add to the mystery, as genuine indirect speech is introduced in 2:10a, it is not with a semantically adequate "saying to me" (אמר לי), but the more fulsome "he replied, saying to me" (ענה דודי ואמר לי). Fox resolves this as follows:

> The maiden speaks of the events as if they were happening in the present, at the time she is speaking (*hinneh zeh* in vv. 8 and 9 is a clear indicator of the immediate present tense), in this way she conveys immediacy and excitement. Nevertheless the events she relates occurred in the past, as is shown by the quoting phrase, "my beloved spoke (*'anah*) and said to me," where the perfect *'anah* breaks the series of seven participles. She is narrating the events to listeners (probably the girls of Jerusalem)... All the youth's words are a quotation encompassed in her narration.[15]

---

15. Fox, *Song of Songs*, 112.

Taking this together with Fox's understanding that 2:17 refers back to 2:9 we could well have a coherent unit addressed to the daughters of Jerusalem in support of the adjuration refrain. As the Shulamite used her own past experience of love-sickness as grounds for the adjuration to waiting, so she offers her own experience of an ardent lover as evidence that such waiting will not be in vain. Both the broad material prior to the adjuration refrain and that which follows it feature lyric praise of consummated love, but the immediate context in either direction is more striking and direct. I would venture the relations *Result*(π[2:4–6],π[2:7]) and *Explanation*(π[2:7],π[2:8–9]), with the latter understood a bit loosely.

a. Consummated romantic love is intoxicating. [2:4–6]
b. so do not seek it. [2:7a–d] Result(πa,πb)
c. but let it seek you. [2:7e] Contrast(πb,πc)
d. for it will not delay. [2:8–9] Explanation(πc,πd)

This understanding provides a coherence to all the text of the Song to the end of the second chapter, but also opens the way to attaching both halves of the third chapter to the same theme, as we will see in the next chapters of the current thesis.

7

Dream (Song 3:1-5)

On my bed, during the nights,	על משכבי בלילות a	3.1
I sought him whom my soul loves;	בקשתי את שאהבה נפשי b	
I sought him, but I did not find him.	בקשתיו ולא מצאתיו c	
Let us get up and go around in the city,	אקומה נא ואסובבה בעיר a	3.2
Through the streets and through the squares;	בשוקים וברחבות b	
Let us seek him whom my soul loves.	אבקשה את שאהבה נפשי c	
I sought him, but I did not find him.	בקשתיו ולא מצאתיו d	

The watchmen found me,	מצאוני השמרים a	3.3
Those who go around in the city.	הסבבים בעיר b	
"Have you seen him whom my soul loves?"	את שאהבה נפשי ראיתם c	
[It was] just a little after passing on from them,	כמעט שעברתי מהם a	3.4
Until I had found him whom my soul loves.	עד שמצאתי את שאהבה נפשי b	
I grasped him and would not let him go,	אחזתיו ולא ארפנו c	
Until I had brought him to the house of my mother,	עד שהביאתיו אל בית אמי d	
To the very chamber of her who conceived me.	ואל חדר הורתי e	

I put you under oath,	השבעתי אתכם a	3.5
Daughters of Jerusalem,	בנות ירושלם b	
By the gazelles and by the does of the fields,	בצבאות או באילות השדה c	
Do not arouse nor awaken Love,	אם תעירו ואם תעוררו את האהבה d	
Until it so desires.	עד שתחפץ e	

Roberts views verses 3:1–5 as a macro-section of the Song. In his reading, each verse is a strophe. He sees them working together as two strophe-pairs, with the section closed by the adjuration refrain. His names for the strophes are: On My Bed (3:1), In the Streets (3:2), The Watchmen Found Me (3:3), I Found Him (3:4), and The Adjuration Refrain (3:5).[1]

Regarding formal cohesion of the unit, the standout feature of the text is the repetition of the phrase "him whom my soul loves" (את שאהבה נפשי), found in each of all four strophes (or verses). But other phrases are also repeated: "I sought him but did not find him" (בקשתיו ולא מצאתיו); and going about in the city (הסבבים בעיר and ואסובבה בעיר). Regarding semantic coherence, there is an *inclusio* or cyclic turn that sees the thread of the narrative move up and away from a bed (על־משכבי) and return into an inner chamber (ואל־חדר).

Other than all strophes being connected by the repeated phrase "him whom my soul loves," the first and second are connected by "I sought him but did not find him" and the second and third by the idea of going about in the city. The third and fourth are connected by the formulaic designation for the one the woman loves. The fourth and first are connected by the idea of returning to an inner chamber, and the fourth and fifth are connected by three "until" (עד ש) phrases, two in verse 4 and one in verse 5 the adjuration refrain.

SDRT analysis sees the first verse as a couple of *Elaboration* relations (in non-canonical order) making more precise the first component of a *Contrast*(π[3:1cα],π[3:1cβ]), where 3:1cα is seeking (בקשתיו) and 3:1cβ is not finding (ולא מצאתיו).

    a. I sought him.

    b. Sought . . . On my bed during the nights.

    c. Him . . . Whom my soul loves.

    d. but I did not find him.

The seeking of clause (a) is elaborated as being metaphorical, as in a dream, in clause (b). It is further elaborated, as being the particular man the woman has become enamored of, in clause (c). The seeking is contrasted with not finding in clause (d). The semantic scope of finding is identical to that of the seeking, with the same object for both verbs, and the same dream scene context for both verbs. The order of the cola could be reversed without changing the semantics. It is just as true to what is being asserted in the text that the woman was not finding the one whom her soul loves during her

---

1. Roberts, *Let Me See Your Form*, 131–45.

dreams at night, as it is that she was seeking him. Indeed, it is actually the failure to find the one sought that occasions her leaving the status quo of her bed. More fully, it is the *Contrast* relation between seeking and not finding that drives the dynamics of the semantics into the next verse. The *Result* of that *Contrast* is that the woman resolves to leave her bed (and her chamber) and go out into the city to find her love.

The second strophe is conceptually parallel to the first. Both conclude in the same way—seeking without finding—and both commence in the same way—establishing the locus of the seeking. The last cola of each strophe (3:1c, 3:2d) are identical, but the only difference between the second last cola of the strophes (3:1b, 3:2c) is the move from perfective (3:1b) to cohortative (3:2c) inflection. The change in mood marks some changes in rhetorical structure such that the final *Contrast* relation, when repeated in the second strophe, follows preceding clauses as a *Narration*, which in turn occasions the *Narration* relations in the following lines and verses. Roberts notes the "continuation of the narrative" while discussing the difficulty of including the adjuration refrain in that narrative,[2] although several other scholars do so read the refrain that way at this point in the text.

It is not difficult to see the coherence of the narrative within this passage; in fact it is clearer than the formal structuring devices, which are also very clear in this instance. What is difficult to understand is how the narrative contributes to wider context in the Song, though its proximity to the adjuration refrain is one potentially fruitful clue as to how that might work. Since the adjuration refrain is a repeated theme in the Song, if the narrative of 3:1-4 meshes with it in some way, then that narrative also meshes with larger themes. Yet again we are looking for dynamic semantic rhetorical structure that engages with the adjuration refrain in establishing the flow of macro-sections of the Song.

Elliot and Exum stand out among recent commentators on the Song in viewing the current section (3:1-5) as closely connected with the preceding section (2:8-17).[3] This is quite natural, since the woman is the speaker throughout, albeit as part of her narration she quotes the man at length in 2:10-14. I am inclined to agree with Exum that 3:1-4 is the second part of a continuous address by the woman. In the first part the man seeks the woman; in the second the woman seeks the man.[4] This is a natural, complementary pair of settings, suited to contrasting with the sense of the adjuration refrain, which appears to caution against seeking, or—as Exum puts

---

2. Ibid., 142.
3. Elliot, *Literary Unity*; Exum, *Song of Songs*.
4. "This time it is the woman who seeks out the man." Exum, *Song Of Songs*, 133.

it—asserts that love has its own timing.[5] Although both adjuration refrain and narrative are articulated as though addressing the present, according to Exum "the woman speaks in the present, telling the women of Jerusalem and us, the poem's ultimate audience, about something that happened in the past."[6] This seems to be correct, and suggests rhetorical relations between the first two instances of the adjuration refrain and the text between them like *Flashback* or *Background* or *Explanation* or *Result*, depending on which refrain we are looking at (2:7 or 3:5), and depending on which half of the woman's narrative we are considering (2:8–17 or 3:1–4).

Roberts notes that dramatists following Delitzsch often see the two sections 2:8–17 and 3:1–5 as a pair of scenes in a single act.[7] This often includes interpreting the final setting of 2:8–17 as being an implicit evening following the explicit morning to fit with the explicit night of 3:1–4.[8] Roberts also provides a long list of non-dramatists who see close connection between the two sections.[9] The strongest case he can see, though, for the connection of the two units, from his strictly formal and poetic approach, is that elements of both are combined in 5:2–8—something I will consider when we reach that section in my own analysis. Roberts ultimately has enough evidence to suggest his own conclusion of a high-level paratactic cohesion across the text of the whole Song, but does not give us insight beyond that static, high-level, "bird's eye view" of formal structuralism. Looking more closely into the text, though, how do we see dynamic semantic movement evolving through the course of changing rhetorical relations between input and output contexts for a reader progressing step by step, strophe by strophe, and section by section? There is certainly a transition between 2:17 and 3:1, from man seeking woman by day in a generic real setting to woman seeking man by night in a generic dream setting. The narrative of 2:8–17 is too hyperbolic to be completely realistic, but something like it is presumed to actually stand behind the woman's narration: she's remembering, not imagining. On the other hand, the narrative of 3:1–4 need not intend to suggest that the woman actually left her bed to seek the man in the streets, but only that she dreamed that she did so. The woman could be remembering what she imagined.

---

5. "If love has a will of its own, how can it be roused before it wishes to be." Ibid., 138.

6. Ibid., 133.

7. These include Goulder, *Song of Fourteen*, 22–27.

8. Roberts, *Let Me See Your Form*, 143.

9. These include: Exum, "Literary and Structural Analysis," 53–56; Carr, *Song of Solomon*, 95–106; Gledhill, *Message of the Song*, 131–46; and Elliot, *Literary Unity*, 67.

Roberts reads the adjuration refrain according to the first of two basic options mentioned by Exum: as a general principle rather than as a narrative detail regarding not disturbing the lovers. However, in keeping with his finding that the refrain closes the sections where it is found, he sees a rhetorical dynamic of the refrain being a natural cautioning based on foregoing material where the woman feels overwhelmed by love. Exum is not so constrained in her interpretation or in how she sees the refrain interacting with other text. Although she has published a change in her mind on the subject, her original thesis was that 2:7 and 3:5 formed an *inclusio* around the woman's first long speech. That reading is unique to Exum and has now been abandoned by her, but I think it has merit, at least in a modified form of argument. *Inclusio* might not be exactly the right terminology to describe why the refrain appears twice—once at the beginning and once at the end of the woman's speech—since other factors are at play in the overall drift of the rhetoric of the Song, if I am not mistaken. The man appears suddenly after the first instance of the refrain. Solomon appears suddenly after the second instance, or at least I shall join others in arguing that it is Solomon who appears in 3:6–11; the matter is not settled among interpreters and Roberts sees the Shulamite in the palanquin. Leaving resolution of that dilemma for the next chapter, if the hypothesis can be granted—for the sake of argument—then the adjuration refrain might achieve several things simultaneously: closure, cohesion, and a contrast or parallel that prepares the ground for a new section.

What I am suggesting is this: following Roberts, both instances of the adjuration refrain close brief narrations where the woman is overwhelmed by love. As such, the refrain stands in a *Result* relation to its preceding context in both cases. On the other hand, partly following Exum, both instances of the adjuration refrain precede the entry of masculine figures seeking, let us say, marital consummation. These seem to stand in an *Explanation* relation to their preceding context (the refrain) in both cases. Love need not be aroused. In Exum's words, it has a will of its own. According to my thesis, that will is embodied in the person of a bridegroom, or a would-be bridegroom. There appears to be a subtle contrast between 2:8–17 where the groom's seeking and finding seems to be within his grasp—depending only on the consent of the bride—and between the bride's or maiden's seeking and finding, which seems to be fraught in various ways, more so in the parallel passage 5:2–8. In either case the watchmen find the woman before she finds her love. There appears to be an asymmetrical gendered element to arousing or seeking love. The lessons of the adjuration refrain appear to be exemplified in complementary ways in the course of the woman's speech, which extends to 3:11 under my reading. The Shulamite is not in the palanquin; she is still the narrator in that passage. She is still articulating the lessons she intends for the daughters of Jerusalem. On the one hand, they need not fear waiting for love to seek and find them; on the other hand, there are dangers in arousing love or seeking love until it seeks and finds them. Exum observes that the Song suggests: "bad things happen to sexually active, forward women."[10]

That is a sketch of what can be said regarding a potentially gendered exhortation from the text, as we have looked at it so far, though the picture will be refined by later sections and in retrospect viewing the Song as a whole work. A distinctive feature of the reading presented here is that it leans towards accepting that there was an insight involved in Exum's original proposal of an *inclusio* between 2:7 and 3:5; reinforced by the gazelle imagery in 2:8–17 (in the first part of the woman's speech) matching the oath of the adjuration refrain; and by the assertions of finding and consummation in the "until" (עד ש) phrases of 3:4 matching the last line of the adjuration refrain. Some of what has been proposed rests on a particular reading of 3:6–11, and to that section we shall now turn.

---

10. Exum, "Ten Things," 30.

8

Bathsheba (Song 3:6-11)

Who is that now? Coming up / Out of the desert	מי זאת עלה מן המדבר	a	3.6
Like columns of smoke	כתימרות עשן	b	
Perfumed with myrrh and frankincense,	מקטרת מור ולבונה	c	
Out of all the powder of the trader?	מכל אבקת רוכל	d	
Look! It is the litter of Solomon,	הנה מטתו שלשלמה	a	3.7
Sixty warriors round about it,	ששים גברים סביב לה	b	
Out of the warriors of Israel.	מגברי ישראל	c	
All of them gripped by the sword,	כלם אחזי חרב	a	3.8
Trained for battle.	מלמדי מלחמה	b	
Each has his sword on his thigh,	איש חרבו על ירכו	c	
Out of the dread of the night.	מפחד בלילות	d	
A palanquin he made for himself,	אפריון עשה לו	a	3.9
Solomon the king,	המלך שלמה	b	
Out of wood from the Lebanon.	מעצי הלבנון	c	
Its posts he made of silver,	עמודיו עשה כסף	a	3.10
Its armrests of gold,	רפידתו זהב	b	
Its seat of purple.	מרכבו ארגמן	c	
Its interior was woven with love	תוכו רצוף אהבה	d	
Out from the daughters of Jerusalem.	מבנות ירושלם	e	
Go out and look,	צאינה וראינה	a	3.11
Daughters of Zion,	בנות ציון	b	
On Solomon the king,	במלך שלמה	c	
On the crown with which his mother crowned him,	בעטרה שעטרה לו אמו	d	
On the day of his wedding,	ביום חתנתו	e	
On the very day of the joy of his heart.	וביום שמחת לבו	f	

ROBERTS DIVIDES THIS SHORT macro-section into four strophes, which he titles: Who is This? (3:6); Solomon's Litter (3:6-9); Decked Out with Love (3:9-10); and The Day of His Joy (3:11).

Roberts observes that not only is the section widely acknowledged as a cohesive unit, even among scholars of the anthological school of thought,[1] but that it has also generated a considerable number of independent studies in its own right, even from scholars who view the Song as a unity.[2] The section appears to be distinguishable from the rest of the Song in at least three ways: the identity of the speaker(s) cannot be inferred with certainty from the text of the section, considered in isolation; it is the only extended span of text where reference to Solomon is sustained as a topic; and it is the only discourse segment where a wedding is explicitly mentioned.[3] Other features of the section have also caught the attention of interpreters; for example, Elliot remarks on an apparently "distinctively majestic tone."[4] Speaker and audience, topic and focus, rather than tone or style, will be the main discourse analytical concerns here; but again we will turn first to summarizing the explicit textual evidence Roberts presents of formal markers suggestive of deliberate structuring.

In this case, there are three strong textual markers of structure: the repeated use of the preposition מן (*min*, "from") providing a marker of cohesion; the initial rhetorical question, מי זאת (*mi zôt*, "Who is she?" or "What is this?") providing a marker of opening;[5] and closure being marked in the final strophe by no less than five consecutive cola with ב-initial alliteration and duplicate *ḥolem* assonance—medially and in the final syllable of each line.

In my translation above, with a little injury to natural English expression (and perhaps to the poet's intended sense), I have marked the six occurrences of מן by using English prepositional compounds involving the word "out" (3:6a, d; 7c; 8d; 9c; 10d). In fact, about half the uses of מן in the

---

1. Roberts offers two examples: Rudolph, *Das Buch Ruth*, 140; and Falk, *Love Lyrics*, 26-27.

2. Of the seven representative examples Roberts provides, the most recent is Provan, "Terrors of the Night," 150-67.

3. Roberts, *Let Me See Your Form*, 148-49.

4. Elliott, *Literary Unity*, 83.

5. There is some debate regarding whether interrogatives function to open poetic units. Roberts cites as being in favor, Pieter van der Lugt, *Strofische structuren in de Bijbels-Hebreeuwse poëzie: De geschiedenis van het onderzoek en een bijdrage tot de theorievroming omtrent de strofenbauw van de Psalmen*, Dissertationes Neerlandicae, Series Theologica (Kampen: JH Kok, 1980), 516-17; as being against, Paul Raab, *Psalm Structures: A Study of Psalms with Refrains*, JSOTSup 104 (Sheffield: Sheffield Academic, 1990), 179.

Song occur either in this passage, or in the following chapter.[6] However, it is not simply an apparently non-random frequency distribution that suggests that usage of מן here is a genuine matter of artifice. The final cola of the first five verses (6-10) all terminate with a phrase beginning with מן : "from all the powders of the merchant" (6); "from the warriors of Israel" (7); "from the dread of the night" (8); "from the wood of Lebanon" (9); and "from the daughters of Jerusalem" (10). As Roberts has it, following the accenting of the Masoretic Text, the opening line of the whole section also ends this way: "from the desert."

Regarding the first colon of the section, Roberts comments that: "Whether it should be reckoned as having a middle caesura depends on how strong a break one sees between the propositional [sic] phrase מן־המדבר and the preceding part of the colon."[7] Additionally, I am attracted by the possibility of an enjambment with the second colon, which then makes all six instances of the prepositional phrase in this section introduce pairs of nouns in construct relationships. In any case, the two מן phrases, one medial and one final to each of the first three strophes, gives the impression of a consciously supplied regularity, counterbalancing the expansive descriptive nature of the passage. This is all the more important as the impression I get from the flow of imagery is one suggestive of a simple gender typology, a shift of conceptual focus: from skillful but dreadful warriors—representatives of national Israel—who are coming up (עלה) out of the wilds and the night; to accomplished and loving daughters—representatives of the domestic economy of the capital—being invited to go out (יצא) of Jerusalem to meet the entourage at the city gates at dawn; thence together to remember mother crowning son at his wedding. A series of מן (from) phrases find fulfillment in a series of ב (at) phrases.[8] Roberts actually sees the same sense of conceptual movement, but with a reversal of the genders, because he reads the opening question as "Who is she?" rather than "What is this?" So he sees the poet directing the reader's gaze first to a princess then to a king. Solomon's bride is (almost) invisible under my reading,[9] but not

---

6. Ian Young counts 26 uses of the preposition in the Masoretic Text of the Song, only one of which is unassimilated, by contrast with 4QCantb, where the Qumran orthography provides seven additional unassimilated uses.; Young, "Notes," 123.

7. Ibid., 150.

8. "The movement, both spatially and temporally, that is implied by מן is now replaced with the arrival and rest in the proper time and place implied by the preposition ב." Roberts, *Let Me See Your Form*, 160; in support of this understanding according to the analytical principles of V. Propp and AJ Greimas, Roberts cites Couffingal, "Le glaive et la couronne: Approches nouvelles de Cantique des Cantiques 3:6-11," *Revue Thomiste* 84 (1984) 607-17.

9. In fact, I suspect the inherent ambiguity of the feminine demonstrative pronoun, a fortuitous and natural feature of Hebrew, may well have been felt by original

womanhood: the Shulamite is doing the talking, and Bathsheba is officiating at a coronation (though a coronation remembered in a fiction, not "live coverage" or an actual epithalamium).

Before turning to the semantics–pragmatics interface, which happens to have a very similar shape to the poetic structures in this section, it is a good opportunity to observe an analogy between that style of discourse analysis and the strict examination of poetics that Roberts is providing, in particular in the matter of the devices seen to be used to signal closure in Song 3:11. Roberts concedes that there are grammatical, semantic, and even higher-level thematic features of the verse that mark section closure, but is specifically looking for lower-level confirmation of such claims, since the lower the language level being observed, the less interpretative and more objective what we find is likely to be. In this case, such firm low-level evidence to back the higher-level analysis of other scholars is indeed found in a very striking sequence of cola in the final strophe, and the evidence lies at the most fundamental and objective level of language—phonetics.

Leaving aside the closing effect of the parallelism of the last bicolon, the more highly marked feature is the initial alliteration on /b/ in the original Hebrew,[10] and it is visible to the naked eye, even to one unfamiliar with Hebrew, since the same grapheme [ב] is repeated at the start of each colon (with anacrusis in the final line). On the other hand, the even more highly marked assonance on *ḥolem* is only clearly visible when vowel pointing is added, as inferred from the consonants and context. This is a good analogy for the current attempt to provide a discourse structuring for the Song. Just as vowels connect consonants, and often do not need to be written explicitly in order for native speakers to be able to infer them, so rhetorical relations between units of text often do not need to be realized as explicit discourse markers. Many such markers do exist in most languages, and are widely used when avoiding ambiguity requires it; at least in prose and languages other than Hebrew, that is typical. In Hebrew poetry, however, it is a well-known hallmark of the genre that ancillary lexical markers are often omitted. On the other hand, it is equally well known that Hebrew poetic use of parallelism assists in pinpointing the semantics of various lemmas in the lexicon of the classical variety of the language. In other words, the medium of Hebrew poetry itself packages information in such a way that various semantic conclusions can be reliably inferred: it is a discourse-structure-

---

poet and audience, in a way that suits the semantic flow of the section.

10. Alliteration and assonance are more highly marked because parallelism, although not quite ubiquitous, is at least unsurprising in Hebrew poetry, whereas alliteration and assonance are not uncommon, but are not so common that they compete with parallelism as candidates for being default distinctives of the genre.

intensive medium of communication. The structure provides information, even when lexical clues are absent. Discourse structure is especially noteworthy in Hebrew poetry, even though such structure is most often implied rather than explicitly marked in the surface form of the text. So, an analogy for the difference between Hebrew prose and poetry is that they stand in a similar relationship to pointed and unpointed Hebrew text. In the same way, supplying rhetorical relations between elementary discourse units (EDUs) of texts—prose or poetry in any language—is rather like supplying the vowel coloring that connects consonants, but is left implicit in consonantal scripts (like Hebrew).

In the current section of the Song, discourse analysis helps resolve the thorny question of pronoun reference in the opening interrogative clause, מי זאת (*mi zôt*), normally seen as a translation choice between only two imperfect options: "Who is she?" or "What is this?" The first observation to be made is that there are actually two distinct deictic lexemes being used, potentially with different referents, and hence not necessarily needing to be in grammatical agreement (in this case agreement along the lines of the personal-impersonal distinction). In other words, מי and זאת need not be coreferential. However, before using text linguistics, let us clarify aspects of the question via the insights of classical techniques.

The grammars admit both readings (Who? or What?) as possible, albeit the second option is claimed only rarely to be attested as the sense of מי.[11] However, Gesenius actually provides no fewer than six examples, which clearly demonstrate the conceptual clarity of such usages.[12]

[Esau] said, "**What** do you mean by all these camp followers that I met?" [Jacob] said, "To find favour in the eyes of my lord."	ויאמר מי לך כל המחנה הזה אשר פגשתי ויאמר למצא חן בעיני אדני	Gen 33:8
Who is Abimelech and **what** is Shechem?	מי אבימלך ומי שכם	Judg 9:28
What is your name?	מי שמך	Judg 13:17
Who am I and **what** is my life?	מי אנכי ומי חיי	1 Sam 18:18
Who am I, Lord Yahweh, and **what** is my house?	מי אנכי אדני יהוה ומי ביתי	2 Sam 7:18
What is Jacob's sin? Isn't it Samaria! **What** is Judah's pagan altar? Isn't it Jerusalem!	מי פשע יעקב הלוא שמרון ומי במות יהודה הלוא ירושלם	Mic 1:5

11. "In rare instances," Keel, *Hoheleid*, 125; "it would be unusual" says Roberts, *Let Me See Your Form*, 149, n. 11; "it is rare" says Hess, *Song of Songs*, 109, citing Dirksen, "Song of Songs," 219–25.

12. GKC §137a

Gesenius proposes that personal מִי rather than impersonal מָה, "is used of the neuter only when the idea of a person is implied."[13] Gesenius's examples are sufficient to cover many different types of context of usage, for example: real questions in direct speech (Judg 13:17; Mic 1:5); indirect speech (Gen 33:8); rhetorical questions (Judg 9:28; 1 Sam 18:18; 2 Sam 7:18); individual reference (Judg 13:17); and plural, mass, collective (Gen 33:8) or generic reference, and synecdoche (Judg 9:28; Mic 1:5) or metonymy (1 Sam 18:18; 2 Sam 7:18), where the deixis or anaphora is ultimately grounded by reference to persons.

In the simplest of Gesenius's examples, Judges 13:17, a direct-speech closed-question (מִי שְׁמֶךָ), the interrogative particle מִי *on its own* is cataphoric, expecting an answer that will identify a person, irrespective of whether that is achieved by a reply involving a proper noun, a definite description, or even a personal pronoun. This stands out by comparison with, say, Genesis 27:18: מִי אַתָּה בְּנִי ("Who are you, my son?"). In the Genesis case the question has the illocutionary force: *Which* of my sons are you? Context tells us that the reply of a name alone was not accepted; Isaac's eyesight was failing, he was being fooled, and in the process of discovering that sad fact, but not with his eyes, nor his ears alone, but by touch. Interrogative מִי seeks an answer that *at least* involves the identification of a person or persons, but *can* involve more than that. In the particular case of Judges, a specific *method* of personal identification is also indicated, by using the common noun שֵׁם (*shem*, 'name') as part of the question; but in *both* Genesis and Judges a personal pronoun (affixed to the noun in Judges) designates the "who" that is to be identified. At the semantic level, the question in Judges is actually a compound question: Who are you? *and* What is your name? or Identify yourself *by* telling me your name. Likewise, in Genesis, the vocative

---

13. Cf. "Furthermore, sources on Biblical Hebrew also typically treat the 'what's up?'-construction (cf. Section I.4.2.3.3.3) as a lack of differentiation between 'who?' and 'what?', as well as the use of *mi(y)* 'who?' with 'things denoting persons', as David Kummerow (p.c.) puts it, or in Joüon's (1965 [1923]:446) words, 'pour les choses [. . .] avec une idée latente de personne' ('for things [. . .] with a latent idea of a person')." Idiatov, *Typology*, 219. And, "Similarly, David Kummerow (p.c.) has suggested that *mi(y)* 'who?' is used here with "things denoting persons". I believe that these examples should not be interpreted as questions involving some non-prototypical combination of values either. In the examples at issue *mi(y)* 'who?' is not used in any special way. Rather, the nouns it occurs with are used metonymically to stand for a group of people the objects these nouns denote contain, belong to, are produced by, etc. A particular inclination to this kind of metonymy appears to be just a general feature of the Biblical Hebrew lexicon. The idea that the use of *mi(y)* 'who?' in (174–178) represents a lack of differentiation between 'who?' and 'what?' is largely due to the misleading translations, which use the primary "thing"-meanings instead of reflecting the intended metonymic extensions." Idiatov, *Typology*, 225–26.

בְּנִי ("my son") provides a semantic constraint on the information being requested: Isaac is requesting information that will serve to distinguish his interlocutor's identity as a particular one out of two twin sons. There is a great deal of complexity to the pragmatics of Isaac's utterance.

These features of interrogatives are not exclusive to Hebrew or Semitic languages. In Malay one asks *Siapa nama Anda?*—literally, "Who is your name?" Language typology finds that many languages form questions by compounding an interrogative particle with a general classifier.[14] In the Malay example, *apa* is a general indefinite particle ("what?"), and *si-* is one of several possible prefixes classifying types of information being requested when it is used to form questions (see also *ber-apa*, *meng-apa*, *ken-apa*, etc.). In other words, interrogative utterances typically involve linguistic markers that indicate a speech act related goal (SARG) of a request for information, often including some marking of the broad *class* of information being requested, and sometimes involving further specification of constraints on the information content expected in a pragmatically felicitous response. The Malay example shows how even a personal interrogative like *siapa* has underlying semantics that can be analyzed as <what? + person>. Malay is only one of many languages that attest the same features.

	English	Malay
1(a)	**Who** are you?	**Siapa** Anda?
1(b)	**What** is your name?	**Siapa** nama Anda?
2(a)	**Where** do you live?	Di **mana** Anda tinggal?
2(b)	**What** is your address?	Di **mana** alamat Anda?

Gesenius goes on to observe that the Hebrew personal interrogative can also be used in what would be considered oblique case uses in Indo-European languages: occasionally the accusative *whom* (1 Sam 28:11; Isa 6:8); often the genitive *whose* (Gen 24:23; 1 Sam 12:3; 1 Sam 17:55, 56, 58; Jer 44:28;); and even the dative *by whom* (1 Kgs 20:14).[15] The syntax of Song 3:6 prevents such oblique case readings, though, since all involve מִי being grammatically dependent on prior verbs, nouns or prepositions. However, Genesis 32:18 provides a nice example of three simple questions with second order embedding in indirect speech (narrator reporting Jacob reporting Esau), two of which involve מִי marking requests for the identity of a person standing in a relationship of ownership to what is explicitly denoted in the text.

---

14. Idiatov, *Typology*.
15. GKC §137b

So Jacob commanded the foreman saying,	ויצו את הראשון לאמר
"When you meet Esau my brother	כי יפגשך עשו אחי
and he questions you saying,	ושאלך לאמר
'To whom do you belong?'	למי אתה
and 'Where are you going?'	ואנה תלך
and 'Whose are these in front of you?'..."	ולמי אלה לפניך

The last question in Genesis 32:18 shows almost exactly the form of words we would expect were Song 3:6 intending to elicit the identity of the owner of something visible: למי אלה. So, were Song 3:6 intending to introduce an answer giving the owner of the litter or palanquin, it would—it seems to me—have said: למי זאת (Whose is this?). Had it done so, the addition of a single prefix would not seem to injure the poetics of the passage in any way, and modern interpreters would have found no difficulty with it, nor the original readers of course. So, either the question in the Song does not intend to elicit the litter as answer, or it is satisfied with a more ambiguous way of presenting the question, probably to harmonize with the other instances of the question in 6:10a and 8:5a, both of which unambiguously refer to the Shulamite, the second being identical in wording to 3:6a.

Let us turn to discourse analysis and deixis. As I read it, there are at least four extra-textual referential domains implied by the question: a person (or persons), a place, a time, and a visible phenomenon. These are constrained in a very natural but Hebrew-specific way in Song 3:6 with only two words, but it may need three words in English to convey the same broad semantic constraints on what would constitute a valid answer. As we have noted, מי serves two roles: it marks the illocutionary force of the utterance as interrogative, and expects the identity of a person, persons, or generic class of people to be a significant part of the answer to the request for information. It approximates to *who?* in English, without being identical to it. Both are pragmatic markers, inviting semantic responses, rather than simply lexemes with their own semantics, and the two languages have different pragmatic conventions governing their usages. "Reinforcement of interrogatives by means of deictic elements is quite common in Semitic."[16]

We should now add that זאת is even more complex than מי,[17] because it can be used in at least four sets of oppositions: singular-plural, *this* and

---

16. Idiatov, *Typology*, 218.

17. Consider also: "The use of a 'reinforcing' deictic is probably best analyzed as clefting. Otherwise, the deictic should be interpreted as a focus marker with no influence on the original syntactic relations. Under the cleft analysis, the deictic itself may be analyzed in a number of ways: as a relative pronoun, as a subject of the main clause in a cleft construction of which the interrogative is the predicate (e.g., [[*it*]sbj [(*is*) *who*]

those (זה-אלה), in which it is unambiguously singular; masculine-feminine (זה-זאת), in which it is potentially feminine; personal-impersonal (מי-זאת), in which it is potentially impersonal; and proximal or distal, *this* and *that* (היא-זאת), in which it is unambiguously proximal, but remains ambiguous as to spatial or temporal distance. If we accept that both מי and זאת are deictic in this context, which is to say that they are in the text in order to introduce one or more new discourse referents from outside the text into the text, and that no personal female referent is mentioned until the daughters of Jerusalem, long after the question has been answered, then two things follow. Firstly, זאת has impersonal reference in this context, and hence secondly, it refers to something different from the person or persons implied by מי. Consider the following in English: passing a football stadium, a child hears crowd noises he has never heard before and asks his father, "What is that?" "Not 'What is that?' but 'Who is that?' my boy. It is the fans cheering on their team." Alternatively, there is the popular cultural phrase: "Is it a bird? Is it a plane? No it is Superman!"

In Song 3:6, the text seems to be best explained by a fictive setting looking east from Jerusalem, in which fine dust—not thick like wood smoke, but more like that of manufactured incense—rises in the still air of the early morning (before the day breathes), backlit by the rising sun perhaps, betraying the presence of an approaching column of troops, marching uphill to mount Zion. The "Who?" question is not answered in the singular, but in a plural, generic or indeterminate way: Who is responsible for what we are seeing here now? The answer to the question is not the litter or palanquin, except by metonymy, nor is the answer a princess, nor even Solomon, but the royal guardsmen, or the whole entourage including Solomon. The זאת is perhaps a proximate demonstrative, if so, because it is temporal rather than spatial, which is to say it means "now": Who is behind this apparition we are observing, at a distance, but *right now*? Perhaps this is reinforced by ancient conceptualizing of visual perception as occurring at the location of the viewer, rather than at the location of what is observed. Additionally, the implied speaker and—in my opinion—*her* audience, including the daughters of Jerusalem, transported with her through time and space in the fiction, are proximate to one another as the same image of rising dust is immediately present to their cognition. Finally, and perhaps most simply and

---

pred]main [*(that)* P]subordinate?), or as a copula. The latter analysis may be preferable because the development from demonstratives to copulas is a common phenomenon in Afro-Asiatic (cf. Section III.2.3.3.2.2 for Egyptian, as well as Frajzyngier 1985:66 for Chadic, who also gives more references). However, what matters most here is the tendency to conventionalize a cleft construction of the structure [interrogative + deictic], which is quite common in other branches of Afro-Asiatic as well." Ibid., 219.

most likely, language typology suggests that proximate demonstratives tend to accompany introduction of new information, whereas distal demonstratives tend to recall old information.

Fox and the Blochs,[18] like almost all others, read מי זאת as coreferring, which we have already admitted would imply a personal and feminine referent, were coreference to actually obtain in this verse. Presumably the reference would be to the Shulamite, as both Fox and the Blochs propose, though it is not impossible to imagine such deictic reference to an anonymous princess-bride. They avoid the difficulty of the apparent answer to the question of 3:6 being supplied in 3:7 as Solomon or his litter (or as I propose, the warriors or the whole formation, including its commander), by considering the question to be rhetorical. I agree with Fox that 3:6 is directly connected to the adjuration refrain in the poet's thinking—strongly so, as we will discuss below—however I do not think it concludes the section 3:1-6 as he does.[19] Although Roberts is unconvinced by some suggestions that connect 3:6-11 with 3:1-5 and with other parts of the Song, and does not mention others that I will propose, I do still think he has succeeded in identifying a genuine seam in the textual fabric of the Song by dividing chapter three the way he does. His rigorous methodology delivers a persuasive and useful conclusion. Roberts's markers of aperture, closure and cohesion are sometimes stronger and sometimes weaker, as he himself acknowledges, but in 3:6-11 all three of them are very strong. It is the cohesion, though, that is decisive in rejecting Fox's reading.

The discourse structure of this section matches the four strophes as presented by Roberts, though I disagree with elements of his interpretation, in particular his reading of the opening question, מי זאת, as *Who is she?* As I take it, it should read *Who is that now?* The topic shifts and zeros in on its target in an essentially monotonic fashion: from the dust kicked up by the warriors (3:6), to the warriors themselves (3:7-8), and the palanquin they guard (3:9-10), finally to its occupant, Solomon himself (3:11), and ultimately to the crown he is wearing, at which point the poet has the Shulamite deliver the "moral of the story": a man's, even a king's, delight (and that of his mother) in his securing of a marriage. It is not a crown of state, but a domestic crown that gives Solomon his joy. The "bottom-line" illocutionary force must be inferred in part from that of the earlier context of the Song, though there are some key textual clues to confirm this reading. The original poet or final editor may well have thought such a reading sufficiently intuitive that it needed little additional marking. It is an intuitive reading

---

18. Bloch and Bloch, *Song of Songs*, 159.
19. Fox, *Song of Songs*, 117-20.

because the section is almost purely descriptive, in a way that pleases the imagination enough on its own to justify the phrases as part of a lyric poem, despite them obviously not progressing the Shulamite's own self-disclosure or vision of love until we reach the closing bicolon.

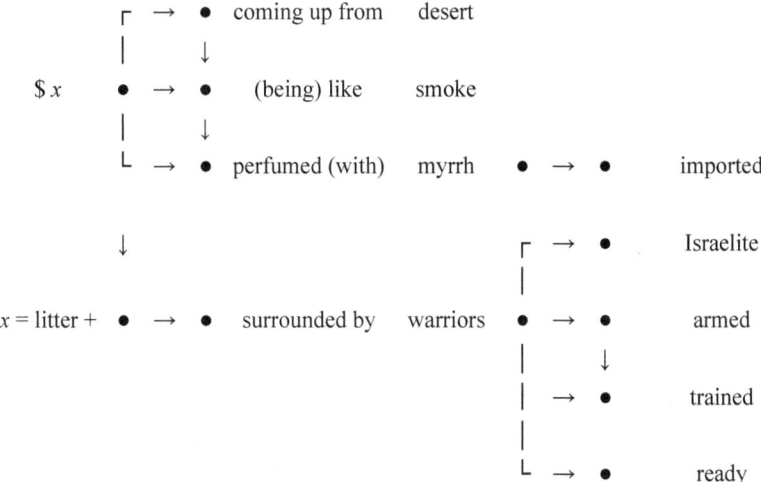

Of course, if Roberts and others are correct to see the Shulamite *inside* the palanquin and silent, rather than outside it and calling attention to it, then there *is* progression in the Shulamite's self-disclosure, and the relationship of the section to the rest of the Song is rather more complicated. Whichever way it is read, however, the elaborate detail does clearly set the *implied* historical context for the Song. The danger with reading the Shulamite into the palanquin mainly lies in additionally viewing the section as engaging with real, rather than imagined and stylized, history. The same danger exists with the Shulamite-as-narrator reading, if it leads to viewing the section as grounding the Song in the *Sitz im Leben* of an epithalamium for Solomon.

Without wanting to claim it is the only possible reading, just a possible and plausible one, how might this section, 3:6–11 suit itself to closing a long speech by the Shulamite, following on from the dialogue concluded at 2:3? According to my reading, 2:4–6 answers to 3:1–4, and 2:8–17 answers to 3:6–11. There are two passages describing the overwhelming nature of consummated love (2:4–6 and 3:1–4), to which context the adjuration refrains of 2:7 and 3:5 stand in a rhetorical relation of *Result*. The Shulamite is asserting that her own experience is typical; that the daughters of Jerusalem should learn from it, and not hasten love until its own desire is aroused.

Consummation is viewed positively, but hedged with a caveat. Consummation is actually what will make waiting more difficult for the maidens in the future. Waiting once in a loving relationship is frustrating, but waiting prior to the awakening of love is something that can be embraced without the fear that one ought to be doing something to make it happen. Love will awaken and pursue consummation. All the maidens need to do is wait patiently and be ready, for love will actually be "just around the corner" (for most of them). This is communicated firstly by the example of the Shulamite's lover literally leaping towards her in 2:8–17, but then by the example of Solomon, perhaps a type of a more stately suitor, making his way inevitably towards the daughters of Jerusalem. Perhaps there is a suggestion that there are warriors enough for each of the daughters of Jerusalem to have her man. The Shulamite's speech ends with an explicit reference to marriage—the only explicit reference in the Song—and in a high-flown description of marriage as the day of the joy of the heart. The following *waṣf* section can be read as elaborating on this joy from a masculine perspective, but the change of speaker helps underline the "bottom line" of the Shulamite's advice regarding marriage. The message of the Song is mainly addressed to the daughters of Jerusalem, not the sons. Chapter 4 of the Song is more of a way of hearing first the man and then the chorus all saying *Amen!* to the Shulamite's words; and to an examination of the first part of that chapter we shall now proceed.

9

The First *Waṣf* (Song 4:1-7)

My mistress's eyes are nothing like the sun;
Coral is far more red than her lips' red;
If snow be white, why then her breasts are dun;
If hairs be wires, black wires grow on her head.
I have seen roses damasked, red and white,
But no such roses see I in her cheeks;
And in some perfumes is there more delight
Than in the breath that from my mistress reeks.
I love to hear her speak, yet well I know
That music hath a far more pleasing sound;
I grant I never saw a goddess go;
My mistress when she walks treads on the ground.
And yet, by heaven, I think my love as rare
As any she belied with false compare.[1]

Look at you, so beautiful, my friend,	הנך יפה רעיתי a	4:1
Look at you, so beautiful!	הנך יפה b	

Your eyes are doves	עיניך יונים c
From behind your veil,	מבעד לצמתך d

Your hair like a flock of goats	שערך כעדר העזים e

1. William Shakespeare, Sonnet 130.

Which descend from Mount Gilead,	שגלשו מהר גלעד	f	
Your teeth like a flock of shorn ewes	שניך כעדר הקצובות	a	4:2
Which come up from the washing	שעלו מן הרחצה	b	
With all of them bearing twins	'	c	
Without any miscarriage among them,	ושכלה אין בהם	d	
Like threading of scarlet your lips	כחוט השני שפתתיך	a	4:3
And your speech[2] is pleasing,	ומדבריך נאוה	b	
Like a slice of pomegranate your brow	כפלח הרמון רקתך	c	
From behind your veil.	מבעד לצמתך	d	

Like the tower of David is your neck,	כמגדל דויד צוארך	a	4:4
Built up with layered stonework,	בנוי לתלפיות	b	
A thousand shields hung upon it,	אלף המגן תלוי עליו	c	
All the metal shields of warriors.	כל שלטי הגבורים	d	
Your two breasts are like two fauns,	שני שדיך כשני עפרים	a	4:5
Twins of a gazelle,	תאומי צביה	b	
That graze among the lilies,	הרועים בשושנים	c	
Until the day breathes	עד שיפוח היום	a	4:6
And the shadows flee.	ונסו הצללים	b	

I will take myself to the mountain of myrrh,	אלך לי אל הר המור	c	
Even to the hill of frankincense.	ואל־גבעת הלבונה	d	
All of you is beautiful, my friend,	כלך יפה רעיתי	a	4:7
Nor is there even a blemish about you.	ומום אין בך	b	

Roberts divides this macro-section into two subunits each of two strophes (4:1c-3 and 4:4-6d).[3] He sees both the overall macro-section and the first subunit as each being introduced by separate bicola (4:1a-b and 4:1c-d). He sees an additional bicolon (4:7) closing the macro-unit, and corresponding closely to the opening bicolon (4:1a-b), thus forming an *inclusio*. However, Roberts finds the penultimate bicolon (4:6c-d, shaded above) to be problematic, since it does not open any subunit and the preceding subunit provides its own strong closure. He notes that scholarly opinion is quite diverse in regard to the function of this bicolon, some going so far as

---

2. See: Psalm 119:161, מדבריך; and Song 4:3 λαλιά (LXX); eloquium (Vulgate); or so your mouth is pleasing.

3. Roberts, *Let Me See Your Form*, 163-64.

to see these two lines as evidence of an addition at the hand of a late editor of the Song.[4]

Yet again Roberts is able to affirm that, with the exception of the difficult bicolon mentioned, there is broad agreement among scholars that these verses do constitute a cohesive unit, irrespective of disagreements about how this unit might be related to the rest of the Song as a text. He will not be able to make the same claim in his next macro-section, however. In this case, what gives the unit cohesion is discussed in literary criticism of the Song along the lines of it broadly fitting within a class of descriptive poem called the *waṣf*. The term derives from a genre of classical Arabic poetry that predates the Islamic era. Attested forms of the Arabic root (و ص ف), from which the word *waṣf* is derived, are described in the supplement to Lane's Classical Arabic dictionary and are rather suggestive: "he attained to the proper age for service" (form i); "he became of full stature, and fit for service" (form iv); "he became characterised by knowledge" (form viii); and in grammatical and literary usage of Classical Arabic, the noun form could be used to denote "an epithet in which the substantive character predominates."[5] The *waṣf* style of poetry is found within the corpus preserved by literate Islamic-world scholarship that documented the oral traditions of pre-Islamic poets. The root is used in the Qur'an thirteen times in verbs (all of form i) and once as a noun (6:139), all involving the sense of attribution (attestation, assertion, affirmation). Poems in the *waṣf* genre are so classified based on their *method* of elaborating on a topic, rather than on any *content* constraints related to topics that might be so elaborated within poems of the genre. In post-classical Arabic terminology, love poetry also gained its own distinct designation, the *ghazal*, which is so well known to the English language that the *Oxford English Dictionary* (OED), even in its first edition,[6] included it as a loanword, with attestations dating from 1800. The Arabic root from which it comes, *ġ-z-l* (غ ز ل), is also the ultimate source, "probably"—according to the OED—via Spanish, for the English word *gazelle*. Lane's dictionary provides many attestations and forms of this root in classical usage.[7] Their relevance to the Song of Songs is striking.

4. Roberts offers examples of three schools of thought. Budde, followed by Landsberger and Müller deletes the verse. Rothstein followed by Jastrow, Rudolph and Loretz swaps the order of verses 6 and 7. Delitzsch and Ginsburg attribute verse 6 to the woman.

5. Lane, *Arabic-English Lexicon*, 3054.

6. "A species of Oriental lyric poetry, generally of an erotic nature, distinguished from other forms of Eastern verse by having a limited number of stanzas and by the recurrence of the same rhyme." Bradley, "Ghazal", 147.

7. Lane, *Arabic-English Lexicon*, 2255-57.

Three major semantic domains are apparent in classical Arabic usage of the غ ز ل root. The predominantly attested references are to amatory and *enticing* (Lane's adjectives) action and *conversation*, especially of young men towards women, often pejoratively of such behavior being frivolous or insincere. Medieval Arabic literary commentary also uses the root to denote text that describes the emotions involved in partings and reunions of lovers;[8] however, reference to this, and to praise of a beloved's characteristics, Lane assesses a little acerbically as actually being post-classical terminology.[9] Nonetheless, the broader usage did enter the language.

A broader second semantic domain is possibly a case of homonymy, but is also tantalizingly suggestive of a prototypical sense for the root. The root is attested in many references to the rotation involved in entwining threads by the industry of spinning, or to participation in this industry itself. The latter may be the primary sense in this usage of the root, but the former is more common in the classical literature available to the medieval lexicographers Lane consulted. The root is used of the sun, and rays of sunlight, explained as metaphorical extensions, as though the sun "spins" its rays. By a more direct metaphor, the root is attested denoting spiders spinning webs.

The third semantic domain is again potentially a case of homonymy, but offers an alternative possibility for a prototypical sense for the root in its references to the gazelle, particularly as associated with characteristics of its life cycle. Perhaps originally this denoted specifically the female giving birth, but it is also used of a young male, as having attained adult capacity for motion, and perhaps as appearing to be using this with excessive enthusiasm.

Not all attested usages of the *ġ-z-l* root are entirely consistent (some specifically exclude references that others presume), which is perhaps evidence for regional as well as diachronic semantic variation. Several of Lane's sources provided folk etymologies involving various conflations of the three semantic domains, and some literary usage appears to play on associations between the three main senses of the root. It is not impossible to imagine an original root meaning something like "flirt" (or more politely, "court") which then provided natural but distinct metaphors for the intertwining of threads, and the youth or fertility of gazelles. The actual chronology of semantic proliferation within this branch of Semitic language usage need not be definitively reconstructed in detail; it is sufficient for purposes of interpretation simply to observe that the Song of Songs clearly shares features

---

8. "Mention of the days of union and disunion," ibid., 2555.

9. "According to a loose and post-classical usage," ibid.

and word associations with some central Semitic poetic traditions, both—especially the latter—probably of some antiquity.

To the two genres of Arabic poetry I have already mentioned, Nögel and Rendsburg present a case for the Arabic poetic genres of *tašbīb* and *hijā'* additionally being relevant for interpretation of the Song of Songs.[10] Theirs is a rather ambitious claim that the Song intends some degree of invective against Solomon. However, to the extent that their argument draws attention to the fact that the figure of Solomon in the Song is presented as remote rather than as being an intimate participant, they speak in concert with most recent commentators.

Although the cohesion of 4:1-7 is intuitively apparent, even in translation, and supported even by the scholars most searching to argue against the unity of the Song, it is still worth briefly observing how an argument based on low-level features of the text can be made even in the current case. It is valuable because if this section is admitted as an unambiguous unity on the basis of high-level features, then if low-level features that accompany this unit (unambiguously cohesive based on the high-level features) are also found in other units (ambiguous as to cohesion due to lack of high-level features), then the occurrence of these low-level features in those other units may serve as evidence to resolve some ambiguity in regards to cohesion. In other words, the current macro-section can be appreciated as a unity without appeal to the way poetry is used in harmony with its unity. In other macro-sections, however, where the unity is less intuitive, the poetic devices there can be examined to see if they suggest the poet used techniques similar to those in the current unit; either intending them to reinforce an idea he thought would be received as a unity, but is eluding our interpretation; or that he used them intentionally to assist an interpreter in perceiving unity where he thought it might otherwise be overlooked.

In fact, most of the poetic devices Roberts appeals to in the current section are indeed drawn from study of the psalms and biblical poetry in general, where textual boundaries for poetry are clearly marked in context: by explicit indicators of psalm divisions, for example; or through change of speaker in a cycle of dialogue, as in the book of Job; or via prose-poetry interfaces, where poetry is embedded in text, as with the Song of the Sea (Exod 15:1-18) or the Song of Deborah and Barak (Judg 5:2-31). To the well-known devices we might add Nicholas Lunn's analysis of word-order variation, where he finds a significant pattern of non-canonical word order being used in biblical poetry more frequently than in prose, *when* this word

---

10. Noegel and Rendsburg, *Solomon's Vineyard*, 129-69.

order is used for the purpose of stylistic variation rather than for discourse marking of topic focus. Lunn considers this feature in relation to verbal rather than nominal, verbless clauses, so although he does note the stylistic variation in ordering of subject and predicate in Song 4:1-7,[11] this does not return any significant data one way or the other in regard to his thesis, because the variation in Song 4:1-7 is all in verbless nominal clauses. Roberts actually remarks on this "nominal and static form of the *waṣf* as a whole."[12]

Intriguingly, Lunn's data reveals but one solitary instance in the Song of the stylistic device he was looking for across a wide sampling of the Hebrew Bible. This effectively identifies the Song as atypical of biblical poetry in general, at least in regards to this specific form of stylistic variation, since the Song does not utilize it. In fact, the Song is even an exception to biblical prose, which *does* use this form of stylistic variation, just with lower frequency. The single instance of non-canonical word order that Lunn found in the Song actually occurs in the verse immediately following the current section, 4:8.[13] Lunn is uncertain as to whether his finding might assist with dating the Song, because other evidence suggests it may serve as evidence of diversity of authorial preference. In any case, what Lunn does say about the rare form of stylistic variation in 4:8, gap-initial parallelism,[14] is that where it is found the commentators tend to consider that it signals aperture.[15] Here then is an example of a poetic device, independently thought to signal aperture, hence confirming the work of scholars of the Song who find a new poetic unit opening at 4:8,[16] but also for those who find independent markers of closure at 4:7.

Roberts mentions four classical markers of closure in 4:7, namely: "ו-initial final colon"; "reversal of the grammatical order of the final colon to form a chiasm"; "the summarising כל of 7a"; and "the non-exceptive phrase ומום אין בך."[17] Expanding attention to correspondences across the whole *waṣf*, he cites Gordis's observation that the way opening and closing components of external *inclusio* structures in biblical Hebrew poetry—like

---

11. Lunn, *Word-Order Variation*, 362.
12. Roberts, *Let Me See Your Form*, 174.
13. Lunn, *Word-Order Variation*, 279.
14. There are only four instances in his data, all from different psalms.
15. Lunn, *Word-Order Variation*, §8.2.3, 188-89, where he cites Terrien; Kidner; Harman; Delitzsch; Krauss; and Anderson.
16. Lunn notes consulting Longman, *Song of Songs*, Murphy, *Song of Songs*, and Carr, *Song of Solomon*.
17. Roberts, *Let Me See Your Form*, 175.

Psalm 49:13, 21 and Job 28:12, 20—are rarely exact,[18] and observes how the closing component typically sharpens the idea of the opening component, rather like synonymous parallelism, but often with the additional feature that it is sharpened in a way that is influenced by the semantics of the enclosed section. In the case of Song 4:1-7, the woman is initially lauded as beautiful, then after the careful consideration of the body of the *waṣf*, she is finally lauded as being without a single flaw. Finally, Roberts notes that the *waṣf* appears to have three "layers" of closure: the second of the two pairs of strophes closes with an עד ש ("until which") clause; the penultimate bicolon semantically implies consummation; and finally, the opening of the *inclusio* is answered with a closing, intensified echo. All three layers have ו-initial final cola.

Discourse analysis of such a "static" and almost homogeneously descriptive span of text is far less interesting than the analysis of the range of poetic devices used within it. Perhaps the most significant thing to note is that although one could analyze Song 4:1-7 according to the List relation of Mann and Thompson's taxonomy in RST, SDRT lends itself to providing a more fine-grained analysis in this particular case. The overarching discourse representation structure (DRS) for the *waṣf* can be represented according to a standard style of diagram in which objects in the world of the discourse context are named in a bar above a box containing constraints or conditions obtaining in regards to those objects and their relations.

---

18. Gordis, *Song of Songs*, 85.

198 GENDER IN SOLOMON'S SONG OF SONGS

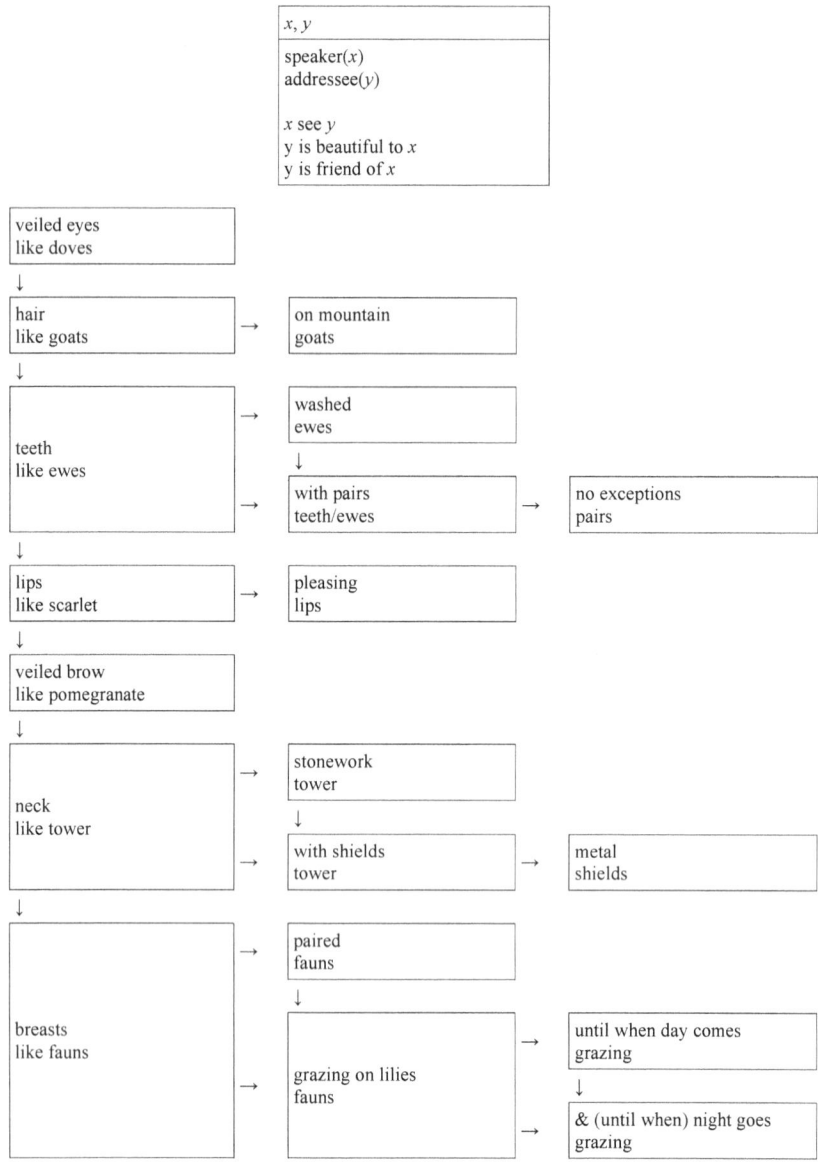

We can also lay out the list of features in such a way that it shows how each of the primary elements of the list is elaborated upon, though some elements are elaborated to greater depth than the others. Observed this way, though intuition alone may suggest it to many readers, there is an appearance of the man waxing eloquent, as though his emotions are betrayed in his increasingly expansive elaborations, with the potential to carry him beyond the constraints of the conventions of Hebrew poetry, which may help explain the dynamism of the penultimate bicolon.

Pulling back from the intimate details of this section, we recall that a man's voice is not a new feature in the text of the Song. The voice of the shepherd lover was heard in dialogue in chapter 1, and—with others who read the Song as a unity—we hear him again, but quoted in chapter 2. In both cases, the man's voice is essentially auxiliary to that of the woman's; her words both precede and follow his, hemming them in. His words are a feature of part of her discourse, but only a part of it. His words answer to the needs of her agenda for communication. At least this is so in the way I have been presenting the dynamics of the discourse of the Song in this thesis, but mostly those who read the Song as a unity observe similar things. Again I would argue that 4:1–7 answers to a pattern set by the woman, in this case by 3:6–11, if I am correct to read those verses as narrated by the Shulamite. They set the pattern and occasion the *waṣf*, as if it were Solomon's own song of joy at that time. They were not Solomon's words, as Delitzsch has it: "This scene contains a conversation between Solomon and his beloved."[19] However, they are the words of the man *as though he were* Solomon. They do not form a third scene of a dramatic act, as Delitzsch would have it, either. The rhetorical relation of the first *waṣf* to its prior context is not one of progressing a narrative. The wedding of 3:6–11 is past to the appearance of the palanquin, and the palanquin itself is most likely a creative metaphor for a homecoming lover, not an actual object, and not arriving in real time. The adjuration refrain is given in real time, the personal details of the Song are past with respect to the Shulamite's conversation with the daughters of Jerusalem. Because the nature of romantic love involves perennial cycles of longing and fulfillment, however, such personal intimations can serve informative roles irrespective of temporal setting. What has been so in the past will be so again. What is being longed for in the future has been longed for before.

In the reading of this thesis, the Song has two distinct halves, with the first half being drawn to a strong and positive closure at 5:1. The analysis of the final section of this first half of the Song involves more dispute about section boundaries than what we have looked at so far, except perhaps the first chapter; so we will turn our attention from the well established unit of the first *waṣf* to issues that require broader consideration before they can fit within the context of our overall thesis.

---

19. Delitzsch, *Commentary*, 70.

10

Consummation (Song 4:8—5:1)

With me from Lebanon, my bride,	אתי מלבנון כלה	a	4.8
With me from Lebanon, come!	אתי מלבנון תבואי	b	
Gaze from the peak of Amana!	תשורי מראש אמנה	c	
From the peak of Senir and Hermon	מראש שניר וחרמון	d	
From lairs of lions	ממענות אריות	e	
From the mountains of leopards.	מהררי נמרים	f	

You have enchanted my heart, my sister, my bride.	לבבתני אחתי כלה	a	4.9
You have enchanted my heart with one of your eyes,	לבבתיני באחת מעיניך	b	
With one pendant from your necklace.	באחד ענק מצורניך	c	

How beautiful your caresses, my sister, my bride.	מה יפו דדיך אחתי כלה	a	4.10
How much better your caresses than wine,	מה טבו דדיך מיין	b	
And the fragrance of your scent than all balsam.	וריח שמניך מכל בשמים	c	

Your lips drip fresh honey, my bride.	נפת תטפנה שפתותיך כלה	a	4.11
Under your tongue are honey and milk,	דבש וחלב תחת לשונך	b	
And the fragrance of your scent like the fragrance of Lebanon.	וריח שלמתיך כריח לבנון	c	

A locked garden are you, my sister, my bride,	גן נעול אחתי כלה	a	4.12
A locked fountain,	גל נעול	b	
A sealed spring,	מעין חתום	c	

Your vegetation a paradise of pomegranates	שלחיך פרדס רמונים a	4.13
With delicious fruits,	עם פרי מגדים b	
Henna bushes with nard plants,	כפרים עם נרדים c	
Nard and saffron,	נרד וכרכם a	4.14
Calamus and cinnamon,	קנה וקנמון b	
With all the trees of Lebanon,	עם כל עצי לבונה c	
Myrrh and aloes,	מר ואהלות d	
With all the best balsam,	עם כל ראשי בשמים e	

A garden spring,	מעין גנים a	4.15
A well of living water,	באר מים חיים b	
And flowing from Lebanon.	ונזלים מן לבנון c	

Stir North Wind!	עורי צפון a	4.16
And come South Wind!	ובואי תימן b	
Breath on my garden!	הפיחי גני c	
May its balsam flow.	יזלו בשמיו d	
May my love enter his garden,	יבא דודי לגנו e	
And may he eat its excellent fruits.	ויאכל פרי מגדיו f	

I have entered into my garden, my sister, my bride.	באתי לגני אחתי כלה a	5.1
I have picked my myrrh with my balsam.	אריתי מורי עם בשמי b	
I have eaten my honeycomb with my honey.	אכלתי יערי עם דבשי c	
I have drunk my wine with my milk.	שתיתי ייני עם חלבי d	

Eat, friends!	אכלו רעים e	
Drink and be intoxicated, lovers!	שתו ושכרו דודים f	

ROBERTS CONSIDERS 4:8–5:1 TO be a single macro-section of the Song. He divides it into four sections, essentially following the changes in speaker: The Man's Invitation and Praise of the Woman (4:8–15); The Woman's Response and Invitation (4:16); I Have Come to My Garden (5:1a–d); and Eat, Lovers, and Drink (5:1e–f).[1] He further subdivides the first section into four subsections, seeing each of these as marked out by the "distinctive" vocative כלה ("bride") which closes its initial colon; though he notes they

---

1. Roberts, *Let Me See Your Form*, 178–98.

all also feature initial tricola which use staircase parallelism, "or a close approximation thereof."[2] Roberts names the four subsections: Come with Me from Lebanon (4:8); You Have Taken My Heart (4:9); You Are Better Than Wine and the Fragrance of Balsam (4:10-11); and You Are a Closed Garden (4:12-15).[3]

Roberts observes that anthologists typically find three segments in these verses—4:8, 4:9-11, and 4:12-5:1—while dramatists and others tend to consider the verses together with 4:1-7 or even 3:6-11 as well (so Delitzsch, as mentioned in the last chapter). Roberts also notes that he divides the section differently even from the small number of commentators who consider it to be a distinct unit, but obviously considers he has adequate structural grounds to do so. The major alternative view to Roberts divides the section 4:8-11 and 4:12-5:1 on the basis of the garden imagery,[4] whereas Roberts's division has the advantage of following the changes of speaker. I will follow Roberts on the basis of my own theory of the Song using cycles to complete units. As this section starts with addresses marked by vocatives, so it closes with vocatives. The whole unit is full of invitation to sensual consumption, which gives it a feel of cohesion, and distinguishes it from the surrounding text. The garden imagery is not the only imagery that is repeated in the course of elaborating the invitations; there is also the prominence of Lebanon, wine, balsam, and honey across the whole section. Jenson says, rather nicely, that the lovers "do not anticipate one another; neither simply assumes the other's complicity; each must be won by the other."[5]

From an SDRT perspective, the section begins with a request that is extensively elaborated in 4:8, followed by an explanation for the request in 4:9: come with me, because you have taken my heart. This is then further explained in 4:10-15. You have taken my heart, because your love is better than wine. This is reminiscent of the first verses of the Song, which is something that also fits yet again with our theory of the Song using cycles to signal completion of units. Up until this point of the Song, it has been the woman who speaks of being overwhelmed by the consummation of romantic love. In this final section of the first half of the Song the mirror image is presented in the man's words. He too finds her caresses to be better than wine (cf. 1:2b). He too finds her scent to be good (cf. 1:3a). But although there are parallels and echoes suggesting similarities between the man and

2. Ibid., 180.
3. Ibid., 180-91.
4. The example Roberts gives is of Elliot, *Literary Unity*, 99-120.
5. Jenson, *Song of Songs*, 52.

the woman, there are also differences. In 4:8—5:1 there is text to signal a return to the opening themes of the Song, but also text that increments the information being presented.

Exum proposes that in the Song as a whole, "Conventional roles for men and women respectively seem to inform the picture of love as something she gives and he takes."[6] This appears to be literally the picture offered in 4:16—5:1d,[7] but not in 5:1e-f, nor more widely in the Song, though the matter is nuanced. One of the things progressed by the text of the current section, beyond what was presented in the opening verses of the Song, is the explicit context of male desire. In this context, the woman's series of three imperatives directed at the winds and three jussives directed at herself and her love are more an expression of invitation than were the jussive, imperative, and cohortative expressions she used at the outset of the Song, which were communicating her own desire—her own appetite. However, the chorus clearly exhorts *both* lovers to eat, drink, and be intoxicated.[8] The final picture is of the consummation of *mutual* appetite, wedding the woman's self-disclosure from the beginning of the Song with the man's self-disclosure in chapter 4.

The sense of closure at 5:1e-f is particularly strong; potentially strong enough to mark no less than the division of the whole Song into two parts. Indeed, we have already noted that all the recent commentators listed in our literature review who find the Song to be a unity nonetheless identify a boundary between subsections between 5:1 and 5:2. Garrett sees 4:16—5:1 as the "centre of a large chiasmus that spans the whole of the work."[9] Carr finds that, "the third division of the poem ends with the couple's companions and guests rejoicing with them and encouraging them to drink their fill of ecstasy and joy in each other's arms—and bed."[10] He also observes of the following section that it stands in a rhetorical relationship to prior context: "This long section marks the working out of the relationship established in the previous chapters."[11] Fox sees the strength in the division lying in the

---

6. Exum, *Song of Songs*, 27.

7. "The woman's invitation in the previous verse ("Let my lover come to his garden!") and the man's reply here in this verse ("I come to my garden," etc.) are complementary expressions of desire gendered in terms of a cultural version of something a woman gives and a man takes." Ibid., 182.

8. This is actually a point Exum freely admits: "'Eat,' 'drink,' and 'be drunk,' plural forms addressed to both lovers, leave no doubt that eating and drinking in the garden is mutual sexual indulgence and satisfaction." Ibid., 183.

9. Garrett, *Song of Songs*, 201.

10. Carr, *Song of Solomon*, 141.

11. Ibid., 142.

continuity of the following section: "The unity of 5:2—6:3, with its continuity of narrative and dialogue, is evident." Goulder's dramatic reading sees the transition from 5:1 to 5:2 as being from the wedding night in 5:1 to the following night in 5:2.[12] "The chorus here will not be the 'daughters of Jerusalem' as elsewhere, but the king's 'comrades' and the princesses 'girls.'"[13] Murphy, like Carr, observes that

> In a wedding context one or other of the lovers might address friends who are participating in the celebration. It seems preferable to interpret the imperatives as addressed to the lovers, and a fitting ending to the description of their love in the preceding dialogue emerges.[14]

Longman goes so far as to connect 5:1 with 1:4, an observation with which I agree: "The chorus is the voice of those outside the relationship who put their imprimatur, as it were, on the relationship."[15] Longman is also decisive about section divisions when it comes to the following section from 5:2: "This lengthy poem is clearly demarcated from what precedes and what follows."[16] Bergant is particularly clear: "Although linguistically this bicolon creates an abrupt shift in the poem, its repetition of some of the poem's significant words clearly creates links within it."[17] She also notes how the following section reinforces a pervasive gender dynamic in the Song: "The man calls and the woman responds ... the woman's search does not accomplish its end."[18]

Exum is adamant that "there are only three clearly distinguishable speaking voices in the poem, and thus only three 'characters,' and all the parts can be assigned to them without difficulty: the woman, the man, and the women of Jerusalem." This is a parsimonious interpretation of the Song with which I agree, especially as Exum's handling of it is sensitive to how the poet uses the voices to address the audience in various ways. This tripartite set of voices provides the context for reading the juncture leading up to 5:1 as being highly marked, just by the transitions between speakers incorporating the full "cast" as they do.

12. Goulder, *Song Of Fourteen*, 41.
13. Ibid., 39.
14. Murphy, *Song of Songs*, 162.
15. Longman, *Song of Songs*, 159.
16. Ibid., 160.
17. Bergant, *Song of Songs*, 58.
18. Ibid., 60.

Although the above labors the discontinuity between 5:1e–f and 5:2ff, what is more important for the case this thesis is attempting to make is the continuity between 4:1–7 and 4:8—5:1. As has already been mentioned, dramatists show some imagination in reconstructing a plot through these sections, even extending back as far as 3:6–11 (and beyond). This is not our methodology however. Nor is it our methodology to observe, as others do, that 4:1–7 has an obvious continuity with 4:8–15 by virtue of all being spoken by the man (Garrett even reads 4:16a–c as being part of the man's speech).[19] We have seen that there is coherence within the man's speech via rhetorical relations of *Explanation*, but what rhetorical relation connects his speech in the current section to the context of the *waṣf* that precedes it? As with other invitations, like that of the Shulamite in 1:4, this appears to be a *Result* relation: because you are beautiful, so then come with me. The reference manual for SDRT annotation has this to say about the *Result* relation.

> **Result.** *Result*(α,β) relates a cause to its effect: the main eventuality of α is understood to cause the eventuality given by β. Thus *Result* is the dual of *Explanation*, which relates an effect to its cause.[20]

Two examples are given in the indicative mood in Reese et al. taken from a sample corpus of 60 *Wall Street Journal* articles.

> 1a. Chrysler stopped output of Dodge Dynasty and Chrysler New Yorker cars yesterday at its Belvidere, Ill., plant.
>
> 1b. Some 1,700 of the plant's 2,900 hourly employees were laid off as a result.[21]
>
> *Result*(1a,1b)

> 2a. The mediator has imposed a new blackout on the two sides,
>
> 2b. so a Big Board spokesman couldn't comment on the talks.[22]
>
> *Result*(2a,2b)

---

19. Garrett, *Song of Songs*, 200.
20. Reese et al., *Reference Manual*, 18.
21. Ibid., 18–19.
22. Ibid., 19.

The classic example in SDRT is the pair of sentences (a) *John pushed Max* and (b) *He fell*, related by *Result*(a,b).[23] However, Asher and Lascerides also provide an example with one component in the imperative mood.

[a] Turn left at the roundabout [b] and you will see traffic lights.[24]

The rhetorical relation *Result* is given a subscript *r* for *request* to mark that the context involves an imperative, so the above could be abbreviated *Result*$_r$(a,b). In our example from the Song of Songs, the imperative follows the indicative rather than the other way around, but the rhetorical relation is still *Result*. Alternatively, since *Result* is the dual of *Explanation*, the relation could be represented as an *Explanation* in non-canonical order with the imperative being the first component of the relation thus adjusted: so come with me, because you are beautiful. In either case, there is coherence in the text of chapter 4 without that being narrative or dramatic coherence. It is possible to interpret the discourse in such a way as to maximize its coherence, making a single author's intention a more likely explanation of the final form of the text than that of even a carefully pieced together anthology. Hence we can consider the significance of apparent thematic connections between the current passage and others from even relatively remote parts of the text of the Song.

First person pronouns in the Song[25]

	denoting woman	denoting man
independent: אני or שאני	12	—
inflected verb: pf. or impf.	40	11
verb or pronoun suffix: "me"	33	8
noun suffix: "my"	59	30

Roberts actually struggles to find formal correspondences between 4:8—5:1 and other parts of the Song, but he radically restricts what he will entertain as potential candidates as correspondences. He is concerned about catchwords and phrases and poetic devices rather than the more elusive and subjective elements of interpretations of symbols. He avoids most features of the semantics and pragmatics of the Song. However, in the current section we actually have important new information in the Song viewed as a whole.

---

23. Asher and Lascerides, *Logics of Conversation*, 462–63.
24. Ibid., 464–65.
25. McGinniss, *Contributions*, 16–17.

The man speaks for himself in an extended passage and makes strong assertions as he closes his speech. In fact, although there are important consistencies between the picture of the man we are given in chapter 4 and how he appears elsewhere, it is something of a high point in his self-disclosure when the text of the Song is viewed as a whole. A good proportion of the first-person references to the man occur in this passage. Part of that is because, in the entirety of the Song, the man has only two long speeches (4:1-15 and 6:4—7:10), a sizeable quote (2:10-14), and some fragmentary dialogue as lines. It is only in his own speeches he can use the first person. Quantifying usage of the first person pronoun can therefore serve as a rough proxy for the weighting in the Song of how much of it is given from the woman's and from the man's perspectives.

As I have already mentioned, Exum finds in the man's first-person perfect verbs towards the end of the section a sense of the woman giving and the man taking. However, not only does the chorus mutualize the conception of the lovers as consuming one another's delights, the man's speech here is distinguished from his speech elsewhere by giving an inside look at his own perspective (4:9). The Song has many passages where the lovers praise one another prior to consummation, and it has some passages where there is praise following consummation (like 1:4c-d and 5:1e-f). It also has passages where the praise of the other person is viewed from the outside as onlookers can also see the person; these are typically matters of external appearance. On the other hand, in the woman's speech especially, there are praise passages that are based on the way the man makes the woman feel. Only rarely do we get such an inside look into the emotional effects the man experiences as a result of his love for the woman, and these are mainly to do with the impact of her external appearance on him. In other words, in the current passage, the fact that we are being given a unique insight into how the man is affected by the woman gives the impression that she is giving and he is taking. Perhaps more modestly, all we are seeing is something that is a necessary consequence of the poet offering us the man's perspective for a change.

When the man speaks elsewhere in the Song we do not get such a sustained picture of his internal experience of desire and satisfaction in its consummation. That the woman is enthusiastic about giving her love is made clear in 4:16, but this does not preclude her taking pleasure from love as well. Articulating her desire to take pleasure in love in this particular passage of the Song, however, is not necessary because it is made clear elsewhere (and in the chorus), and keeping that aspect of their love silent allows a fuller sense of the man's experience to be presented without being diluted by other elements. The Song does offer dialogue to indicate mutuality in places. It asserts mutuality in others. It implies mutuality in yet others. But the majority of the Song is constructed by sustained speeches from particular perspectives. Chapter 4 presents a kind of central chapter, an insight into the man that is assumed throughout the Song. We are given a window into what it is that would lead the man to kiss the woman with the kisses of his mouth, and what it is that would lead him to be like a gazelle or stag on the mountains of spices.

Chapter 4 is the exception that proves the rule in regards to the main thesis of the current study. The Song of Songs appears to be written to communicate a woman's perspective on romantic love. This does not mean the man's perspective is entirely absent; it is just not developed to the same extent; it is not the main focus in the flow of the presentation. This is as one might expect by analogy with the apportioning of text to the main voices in the Song: the Shulamite has most of the lines and our thesis is that the whole Song is in a sense structured such that it is "her" presentation on romantic love with her lover playing a supporting role in that presentation. The Shulamite has most of the lines, but not all of them; yet it is still "her" Song. So, likewise, although the Song, it is being argued, is ultimately aimed at communicating advice to young women (and men) based on the presentation of a fictive, somewhat exaggerated, stereotypical woman's internal engagement with the joys and trials of love, a man's perspective cannot be completely excluded, is to some extent part of the presuppositional background of the Song, and is made explicit most clearly in this "central" speech of his in chapter 4, as though he were Solomon rejoicing on the day of his wedding.

II

Nightmare (Song 5:2—6:3)

I was sleeping but my heart was aroused.	אני ישנה ולבי ער	a	5.2

The sound of my love, knocking.	קול דודי דופק	b

Open for me, my sister, my friend,	פתחי לי אחתי רעיתי	c
My dove, my perfect one,	יונתי תמתי	d
For my head is full of dew,	שראשי נמלא טל	e
My hair with the droplets of night.	קוצותי רסיסי לילה	f

I have stripped off my garment.	פשטתי את כתנתי	a	5.3
How can I get dressed [again]?	איככה אלבשנה	b	
I have washed my feet.	רחצתי את רגלי	c	
How can I soil them [again]?	איככה אטנפם	d	

My love moved his hand in from the latch,	דודי שלח ידו מן החר	a	5.4
And my emotions were stirred because of him.	ומעי המו עליו	b	

I got up to open for my love,	קמתי אני לפתח לדודי	a	5.5
And my hands dripped myrrh,	וידי נטפו מור	b	
My fingers flowing myrrh,	ואצבעתי מור עבר	c	
On the handles of the bolt.	על כפות המנעול	d	

I opened for my love,	פתחתי אני לדודי	a	5.6
But my love had turned away and passed on.	ודודי חמק עבר	b	

My soul went out at his deserting me.	נפשי יצאה בדברו	c

I sought him but I did not find him;	בקשתיהו ולא מצאתיהו	d	
I called him but he did not answer me.	קראתיו ולא ענני	e	
The watchmen found me,	מצאני השמרים	a	5.7
Those who go around in the city.	הסבבים בעיר	b	
They struck me; they bruised me;	הכוני פצעוני	c	
They took my shawl from me,	נשאו את רדידי מעלי	d	
Those who guard the walls.	שמרי החמות	e	

I put you under oath,	השבעתי אתכם	a	5.8
Daughters of Jerusalem,	בנות ירושלם	b	
If you find my love,	אם תמצאו את דודי	c	
What will you tell him?	מה תגידו לו	d	
That I am weak with love.	שחולת אהבה אני	e	

How is your lover better than other lovers,	מה דודך מדוד	a	5.9
Most beautiful among women?	היפה בנשים	b	
How is your lover better than other lovers,	מה דודך מדוד	c	
That you swear us to this?	שככה השבעתנו	d	

My love is bright and ruddy,	דודי צח ואדום	a	5.10
Outstanding beyond a multitude.	דגול מרבבה	b	

His head is refined gold,	ראשו כתם פז	a	5.11
His locks palm branches,	קוצותיו תלתלים	b	
Black like a raven.	שחרות כעורב	c	
His eyes are like doves,	עיניו כיונים	a	5.12
By streams of water,	על אפיקי מים	b	
Bathing in milk,	רחצות בחלב	c	
Sitting on brimming pools.	ישבות על מלאת	d	
His cheeks are like a bed of balsam,	לחיו כערוגת הבשם	a	5.13
Perfumed towers.	מגדלות מרקחים	b	
His lips are lilies,	שפתותיו שושנים	c	
Dripping flowing myrrh.	נטפות מור עבר	d	

His arms are rods of gold,	ידיו גלילי זהב a	5.14
Set with precious stones.	ממלאים בתרשיש b	
His abdomen is a panel of ivory,	מעיו עשת שן c	
Covered with sapphires.	מעלפת ספירים d	
His legs are pillars of alabaster,	שוקיו עמודי שש a	5.15
Established on refined pedestals.	מיסדים על אדני פז b	

His appearance is like Lebanon,	מראהו כלבנון c	
Choice like the cedars.	בחור כארזים d	
His mouth is sweet,	חכו ממתקים a	5.16
And all of him is pleasant.	וכלו מחמדים b	

This is my love and this is my friend,	זה דודי וזה רעי c	
Daughters of Jerusalem.	בנות ירושלם d	

Where has your love gone,	אנה הלך דודך a	6.1
Most beautiful of women?	היפה בנשים b	
Where has your love turned?	אנה פנה דודך c	
And let us seek him with you.	ונבקשנו עמך d	

My love has gone down to his garden,	דודי ירד לגנו a	6.2
To the beds of balsam,	לערוגות הבשם b	
To pasture in the gardens,	לרעות בגנים c	
And to pick lilies.	וללקט שושנים d	
I am my love's and my love is mine;	אני לדודי ודודי לי a	6.3
He pastures among the lilies.	הרעה בשושנים b	

ROBERTS REPORTS THAT THIS section, despite its length, is still "often treated as a single song,"[1] even among anthologists, citing Falk and Gordis.[2] He claims that among all commentators its unity is "more widely accepted than

---

1. Roberts, *Let Me See Your Form*, 201.
2. Falk, *The Song of Songs*, 34–37, 77–79; Gordis, *Song of Songs*, 87–88.

that of any other extended part of the Song."[3] He treats the section as a unit himself because of its "sustained narratalogical and dialogical cohesion," which he considers is "unmatched in any other part of the Song."[4] Our own review of recent commentators found that, without exception, not only did those who viewed the Song as a unity see 5:1 and 5:2 as closing and opening sections respectively, so too did they see 6:3 and 6:4 doing so as well. However, is there any hint that this new section is rhetorically related to the preceding one? Several dramatists think so, seeing *Narration* joining 5:2—6:3 to 4:8—5:1. In Delitzsch's view, the night of 4:8—5:1 is the second night after Solomon's wedding. My own view is that the relation is the opposite of *Narration*; it is *Flashback*. The text of the current section relies on what has already been established in the Song and extends it in new directions.

Roberts's analysis of the substructure of the section at its highest level follows the view common among anthologists that divide the verses 5:2–8, 5:10–16, and 6:2–3, with 5:9 and 6:1 as "redactional addition,"[5] though Roberts posits no later editor. This is quite complicated to represent in two dimensions, as the range of levels of boundary markers in the translation above indicate, which simply follows Roberts without any attempt at critical engagement. A more descriptive, two-dimensional representation is offered in the appendix to this thesis, though that too is complex. Rather than attempt to supply a prose summary of such intricate material, the passage will be examined in the three main segments proposed by Roberts, remembering that these segments are not viewed as distinct macrosections or separate poems, but parts of what is generally considered to be one united whole. From an SDRT perspective, the second and third panels of 5:9–16 and 6:1–3 are simply elaborated question and answer pairings—$QAP(\pi[5:9],\pi[5:10-16])$ and $QAP(\pi[6:1],\pi[6:2-3])$—whereas the first section is typified by *Narration* relations, as the commentators suggest.

The first subsection, 5:2–8, is rich with self-disclosure from the woman. In an effort to piece together some kind of chronology, it is easy to overlook that it is not so much the night setting that is significant, but the way the woman is moved by the nocturnal events. The night setting is used throughout the passage with various references depending on it for their full significance to be appreciated; but the night remains background and the woman's personal experiences remain foregrounded throughout. So, for the purposes of our research questions at least, it is not so much that the woman was sleeping (יְשֵׁנָה) that should catch our attention, but that she was

---

3. Roberts, *Let Me See Your Form*, 201.
4. Ibid., 199.
5. Roberts, *Let Me See Your Form*, 201.

aroused (עוֹר); the same verb as is used in the abjurations of the adjuration refrain. Indeed, one popular interpretation of the adjuration refrain turns on this sense of the verb as "to awaken." However, this cuts both ways. It is also possible that the woman was already troubled in her sleep, or that the whole night scene is a description of her troubled dream. This too is a reading of the adjuration refrain: that the lovers are not to be troubled or disturbed. Yet another possibility is that of arousal. The woman is, let us say, romantically aroused in her dream, dreaming of her lover coming to call upon her. The text blurs the boundaries of dream and reality,[6] though it is quite natural to dream of being woken from sleep when the context is lovemaking. In any case, the woman's body is sleeping—an external perspective on the woman's circumstances—but her heart (לבב) is aroused—an internal perspective on the woman's circumstances. It is the way the woman's inner world (מעה) moves within her (המה), or how her psychology (נפש) influences her emotions (יצא), that constitutes the real narrative thread of the verses. The insights we are given go far beyond what the man disclosed in the previous chapter, or what he discloses elsewhere. There is more depth, intimacy, and intensity. One might dare to say we are dealing with a naked woman,[7] even naked to her very soul.

The current thesis proposes that the Song is written from a woman's perspective deliberately to make that perspective available to readers. The current section is clearly an example of this, though the question of whether the proposal holds in some sense for the whole of the Song requires considerably more work. What makes that work easier is that 5:2—6:3 has many similarities to other parts of the Song. Although the usual connection made is between the current dream sequence 5:2-8 (על משכבי בלילות) and that of 3:1-5 (אני ישנה), there is also a similarity between 5:2 and 2:8ff with both sections featuring the phrase "The sound of my love" (קול דודי). Here too, in 5:2, we get the man's words quoted by the woman, though he never quotes her. We also have the woman's *waṣf*, ostensibly a parallel to the man's, but with the distinctive feature that whereas his *waṣf* is addressed to the woman

---

6. "The poem begins with the woman stating that she was sleeping yet awake, an expression that only creates ambiguity and opens the passage to a variety of interpretations. Some commentators think that she is either dreaming [Gordis], in a state of semiwakefulness [Pope], or merely fantasizing [Murphy]. . . . The reference to sleep and wakefulness can probably be best understood as a poetic fiction that draws its images from both the world of dreams and the world of reality." Bergant, *Song of Songs*, 60.

7. "The garment of which she speaks was a loose-fitting, ankle-length undergarment. In warm weather, it was often worn by itself but removed at bedtime. If she had taken it off, she is naked." Bergant, *Song of Songs*, 63.

in the second person, her *waṣf* is couched in the third person, and explicitly addressed to the daughters of Jerusalem. The woman's self-disclosure is direct, whereas the man's self-disclosure is indirect. What we learn of the man fits within norms of what might be considered proper to public discourse. What the woman discloses, however, seems to cross the boundary of what is properly public into a private and personal world; perhaps not so very private that it does not include intimates like the chorus of daughters of Jerusalem, though it is hard to gauge conventions of etiquette so remote to our own experience as the culture of ancient Israel. Not all cultures are shy about sexual matters.

Exum sees 5:2—6:3 as a fusion of the earlier accounts 2:8–17 and 3:1–5. "What were two episodes in her earlier story are thus seemlessly combined to create a single, finely crafted unit, whose integrity is recognized by virtually all critics."[8] She lists parallels between the two passages,[9] including features specific to the man's calling upon the woman: the phrase *qôl dôdî*, "the voice of my lover"; the man is outside; he invites the woman to "rise up" or to "open"; he uses the epithets "my friend" and "my dove"; he offers a reason for his invitation (springtime or nighttime); and, in one case he calls the woman outside, in the other he calls to be let inside. The mutual possession refrain is found in 2:16, but also at 6:3, in reverse order. There are also parallels involving features specific to the woman's seeking and finding: the setting is at night; she sought but did not find; the watchmen, who go around in the city, find her; an oath is placed on the daughters of Jerusalem. To these observations, Roberts adds that "The phrase חולת אהבה אני at the end of the modified adjuration refrain here in 5:8e is an exact repetition from 2:5c, where it is tied in with the complex of features that always precedes the adjuration refrain in its regular form."[10]

Roberts also sees the macro-section as connected with the preceding section, not in a narrative way like the dramatists, but in three more formal than semantic features, though they are semantic at a surface level. Firstly, he notes the vocative אחתי in 5:2.[11] This epithet for the woman is only used in 4:8—5:1 (four times) and in 5:2 (once). Secondly, both passages end with the man entering his garden and eating—clearly metaphorical for the taking of pleasure in lovemaking from the man's perspective.[12] With the exception of 8:13–14, it is only in 4:8—5:1 and in 6:2 that גן ("garden") and בשם ("balsam") are intended to refer to the woman. Thirdly, by Roberts's reckoning, there is a structural similarity of a final independent bicolon closing the two

---

8. Exum, *Song of Songs*, 186.
9. Ibid., 186–87.
10. Roberts, *Let Me See Your Form*, 228.
11. Ibid., 227.
12. Ibid., 228.

macro-sections.[13] The 4:8—5:1 macro-section is closed by 5:1e-f, an independent bicolon, where the chorus urge on the lovers. The present section, 5:2—6:3, is closed by 6:3, another independent bicolon, which features the mutual possession refrain.

So, although scholarly commentary sees 5:2—6:3 as a long independent macro-unit of the Song, it also sees it as intimately connected with large sections of the rest of the text, especially the three chapters preceding it. In a sense, although Exum reads the Song as a unity, her analysis of how the "stories" of chapters 2 and 3 are intertwined in 5:2—6:3 almost reads as though she were showing how the latter passage were redacted from the earlier two "source texts." This impression is strengthened if we view the woman's *waṣf* in chapter 5 as answering to the man's in chapter 4. We end up with 5:2—6:3 as a kind of précis of the Song so far, yet it clearly contains new material, and it contrasts with, rather than simply repeating, some of the earlier material it seems to parallel. The way I take this is that the Song is "punctuated." The Song really is a song of songs, with these songs having aperture, cohesion, and closure. However, following Roberts, it is clear that the songs interact with each other such that there is a higher-level cohesion over the whole of the Song, making it one work and not many. Additionally, I observe what comes across as analogous to a paragraph, or a couple of paragraphs of text. In the terms of this analogy, the component songs of the overall Song are like sentences within one or two paragraphs that make up the totality of the Song. I say two paragraphs because I think the division of the Song, between 5:1 and 5:2, is a substantial and deliberate division of the Song into two halves. The completeness of 5:1e-f followed by the integrity and sheer length of 5:2—6:3 appear to convey a deep break in the flow of the text. It allows for 5:2—6:3 to re-establish the discourse of the Song according to authorial intentions complementary to those involved in laying out the first half of the text. Alternative perspectives are explored. The level of intensity is raised a notch. The rhetoric of the Song progresses it towards an intended climax.

Whatever we observe in regards to structure, the fact remains that in the current section we get a particularly compelling view of the woman's psychology.[14] It is not unfamiliar to us: her language of being weak with love is repeated in 5:8e from 2:5c as I have already mentioned. But that is not the only familiar theme. The watchmen mistreat the woman worse than her brothers did, if I am right to keep viewing the solo female voices in the discourse as belonging to one individual. This is a reminder that even in

---

13. Ibid.

14. "The woman's reaction to the man's action is quite dramatic. Her innards, the seat of emotion (see Isa 16:11), are profoundly stirred for him." Bergant, *Song of Songs*, 63.

chapter 1 there is a seeking and finding theme, where the woman seems to suffer before finding her love. There is a veiled threat of menace about male characters other than her love. First it is the brothers and perhaps shepherds, then it is the city watchmen, though the warriors around Solomon's palanquin are also fearsome in their way, albeit no threat to the Shulamite nor the daughters of Zion, with whom they are presented as being in a kind of alliance, guarding the palanquin that involves loving workmanship by the daughters.

The narrative section, 5:2–8, hinges on the Shulamite opening the door, despite her foregoing protests that she was undressed and washed for the night. This change of mind is not explained in the text, just as the disappearance of her love by the time of her opening goes unexplained. Bergant observes that even the woman's reluctance to open, despite her explanations, is "puzzling."[15] However, Bergant also notes a consistency of imagery between the woman as keeper of her own "door," and the image of her as an enclosed garden and sealed fountain in the preceding macro-section of the Song. In the present section, "Here she is enclosed once more, and it is up to her to open to whomever she chooses."[16] Even where the Song provides narrative, it seems to withhold full development of that narrative in order to re-evoke themes, and sometimes to play on those themes in contrasting rather than repetitive ways. Are we to conclude that the woman was unusually slow to respond to her love and things did not end well as a result? Or are we to conclude that her venturing out to seek her love is a risky option? It is questions like these that have more hope of an answer than filling in the details of the Song's sparse fragments of narrative. But it is precisely questions like these that require the Song to be a unity with an authorial intention guiding the development of its themes. The current thesis does not attempt to propose a detailed explanation of thematic development, but it does seek to argue that the Song was written to present such a thematic development rather than present a narrative, as with the historical allegorical readings or with the dramatic readings. And it seeks to show that it is themes revolving around the woman's psychology that are the main thread of the discourse of the Song. Up to the current point in the Song, the man's voice can be explained as ancillary to that of the woman, but the following extended sections involve much more input from him, prior to the Song's closure, again with the woman's voice predominating. As such, it is in our next chapters that our thesis is really put to the test.

15. Bergant, *Song of Songs*, 62.
16. Ibid., 62–63.

12

The Man's Second *Waṣf* (Song 6:4–10)

You are beautiful, my friend, like Tirzah,	יפה את רעיתי כתרצה a	6.4
Lovely, like Jerusalem,	נאוה כירושלם b	
Awe-inspiring, like a host with banners.	אימה כנדגלות c	

Turn your eyes away from me,	הסבי עיניך מנגדי a	6.5
For they overwhelm me.	שהם הרהיבני b	
Your hair is like a flock of goats	שערך כעדר העזים c	
Which descend from Gilead,	שגלשו מן הגלעד d	
Your teeth like a flock of shorn ewes	שניך כעדר הרחלים a	6.6
Which come up from the washing	שעלו מן הרחצה b	
With all of them bearing twins	שכלם מתאימות c	
Without any miscarriage among them,	ושכלה אין בהם d	

[Like threading of scarlet your lips	כחוט השני שפתתיך a	6.7
And your speech is pleasing,]	ומדבריך נאוה b	
Like a slice of pomegranate your brow	כפלח הרמון רקתך c	
From behind your veil.	מבעד לצמתך d	

There are sixty queens,	ששים המה מלכות a	6.8
And eighty concubines,	ושמנים פילגשים b	
And maidens without number.	ועלמות אין מספר c	

My dove, my perfect one, is unique.	אחת היא יונתי תמתי a	6.9
She is unique to her mother.	אחת היא לאמה b	
She is pure to the one who gave birth to her.	ברה היא ליולדתה c	

Daughters saw her and blessed her,	ראוה בנות ויאשרוה d
Queens and concubines, and praised her.	מלכות ופילגשים ויהללוה e

---

Who is this looking down like the dawn,	מי זאת הנשקפה כמו שחר	a 6.1
Beautiful, like the moon,	יפה כלבנה	b
Pure, like the sun,	ברה כחמה	c
Awe-inspiring, like a host with banners.	אימה כנדגלות	d

ROBERTS READS THIS WHOLE section as a *waṣf*,[1] and considers it to be a distinct macro-section because of the *inclusio* formed by 6:4c and 6:10c (אימה כנדגלות), or more broadly the strophes 6:4 and 6:10.[2] He notes that anthologists and others divide the section into two parts,[3] 6:4–7 and 6:8–10, where yet other writers consider the current section together with 6:11–12 and sometimes beyond that as well.

Clearly there is a change of voice between that of the Shulamite answering the daughters of Jerusalem to that of the man, though there is no simple textual cue as to why the voice changes, unless 6:4–10 follows 6:3 as 4:1–7 may follow 3:11. The man's first *waṣf* might follow 3:11 as though it were a song of Solomon's joy; likewise this second male-spoken *waṣf* follows the man entering his garden and pasturing among the lilies. The verses do also copy a substantial portion of the first *waṣf* word-for-word. After the fact, the man's speech fits with context, but there is no certain cue for its onset.

This lack of cuing is not the case where the man speaks in earlier parts of the Song. In other parts he is involved in dialogue with the woman, often initiated by her, or his voice only arises as she quotes him as part of painting a picture of a larger scene. Also, as I have just mentioned, the first *waṣf* and the man's ongoing invitation and praise in chapter 4 can be read as answering to the typology of Solomon's joy on the day of his wedding. This is still the case, even if we do not read it as the dramatists do, as being literally the wedding song of Solomon.

Two words, however, are suggestive that this second *waṣf* from the man does follow naturally from the woman's intimate disclosures of chapter 5. The colon that marks the *inclusio*, if indeed it is an *inclusio*, speaks of the

---

1. Roberts, *Let Me See Your Form*, 230.

2. Ibid., 231.

3. Roberts cites Gerleman, *Ruth/Das Hohelied*, 180–87 as an example typical of anthological accounts of the verses.

woman as being awe-inspiring (אים) in 6:4c, and this is followed up in 6:5b by the man speaking of being overwhelmed (רהב). This language is at odds with Exum's sense that love is something the woman gives and the man takes. It is more in keeping with the woman's perennial issues of unfulfilled longing, and her weakness in the face of consummation in chapter 2 or in the face of separation in chapter 5.[4] The man of 6:4-10 is not so composed as to be taking what he wants, so much as being overwhelmingly thankful for what another wants to give him.

As we saw a reworking of the adjuration refrain in chapter 5, here we see a reworking of the *waṣf* of chapter 4. In the earlier context, as with the earlier contexts of the adjuration refrain, we interpret the text according to the positive context of consummation. But here, as with the modified adjuration refrain of chapter 5, we interpret the *waṣf* in a context where the lovers are apart again. There is insufficient elaboration of the narrative to place them exactly. He vanishes mysteriously only to reappear here just as mysteriously, but we are nonetheless left with both voices returning to speaking as though in longing rather than fulfillment. Part of this may be a deliberate effect intended by the poet to suggest that consummation is never perfectly complete. It has its moments, but these only lead inevitably to a renewal of longing over time. Passionate romantic love, sexual love, has an addictive cycle about it. This is true even without physical consummation, which gives the Song room to tastefully explore the topic without being explicit.

One striking element of the current *waṣf* is the man's use of the third person for the woman in verse 6:9. He uses an independent pronoun three times. It is this feature, together with others in verses 8 to 10 that give the second half of the *waṣf* quite a different flavor to what we have come to expect from the man. Is he addressing the daughters of Jerusalem or the audience? It is probably better to take the enallage as stylistic; not dissimilar to the woman's voice in 1:2-4. But just as the man uses the first person of himself much less than the woman uses it of herself, so he uses the third person of her less than she uses it of him. This fits with the woman having a dialogue with her intimates, the daughters of Jerusalem, whereas his dialogue is only with the woman uniquely. Indeed, it is the uniqueness of the woman that is pointed up in the third person passage, and that might

---

4. "Once again [in 5:8] the woman claims that she is 'faint with love.' Here too there is a difference in what this phrase implies. In the earlier passage (2:5), it was the pleasure that she enjoyed while in the arms of her lover that made her faint. Here her emotion is just the reverse; she is faint from longing for him. We see here how the context of the poem can produce a meaning quite different from that of the same words in a completely different context." Bergant, *The Song of Songs*, p. 67.

explain the poetics of the usage. The man is pointing away from the woman to queens and concubines and maidens (even the daughters of Jerusalem), and selecting out of that crowd just one unique "blessed" and "praised" woman for consideration. The third person forms help open up the context before narrowing it down again with the closing question, "Who is this?" Who is this out of so many who is so outstanding? It is clearly a rhetorical question, as hyperbolic as the language of which it is comprised and as the language found throughout the *waṣf*.

From an SDRT perspective, the current passage is uniformly elaborative, as was the first *waṣf*. It is hard to decide on a relation between 6:4–10 and its prior context. Perhaps it is a *Narration* with an implicit ". . . and then he said . . . ." Or perhaps it is an *Elaboration*, where the *waṣf* denotes the same kind of thing that pasturing among the lilies denotes: the man engaged in enjoying the pleasure of his lovemaking with the woman. Each literary gloss is a different way to evoke the idea of a man enjoying a romantic relationship. The first describes him from the outside as acting: pasturing among the lilies; the second describes him from the inside, allowing his own voice to articulate what is on his heart.

Carr titles his consideration of this passage "The lover overwhelmed."[5] Fox observes the expansive nature of the second part of this second *waṣf*: "He is expanding on the praise he gave her earlier (4:1–3), to which he adds the praise of queens and concubines, projecting his own impressions onto observers who are both neutral and noble, though hypothetical."[6] Goulder has Solomon as the speaker of the verses: "He opens by restating . . . and . . . repeats . . . his praises . . . But this time . . . the point now is that she outshines all his harem."[7] Murphy notes the man "speaks as if appearing out of nowhere,"[8] and that "there is no obvious explanation of the repetition" of the lines from the *waṣf* of 4:1–3. Longman stresses that the verses assert the uniqueness of the Shulamite, "the woman's beauty is superior, even unique, compared to the beauty of others—represented by the sixty queens, eighty concubines, and countless young women."[9] He also stresses the emotional affect induced by the woman's beauty on the man: "The woman's beauty is so great that it shakes the man to the very core (v. 5)."[10] Bergant titles her

---

5. Carr, The Song of Solomon, p. 159.
6. Fox, The Song of Songs, p. 150.
7. Goulder, The song of fourteen songs, p. 49.
8. Murphy, The Song of Songs, p 177.
9. Longman, Song of Songs, p. 177.
10. Ibid.

discussion of the *waṣf* "A Woman of Singular Beauty."[11] She also notes the change from second to third person: "The *waṣf* (vv. 5–7) is spoken directly to the woman; a boasting song is spoken about her (vv. 8–9)."[12]

Garrett reading the Song as a unity goes so far as to suggest that:

> The verbatim or near-verbatim repetition here of certain lines from chap. 4 is more than the use of formulaic expressions. By repeating his previous words of admiration for her, the man implies that his desire for the woman is undiminished by his having consummated the relationship with her. She is still as desirable to him as ever before.[13]

This is a nice thought, but more than our methodology can confirm. Hess summarizes the section in ways that point up the things we and other writers have discussed above: the expansive nature of the *waṣf* by contrast with 4:1–7 in the terms it uses to describe the woman's unique influence over the man.

> Here the words summarize and generalize the beauty of the female to emphasize the power of that beauty, a power that can overcome her lover's defenses with a gaze of her eyes and that can evoke praise from the finest women in the land. The central statement, that of v. 9, emphasizes how unique and therefore how special the female is.[14]

Jenson, a contemporary champion of the allegorical reading of the Song, before exploring allegorical possibilities notes how abrupt is the transition to talk of the "harem." "The final part of the passage begins with an abrupt comparison of the woman with the members of an unidentified harem. Indeed the transition is so abrupt that one is tempted to treat also verses 8–9 as a separate poem."[15]

Assis is not quite a dramatist, though he is explicitly a narrativist, seeing the Song as having a beginning, middle, and an end—a real plot—with a climax in the center. He explains the similarity between the *waṣf* of chapter 4 and the current one in terms of their contexts in the narrative plot he discerns in the Song.

---

11. Bergant, *The Song of Songs*, p. 75.
12. Ibid., p. 77.
13. Garrett, *Song of Songs*, p. 229.
14. Hess, *Song of Songs*, p. 205.
15. Jenson, *Song of Songs*, p. 63.

Is it possible to explain the close affinity between these poems? It seems to me that the position of the two poems in their context can shed light on the issue. The descriptive poem in 4:1–7 comes before the climax of the book, the intimate assignation between the man and the woman. After the realization of the great desire in Unit III comes the ebb of the relationship and a separation between the man and the woman, which are described in Unit IV. Now we have reached Unit V. In this Unit the reader expects to see a resolution of the tension that was created between the realization of the great desire in Unit III and the distancing in Unit IV. Unit V begins with descriptive motifs of the woman by the man which recall the man's courtship of the woman which had led to their rendezvous in Unit III. The intention of the clear analogies between the two poems is to recall the memory of the peak moments of their meeting. Through these analogies the poet wants to give the reader a feeling that the loving couple is now, after the ebb, about to have another meeting, like that in Unit III, which has now been recalled in the reader's consciousness, and that after the peak and the ebb, another peak is on the way. The reader now has only to expect how the relations between the lovers will develop, after they had made a good start.[16]

Assis views his methodology as form critical, but it is here also discourse analytical. With modifications, there is scope for our own reading to appropriate some of his insights. Yes, there is something climactic about 5:1e–f and the text that leads up to it; and, Yes, if the Song is the work of a single author, or even a single redactor, some purpose seems likely to the almost verbatim reworking of the first part of the earlier *waṣf*.

As the last section of the Song, 5:2—6:3, is in many ways the best evidence that the Song is written from the woman's perspective, so the current section is perhaps the most difficult to fit with that thesis. Yet it is not so difficult as it may seem, and if achieved becomes some of the strongest evidence for the case, since it is the least likely candidate for the purpose. For a start, the woman is the topic of the man's *waṣf*. So we are not dealing with verses that really exclude the woman, just verses that give us rare insight into the man's emotional disposition. The contrast needs to be with the woman's *waṣf* about the man, and her intimate self-disclosure in that context. The core difference is that the woman explicitly addresses the daughters of Jerusalem, and so represents the poet addressing the audience in a way the rest of the Song has accustomed the reader to expect. In the current case, the man does indeed revert to the third person to make a point, but in a way

---

16. Assis, *Flashes of fire*, pp. 195–96.

that seems abrupt to some commentators. This is precisely because there is no explicit audience, other than perhaps the Shulamite, for us to interpose between poet using the man's voice and the reader. But the Shulamite as audience is enough to take the edge off the apparent incongruity of the man suddenly addressing the audience. She is explicitly not only topic but also audience for the first half of the *waṣf*. By 7:1, the Shulamite is again explicitly the audience. Unless we are missing something in 6:11–12, which is a real possibility, we do need to conclude that the man's voice in the Song is almost entirely addressed to the Shulamite and not to the daughters of Jerusalem, and through them to the audience of the Song. This passage has the beginnings of a possible counterexample to the thesis of the current study, but that counterexample does not ultimately materialize.

The current passage, the man's voice, also seems to depend on the foregoing text, the woman's voice, in all the three subsections of her words. Our chapter's verses, 6:4–10, answer to the woman's leaving her bed to seek her love in 5:2–8. Here is the one we are to tell she is weak with love for. The verses also answer to the woman's *waṣf*, in 5:9–16, even perhaps by half of it reverting to the third person, echoing her own style of praising her love. Finally, the verses 6:4–10, the man's second *waṣf*, answer to 6:1–3 where he is described as pasturing among the lilies. In some ways, as striking as is the man's appearing out of nowhere to speak, he has actually been summoned in 5:2–8, conjured by description in 5:9–16, and declared to be present in 6:1–3.[17] Thus our current text is rhetorically related to all major elements of immediately preceding context, and there is a degree of coherence evident in the dynamic flow of the Song. Additionally, the masculine voice remains a foil for the feminine voice. In the wording of the Song it is the man who calls the woman out into public space, but as regards speech, it is the woman who induces the man to articulation. Neither is so much a social norm—certainly not the latter—so much as they are patterns sustained in the unfolding poetry of the Song that come to give character to the male and female voices. Suffice it to say, in the current case, however, that the man's speech in 6:4–10 is no exception to the general rule that the woman's voice is controlling the flow of the discourse.

Landy's second essay on the Song in his book *Paradoxes of Paradise* has much to say about the relationship between the lovers, which is the title

---

17. This idea is due to Exum: "The woman has just finished a long speech in which she first tells a story about seeking her lover and then 'finds' him by praising his physical charms, one by one, until she has successfully conjured him up. In response the man now launches into a long speech in which he conjures her up by praising her physical charms in detail, not once but twice." *Song of Songs*, p. 214.

of its second chapter.[18] Having much to say about a relationship between characters is not surprising in an analysis of a love poem, and especially a long love poem. However, he notes that with the Song we often have to translate from incidents to the general composition.

> One does not approach the relationship as in a narrative, where characters are distinct, identifiable in a more or less realistic and continuous story. The lyric is broken up into many snatches or glimpses, typical amorous moments, just as the characters appear through multiple conflicting personae.[19]

The relationship between the lovers is indeed the topic of the Song, but it is handled in a different manner to that of a continuous narrative. Landy works to "make a few limited generalizations that give us at least a silhouette of coherent figures."[20]

> First of all, since it is most obtrusive, is the dominance of the woman as a voice and presence. It is not simply a question of quantity, though the woman has more to say; it is also that the combined speeches of both lovers, with their different styles and concerns, focus on defining her image. Of the two lovers, only the woman is preoccupied with self-definition, from "I am black and/but comely" in 1.5 to "I am a wall" in 8.10. Only she uses the first person pronoun "I" as if to stress this introversion (Goitein 1957:302).[21]

"If there is a story in the Song of Songs, it is of her self, shaped by suffering, pleasure and self-reflection."[22] This stands out precisely because of its contrast with the man, who "hardly talks about himself at all; there is no self-examination, and hardly any narration. He shows us the woman from the outside."[23]

The remaining macro-sections of the Song, according to Roberts's accounting, present only one further sustained potential challenge to our thesis that the Shulamite's voice shapes the discourse. The final two macro-sections are clearly shaped by the Shulamite's voice, so provide no challenge, and the section immediately following the current one is too brief and too obscure to do so. It is only in 7:1–11 that the man's voice rings out once

---

18. Landy, op. cit., pp. 55–129.
19. Ibid., p. 60.
20. Ibid.
21. Ibid.
22. Ibid., p. 61.
23. Ibid.

more with potential to challenge the Shulamite's voice as decisive for determining the overall flow of the text. There are complexities to all these sections that we will explore in due course, and it is highly significant that the Shulamite completes the man's final sentence in 7:10, which we will discuss further as we consider the text of 7:1–11 in detail. But we can already see at this point that the man's contributions to the Song are essentially only found in chapter 4, here in chapter 6, and then in chapter 7. Were they written differently, were he more introspective, then he would make himself more of a character available to a reader, akin to that of the woman, and there would be scope, despite his lower volume of words, to be considered as having as much depth as the woman, truly an equal party to her in the discourse. But this is not what we find. He is a complementary character, sure enough, but strictly a complementary character, i.e., he completes the woman's self-description of "her" romantic relationship, mainly as a mirror of her *external* appearance. She tells us of her internal life; he does not tell us about that, nor even of her external life other than her appearance. It is not even clear that he offers a character reference for her; he tells us only what we would presumably know for ourselves were we to view the Shulamite for ourselves. She defends her own reputation.

Such at least is the case that I trust appears to a reader of this thesis as plausible, and a parsimonious explanation for much of the character of the text of the Song as we encounter it. It could be advanced as an argument in its own right for the unity of the Song, but the likelihood of it being the correct reading is all the stronger if the unity of the Song is suggested along independent lines first. The dynamic semantics of the Song appear to argue for its coherence, confirming the formal poetic cohesion suggested by Roberts's analysis. Given this unity, the centrality of the Shulamite appears to be part of the poet's deliberate message, as I will discuss in the conclusion to the thesis. For now, though, we shall turn to the most cryptic verses of our text.

13

Obscurities (Song 6:11–12)

I went down to the garden of walnut trees,	אל גנת אגוז ירדתי a	6.11
To see the fresh growth of the valley,	לראות באבי הנחל b	
To see if the vines had budded,	לראות הפרחה הגפן c	
And the pomegranates bloomed.	הנצו הרמנים d	
I did not understand; my soul	לא ידעתי נפשי a	6.12
Set me beyond the chariots of my noble people.	שמתני מרכבות עמי נדיב b	

ROBERTS TREATS THESE TWO difficult verses separately to other sections, because his methodology cannot connect them either to the preceding or to the following macro-sections.[1] Several scholars view the verses as standing independently as a unit,[2] though many do attach them to foregoing or later text that they view as being contiguously connected.[3]

Carr asserts, "Commentators are unanimous that this verse is the most difficult in the Song, and one of the most difficult in the Old Testament."[4] Exum calls the verses a "notorious crux."[5] She considers that it is "impossible to say with any confidence how these verses are related to the preceding

---

1. Roberts, *Let Me See Your Form*, 246.
2. Ibid.
3. Gordis, *The Song of Songs and Lamentations*, p. 67 attaches these verses to 6:10; Gerleman, *Ruth/Das Hohelied*, 94 attaches them to 7:1.
4. Carr, *Song of Songs*, 165–66.
5. Exum, *Song of Songs*, 222.

and following verses."⁶ It is not even clear whether the man or woman is speaking, let alone to what purpose. She refers the reader to Pope for detailed treatment of the various interpretations that have been offered. Pope considers each of verses 11 and 12 separately, and starts his report of interpretations with the Targum, which views the intended sense of the verse as describing Yahweh entering the second temple to see if Israel has become fruitful in good works.⁷ Midrash Rabbah makes many moral suggestions based on the allegory of the nut tree. These are numerous and detailed, but represent more of a way of using a canonical Scripture for moral homiletics than the linguistic exercise of determining the intended sense of the text in its original context. The Jewish allegorical readings teach us more about what was valued in Rabbinic scholarly community than what the text meant to its first hearers. Likewise, Christian allegorical readings teach more about the theological propositions that were valuable to the Christian teachers who allegorized from the Song. Generalized, Pope notes they taught that

> The vines flourish when children are brought up in the faith of the Church and the pomegranates bud when the perfect edify their neighbors by example, holy conversation, preaching, and exhibition of good works.⁸

Augustine provided a tripartite analysis of the significance of the nut, where Rabbinic writers had seen quadripartite significance in the same object. Augustine was concerned to reinforce the doctrine of the union of the divine and the human in the person of the Christ.⁹ The rabbis were concerned to stress the moral and practical virtues of studying the Torah.

Pope starts by acknowledging of verse 12: "This verse is generally conceded to be the most difficult in the Canticle and it continues to vex translators and commentators."¹⁰ This is an ancient problem, since both the Septuagint and Vulgate "tamper" with the text, according to Pope. The Septuagint takes *nephesh* (נפש), "soul," as subject of the verb "to know" (ידע), hence changing first person to third person. The Vulgate changed the semantics of the second verb. Pope actually despairs of reviewing the full diversity of exegesis of the verse, reverting to offering seven English translations, all of which differ from one another.¹¹ "A thorough history of

6. Ibid.
7. Pope, *Song of Songs*, 583.
8. Ibid., 584.
9. Ibid.
10. Ibid.
11. Ibid., 585.

the exegesis of this verse would be a major undertaking."[12] Pope does offer several pages of review of modern attempts to emend the text in various ways, but without such offerings winning his approval. Exum's attempts to at least ascertain whether verse 11 is spoken by the man or by the woman are more concise and useful for the current thesis, but are still inconclusive.

The main clue regarding speaker in 6:11 discussed by commentators is that similar wording is repeated in 7:13. Exum presents literary arguments for and against the proposal that it is the woman speaking in 6:11, as she does in 7:13. Without the words being in the woman's voice in 7:13, we might expect them to be the words of the man, because it is the man who goes to the garden in the Song, especially in chapter 4. Reference to a garden here is thus suggestive that it might be the man we continue to hear speaking, following on from his words in 6:4–10. I actually prefer this reading, since the wording of 7:13 is importantly different to 6:11. Yet again we see that the very same words repeated in the Song, but in different contexts, can have different preferred interpretations. In 7:13 the context is of both lovers joined together, and together they go "to see if the vines have budded and the pomegranates bloomed." This allows that the woman could be understood to be agreeing to accompany the man in this activity, rather than her initiating it *ex nihilo*. It could presume that 6:11 is still activated in the minds of the audience, explaining 7:13. So, I am also inclined to read 6:11–12 as probably fitting with following context rather than preceding context for this reason. However, Exum raises a subtle but powerful point regarding the style of discourse of the woman and the man. The point is valuable in itself, irrespective of how it bears on resolving what will probably remain an ultimately intractable question.

Exum sees that 6:11 is a mini story, as the woman rather than the man is wont to tell. This is part of what this thesis means by proposing that the Song is articulated from the woman's perspective. The narrative mode is dynamic, and the Song has a dynamic semantics—an unusually constructed style of discourse, but a recognizable one nonetheless. It is the woman, rather than the man, who normally progresses the discourse of the Song. The man "stands and delivers" his lines in a more static way. Exum says he looks at and describes what he sees as his characteristic mode of speaking. There are exceptions to Exum's characterizations, but the patterns are widely attested.

The verses are too short to really fit them to patterns and allocate them to speakers accordingly. The meaning of 6:12 is also beyond the scope of the methodology or purpose of this thesis to establish. SDRT analysis simply observes the obvious about 6:11; that the subordinate cola stand in

12. Ibid.

an *Explanation* relation to the matrix clause of going down to the garden. Without better comprehension of the meaning of 6:12, neither the relation of 6:12b to 6:12a, or even its colometry, can be certain, let alone the relation of the verse to prior context. Given this impasse, I will gloss over these verses in the larger analysis, to which we will return by moving on to a consideration of verses 7:1–11.

14

The Man's Third *Waṣf* (Song 7:1–11)

Come back, come back, O Shulamite!	שובי שובי השולמית a	7.1
Come back, come back, so we can gaze on you!	שובי שובי ונחזה בך b	
Why would you gaze on the Shulamite,	מה תחזו בשולמית c	
As if on the dance of the two camps?	כמחלת המחנים d	

How beautiful your feet in sandals,	מה יפו פעמיך בנעלים a	7.2
Daughter of a nobleman!	בת נדיב b	
Your curved thighs are like jewels,	חמוקי ירכיך כמו חלאים c	
The work of the hand of an artisan.	מעשה ידי אמן d	
Your navel is a round bowl,	שררך אגן הסהר a	7.3
That never lacks blended wine.	אל יחסר המזג b	
Your belly is a mound of wheat,	בטנך ערמת חטים c	
Surrounded by lilies.	סוגה בשושנים d	
Your two breasts are two fawns,	שני שדיך כשני עפרים a	7.4
Twins of a gazelle.	תאמי צביה b	
Your neck is like a tower of ivory.	צוארך כמגדל השן a	7.5
Your eyes are pools in Heshbon,	עיניך ברכות בחשבון b	
By the gate of Bath-Rabbim.	על שער בת רבים c	
Your nose is like the tower of Lebanon,	אפך כמגדל הלבנון d	
Looking out over Damascus.	צופה פני דמשק e	
Your head upon you is like Mount Carmel,	ראשך עליך ככרמל a	7.6
And the hair of your head like purple.	ודלת ראשך כארגמן b	
A king is bound in the braids.	מלך אסור ברהטים c	

How beautiful you are, and how pleasant,	מה יפית ומה נעמת a	7.7
My love, the daughter of delight.	אהבה בתענוגים b	

Your stature resembles a palm tree,	זאת קומתך דמתה לתמר a	7.8
Your breasts clusters of fruit.	ושדיך לאשכלות b	
I say, "I will go up the palm tree,	אמרתי אעלה בתמר a	7.9
And take hold of its branches."	אחזה בסנסניו b	
Let your breasts be like clusters of grapes.	ויהיו נא שדיך כאשכלות c	
	הגפן	
And the fragrance of your breath like apples.	וריח אפך כתפוחים d	
Your mouth is like the best wine,	וחכך כיין הטוב a	7.10
Going straight to my love,	הולך לדודי למישרים b	
Flowing over the lips of those who sleep.	דובב שפתי ישנים c	

I belong to my love, and his desire is upon me.	אני לדודי ועלי תשוקתו a	7.11

ROBERTS DIVIDES THE CURRENT macro-section into two parts: The First Description of the Woman (7:1–7) and The Second, Interactive Description of the Woman (7:8–10). He sees these opened by The Shulamite Strophe (7:1) and closed by a version of the mutual possession refrain (7:11).[1] He further divides the first description into four parts and the second description into two strophes. He notes: "There is little agreement about whether the units contained herein actually belong together as a structured section. Nor is there agreement about the exact boundaries of the elements included within it to begin with."[2] The most controversial verses are 1, 7, and 11. Each of these can be viewed as opening, or closing, or as independent.

Carr considers the current verses within a very large macro-section stretching from 5:2 to 8:4. He considers that whole section to be "the working out of the relationship established in the previous chapters."[3] He calls the whole section "Lost – and Found". Within that large picture, he sees verses 1–6 working together as a unit. Carr treats the second part of our current verses, 7:7–10a, as a separate subsection of his macro-unit, and stops before the voice changes to that of the woman in 10b. Ultimately, this is

---

1. Roberts, *Let Me See Your Form*, 259-91.
2. Ibid., 260.
3. Carr, *Song of Solomon*, 144.

not so different to Roberts, though Carr is free to allow his interpretation to guide his divisions. Roberts considers verse 7 together with the earlier subsection and adds 10b–11 to the second one. Carr actually proposes a change in voice from 7:7 to 7:8. He reads verses 1–6 as being the voice of "onlookers," whereas 7–10a he reads as being the voice of the man. He also places this in the context of an inferred plot: "After the detailed description of the beloved's beauty by the onlookers, the lover himself again adds his praise, speaking out of the remembering of the wedding night just past (cf. 1:8; 4:10)."[4] Carr's assumed plot and his interpretation of 7:1 inform one another in coming to this conclusion.

> The onlookers (wedding guests?), who would stay for several days to celebrate, urge the bride to put in an appearance and join the festive dance. She demurs with a question, Why me? [7:1b], and they reply [7:2–6] with their praise of her beauty. Her lover/husband then joins in with his adoration [7:7–10] and she renews her commitment to him [7:11–8:4].[5]

Carr's reading, like that of many others concerned to reconstruct a plot from the Song, and to keep that plot in harmony with the sexual propriety of the Hebrew Scriptures, needs to find a way to explain how the Song consistently speaks to an audience about consummation as though it is in the present or recent past, and as though it is something surprising and unexpected, almost as though marriage had not actually rendered it a natural expectation. This pushes such interpreters towards a narrow setting of an assumed wedding, perhaps with a week-long celebration afterwards. The key element pushing such interpretations, however, is their attempt to take the sense of the present seriously, and to read the text as sequential narrative.

There is enough flexibility with the way consummation is described in the Song that several such readings are possible, finding *first* consummation at different points in the text. Marriage, of course, is then read in to the text somewhere earlier. The highly stylized nature of the text of the Song makes this possibility relatively easy. However, as we have been mentioning in passing at various points, it is quite possible, indeed preferable, to view much of the text that is suggestive of consummation as being events of the past, just described with exuberance as though they were present. There is no shame in the lovers being public about them. The voices of man and woman in the Song evoke a picture of newlyweds reflecting on courtship,

4. Ibid., 175.
5. Ibid., 167.

first consummation, and early marriage, repeated consummations, yet in such a way as the imagery can be appropriated by any affectionate couple with more maturity in years of marriage. Love is not so much asserted as being evergreen; it is being illustrated as evergreen. If the Song can be taken as a poetic version of a morality play, it is not that marriage must precede consummation that is being taught to us, but rather that consummation must *repeatedly* follow marriage. Better still, it is describing rather than prescribing marriage as a *state* of ongoing consummations, and of periods of separation and longing.

Having said that, Carr and narrative readings are not necessarily the preferred option, making for more assumptions than are necessary. What they do illustrate is that a dynamic reading of the second half of the Song is possible. They share with the current reading, and in a more direct way, a view of the text as being coherent, albeit that some degree of inference is necessary to come to that conclusion, or to support that assumption.

Fox, like Roberts, approached the current verses with caution: "The results of any attempt to divide 6:11—7:14 (and beyond) into units are inevitably uncertain."[6] He views 7:1 as one "of three obscure verses, 6:11, 6:12, and 7:1."[7] On the basis of the first and second person plural forms of 7:1b and 7:1c respectively, and their obvious exclusion of the Shulamite by referring to her, Fox concludes that in 6:11–12 the Shulamite has already excluded herself from those who come to be talking about her, and indeed come to be calling her back to join them. Roberts sees something similar, specifying the speakers in 7:1a-b as the daughters of Jerusalem and in 7:1c-d as the man, correcting the girls for their lack of respect for the Shulamite.[8] Fox rejects Gordis's (and Carr's) suggestion that the background for these early verses of chapter 7 is that of a wedding as "strange."[9]

Goulder's Song 11 (of 14 songs) is almost identical in its span to that of Roberts. He leaves the mutual possession refrain to open his Song 12. He has the Shulamite speaking on her own behalf in 7:1c-d. As a modern dramatist, he considers that in this section: "The plot moves forward."[10] The key element in that is the "princess" becoming the new favorite out of the whole harem.

---

6. Fox, *Song of Songs*, 155.
7. Ibid.
8. Roberts, *Let Me See Your Form*, 261.
9. Fox, *Song of Songs*, 155.
10. Goulder, *Song of Fourteen*, 55.

Murphy thinks that in the early verses of chapter seven "the identity of the speaker(s) is left vague."[11] In verses 8–10, however, it is "certainly the man who continues."[12] Murphy sees "several literary genres . . . tied together by the sequence of the dialogue."[13] His span for this dialogue extends all the way up to 8:4, so includes considerable material spoken by the woman, including the mutual possession refrain (modified) and the adjuration refrain. What is significant to us is this perception that the sequence of dialogue lends coherence to otherwise distinct literary set pieces. There is something that scholars like Carr and Murphy sense in the text that leads them to hold together disparate elements on the basis of higher-order unity. Carr is aided by reading text in the context of a possible plot line, into which particular spans of text can make contributions; Murphy is more pushed simply by the pattern of a flowing dialogue; but both scholars find a type of coherence, over and above the cohesion that they also detect at lower levels of text organization.

Longman takes an identical division of the verses to Roberts, and he helpfully articulates a rhetorical relation between the *waṣf* of 7:2–6 and the praise poem of 7:8–11, where he notes his understanding of the relationship between the poems is *causal*: "The man's description of the woman's physical charm leads him to express his admiration and his desire for sexual union."[14] In SDRT terms, this is *Result*(7:2–6,7:8–11). Likewise, Longman sees a rhetorical relation between the *waṣf* and the preceding context of 7:1 in which the issue of gazing at the Shulamite is raised: "we take the reference to gazing at the Shulamite as the motivation for the description of her physical charms that follow."[15] It could be read that the *waṣf* actually answers what is more than a rhetorical question in 7:1c–d. In this case we have the motivation for the *waṣf* in answering the question: Why gaze? Because she is beautiful. This is a question–answer pair or *QAP*(7:1c–d,7:2–6). As such Longman proposes a dynamic coherence over the course of the unit that is clearer than is the coherence over the broader span of 5:2—8:4 or even the whole Song, per Carr, but also in our own view—just without assuming, with Carr, a narrative dynamic to the overall text of the Song.

Bergant notes: "The introductory verse of this *waṣf* yields several interpretations, all of which depend upon how the preceding passage was

---

11. Murphy, *Song of Songs*, 185.
12. Ibid.
13. Ibid.
14. Longman, *Song of Songs*, 188.
15. Ibid.

understood."[16] This is, of course, true of all text, but especially noticeable in difficult and highly underspecified texts like the Song of Songs, and it motivates our own attempt to discern rhetorical relations between new spans of text and their prior context. Bergant sees a macro-section of the Song stretching from 6:4 to 8:4, and within this section treats our current verses in two separate parts (also leaving off the woman's completion of the man's sentence and her repetition of the mutual possession refrain). She sees a distinct dynamic progressing the text between 7:1–6 and 7:7–10a. "Most [interpreters] maintain that the celebration of the woman's beauty found in the preceding *waṣf* now moves into anticipation of enjoying the delights that her alluring body can afford."[17] Perhaps key to the way the text evokes this movement is the way the man seems to approach the apparent inaccessibility of the woman: he is not deterred; he will climb the palm tree and grasp hold of its fruit.[18] The reader senses movement in the text because what has been praised already is now being put forward as the goal of future action, even imminent action.

Garrett is of the school that reads from 7:2 as far as 8:4 as being what seems to its proponents to be a macro-unit of the Song. At a lower level of abstraction, he separates the two sections we are looking at, the *waṣf* from the praise poem, but offers a clever antiphonal reading of verse 10, where the voice of the man returns in 10c, with the woman retaining 10b and 11 as her lines. He sees a purposeful dynamic movement in the text, as do other writers, but argues it from what he sees as being implicit in the reverse direction of the *waṣf*: its movement upwards from feet to hair.

> First, the man gives an admiring description of various parts of the woman's anatomy; he then graphically describes his strong intention to make love to her. Notwithstanding the attention he gives to her breasts in the second stanza, vv7–9, the movement here from the feet upward is meaningful. The goal and focal point of the first stanza are her face and head. This focus conveys an appreciation for the person and personality of the woman since the face, more than any other part of the body, physically presents a person's individuality.[19]

Hess considers verses 2 to 10a as a unit, but views verse 6 as the "middle verse" of a *waṣf*, though he notes it is "followed by a general exclamation of

16. Bergant, *Song of Songs*, 80.

17. Ibid., 88.

18. "The inaccessibility of the woman's charms does not deter the passionate man." Ibid., 89.

19. Garrett, *Song of Songs*, 250.

beauty" in verse 7.[20] He sees what others consider to be a praise poem to be "the climax of the *waṣf*" and connects it with the other *waṣf* passages and the whole Song. He observes that it is the breasts and mouth of the woman that are praised in the climax of the current *waṣf*, which also occurred in the first *waṣf* but not the second addressed by the man to the woman; and the man's mouth is praised at the beginning of the Song (1:2), with the woman's breasts being the last things praised (8:10).[21] These are formal and stylistic observations, like those of Roberts. They are static and tell us of the poetics of textual cohesion. They are a fair argument towards the inference of poetic unity for the Song, but Hess goes further and notes, with others, that the dance of verse 1 points us towards the feet, which is where we start in the *waṣf*. So Hess says of verse 2 and following that the text

> also forms a logical connection with the statements of the chorus that immediately precede it. There the emphasis was on gazing at the female's dance. Although the whole body may be active in a dance, there is no dance without the motion of the feet. The feet and legs for a natural bridge between a vision of the female dancing and the *waṣf* that begins with this text.[22]

Exum takes some time to critique the reading of the *waṣf* and praise poem as parody or comedy, grotesque or pornographic.[23] This leads her to an assertion of rhetorical relationship between the *waṣf* and the concluding or reopening verse 7, which she sees as summation.[24] Her point seems to be that although there may be various associations that the metaphors of the *waṣf* might have raised for an original audience, these need to remain compatible with the overall statement that is unequivocal about the delight of beauty. Exum is skeptical of both the setting of a dance, and the suggestion by some writers that the dance is performed naked. She says, "This is to build one unwarranted assumption on another."[25] And she makes the profound and nicely stated point that in the Song, "the body is clothed in metaphors that obscure as much as they promise to reveal."[26]

---

20. Hess, *Song of Songs*, 211.

21. "The Song begins by relishing the joy of the male's mouth (1:2) and concludes with the breasts of the female as the last physical attribute mentioned (8:10)." Ibid.

22. Ibid., 211–12.

23. Brenner 1993; Whedbee 1988; Black 2000; Boer 1999: Ibid., 57–70.

24. "One may allow for an ambivalence toward beauty in the Song . . . while still recognizing the individual metaphoric descriptions in these verses as illustrating the summation in v. 6." Exum, *Song of Songs*, 231.

25. Ibid., 232.

26. Ibid.

Jenson thinks "It probably makes little difference whether we take these verses [7:1–5] and 7:6–9 as two poems or one."²⁷ But he considers the two sections separately. He also describes the praise poem as offering the most "bluntly lustful" verses in the Song.²⁸ There is something to be said for this honest appraisal, and it bears on our study of gender across the Song as a whole. Although the man says little about his own internal world, in fact he uses the first person rarely, he uses it here in his talk of climbing the palm tree, and we have a striking disclosure of appetite. The man is not just an appreciative spectator with regard to the woman; he is moved to be an active agent towards her body. Here we have an echo of 5:1a–d, in some ways more directly evoking the passion of consummation from the man's perspective. Jenson's comment helps to remind us that there is something mysterious about the physical nature of consummation. It is not just a matter of idealized appreciation at a distance, nor even of pleasant, gentle, glancing contact between two enamored individuals. At some point there is an even more profound physical engagement. The Song does not really explore that beyond the niceties I have already mentioned, but is bold enough to suggest it here (and more elliptically in 5:1a–d). The Song seems to want to encompass the full gamut of the course of eroticism, but chooses to place its focus on the niceties. Perhaps this too reflects a feminine perspective. There is much debate about female sexual appetite. Ancient Near Eastern songs are not shy about it,²⁹ even if they are not entirely realistic about it. The Song is restrained in its way, though clearly being unashamed about real feminine physical longing, and that of masculine appetite also. Jenson gives eroticism an allegorical theological discussion that I will not critique here.

Our verses are essentially the same as Assis's Poem 3 of his Unit V, where he leaves out the mutual possession refrain. He breaks the section into five subsections, not too dissimilarly to Roberts's analysis. Assis is concerned with various details of exegesis while discussing the opening "Shulamite Strophe," as Roberts calls it, and while considering the *waṣf*. But with verses 6 and 7 Assis is confident they "are a direct continuation of the previous description (vv. 2–6 [1–5])." This is appreciation of a rhetorical relation: *Continuation*(π[7:1–5],π[7:6–7]). Assis also feels there is significance in a change in propositional content, though he does not call it that. Rather than describing the Shulamite from the outside, objectively as it were— albeit that objectivity can be highly questioned—the man shifts

---

27. Jenson, *Song of Songs*, 73.

28. "There is no other poem in the Song quite so bluntly lustful as verses 6–9." Ibid., 76.

29. See Leick, *Sex and Eroticism*.

to making assertions that more definitively imply his personal involvement and the impression the Shulamite is making upon him.[30] These verses are transitional to the man going yet one step further and asserting that he will act in response to what he feels about what he is seeing. This is more than poetic cohesion, as in the parallel descriptive metaphors of the *waṣf*; it is a form of textual coherence.

All told, and without needing to assume a narrative, commentators see a broad progression of thought, perhaps with increasing intensity of intimacy, across the second half of the Song. This is seen even within the current macro-section, and among several scholars it is seen to continue up to 8:4. It is to these additional verses we now turn, since Roberts views 7:11 to 8:4 as the next, and antepenultimate, macro-unit of the Song.

---

30. "So far in the poem the man had referred to the woman's beauty, but now he is referring to her impact on him." Assis, *Flashes of Fire*, 211–12.

15

Pivot Piece (Song 7:12—8:4)

Come my love! Let us go out to the fields.	לכה דודי נצא השדה	a	7.12
Let us spend the night among the henna.	נלינה בכפרים	b	
Let us go to the vineyards early.	נשכימה לכרמים	a	7.13
Let us see if the vine has budded,	נראה אם פרחה הגפן	b	
The blossoms have opened,	פתח הסמדר	c	
The pomegranate bloomed.	הנצו הרמונים	d	
There I will give my caresses to you.	שם אתן את דדי לך	e	
The mandrakes give off a fragrance,	הדודאים נתנו ריח	a	7.14
And at our door are all excellent things,	ועל פתחינו כל מגדים	b	
Both new and also old.	חדשים גם ישנים	c	
My love, I have kept [them] for you.	דודי צפנתי לך	d	

Who would give you to be like a brother to me,	מי יתנך כאח לי	a	8.1
Nursed at my mother's breasts?	יונק שדי אמי	b	
Were I to find you outside I would kiss you,	אמצאך בחוץ אשקך	c	
And they would not scorn me.	גם לא יבוזו לי	d	
I would goad you, I would bring you	אנהגך אביאך	a	8.2
To the house of my mother; she would teach me.	אל בית אמי תלמדני	b	
I would give you spiced wine to drink,	אשקך מיין הרקח	c	
From my pomegranate juice.	מעסיס רמני	d	

| His left hand is under my head, | שמאלו תחת ראשי | a | 8.3 |

And his right arm embraces me.	וימינו תחבקני	b
I put you under oath,	השבעתי אתכם	a 8.4
Daughters of Jerusalem,	בנות ירושלם	b
Do not arouse nor awaken Love,	מה תעירו ומה תעררו את האהבה	c
Until it so desires.	עד שתחפץ	d

ROBERTS VIEWS THIS MACRO-SECTION as comprised of two units: Vineyards in Bloom (7:12-14) and To My Mother's House (8:1-4).[1] He sees each of these as "a well defined and cohesive segment."[2] However, he considers there are features about the two segments that suggest they should be joined together. Additionally, he believes that all of 7:1—8:2 can be analyzed as a single passage of four strophes in which the woman describes her longing for the man. Thus, the two divisions marked in the translation above are alternative ways of viewing the text, not two conjoined divisions: they are disjunctive not conjunctive. This is not the only place in the Song where Roberts sees potential for such structuring by the poet, of overlapping sections at higher levels of abstraction than the strophe.

Roberts argues that 8:1-4 follows from 7:12-14 in several ways. The first and most objective is grammatical, via pronominal anaphora: first-person pronouns refer to the woman throughout, and second-person pronouns to the man.[3] This is because no change of discourse referent is marked, by a vocative say, to change the denotation of the second-person suffixes.[4] There is a subtle shift in the first-person pronouns, however, from inclusive plural cohortatives to singular cohortatives. But this does not involve a change of speaker.

Roberts finds more poetic evidence in the "repetition of נתן as a key word."[5] This, he sees as linking 7:12-13 with 7:14 and both to 8:1-2 due to its occurrence in 7:13e, 7:14a, and 8:1a. Imagery also features in the poetic cohesion, with the vineyards and pomegranates of the invitation verses being echoed by the longing to serve wine and pomegranate juice in the

---

1. Roberts, *Let Me See Your Form*, 292-317.

2. Ibid., 292.

3. "The first person speech of the woman addressing the man directly in the second person continues all through 7:12-14 and right into 8:1-2." Ibid., 312.

4. "Given ... the absence of any vocative or other identification of the man in 8:1, it is virtually impossible to read the second person masculine singular suffix on יתנך in 8:1a in any other way than anaphoric to the man of 7:12-14. The same would then apply to all the following masculine suffixes in 8:1-2 as well." Ibid., 312-13.

5. Ibid., 313.

maternal home. More subtly, though Roberts thinks more powerfully, there is a pattern of closures across the strophes where they conclude with the woman offering her love.

> Each of these three segments consists of the woman expressing a wish for union with the man, and each finds its closure in the woman making some kind of promise to give herself to the man. 7:12-13 closes with the unadorned monocolon, שם אתן את דדי לך, while 7:14 ends with the symbolic צפנתי דודי/ישנים גם חדשים לך, and 8:1-2 likewise ends symbolically with אשקך מעסיס רמן/ מיין הרקח.[6]

There is also evidence of a cyclic pattern, with regard to the contrast of indoors and outdoors, not unlike 2:8-17. In this case it is the woman inviting the man both outdoors and indoors, but the same pattern of ending where things began is in evidence.[7]

Roberts is not as confident of the close connection of 7:12—8:4 to 7:1-11 as are some other authors. He lists a range of words and images that are common to both sections, but feels they are too ubiquitous across the Song to signal cohesion at this particular point. He observes:

> More broadly, one could certainly say that 7:1-11 depicts the longing of the man for the woman, while 7:12—8:4 depicts the corresponding longing of the woman for the man. But the focus of this study is to find structural features that would support just such a thematic correspondence.[8]

Roberts wants to base associations on structural features strictly prior to exploring thematic associations, given the license with interpreting its thematic significance the text allows to the reader. He does assert, however, that were the enigmatic 6:11-12 to be the opening verses of a macro-section including 7:1-11, then the case for viewing 6:11—8:4 as a structural unit would be "substantially enhanced."[9] This should once again give us confidence in Roberts's discipline in apportioning text to macro-units, while also giving us a caveat that even his rigorous methodology cannot deliver certainty about textual boundaries.

Roberts has reasserted his "static" approach to discerning textual cohesion. We need to turn once more to commentators to pick up more discussion of dynamic semantic threads in the Song. Roberts offers an almost

6. Ibid.
7. Ibid., 314.
8. Ibid., 315.
9. Ibid.

artificially "pure" methodology, whereas intuition suggests that a poet expected readers to discern "movement" in the Song and to use that in grasping its intentions. Our commentators are not all alike in the prominence they give to remarking on textual "flow." There is a tendency to establish the static semantics of particular words and significance of particular phrases as the bulk of their observations. But scholars who view the Song as a unity provide considerably more consideration of features pertaining to dynamic semantics than do anthologists, for the obvious reason that anthologists do not admit that there is any dynamic flow of content under a poet's overarching goals in communication.

Carr is a classic example of a commentator who sees an all-encompassing development over the course of the Song; in particular he sees it as providing the framework for a narrative. Without pressing too hard for details of that narrative, it is a plausible reading. It may not be the intended sense of the second half of the Song, even if the Song is the unity I am arguing it actually is, but by accident or by indirect consequence, the second half of the Song does permit of itself that it be read as an abstracted narrative. If the Song is an abstracted presentation as I am arguing, the contours of that abstraction can be read by some as more concrete narrative. A poor workman blames his tools, it is said, which intends to apply broadly and abstractly, though it is envisioned by most hearers quite concretely.

Carr captures what I would consider to be the flow of the second half of the Song in a strong statement about the crux the current verses offer in interpreting that second half. He considers that the section "capsulizes the fourth major division of the Song. The girl, who has been the object of the attention of the assembled crowd, now responds with a reaffirmation of her commitment to her lover/spouse."[10] Clearly Carr has a broad idea of a plot with concrete characters here, however an abstracted reading with similar characteristics is possible. The voice that dreamed of her lover visiting by night and then vanishing is here reunited with him. Indeed, there is even talk of spending the night together outside the home, and the day together inside it. This is fine as an abstract typology of lovers' longings without it needing to progress a plot with fictional characters, and certainly without it needing historical characters.

To their credit, allegorical readings of the Song did grasp that the text was not tightly associated with the persons of the voices that speak in its verses. However, the Song is not concerned about the sorts of details that make stories coherent; in particular, it is not concerned with precise timings. If it is not a story, then it is not an allegory. It is, however, concerned with

---

10. Carr, *Song of Solomon*, 178.

matters beyond the voices it purports to present. It is every woman's song and every man's song. The voices are stripped down to represent only what they need to represent as types of lovers anywhere. Or so I read it. There is a dynamism to what the voices express that accords with the actuality of the ebb and flow of romantic and erotic love. Sometimes this dynamism comes across as a backwards and forwards complementarity of give and take, other times it comes across as cyclical. Time in the Song is "relationship time." It is not measured by the ticking of a clock but by the beating of hearts. It is not suggestive of an absolute and linear, external and objective measurement, but a relative and circular, internal and subjective experience. But again, this is how I read the Song, which allows us to find accord with commentators like Carr as regards a very generalized dynamics of textual presentation, without following him all the way to narrativization. By contrast with our reading, Carr ties down the Song to being more specific than I consider the text actually requires, or in fact supports.

Fox divides the text of our verses such that the verses from chapter 7 are separate from those of chapter 8. Regarding the verses from chapter 7, he argues:

> This unit is not disjunct from the preceding one, for the boy's detailed praise of his beloved in 7:2–7 implies an intention to enjoy her charms (vv. 8–10aα).... The youth expresses his desire to embrace his beloved and to enjoy her love (7:8–10aα), and she immediately consents and invites him to go with her to the countryside (10aβ–14). The formulation of her invitation closely resembles his invitation in 2:10–13 and the statement in 6:11 about the nut garden.[11]

The resemblances are important in the Song for maintaining a sense of consistency of characterization, not just for marking structural cohesion. The way Fox divides the verses accords with his own comparisons with the ancient Egyptian love poems, which lead him to consider all of 6:11–7:14 as one single "Admiration Dialogue" (Fox's capitals).[12] The dialogue gives a dynamic feel to the verses. They make sense in juxtaposition rather than as isolated units. It may be remembered that Roberts was also tempted to divide the text this way, but could not do so, only because of the Spartan nature of what his methodology allows as evidence of structural unity. What is surprising, then, about Fox's division is the heavier weight he gives to dividing 7:10b–7:14 from 8:1–4. He argues for this because he reads a change of scene between the sections. He takes the setting more literally than this

11. Fox, *Song of Songs*, 162.
12. Ibid.

thesis's reading as I have just described it: "The scene has changed. The lovers are now lying in each other's arms, perhaps in the bower to which the Shulammite invited her lover in the preceding unit. The setting is like that of 1:9–17, 2:1–7, and probably 3:7–11."[13] Again Fox is strong on seeing the global thematic correspondences across the Song, it is just that he pushes to make them more concrete in their immediate contexts than is absolutely necessary. Does it really matter where the Shulamite and her love are as verses 7:12 to 8:4 are uttered? Nor does it really matter when. What matters more is to whom she is speaking and what she is conjuring up as a picture of her desires. The more precisely we seek to situate the voices of the Song, the more we fragment the text, as Fox does here in driving a small fault-line between parts of the same speech.

On the continuum of literal appropriation of the Song, Fox is less tied to narrative literalism than Carr, and Carr is less tied to it than Goulder with his dramatic reading of the Song. Goulder begins his Song 12 (of 14) with the mutual possession refrain, but ends his consideration of the current verses, like Roberts, at 8:4. Goulder is so literal he is historical: "The dance has brought the princess's triumph; she has eclipsed even the beautiful Abishag."[14] Unfortunately, such literalism is fruitful for speculation that depends on the veracity of the assumed correspondence with reality. In Goulder's case, his assumptions give room for a logical explanation for the woman's invitation:

> It is she that the king desires, and she capitalizes her advantage. As long as he merely visits her in her room, as in chs. 4–5, she is on a par with any of the other women. What she wants is a unique and public position, to be Queen, because she loves him (8.6), as well as for any more worldly motives. So she suggests that they go out into the country.[15]

With such readings, it is not hard to find a dynamics to the semantics as the text is propelled along by the narrative, with an elapsing of time as part of the embedded presuppositions, as narrative requires. Additional rhetorical relations associated with logical rather than chronological associations are also possible. Although I cannot use Goulder's reading to establish rhetorical relations that I would accept in my more conservative methodology, I can abstract a little from Goulder, and it harmonizes with Carr and other scholars. The king's desire that Goulder speaks of provides a context for

---

13. Ibid., 166.
14. Goulder, *Song Of Fourteen*, 61.
15. Ibid.

the woman's expressions of reciprocal desire, whether we consider her to be a princess or not. If we strip the voices of the royal fiction the Song does use, we are left with a real basis for a rhetorical relation of *Result*: because you desire me and because I desire you, so then let us spend the night in the countryside. Fox appreciated the dynamic sense that connects the articulation of requital of proffered love such that the king's speech, then the woman's speech, are naturally joined as more than just the sum of two independent parts. Goulder goes one step further and sees consummation as a natural third step in dramatically related units. Carr views the verses as a second consummation. They can read like part of a plot that extends over the course of the majority of the second part of the Song of Songs.

Like Fox, Longman divides the current verses into two poems separated over the chapter break. Two reasons for this seem to be implicit in what Longman says in his commentary: firstly the genre of the two poems is different; and secondly the setting is different. Both points are reminiscent of Fox. Longman sees 7:12–14 as "a love monologue—more specifically, an invitation from the woman to the man."[16] However he sees 8:1–4 as "yearning for union".[17]

Bergant is also of the same school as Fox and Longman in viewing the text as two poems. Rather nicely, she points to a sense of progression in the text created by the lexical semantics of 7:12–13. "The first three cohortative verbs invite movement toward a place; the fourth is an invitation to observe the signs of spring. The purpose of the visit to the vineyards is to observe the progress of spring growth." This is an additional insight; over and above the one noted by other writers that the cohortative mood answers with assent to the man's praise poem with his asserted desire to climb the palm tree. It is not just the mood of the verbs but their content that evokes continuity through progressing the psychological drama of the text, whether we physically situate it in the sort of terrain of which it speaks or not.

Our verses correspond to Garrett's fourth and fifth stanzas in his "The Second Song of Mutual Love." "The fourth and fifth stanzas (7:12—8:2), describing the woman's longing for the man, are her response to the tenor's [man's] words in the first two stanzas."[18] Hess says, "The interruption of the female nevertheless continues the thought of the male. The wine imagery that describes their kisses becomes a picture of an intimacy that they share as it flows back and forth between them." So he sees a coherence that can be described as a continuation of thought. Additionally he sees the imagery

16. Longman, *Song of Songs*, 199.
17. Ibid., 203.
18. Garrett, *Song of Songs*, 238.

working to suggest properties of an abstraction, namely the lovers' mutual desires for each other. This is something that flows, and does so backwards and forwards, cyclically.

Exum, like Fox, Longman, and Bergant, divides our current verses over the chapter division. She sees a clear rhetorical relation between what she terms the woman's reply and the man's long speech that precedes it.[19] "Since 7:10-13 is clearly her reply to his desire for intimacy expressed in vv. 7-9, these verses belong with the preceding."[20] Exum notes how this second scene of consummation is the reverse of the first in 4:16—5:1. There the woman invited, and the man acquiesced enthusiastically. Here the man invites, and the woman acquiesces enthusiastically. The woman's invitation of 7:12-13 is a direct response to the man's expressed desire in 7:8-10a. Her words complete the picture of consummation in the current verses where his words, and those of the chorus, completed the picture at the conclusion of the first half of the Song. This is suggestive that we are, in fact, dealing with the highest order of structuring in the Song. The Song began with a dialogue about love, and then with the woman's testimony about the progress of her own amorous adventures which concluded with the chorus acknowledging the consummation. The Song then takes a second perspective: the lost and found perspective rather than the distant love perspective of the first half of the text. This second perspective, partly by night, complements the first perspective, mostly by day. Then the Song returns to a final dialogue about love, or so Exum reads the final chapter. The other structural observations are my own. In introducing chapter 8, Exum summarizes the Song thus:

> The woman and the man have each had two long speeches, in which the poet portrays them speaking in distinctive ways about their mutual desire and infatuation. In this way the poet presents a vision of love that includes both points of view, a woman's and a man's. Now the Song returns to the mode in which it began, with a series of shorter speeches, where the voices of the woman, the man, and the women of Jerusalem intermingle, and the transitions from one topic to another are more abrupt. Like 1:2—2:7, these verses are a kind of montage.[21]

Jenson divides our macro-section over the chapter division like many others, though he does so with a view that chapter 8 is a kind of appendix, provided by the editor of the final form of the Song, in which disparate

---

19. "Once again, the man's long speech gives rise to the woman's invitation to love." Exum, *Song of Songs*, 240.

20. Ibid.

21. Ibid., 244.

material is all passed on for posterity, but in which no particular cohesion or coherence can be assumed to obtain.[22] Assis divides the text very much like Roberts does, though with the addition of the mutual possession refrain as opening, and the Who is this? verse at 8:5 as closing the unit, Poem 4 of Unit V by Assis's reckoning.[23]

As a generalization, our authors tend to see the current verses as coherently connected, even cohesively connected, to foregoing context, particularly as expressing the requital of sentiment and a culmination in the fulfillment of consummation. In most cases, this is also held to be so anticipatory to treating the bulk of chapter 8 as dealing with grander, more climactic, and generalizing themes in the Song. Chapter 8 is also commonly seen as manifesting a different genre of lyric poetry to that of the bulk of the Song, excepting its first chapter and a half. There are more abrupt changes of topic and conversational turns. But of all the remaining verses of chapter 8, beyond the four we have already considered, the next verses 8:5–7 are commonly seen as the climax of the Song, and to these verses let us now turn our own consideration.

---

22. "One possibility is that we accept the appearances: chapter 8 looks very much like the repository of an editor's frustration.... The alternative suggestion is that the bits of chapter 8 shift about so in topic and personae because they are dialogue." Jenson, *Song of Songs*, 83.

23. Assis, *Flashes of Fire*, 219–23.

16

Love (Song 8:5–8:7)

Who is this coming up from the desert,	מי זאת עלה מן המדבר	a	8.5
Leaning on her love?	מתרפקת על דודה	b	
Under the apple tree I roused you,	תחת התפוח עוררתיך	c	
Where your mother conceived you,	שמה חבלתך אמך	d	
Where she conceived and gave birth to you.	שמה חבלה ילדתך	e	
Set me like a seal on your heart,	שימני כחותם על לבך	a	8.6
Like a seal on your biceps.	כחותם על זרועך	b	
For love is strong like death,	כי עזה כמות אהבה	c	
Jealousy stubborn like Sheol.	קשה כשאול קנאה	d	
Its arrows flaming arrows,	רשפיה רשפי אש	e	
The very flame of Yahweh.	שלהבתיה	f	
Many waters are not able	מים רבים לא יוכלו	a	8.7
To quench love	לכבות את האהבה	b	
Nor rivers overwhelm it.	ונהרות לא ישטפוה	c	
If a man gave	אם יתן איש	d	
All the wealth of his house for love,	את כל הון ביתו באהבה	e	
It would certainly be despised.	בוז יבוזו לו	f	

ROBERTS HAS TO ADMIT that "the unity of 8:5–7 is much disputed,"[1] and that "it must be acknowledged that any cohesive reading of these verses depends ultimately on their relationship to the larger context of the Song."[2] In the

---

1. Roberts, *Let Me See Your Form*, 318.
2. Ibid.

layout above, although I agree with Roberts and others that 8:7 is actually prose, the colometry of Krinetski has been adopted for the sake of consistency with the rest of the poem where lines are shorter than 8:7A = 8:7a–c and 8:7B = 8:7d–f.[3]

Citing Delitzsch and others,[4] Roberts reports that "the identification of 8:5–7 as a unit is not particularly unusual." However he also reports that the more dominant view over the course of the twentieth century has been to see 8:5a–b and 8:5c–e as "unconnected fragments," though there has been support for seeing 8:6–7 as a "complete poem."[5]

Most tellingly for our current research questions, Roberts warns that "Even among those inclined to holistic readings of the Song, the perception of a lack of coherence in 8:5–7 often leads to some part of the verses being assigned either to what precedes or to what follows."[6] However, he ends his introduction to the section with the positive affirmation that, regarding our current section, "Quite a number of interpreters treat it as the first segment of 8:5–14 so that it is the introductory statement to the concluding section of the Song."[7] Roberts cites Carr, Elliott, and Dorsey as examples.

Carr acknowledges that "there are difficulties in any suggested grouping" for the subsections of the final chapter of the Song.[8] However, he finds it decisive that,

> The third section of the Song (3:6—5:1) opens with these same words [מי זאת] as this one and they both close with the consummation of love. Here we have a series of short references to, or comments from, all the participants in the Song—the companions, the brothers, King Solomon, the mother, the beloved, and the lover—as the commitment of the lovers to each other is re-affirmed and re-consummated.[9]

As Roberts states, a sense of coherence regarding the final chapter depends heavily on seeing it as rhetorically connected to the prior context of the Song. Instead of what we have often found, that relatively short macro-units have an internal cohesion and coherence, which then can be extended to fit with the prior context of the Song in a coherent manner, here we find

---

3. See Krinetski, *Kommentar zum Hohenlied*, 219.
4. Delitzsch, *Commentary*, 10.
5. Roberts, *Let Me See Your Form*, 319.
6. Ibid.
7. Ibid., 320.
8. Carr, *Song of Solomon*, 185.
9. Ibid.

the inferring of coherence works the other way around. However, as Carr indicates, there are many such thematic cues to suggest chapter 8 is one part of a greater whole and not an independent anthology of fragments.

Fox considers 8:5a–b as the conclusion of the preceding section. Were we to feel free to edit the received text, it would involve moving 8:5 so it concluded 8:1–2, but it is also evident that those verses complete their own section in an already harmonious way. Fox also comments that 8:5c–14 "lack clear continuity from one to the next" but that they "together form the Song's finale" anyway.[10] He gives particular attention to the question of a rhetorical relationship for 8:5c–e, both with respect to its prior context and with respect to how the later context might relate to it.[11] Fox reads 8:5a–b as the words of the daughters of Jerusalem in response to the Shulamite's abjuration towards them, and 8:5c–e as a prelude and rationale for her adjuration towards her love. Hence, in SDRT terms, Fox reads $Result(\pi[8:5c-e],\pi[8:6-7])$. In his own words,

> I include it [8:5c–e] in this unit rather than having it close the preceding one because after the exclamation by the girls of Jerusalem (v. 5a), an isolated remark by the Shulamite to the boy seems awkward, whereas this remark may be an appropriate prelude to her demands for everlasting faithfulness: we have made love; now our bond is eternal.[12]

Fox also notes that 8:6–7 stand in a logical relationship to the rest of the Song. They generalize beyond the personal experience of the Shulamite, or the feminine voice the poet has created. The rest of the Song has established that the woman knows what she is talking about when she makes the assertions of 8:6–7.[13]

Goulder finds less trouble than others weaving his narrative through the final chapter of the Song, armed as he is with the ability to supply the details needed to make such a reading plausible. The princess who had called the king to spend the night outside the city now returns in 8:5 with her plan having achieved its purpose: "She is his favorite consort, acknowledged in public."[14] The connection between 8:5 and 8:1–2 that other scholars of

---

10. Fox, *Song of Songs*, 167.

11. "It is not clear what relation 8:5b has to its context, whether looking ahead or looking back." Ibid.

12. Ibid.

13. "Vv. 8:6–7 are the highpoint of the poem, its moment of greatest generality, where it draws a conclusion from the particular experience it has been portraying." Ibid., 168.

14. Goulder, *Song of Fourteen*, 65.

the Song-as-unity school sometimes seek is more readily available to the dramatist. Goulder's ingenuity also makes it possible for him to connect verse 7 with verses 8 and following, by proposing a conversation between wedding guests and a wealthy but unwise suitor for a ten-year-old girl.[15] Given his narrative, he extends his thirteenth of fourteen songs as far as verse 10, though I will not follow his reading here.

Murphy has a good deal to say about verses 6 to 7. Like Fox and many commentators he describes them as a "climactic point."[16] He also notes that the strong imagery of flames in verse 6 is matched by its opposite, water, in verse 8.7a–c. Murphy makes no attempt to connect verse 5 in whole or in part with verses 6 to 7, though he does begin his final section at verse 5. He does however comment that verses 8 to 12 seem to him to "introduce a vignette that has no obvious connection with the immediate context."[17] He sees the purpose of the lines as providing "a kind of inclusio, echoing the reference to the 'brothers' of 1:6."[18] Importantly, I think, he attributes all the lines to the woman, providing a direct quote of what was said of her when she was younger, but to which she now replies as one who is now mature.[19]

Our current section is identical with Longman's twentieth poem in his division of the Song. Longman provides a rhetorical motivation for 5a–b preceding 5c–e in that the chorus could be reintroducing the woman before she continues into the next part of her speech, this time with such sweeping but convincing generalizations about love.[20] Bergant's first observation regarding these verses considers the rhetorical issue: "Neither the form nor the content of this poem flows easily from what precedes it."[21] Like Roberts, Longman, and Bergant, Garrett also considers 8:5–7 as a unit. He asks the same questions as other authors regarding the rhetorical occasioning of the current verses: "Why does this canto begin with an arrival motif? It does not seem a necessary or even congruous introduction to the somber analysis of the power of love that follows."[22] Although he asks the question, he finds an

---

15. Ibid., 66.
16. Murphy, *Song of Songs*, 196.
17. Ibid., 198.
18. Ibid.
19. "The lines of vv 8–12 are to be attributed to the woman, who first quotes directly words spoken about her, when she was younger, by her brothers (vv 8–9) and then replies to the (v 10) from the viewpoint of a mature woman." Ibid.
20. "The function may be in part to provide a poetic echo with 3:6 as well as to introduce the woman who then speaks in verses 5b–7." Longman, *Song of Songs*, 206.
21. Bergant, *Song of Songs*, 96.
22. Garrett, *Song of Songs*, 256.

answer along the same lines as Longman: "on close inspection, it is an appropriate prelude to the woman's song."[23] Also like others, Garrett points to echoes of 3:6–11, where the "arrival canto" serves, in his view, to giving the couple "a grand and heroic status."[24] Where 3:6–11 suggests grandeur, 8:5–7 suggests the wisdom of intimate knowledge. Garrett proposes that "the choral prelude informs the audience that the woman has sufficient stature and experience to make the profound pronouncements on love that follow."[25]

Rather nicely, Garrett comments that: "The comparison to death probably has another implication: to marry is to give one's life to another, and whoever marries has died to all others."[26] After elaborating on this point, he goes on to suggest that it is not really a new point the Shulamite is making, but one consistent with the abjuration she declaims thrice to the daughters of Jerusalem, not to take love lightly. In other words, there is a rhetorical relationship between the climactic verses of the Song and the theme of the adjuration refrain. Garrett says, "It is hardly out of character for the woman's part to give the audience such warnings about the power of love. She has already three times called on the Jerusalem girls not to arouse love before it is ready (Song 2:7; 3:5; 8:4)."[27]

Hess also treats 8:5–7 as a unit within his final macro-unit of the Song, though he separates out the voice of the chorus in 5a. He is also open to the brothers' voice in the next section to be quoted by the woman. Like most writers he sees this section as forming "a climax to the entire book," though he goes an extra step in suggesting they "provide an interpretive key for understanding the whole of the Song."[28] The current thesis is inclined to agree with Hess's bold proposal, as we shall discuss when summarizing what the methodology we are using suggests about the Song. Hess proposes:

> The focus of the Song may be found in the following two lines. The strength of love likened to death, and the difficulty of overcoming death is likened to the hold of the grave (8:6). No mere mortal can escape these, and thus they testify to the most powerful forces known. Their power cannot be overcome and their hold is eternal.[29]

---

23. Ibid.
24. Ibid.
25. Ibid.
26. Ibid., 257.
27. Ibid.
28. Hess, *Song of Songs*, 235.
29. Ibid., 238–39.

Hess actually sees the key to the Song as caught up with theological implications at this point, as the quote above begins to suggest. As love is portrayed as belonging properly in the realm of the forces of life and death, so it enters into the realm of metaphysics and theology. There is merit in this argument and, in fact, I share the same convictions as Hess about the matter, but I believe the Song can still be grasped without making the theological "leap." Verse 6 can still be seen to be key to the Song via mundane linguistic and literary techniques, and can still have a practical wisdom application without appealing to theology. Several writers do observe that it is not just allusions to Yahweh that might be found in this verse, but other gods from the pantheons of ancient Israel's cultural neighbors. It is not accidental that the minds of commentators are drawn this way. The text is pushing to identify erotic love *of the right sort*, with the right sort of awesome Providence. The Song reaches a crescendo in calling for a covenant commitment associated with erotic and romantic love. Calling for divine witness to such human coupling is the very opposite of shame. That the Song reaches such a crescendo says much about where the rest of the text may have been pointing all along, just in case we had missed the point.

Exum treats 8:5a-b separately to 8:5c-7, with a focus on how 8:5a-b are reminiscent of 3:6. She views the function of the verses thus:

> By having the women of Jerusalem speak at this point, the poet once again reminds us of the presence of an audience, onlookers who participate in the unfolding of the lovers' relationship, and so encourages the readers' involvement.[30]

It is one of the several strengths of Exum's commentary that she consistently presents the text in terms of how it mediates communication between poet and audience, without either really being so obvious to casual inspection. Exum is particularly strong in pointing out that neither the woman's nor the man's voice is that of the poet. This is something that is less clear in dramatic and narrativistic readings of the Song. In such readings there is a tendency to conflate the words of the discourse participants with those of the poet. The Song works at one step removed from typical discourse, which normally has author and audience interfacing directly. This is important in thinking through how the dynamics of the overall presentation are worked out through the medium of the sequence of cameos of which the Song is comprised.

---

30. Exum, *Song of Songs*, 248–49.

Regarding the key verses, 6–7, Exum speaks of them as the "Song's only didactic pronouncement."[31] Again she notes:

> Although the poem's readers are its ultimate audience, within the world of the poem this succinct credo on the subject of love is spoken by the woman to her lover, for the poet is too subtle, and too good a poet, to preach or teach, and never addresses the reader directly.[32]

Even more tellingly, Exum pinpoints how these verses serve as a key to the whole of the Song. It lies in the personification of love as a force with a will of its own. This connects the climactic verses of 8:6–7 to the abjurations not to arouse this force until it so has a will of its own.

> Love in these verses is virtually personified as a force that contends with cosmic powers. This personalizing of love is also found in the adjuration refrain in 2:7, 3:5, and 8:4, where love is spoken of as having a will of its own. The affirmation of love's power here thus sheds light on the meaning of the oath the woman places upon the women of Jerusalem: the injunction not to awaken love is rhetorical, for why seek to rouse love, since love cannot be denied when it wishes to be roused.[33]

Jenson splits the current verses into three fragments: 8:5a–b, 8:5c–e, and 8:6–7. He is explicit about seeing the first two as fragments: of 8:5a–b he says, "since this verse appears in the jumble of chapter 8, we perhaps should treat it as a fragment";[34] and of 8:5c–e he says, "in the case of these lines there can be little doubt that here is a mere fragment."[35] He is inclined to read 8:6–7 as a poem, though he states "we can not be sure that they are."[36] He does make an effort to check rhetorical relations and logical coherence regarding the woman's assertions in verses 6 and 7: "It is not at first sight obvious that these lines, grand as they are in poetic form and rhetoric, actually support her claim. We must work step by step."[37] He actually concludes: "The woman's claim is justified only if love defeats death, if lovers' jealousy defeats the grave."[38] This is a carefully discerned insight, and one lost in other writ-

---

31. Ibid., 249.
32. Ibid.
33. Ibid.
34. Jenson, *Song of Songs*, 86.
35. Ibid., 88.
36. Ibid., 90.
37. Ibid.
38. Ibid., 92.

ers following the high-flown spirit of the verses with more enthusiasm than critical appraisal.

Assis takes 8:6–7 as Poem 5 of Unit V in his division of the text of the Song, and titles his whole commentary with an image drawn from verse 6. Assis draws attention to the contrasts between the generalized conception of love in these verses and the personal intimacy of the rest of the Song, in particular noting that, "It is surprising that in the only poem that is intended to explain love, the description of love is in such harsh terms. The poet uses concepts such as death and the nether-world, jealousy, conflagration and enormous amounts of water."[39] This leads Assis to question just what motivates the poet to speak, what vision of love is the "take home message"? He decides:

> The poet here has not intended to present the pleasures of love. Even the satisfaction that love provides is not the theme of this poem. The love which the poet speaks of in this poem is the yearning for what is long awaited. The grand concepts the poet employs here represent the passions experienced by the lover who has powerful desires for his beloved.[40]

Assis sees the poet surprising the reader, "raising the stakes" to the topic of love, and presenting memorably a striking seriousness to the subject.

Such are the insights of recent commentators on the Song concerning features of the text that bear on our research questions. I will have more to say about these in a concluding summary with discussion, prior to considering the work of André LaCocque, and then concluding the whole thesis. But before we can pursue those matters, we will see what we can make of the final macro-unit of the Song.

---

39. Assis, *Flashes of Fire*, 241.
40. Ibid.

17

Postscript (Song 8:8–8:14)

We have a little sister,	אחות לנו קטנה	a	8.8
And she has no breasts.	ושדים אין לה	b	
What should we do for our sister,	מה נעשה לאחתנו	c	
For the day which she is spoken for?	ביום שידבר בה	d	
If she is a wall,	אם חומה היא	a	8.9
We will build a battlement of silver upon her.	נבנה עליה טירת כסף	b	
And if she is a door,	ואם דלת היא	c	
We will enclose her with planks of cedar.	נצור עליה לוח ארז	d	
I am a wall,	אני חומה	a	8.10
And my breasts are like towers.	ושדי כמגדלות	b	
Thus I have become in his eyes,	אז הייתי בעיניו	c	
Like one finding peace.	כמוצאת שלום	d	

Solomon had a vineyard in Baal Hamon.	כרם היה לשלמה בבעל המון	a	8.11
He gave the vineyard to guards,	נתן את הכרם לנטרים	b	
Each to bring a thousand silver pieces for its fruit.	איש יבא בפריו אלף כסף	c	
My vineyard is for me alone.	כרמי שלי לפני	a	8.12
The thousand are for you O Solomon,	האלף לך שלמה	b	
But 200 for those who guard its fruit.	ומאתים לנטרים את פריו	c	

You who dwell in the gardens,	היושבת בגנים	a	8.13

Companions are listening.	b חברים מקשיבים
Let me hear your voice!	c לקולך השמיעיני

Flee, my love,	a ברח דודי	8.14
And liken yourself to a gazelle	b ודמה לך לצבי	
Or a young deer stag	c או לעפר האילים	
On the mountains of balsam.	d על הרי בשמים	

ROBERTS ONLY TREATS THE final verses of the Song together for the purposes of discussing whether they have relationships to one another, not because he is asserting that they do. In fact, he finds "three separate units which do not have any transparent relationship to each other."[1] As other writers note also, "the section bears a resemblance to the opening section of 1:2—2:7, which also consists of a series of segments—mostly strophic pairs—with no transparent connection to each other." Mind you, again as other writers comment, there do appear to be allusions in the final verses to themes addressed in the opening verses.[2] If the opening and closing verses do not seem to cohere among themselves, there does appear to be a hint of them being associated with one another. The current thesis will present the view that the Song is frequently circular, very likely deliberately so, and that this is supported by associations between the opening and closing verses. But it must be admitted that such a view is not transparent when viewing either the opening or closing verses in isolation, as we are doing in the current sequential examination of the text.

Roberts names the three sections: What Will We Do for Our Sister? (8:8–10); Solomon's Vineyard and Mine (8:11–12); and Upon the Mountains of Balsam (8:13–14). He considers each as though it were an independent major unit of the Song, identifying internal connections, contiguous connections, and remote connections for each, as he did for the sections within 1:2—2:7. Regarding the first section, Roberts finds it strongly internally cohesive,[3] yet with "no structural or poetic basis at all for connecting this segment with the preceding segment of 8:5–7."[4] From an SDRT perspective, there is not such a dire state of affairs, as it is quite reasonable to infer that either *Background* or *Flashback* or both connect the verses about the

---

1. Roberts, *Let Me See Your Form*, 340.

2. "This overall resemblance is sharpened by the presence of some features in this section that seem to be allusions to features in 1:2—2:7." Ibid., 341.

3. "The lack of a strong opening, however, is compensated for by exceptionally strong cohesion in this segment, clearly marking its boundaries as well." Ibid., 350.

4. Ibid., 151.

brothers with the grand climactic verses about love. With respect to remote connections, Roberts reports that "The role of brothers in authority over a sister certainly recalls the brothers of 1:6, and a number of interpreters have found an inclusio for the Song as a whole in the two references."[5] He cites Rendtorff and Dorsey,[6] but not Exum.[7]

Roberts observes that the second section is "widely accepted" as a unity, due to "being clearly delineated by the vineyard theme." He cites Gerleman and Keel,[8] "both observing that the distinctive theme of vv. 11–12 leaves the boundaries of this unit in no doubt."[9] Roberts finds additional evidence supporting the cohesion of the verses as a united whole.[10] Regarding contiguous connections for the verses, he notes that interpreters who allocate the vineyard strophes to the woman's voice, most commonly dramatists, often see connection on the basis of continuing voice from 8:8–10 through 8:11–12.[11] Overall, Roberts is not persuaded of any contiguous connection:

> In short, it appears that we have two segments that are built on the entirely different images of the city fortifications on the one hand, and vineyards on the other. Moreover, the images are developed differently, and the cast of characters is different. This is not to say that the segments might not eventually be shown to have some connection by virtue of a role in some larger structural pattern. But they are not, in themselves, obviously connected to each other.[12]

Once again, Roberts is more positive about remote connections regarding verses 8:11–12.

> The most obvious external connection is the link with 1:6, where the woman is appointed to keep (נטר) the family vineyards, and then declares that she has not kept (נטר) her own vineyard (כרמי שלי). These two passages provide the Song's only occurrences of נטר, of שלי, and of the singular of כרם. Naturally, the intensity and exclusiveness of this link is of great importance to those

---

5. Ibid., 352.
6. Rendtorff, *Old Testament*, 262; Dorsey, *Literary Structure*, 212.
7. Exum, "Literary and Structural Analysis," 75–76.
8. Gerleman, *Ruth, Das Hohelied*, 222; Keel, *Hohelied*, 280.
9. Roberts, *Let Me See Your Form*, 353, n. 60.
10. Ibid., 358–59.
11. Ibid., 359–60.
12. Ibid., 360.

who find vv. 11–12 part of a closing *inclusio* (usually including all of 8:5–14) that is the counterpart of 1:2—2:7.[13]

The third section again draws Roberts to assert on the one hand that there is "little basis to connect this segment structurally with the preceding one,"[14] yet on the other that "this final segment of the Song is rich, perhaps above any other segment, in its connections with other parts of the Song."[15] Firstly, Roberts notes that there is a reappearance of companions (חברים), although these companions may be a different group.[16] In chapter 1 they were shepherds; in chapter 8 it is not so clear who they are. In chapter 1 they were the companions of the *man*, whereas in chapter 8 they could well be the companions of the *woman*, hence the daughters of Jerusalem. Nevertheless, the lexical selection provides a poetic effect. But this is not the most "substantial" external link that Roberts identifies.[17] Characterizing the woman as one who dwells in the gardens recalls the "dominant imagery for the woman in 4:12—5:1 and then again in 6:1 and 6:11."[18] The reactivation of the garden metaphor is reinforced by the use of "balsam" (בשׂם) as the final word of the Song, since although the word is common in the Song, it is especially pronounced in the passages that liken the woman to a garden, as though balsam characterizes the spices imagined to be present in the garden. But what Roberts considers to be "the most substantial external link" between 8:13–14 and the rest of the Song is the way 8:14 has a closing function akin to 2:17 in 2:8–17.[19] Additionally, the man is likened (דמה) to a gazelle (צבי) disjunctively (או) with a young stag (לעפר) of the deer (האילים), all vocabulary from chapter 2. Also, in chapter 2, the man calls on the woman to speak so that he might hear her in 2:14d (השמיעיני את קולך), as he does again here in 8:13c (לקולך השמיעיני). Roberts goes so far as to say that, "8:13–14 is in some ways a miniature of 2:8–17."[20] Even more strikingly, he notes:

> Thus, with varying degrees of intensity, this final two-strophe segment of the Song may be linked with most of the preceding

---

13. Ibid.
14. Ibid., 366.
15. Ibid., 367.
16. "The reappearance of the חברים of 1:7 is often noted first by those who are interested in indicators of some inclusio relationship between 1:2–2:7 and this last part of the Song." Ibid.
17. Ibid.
18. Ibid.
19. "We have already noted the near identity of v. 14 with 2:17, and the closing function of both." Ibid.
20. Ibid.

sections, including 1:2—2:7 (חברים and the צבאות and אילות of the adjuration refrain); 2:8–17 (השמיעיני את־קולך and all of 2:17, along with other items); 3:1–5 (adjuration refrain with צבאות and אילות [again]); 4:1–7 (עפרים תאמי צביה; breasts as mountains of spices); 4:8—5:1 (mountains; spices, including especially בשם; garden); 5:2—6:3 (garden and בשם); and 6:11 (garden).[21]

Carr says tersely of verses 13–14: "The lover calls for her response to his presence (cf. 2:14). His request draws an immediate response from his beloved, and her invitation is a reprise of many of the longings of earlier passages in the Song."[22] But of the whole section we are looking at he observes that, "For many commentators the Song ends with 8:7. These last few verses are often relegated to the category of 'appendices.'"[23] Like Roberts, he notes that, "Verses 8 to 10 seem to go together, but there is no universal agreement on this division. Nor is there consensus on the identification of speaker/speakers, nor on the number of women being discussed in the verses."[24] Carr cites Delizsch, Pope, and Gordis regarding various permutations of reading among interpreters, and he concludes: "No proposal has won the allegiance of the commentators, although it seems most probable that the brothers are speaking here, and the object of their attention is the heroine of the Song."[25] Carr actually ends up allocating all of 8:11–14 to a single section, which he calls Communion.[26]

Fox concludes, as Roberts does, that these final verses are best apportioned as three distinct units. Regarding the speaker or speakers in 8:8–10, Fox thinks "It is probably the brothers, mentioned in 1:6, who are speaking in this difficult unit, offering reconciliation in place of their earlier rebuke."[27] He does, however, concede that Exum could be right to allocate the verses to the daughters of Jerusalem.[28] But he considers the possibility to be "unlikely."[29] While dealing with the difficulties of interpreting the

21. Ibid., 368.
22. Carr, *Song of Solomon*, 191–92.
23. Ibid., 187–88.
24. Ibid., 188.
25. Ibid.
26. Ibid., 189.
27. Fox, *Song of Songs*, 171.
28. Exum, "Literary and Structural Analysis," 75.
29. "It is unlikely, though not impossible, that the girls of Jerusalem speak here (thus Exum, 1973:75f.), for the responsibility of caring for the girl's needs at marriage would fall upon the brothers." Ibid., 75–76.

intention of references to walls, doors, and towers, he opines, "The note of playful banter in this exchange has escaped notice of the commentators."[30] Regarding the vineyard verses, Fox settles on the man as speaker—"The boy is speaking here, not the girl"—but, like Roberts, makes most of the echoes of 1:6 that arouse the reader's curiosity.

> This short unit recalls motifs and phrases from the girl's statement in 1:6: vineyards, the tending (NTR) of vineyards, and the phrase *karmi šelli*, "my vineyard." Here the motif of tending vineyards appears immediately after the brothers' reconciliation with the Shulammite; in 1:6 it appears right after she speaks of the mistreatment she received from them.[31]

Fox strikes a resounding note in regards to the last section, however, one shared with some other commentators and the current thesis. Not knowing what to make of the verses, he despairs and speculates that the end of the scroll may have been lost, "And yet the poet may intend to leave the reader *in medias res*, where the Song began, for love is an ongoing experience, and marriage not the end of the story."[32] This is precisely the interpretation I think is most plausible, supported by many lines of evidence. It does not really matter whether there is a formal *inclusio* operating between chapters 1 and 8, nor even if the vocabulary of 8:13-14 recaptures the key themes of the Song. In various ways, a circularity is suggested, and a circularity that imitates the very phenomenon that is explored throughout the Song of Songs: romantic love.

Goulder apportions our verses such that 8:8-10 are the concluding part of Song 13 by his reckoning, and 8:11-14 are the final song 14. He says,

> Two things make it probable that we should see Song 13 as ending at 8.10, and a short final Song (14) as beginning here [at verse 11]. First the location and dramatis personae change. Song 13 opens with the royal couple coming up the desert road back into the city, while 14 is in the palace garden (v. 13).. . . Secondly, the theme of Song 13 was the power of love as greater than money, and this closed with the development of the city-tower-gate-wall imagery in 8.10: now we have the different, vineyard image, which forms an inclusion with Song 1 (1.6), and completes the whole poem.[33]

---

30. Fox, *Song of Songs*, 172.
31. Ibid., 174.
32. Ibid., 176.
33. Goulder, *Song of Fourteen*, 69.

Although we may question the specificity with which Goulder allocates voices to characters in his dramatic reading, his general points regarding setting and imagery are consistent with other commentators.

In direct opposition to Fox who sees "playful banter" in the verses regarding the brothers and sister, Murphy declares,

> There is a rather solemn air about the announcement of the brothers concerning their little sister, whom they formally introduce as a child in v 8a. But she becomes the 'problem' in v 8b. What will be their responsibility to her when she reaches marriageable age? There is an almost riddle-like quality to the solution (v 9) which the brothers propose to their own question.[34]

He decides, "The brothers mean to take harsh measures if necessary to protect their sister. If she fails to remain chaste, they will take steps to board her up."[35] Murphy considers the next verses, 8:11–12, to be a "boasting song, comparable to 6:8–9, in which the man prizes the beloved beyond the entire harem of Solomon."[36] He is ambivalent about whether the verses are to be attributed to the woman or not, and about whether there is any genuine connection between the references to keepers and vineyard that echoes chapter 1. He does accept that in general terms, "it is worth noting that several themes in chapter 1 reappear in the last part of chapter 8 (vineyard, keepers, brothers)."[37] Regarding the last verses, Murphy like Roberts and others also recognizes the echo of 2:17. He generalizes, "The concluding verses epitomize the tantalizing shifts of person and scene that are characteristic of the Song as a whole."[38]

Longman treats the three sections of our final set of verses as three separate poems, twenty-one through twenty-three by his accounting. He agrees with Fox that the verses about the brothers and sister are "playful," indeed "perhaps providing relief after the intensity of the previous poem."[39] Longman, however, sees that the vineyard section "is filled with enigmas, beginning with the question of who is the speaker."[40] He agrees with Murphy about the section being a "boasting song," if we "hear the voice of the

---

34. Murphy, *Song of Songs*, 198.
35. Ibid., 199.
36. Ibid.
37. Ibid.
38. Ibid., 200.
39. Longman, *Song of Songs*, 215.
40. Ibid., 218.

woman here."[41] Longman also observes the unfinished, incomplete impression with which the final verses leave the reader. "It honestly seems an odd way to end a poem; we might expect that the conclusion would bring complete and unbreakable intimacy. Perhaps, however, this better expresses love in the real world."[42]

Regarding the unmarried sister, Bergant nicely balances the somber and playful readings, saying:

> The harshness of the military imagery is qualified by the addition of precious adornments that signal the extraordinary value and beauty of the woman. The man used a similar poetic device when he likened the woman's neck to the tower of David embellished with military banners.[43]

Bergant, like Murphy and Longman, reads the vineyard verses as a boasting song, though she reads it as the man boasting.[44] Like other writers, she sees that "the change in speaker and content clearly sets this section off from what immediately precedes it," but like Roberts also sees that "the poem does not stand isolated from the rest of the Song of Songs."[45] She sees two chief connections: firstly the linguistic connection between the words *shalom* and *Solomon*, and secondly the thematic connection where the both passages "acclaim the incomparable value of the woman."[46] She also finds the usual remote connections found by other writers, but is more sanguine than others in regards to connecting 8:11–12 with 8:8–10. Bergant also notes commonality between 8:13–14 and 2:14–17 like other writers, and says of the way the Song of Songs ends that it does so

> on a note of separation with a plea for union. As incomplete as this may sound, it is also quite true of authentic love. Loving relationships are never complete; they are always ongoing, always reaching for more. Regardless of the quality or frequency of lovemaking, there is always a measure of yearning present.[47]

Garrett treats 8:8–12 as a unit and 8:13–14 as a "farewell." He still treats 8:8–10 and 8:11–12 as separate stanzas under the rubric of "The Virgin's

---

41. Ibid.
42. Ibid., 220.
43. Bergant, *Song of Songs*, 101.
44. Ibid., 102.
45. Ibid.
46. Ibid., 103.
47. Ibid., 105.

Education II."[48] This deliberately matches his title of "The Virgin's Education" for Song 1:5–6. Most of Garrett's general comments about form, structure, and setting revolve around which voices are singing in the verses. He allocates the bulk of the lines to the chorus. In his even more general comments in "explanation" of the 8:8–12 passage, he successfully abstracts issues such that they suit our own analysis of the verses in terms of *Background* or *Flashback* with respect to prior context.[49] Garrett summarizes the farewell as follows: "The man and the woman thus depart into the countryside and leave the audience, and the reader, with a distant, wistful vision of love."

Hess considers the woman to be defending herself in 8:10 against a charge from the brothers in 8:8–9. He discusses the sections separately and mainly concentrates on the cultural background that may inform interpretation. How far are the brothers acting to protect their sister or acting in perceived self-protection, "the honor of the family and particularly that of the brothers"?[50] Hess then turns to the difficulties of the vineyard verses, looking at them in the broader context of the Hebrew Bible.[51] Like others, he also considers the difficulty of who is speaking.[52] More apposite for our considerations of rhetorical relations, Hess makes the following observation of 8:11–12.

> As a note that follows upon the evaluation of love as a binding commitment (vv. 6–7), the female expresses the strength of that relationship by her refusal to substitute any earthly offer, however desirable it may seem at the time.[53]

Hess concludes his final segmentation of the Song with individual treatment of each of the last two verses, noting similar coinciding elements of vocabulary, as do other authors.

Exum views verses 8–14 as making a deliberate turn to a different style of poetics: "Saying more on the topic of the strength of love would risk allowing the poem to slip into sentimentality—and the poet knows well that showing is better than telling."[54] She observes, as have others, that "as it nears its end, the Song reverts to themes and motifs from the beginning."[55]

---

48. Garrett, *Song of Songs*, 258.
49. Ibid., 262.
50. Hess, *Song of Songs*, 244.
51. Ibid., 246–47.
52. Ibid., 247.
53. Ibid.
54. Exum, *Song of Songs*, 254.
55. Ibid., 255.

Structurally, Exum views 8:8–14 as a unit within 8:1–14, and each of 8:8–10, 8:11–12, and 8:13–14 as units in turn within it, again like other scholars we have considered above. Regarding verses 13 to 14 she says,

> The Song ends, as it began, with the erotic imperative, the call to love addressed directly, and urgently, to the beloved.... Far from being anti-climactic or mystifying as a conclusion, as many critics have observed, these verse provide an inspired ending to the Song. Rather than bringing the poem to closure, they lead us back into it.[56]

And back into the Song we shall now ourselves proceed as we summarize what we have discussed regarding the dynamic semantics of the Song of Songs, augmented by some additional proposals of my own.

---

56. Ibid., 261.

18

Da Capo al Fine

We have seen how most of our commentators consider the Song's final strophes to be pointing beyond themselves, evoking something of the ever-unfinished business of love. Exum and Roberts are clearest about seeing the verses not only doing this, but doing it in a way that points back into the Song.

It is hard to discern how the poet intended his final words to be taken, for since the topic of love has been the theme of the Song throughout, final words that point to ongoing love will also point to the continuation of the topic. The difference is the difference between semantics and poetics. The poet may have been untroubled by the distinction. It may be safest to credit the poet with having the abundantly demonstrated skill to achieve both semantic communication and artful poetics simultaneously. If a reader captures the communicative intention of an implied proposition that ideal romantic love is never fully consummated, that is sufficient for the poet. His success can be measured by modern readers who grasp his point centuries later. However, if a reader also appreciates a genuine flourish of artistry, noticing that the Song does close, in a sense, on itself as a window through which idealization of love can be apprehended, then all the better. The vocabulary as well as imagery and thematic echoes explicit in the final strophes do give a strong indication that either summary or *inclusio* were intended as part of some such deliberately artistic flourish.

Although the main case of the current thesis does not depend on it, pressing the scrutiny of Roberts and insight of Exum a little harder gives a reading of the Song that helps clarify the main points at issue in the current thesis. The Song may be read as having a circular structure, or at least so shall I now present that view here. The claim is asserted baldly for the sake of clarity, though the claim ought to be appreciated as being hedged with caveats. The original poet may have had precisely the intention I shall attribute to him, but thought of it by a different metaphor to that of the circle, indeed by something more apposite to the text and topic of the Song, but circularity could have been his intention in a very direct way. To see it we need only to observe that 8:13 appears to describe something very like 1:2–4.

היושבת בגנים

O dweller in gardens,

חברים מקשיבים

[while your] companions are hearkening,

לקולך השמיעיני

let me hear your voice!

It does not matter whether we allocate the logically redundant "to your voice" (לקולך) as indirect object of the verbal idea of hearkening (קשב) or of listening (שמע). I have simply accepted Roberts's colometry.

If this were a deliberate structuring device, planned by the poet, then the poet was signaling the unity of the Song. It is consistent with the subsections of the Song which often conclude by returning to a setting in which they began.[1] Fox says, "Two rather enigmatic verses (8:13–14) set us back to a point earlier in the cycle as the boy again asks to hear his beloved's voice."[2] More poetically he offers, "The Song takes a single romance and turns it around and around like a gem, displaying all its facets. The reader finally sees the gem as a whole, and the order in which the facets were shown does not much matter."[3]

Also if it were true that the end of the Song deliberately leads the reader not just back into the Song as Exum, I believe rightly, proposes, but leads the reader back specifically to its very beginning, the way this is done suggests that the Song may well be primarily about making a woman's voice heard among companions, to the delight of a man who loves her. As such I am

---

1. "On the whole, the Mesopotamian corpus could best be described as narrative, or dramatic, poetry rather than lyric poetry. The action, especially when accompanied by a narrator who reports events in sequence, progresses in a linear fashion. This is quite unlike the lyric poetry of the Song, where the movement is circular." Exum, *Song of Songs*, 51.

2. Fox, *Song of Songs*, 226.

3. Ibid.

drawn by the possibility that the man's voice in 8:13 is the poet in disguise, giving us the key we need to unlock the framework within which we should interpret the Song. But this is done subtly and cleverly so that it is quite natural. It is really the only place in the Song where the man commands the woman's speech, whereas often she controls his speech by asking questions, quoting him, even finishing a sentence for him.

Were 8:13 to caption the Song instead of the cryptic title we have regarding Solomon, the Song would not seem to start so abruptly. Yet the abrupt start sets a tone that is carried on throughout the Song with its major changes in topic typically being introduced by the woman, just as in 1:2.

Is there any reason the poet chose to make the woman's voice more prominent in the Song? Was it just gallantry? Is there something about the topic of romantic love that culturally or biologically does center the perspective of women, suiting it to being presented through the literary device of a (slightly more) mature woman advising younger women about how to conduct themselves in matters of the heart? I will defer consideration of this question to the next chapter where we will interact with André LaCocque's reading of the Song as the work of a female poet.

Whether or not the Song has an overall circular structure, a circle is still a line. In the case of the Song, even if the line is thematic rather than narrative, it must still be a line if it is to be completed by some device that also makes it a circle. What then is the structure of that line if it is not narrative? I have attempted to gather data in the foregoing chapters that helps us to see this line.

In 1:2—2:7 we have the woman calling for and apparently finding consummation. She is overwhelmed by love both before and after consummation. In 1:2–4 she articulates being so intoxicated by love that she wants consummation, then in 2:4–6 she articulates being intoxicated by love *after* consummation. Or at least thematically we may propose this. A combination of narrative and puritan reading will resist seeing consummation intimated so early in the Song, but this is not necessary, and is rather forced. Roberts stresses that the refrains of the Song mark closure, and I think this is correct. The first section of the Song, although it is an eclectic section in the material it presents, concludes with the most prominent refrain of the Song, the abjuration against arousing love before it so desires. This is quite a natural conclusion arising from the hyperbole of the intoxication of being in love, especially if such love is consummated. As such, the first section of the Song is internally coherent if we are appreciating it as it was intended.

I argue that the second section of the Song also follows naturally from the adjuration refrain. If one is to wait for something that is powerfully good, then the fear is that the good may not actually eventuate. If this understanding is correct, then 2:8–17 defuses the fear by suggesting a lover is just "over the hill" and energetically bounding towards a woman inclined to enjoy love. The call to love will come in the right season. The following section, 3:1–5, complements 2:8–17, and indeed is marked for closure by a return to the adjuration refrain. The complementarity lies in the woman taking the initiative to find her love. In 2:8–17 he initiates; in 3:1–5 she does. But the complementarity is incomplete. What he does by day, she does by night, and the feel of the second set of verses is that of a dream. In her *dreams* she takes initiative. This reading depends on other general thematic currents in the Song, and the adjuration refrain. In her dreams the woman does not model her advice.

Verses 3:6–11, if they are delivered by the woman about Solomon, echo the pattern of 2:8–17 and confirm with regal authority the pattern of the bridegroom acting to establish consummation of his desire rather than the bride seeking the groom. A normative cultural pattern is being upheld, rightly or wrongly—let the reader decide. This bridegroom then speaks in 4:1–7, suggesting from the masculine perspective what we have already heard from the feminine. This is extended into 4:8—5:1, including a closing dialogue that confirms female invitation, male initiative, and social approval.

At this point in the Song we get a clear break. Whether we have followed the intended trajectory of the discourse correctly or not, the major "punctuation" of the Song occurs after 5:1.[4] "A number of the surviving medieval manuscripts of the Song have only one break—after 5:1!"[5]

In 5:2—6:3 a new thematic setting replaces the stream of thought that came to completion at 5:1. It is not unprecedented. The woman had sought her love among the shepherds in 1:7–8 and left her bed at night in 3:1–5, but almost the whole of the second half of the Song of Songs can be interpreted under the overarching theme of seeking (בקש) and finding (מצא). Indeed, even in the final lines of the Song (8:10), the woman's boast includes her becoming like the "finding of peace."

It is impossible to be certain, but the adjuration refrain may govern interpretation. Both the man and woman seek each other in the Song, though the woman does so in dreams with words, whereas the man appears to act to find what he seeks. The woman seeks to be found, though she is openly inconsistent about this. She seems to be on the brink of being sexually forward without actually crossing the line. Although it is impossible to

---

4. "The major incision exists behind verse 5:1". Kessler, *Poetical and Structural Features*, 42.

5. Segal, *Song of Songs* 175, citing Cohen, *Studies*, 33.

be certain if this characterization of the woman is at the heart of the Song's message, or even part of it, the very difficulty of pinning it down rescues the Song from being too tidily moralistic. There are no rules for couples as to who initiates erotic love within a lasting relationship, yet there is commonly acknowledged to be a tendency for women to fantasize about the initiatives of ardent lovers, and a thriving popular literature industry catering to that market. The Song seems to fit with this stereotype, but tastefully, skillfully giving a real impression of a tendency without making it so concrete it actually *loses* realism. Even so, at its plainest, in the abjuration to the young women against rousing love and the abjuration to the man to "seal" love for a lifetime, there *are* plain words suggesting absolute and gendered boundaries on erotic initiatives.

Through several stages—dream, *waṣf*, and question and answer with the daughters of Jerusalem—the woman "conjures up" the man in 5:2—6:3, and he appears, just as she longs for him to do. There is a different dynamic to the first half of the Song where the lover appeared promptly. This could be another example of complementary pairings in the Song. Having arrived back on center stage, the man delivers two *waṣfs* (6:4–10 and 7:1–11) and an enthusiastic call to consummation before surrendering center stage once again to the woman, if ever she left it, since all his words are about her. The woman responds with an invitation, underlining the mutuality of the love the man has so clearly articulated he wants to share, in a very direct and physical way. Hence 7:12—8:4 bring to a close the main flow of the seeking and finding theme of the second half of the Song.

The climax of the Song is then presented in 8:5–7, a concise vision of love, with tightly formal poetry in verse 6, consisting of more classical parallelism than has been typical of the rest of the Song. In verse 7 there follows elevated prose with similar effect to verse 6.

The final section relaxes away from the high flown phrases of 8:5–7 as we are led back to more intimate and concrete themes reminiscent of chapter 1, concluding with the invitations of man to woman and woman to man in 8:13–14, perhaps intended to signal an invitation to the reader to reread the Song of Songs from beginning to end, *da capo al fine*.

While dramatists have found it possible to reconstruct a narrative out of these broad thematic movements, which is satisfying to some readers, that does not seem to be demanded by the text; in fact, it takes away some of the generality of the text. The poet appears to have worked hard to keep the text free of specificities that would distance a reader from appropriating the Song as a text addressed to her, or to him. As narrative, the Song is fragmentary and full of gaps that allow a reader to imagine his or her circumstances, or those of friends, into the text. But as a working through of themes associated with romantic love, the Song appears to be well rounded and balanced. As a thematic treatment of romantic love, then, we find it to have both poetic cohesion and semantic coherence. It is a unity, and it has some simple and direct things to say in the adjuration refrain and the short hymn to love with which it closes.

Such is the conclusion of my discourse analysis, but what of the centrality of the woman's voice? How, if at all, is that related to the message of the Song? I read the woman as implied author of the Song, but André LaCocque reads a literal female author. So we turn to his "hermeneutical essay" on the Song for more insight into the woman's voice.

19

Support: André LaCocque, Daniel Grossberg, and George Schwab

IN CHAPTERS 5 TO 17, we looked at the structure of the Song according to a discourse analytical approach. In chapter 18, we took the abductive step to forming a gynocentric hypothesis. In this chapter, we look at some independent support for that thesis, mainly that coming from André LaCocque, who is famous for his monograph on the Song that includes articulation of his own view that the actual author of the Song was a woman. André LaCocque says of his own thesis, "I contend here, the author of the Song was a female poet who intended to 'cock a snook at all Puritans.'"[1] I have reservations about both parts of this thesis, in that female authorship only works at the level of the implied author, and that the poet is actually writing in support of the institution of marriage without being explicit about that. However, I would agree with LaCocque that the centrality of the female voice is significant, and scholarly commentaries do not always make as much of it as could be made of it, and that the lack of explicit references to formalities of marriage and weddings are also important, with the scholarly commentators often assuming too much by way of the Song's harmonization with social conventions surrounding the institutionalization of human pair bonding.

LaCocque divides the Song into subsections very similar to those we have already considered above in detail. That facilitates comparing his reading with the writers we have already consulted on similar terms, the only difference being his basic interpretive presuppositions: a female author, and a radical agenda. He also views the poet as reworking prophetic imagery

1. LaCocque, *Romance, She Wrote*, xi.

of the relation of Yahweh to Israel as that of a marriage back to its original source in human marriage.² LaCocque provides an explicit framework for interpreting the "dialogical quality" of the text, not too dissimilarly to how I have posited this above in various places.

> The dialogical quality of the work is eminent. True, the readers are never overtly addressed by the Canticle as "you," but the address is never covert either: the "you" is implied in the third person of the narrator. Furthermore, the poet has multiplied dialogical devices: the lover speaks to the beloved; the beloved to the lover; they both speak to "companions," to "daughters of Jerusalem." This way, the reader is not permitted to stay out as an onlooker (a Peeping Tom?). The reader is among the male friends, among the female chorus, and is exhorted not to precipitate the action ("do not stir love . . ."), not to hide the lover from the beloved, but to participate in their mutual quest. The reader is eminently *active*.³

Looking at the first chapter, and first verses of the Song, LaCocque sees the poet reworking the idea of Jeremiah 31:3: "I have loved you with an everlasting love; therefore with lovingkindness I have drawn you" (NKJV). This is recalled to LaCocque's intertextually inclined mind by "Draw me after you!" in Song 1:4. He also notes that, "Elsewhere in Scripture, 'the king' might be in reference to God the Lord, but here it is the lover who is called by that term of endearment."⁴ LaCocque also considers various references to "chambers" (חדר) in the corpus of the Hebrew Bible, and to the temple, which stood next to Solomon's royal chambers. He goes on to opine, "The allusions to the temple continue in the following verse (1.5), where the 'curtains of Solomon' recall the priestly usage of the term *curtains* in the Pentateuch designating the 'curtains of the tabernacle' (cf. Exodus 26; 36)."⁵

LaCocque attempts to place the "maidens" (עלמות) in context, historically, intertextually, and within the Song. He quotes Boyarin who observed that the maidens in the Song are "desiring subjects and not . . . desired objects,"⁶ asking, "Does this render ancient Hebrew society any less

---

2. "In summary, language has come full circle, from the horizontal plane to the vertical through prophetic metaphorization and to horizontal again through poetic defigurativation and refigurativation." Ibid., 56.

3. Ibid., 57.

4. Ibid., 70.

5. Ibid., 71.

6. Boyarin, *Intertextuality*, 123.

patriarchal? I rather doubt it, but it does perhaps further unsettle 'literature' as a univocal reflection of other social practices."[7]

After extensive consideration of what LaCocque believes to be radical reworkings of prophetic and other biblical imagery, he concludes regarding the first chapter of the Song:

> A large part of the discourse is set in the female's mouth. She is certainly the centrefold.... The female expresses that much in a language that deserves our utmost attention, for the imagery is permeated with "biblical" reminiscences. The poet uses the well-known language of prophets – their talk of shepherding, of leading the flock to shaded and watered spots, of protection against the "smiting" sun, and the central event of Israel's escape from Egypt.... But now, the shepherd is just that, a shepherd; the nard is a woman's perfume; and the temple chambers are trees of the forest extending their branches to cover clandestine loves!... Canticle 1 has thus accumulated cameos and sketches with the purpose of creating the atmosphere that prevails in the Song.... Already at the rhetoric level, there is some kind of derision of the chastened language of contemporary scribes.[8]

While there is much here to question there is also much to accept. We can accept that the woman speaks and is the central character as well as central voice. We can accept that there is a concatenation of cameos that coherently builds a cohesive set of themes. How much the language of the poem deliberately reflects other biblical passages is, however, questionable. LaCocque is almost as creative as were the allegorists in his ability to find connections between ideas in the Song and those of other parts of Scripture. Where LaCocque differs is in his ability to present plausible suggestions that the Song rereads canonical literature "against the grain."

Even more stark is LaCocque's treatment of the oath of the adjuration refrain. "*YHWH ṣebaʾōt* has become *ṣebaʾōt*; while *El Shadday* has been changed into *ʾayᵉlôt haśśadeh* ... In the Song of Songs, the devotional discourse is redirected towards another purpose with a smack of scandal."[9] He mentions this in dealing with 2:1–7, but refers to it briefly again in his treatment of 3:1–5. "The next section, 3.1–5, contains at least four subversive elements: (a) a reference in verse 1 to premarital sexuality."[10] While it is fair to suggest that the Song does not clearly identify a socially approved

---

7. Ibid., 158, n. 23.
8. LaCocque, *Romance, She Wrote*, 81–82.
9. Ibid., 86.
10. Ibid., 93.

ceremony preceding the romantic and erotic coupling of the main protagonists of the Song, it is probably equally fair to suggest that it does not clearly identify any extramarital (including premarital) sexuality either, unless we look at the potential for a plurality of queens and concubines to suggest polygamy. For the main characters, the specifics of having their paperwork in order simply do not enter the picture. Paperwork may be put in its place by the Song, but this is not necessarily scandalous. The other subversive elements LaCocque finds in 3:1–5 are: the nocturnal search by the woman for her lover; the drawing of attention to her mother's house; and the oath of the adjuration refrain. As with the claim of 3:1 suggesting premarital sex, LaCocque's other proposed "subversive elements" need not have been as shocking to sensitivities as he proposes, albeit that they do lie outside the norm we find in other books of the Hebrew Bible corpus.

It is easier to appreciate LaCocque's helpful perspective on 3:6–11 where he observes as follows.

> King Solomon is protected by sixty bodyguards, but his real entourage is made of women (v. 11). As he is the paragon of love, this is not unexpected. The feminization of the scene, however, is so total that it cannot but reflect upon the male royal character inside the palanquin. Solomon is surrounded (drowned?) not only by females everywhere but also by their work ("decked in love by the daughters of Jerusalem"; v. 10b). Although it may be that women were employed in the temple for some specific works, their mention at this point by the Canticle enhances the feeling of voluptuousness and of decadence created by the whole description. A surprising detail, the crown put on the king's head by his mother is puzzling.[11]

It is certainly true that one could read the final verse of the third chapter of the Song as the crowning verse of all three chapters in a movement that gives prominence to woman as the greatest joy of man. Indeed, this well suits itself to supporting our own reading of 3:6–11 as being in the voice of the woman, and of 4:1–7 being a natural, even overdue, voice of man articulating precisely this joy.

LaCocque is also helpful, though he is not alone, in noting something of a correction given to the man by the woman in 4:8—5:1. He speaks of her as a locked garden, but she declares that the locking of the garden would be pointless were it not offered to one to enjoy it. She offers her garden to him.

---

11. Ibid., 101.

> In conclusion, the response of the woman to the ravished wonderment of her lover is an invitation to enjoy her delights. They are meant for him. They are not to be kept as a "garden locked up and a sealed fountain" (see 4.12). Her fragrance, her perfumes, her nectar, milk and honey, her fruits, her wine and oil and spices, mean nothing if he does not "come to *his* garden."[12]

LaCocque continues his work of exploring possible biblical allusions lying behind the text of the Song through the second half of the poem. He brings this to a conclusion with a discussion of how the final verses of the Song, 8:13–14, are suggestive of the Song having a circular structure, as I also propose.

> It is not surprising and unexpected that the Song of Songs is built as a cycle. Verses 13–14 of Canticle 8 build an end that is, at the same time, a rebound of the whole poem, a return to the beginning. And thus the Canticle is an endless song. . . . Cant 8.13–14 simply repeats 2.17, almost verbatim. This and other factors . . . lead me to conclude that the Song of Songs is indeed a *round*, the *rondeau* of the Middle Ages, that is, an endlessly repeated song. This feature is a strong argument in favor of the unity of composition and of authorship.[13]

He also says that this "has passed unnoticed by commentators, although some of the close readers put us on the right track." The closest he finds to the thought is Denis Buzy,[14] whom he paraphrases as saying that, "the Canticle's poems are variations on the same theme without progression of thought."[15] I would argue that Buzy's is too static a reading of the Song in general. It is rather like Roberts's reading, though Roberts was forced to a static reading by his methodology.

Overall, LaCocque's reading of the Song only really makes use of the speculation about a female author insofar as a female author, being outside the regular authorized public spokesmen of the religious community of ancient Israel, might have been suitably placed to reflect upon canonical literature and community conventions as an "insider-outsider" critic. On the other hand, I want to argue that by the poet making the woman in the Song to be visibly the "mistress of ceremonies," holding center stage, that

---

12. Ibid., 112–13.
13. Ibid., 90.
14. "D'un poème à l'autre, la progression est nulle, puisque chque fois tout recommence, pour s'achever de nouveau et recommencer encore." Buzy, "La composition littéraire,"169–84.
15. LaCocque, *Romance, She Wrote*, 190.

we are dealing with something deliberate and significant about the Song, something associated with its basic intended message.

We are dealing with a feature of the Song that resonates with the circularity of its subunits, and overall circularity, in a way that suggests an individual author with specific intent, a specific intent literally centered on woman. As such I read the Song as a literally gynocentric poem, both in the sense that a woman's voice is at its center and that its message is centrally about woman: woman in her romantic engagement with man. Sometimes the orbit of the thematic treatment of romantic love in the Song is large and other times it is narrow. In 2:8–17, for example, the orbit is large. The man comes, perhaps from Lebanon, in the imagination of the female voice, and he invites her out into the springtime world to roam with him in his sphere of action in the world at large. At other times, the orbit of the thematic treatment of love is narrow, so narrow it is more a to-and-fro backwards and forwards between lover and beloved, as in the mutual possession refrain. The nature of the topic of romantic love necessitates the semantics of two bodies in orbit around each other, but to give it more than just an artistic representation in generalized terms, it is "brought down to earth" by viewing it from the woman's perspective. Nevertheless, two distinct, concrete applications are volunteered for the reader to take to heart. The adjuration refrain calls young women to wait for their young men. The final climax of the book calls young men to seal their hearts for life with the young women they come to be bound together with in love. Different claims are made on men and women, but both are made on the basis of female emotional engagement rather than on male emotional engagement.

The Song could have been written by a woman, but it seems unlikely that we could ever know. More likely, the Song was written by a man; but that it was a single poet and not several poets loosely worked together by an editor is supported by the consistency of the style of all the component pieces of the Song, particularly in how they are held together by a female voice that seems decidedly uniform throughout. To this reader, the Song sounds like it is the song of a woman, about herself, and her love, and how she thinks those exemplary for other women and men.

So much for some external support in broad terms for the gynocentric hypothesis of this thesis. There is also support for the reading of overall unity, quite apart from whether a woman's voice is key to its unity or not. Indeed there is much support, but a significant writer in favor of reading the Song as unity has gone unmentioned up to this point. Daniel Grossberg sees the Song, like all poetry, as having "centrifugal" as well as "centripetal" aspects. He gets the terminology from Stankiewicz.[16] Various characteristics of a poem radiate tangentially from its core idea or form, whereas other characteristics draw its notions or devices towards its core. This can also be expressed as a weighting towards highlighting the whole or the parts of a poem:

> Some poetic texts tend to highlight the unity of the whole; others tend toward a dominant emphasis on the parts. Poetic works, therefore, can be typed by determining the location of their compositional structuring on a centripetal/centrifugal continuum.[17]

With regard to the Song of Songs, Grossberg finds "Our identification of an array of compositional features in the Song leads us to fix its structural character nearer to the centrifugal extreme of the continuum with strong balancing centripetal features."[18] In particular he notes the following.

> "While progressing through the Song of Songs, the reader constantly recalls the multiple evocative verses already read. Our examination of the associations and repetitions of 1:2 throughout the Song highlights their centripetal power. In the face of fragmenting figures, the recurrence of words, themes, sounds, and images constantly brings the parts back to an equilibrium with the whole."[19]

Like Roberts, Grossberg finds an array of devices that operate at a higher level than bicola or strophes, suggesting a unity to the Song at a higher level of abstraction than needed for understanding any of the self-contained cameos of the Song considered in isolation. More specifically, this is somewhat circular in Grossberg's reading, as has been the proposed reading of this current thesis, though not so much a feature in Roberts's analysis.

Besides finding support for key elements of this thesis—viz., a unified (circular) poem, and articulated in a woman's voice—there is also independent support for the interpretation, the message of the Song, as we have read it above. Schwab reads the Song, as we do, as essentially a cautionary sapiential work on its topic of romantic or erotic love. Schwab establishes this in some detail in a monograph devoted to the point.[20]

---

16. Stankiewicz, "Centripetal And Centrifugal Structures, 217-42.
17. Grossberg, *Centripetal and Centrifugal Structures*, 5.
18. Ibid., 56.
19. Ibid., 76.
20. Schwab, *Songs' Cautionary Message*.

Having presented an abductive argument for a reading of the Song of Songs, and provided some pointers to other writers who support key parts of that argument, we are left at the point of concluding the presentation of the thesis.

20

Conclusion: Gender in Solomon's Song of Songs

THE BULK OF THIS thesis has critically interacted with Roberts's finding of an overall cohesion to the Song, seen in use of various poetic devices. In Grossberg's terminology, there are centripetal features of the Song counteracting the centrifugal nature of the elaborate excursuses the Song is so famous for. I have attempted to show that in addition to such centripetal cohesion there is a centripetal coherence based on the *semantic content*, not just the poetic form, of the Song.

If we read the Song as essentially an exuberant presentation of wisdom about love from a married woman to young virgins, written such that all may eavesdrop on this conversation to their edification, then the colorful cameos of the various panels of the Song can be seen to progress in a fairly logical manner, even being concluded by artistic devices to draw the reader back into reconsidering them again from the beginning. Two things that are particularly striking about this reading are that: (1) we have a woman's voice presenting these many verses of the Hebrew Bible; and (2) that it is largely her own experiences that form the subject of concern. That is, the Song is sung (1) by a woman, and (2) about women. Expanding on the significance of this should be an apt conclusion to a thesis that sought a basic foundation for an appreciation for how gender issues are present in the Song.

Consideration of these issues is only now entering the literature on the Song according to Exum.[1] She also proposed that further research would

---

1. "To my knowledge, the present commentary is the first to examine systematically gender differences." Exum, *Song of Songs*, 81.

CONCLUSION: GENDER IN SOLOMON'S SONG OF SONGS

seek to see how different claims were made on male and female readers.[2] This thesis has proposed two such differing claims: men to commit to exclusive romantic relationships; and women to wait until they can accept overtures from such men. This hardly completes the research project suggested by Exum. The thesis above may prove helpful in framing further research into the differing expectations for male and female hearers in the original audience for the Song. But let us conclude the study, as promised above, with an excursus regarding the significance of the reading of the Song as having an implied fictive female author who uses her fictive life experience as exemplary in educating young women, and in educating the whole community through their paying attention to what transpires in the woman-woman dialogue—arguably the meta-dialogue—within which the male-female dialogue takes place.

It has often been observed that the voice of women—either in distinction to men, or even in solidarity with them—is under-represented in the Hebrew Bible. Exum asserts, "In the narratives of the Bible, women are usually minor characters in the stories of men."[3] Even books named after a female lead disappoint us. Mordecai might be the principal protagonist of the book of Esther,[4] though the matter is disputed and complex. Similarly, Boaz might be considered to be something approaching a classical herotype in the romance of Ruth; though here too there is a complex interplay between the main characters. It is, after all, Ruth who is presented twice as voluntarily, even willfully, making exemplary decisions related to personal status that secured the future of Israel. Initially, against her mother-in-law's urging, Ruth chooses to bind her destiny (and that of potential offspring) with Naomi's family, and the extended family in the nation of Israel. So Ruth is first contrasted with Orpah, who "returned to the home of her mother" (שבנה אשה לבית אמה).[5] Later, at the crux of the narrative, Ruth gleans a husband in Boaz, while being contrasted with other women, wont to "go after younger men" (לכת אחרי הבחורים).[6] Yet as countercultural as Ruth may have been in making her choices, the praise associated with them comes

---

2. "How the Song makes different claims upon female and male readers." Ibid., 82.

3. Exum, *Fragmented Women*, 9.

4. "Mordecai is the most important figure in the book." Frederick Bush, *Ruth/Esther*, Word Biblical Commentary 9 (Nashville: Thomas Nelson, 1996), p. 318. See also Fox, *Character and Ideology*, 185.

5. Ruth 1:8; compare Song 8:2 "I want to goad you to enter into my *mother's house*" (אנהגך אביאך אל־בית אמי).

6. Ruth 3:10; compare Song 1:4 "Draw me *after you*, let us run" (משכני אחריך נרוצה).

because of her kindness, not just because of the value of her contributions to a team effort.

The scrolls of Esther and Ruth are somewhat atypical of biblical literature in their explicit presentation of female characters as willful—or even merely explicitly consenting—partners in shaping Israel's history. That is the issue Exum wanted to address in *Fragmented Women*. In fact, Esther and Ruth are typical of a vast host of women who have shaped human history in all times and cultures, but unlike Esther and Ruth, have been generally passed over in its retelling. Exum cites some of Lerner's views in regard to this, to which some extra context is worth adding.

> Like men, women are and always have been agents in history. Since women are half and sometimes more than half of humankind, they always have shared the world and its work equally with men. Women are and have been central, not marginal, to the making of society and to the building of civilisation. Women have also shared with men in preserving collective memory, which shapes the past into cultural tradition, provides the link between generations, and connects past and future. The oral tradition was kept alive in poem and myth, which both men and women created and preserved in folklore, art, and ritual.[7]

In the context of biblical literature, it is particularly interesting to note the common association of women's voices with poem, song, and wisdom.[8] However, it remains fair to say that biblical literature is rather like world literature in microcosm; "the female perspective is muted, if not altogether excluded."[9]

It is the argument of this thesis that Solomon's Song of Songs is precisely the opposite: not only is the female perspective included, it is foregrounded; indeed, it is the Shulamite's lover who is "a minor character in the story of a woman." In the context of the received corpus of canonical biblical literature, that is a notable enough thesis in itself, though it is not an entirely new observation. It is not, however, a radical new biblical perspective on gender, despite some creative readings to that effect, especially in the two volumes of essays on the Song in the Feminist Companion to the Bible series.[10] The Song does not present a feminist utopia—or perhaps it does,

---

7. Gerda Lerner, *Creation of Patriarchy*, 4.

8. Note that Exum was careful to pick out narrative in particular for her criticism, though prophets and psalmists may also be argued to flood poetic biblical literature with male perspectives also.

9. Exum, *Fragmented Women*, 10.

10. Brenner, A *Feminist Companion*, and Brenner and Fontaine, *Song of Songs*.

though that depends very much on what type of feminism we are talking about. The Song implies typical "gender roles," and not such that they are comfortable for the woman, albeit she controls the discourse. Her brothers and the watchmen of the city are problematic characters. She is constrained by convention and wishes she were not, so she could kiss her love in public. In fact, it is pretty much only the discourse that the woman controls, and the free gift of her body and soul to her love. Yet this "space" in which the woman is sovereign expands to being the whole of the universe of the Song. Her sovereignty is not such that her love is uniformly subject to her desires, but rather that there is no conflict of interest between the lovers as they offer and receive love backwards and forwards in the various cameos detailed in the text. But what we see in this relationship of mutual possession is not a "balance of powers." There is power in the Song, and it is balanced; however, romantic love, dyadic male–female love, is not presented as being about minimizing conflicts but about maximizing pleasures. In the Song's vision of gender relations, power is something both lovers experience as overwhelming them. Love itself is the power, and it is a benevolent power that does not set couples against one another, but brings them together.

> There is no other female character in the Bible whom we get to know so well through her intimate and innermost thoughts and feelings.[11]
>
> – Cheryl Exum

שובי שובי השולמית

Come back, come back, O Shulamite!

שובי שובי ונחזה בך

Come back, come back, so we can look at you!

---

11. J. Cheryl Exum, *Fragmented Women*, 25.

Bibliography

Acta Synodi Nationalis, in nomine Domini nostri Iesu Christi. Dordtrecht: Elzevir, 1620.
Alexander, Philip S. *The Targum of Canticles: Translated with a Critical Introduction, Apparatus, and Notes*. The Aramaic Bible 17A. Collegeville, Minnesota: Liturgical, 2003.
Almond, Richard. "Psychological Change in Jane Austen's *Pride and Prejudice*." *Psychoanalytic Study of the Child* 44 (1989) 307–24.
Alter, Robert. *The Art of Biblical Poetry*. New York: Basic Books, 1985.
Ancona, Ronnie, and Ellen Greene, eds. *Gendered Dynamics in Latin Love Poetry*. Baltimore: John Hopkins University Press, 2005.
Anthony, David W. *The Horse, the Wheel, and Language: How Bronze-Age Riders from the Eurasian Steppes Shaped the Modern World*. Princeton: Princeton University Press, 2010.
Appel, Alfred, Jr., and Vladimir Nabokov, "An Interview with Vladimir Nabokov." *Wisconsin Studies in Contemporary Literature* 8 (1967) 127–52.
Arbel, Daphna (Vita). "My Vineyard, my Very Own, is for Myself." In *The Song of Songs, A Feminist Companion to the Bible* (second series) 6, edited by Athalya Brenner and Carole R. Fontaine, 90–101. Sheffield: Sheffield Academic, 2000.
Asher, Nicholas. *Reference to Abstract Objects in Discourse*. Studies in Linguistics and Philosophy 50. Dordrecht: Kluwer Academic, 1993.
Asher, Nicholas, and Alex Lascarides. *Logics of Conversation*. Cambridge: Cambridge University Press, 2001.
Assis, Elie. *Flashes of Fire*. Edinburgh: T&T Clark, 2009.
Austin, John Langshaw. *How to Do Things with Words*. Oxford: Oxford University Press, 1962.
———. *Sense and Sensibilia*. Reconstructed from the manuscript notes by G. J. Warnock. Oxford: Clarendon, 1962.
Baehrens, Willem Adolf, ed. *Kommentar zum Hohelied in Rufins und Hieronymus' Übersetzung*. Die Griechische Christliche Schriftsteller (GCS) 33. Origenes Werke 8. Leipzig: Hinrich, 1925.

Barbiero, Gianni. *Song of Songs: A Close Reading*. Translated by Michael Tait. Supplements to Vetus Testamentum 114. Leiden: Brill, 2011.

Barlow, Adrian. *World and Time: Teaching Literature in Context*. Cambridge Contexts in Literature. Cambridge: Cambridge University Press, 2009.

Bede, The Venerable. *On the Song of Songs and Selected Writings*. Translated by Arthur G. Holder. Classics of Western Spirituality. Mahwah, New Jersey: Paulist, 2011.

Beekman, John, et al. *The Semantic Structure of Written Communication*. 5th revision. Dallas: Summer Institute of Linguistics, 1981.

Beekman, John, and John Callow. *Translating the Word of God*. Grand Rapids: Zondervan, 1974.

Begin, Menachem. *Knesset Record* 46. Jerusalem: August 31, 1966.

Bekker, Immanuel, ed. *Aristoteles Graece*. Volume 2. Berlin: Royal Prussian Academy, 1831.

Belinsky, Vissarion Grigoryevich. "Eugene Onegin: An Encyclopedia of Russian life." In *Russian views of Pushkin's Eugene Onegin*, edited and translated by Sona Stephan Hoisington. Bloomington: Indiana University Press, 1988.

Belwood, Peter. *First Migrants: Ancient Migration in Global Perspective*. Chichester: Wiley-Blackwell, 2013.

Bergant, Diane. *Song of Songs*. Berit Olam. Collegeville: Liturgical, 2001.

Bergen, Robert D., ed. *Biblical Hebrew and Discourse Linguistics*. Summer Institute of Linguistics, 1994.

Berichto, Sidney. *The Song of Songs: With the Book of Ruth, Lamentations, Ecclesiastes and the Book of Esther*. The People's Bible. London: Sinclair-Stevenson, 2000.

Berlin, Adele. *The Dynamics of Biblical Parallelism*. Revised and expanded. Grand Rapids: Eerdmans, 2008.

Berndt, Ronald Murray. *Love Songs of Arnhem Land*. West Melbourne: Nelson, 1976.

Bettan, Israel. *The Five Scrolls: A Commentary on the Song of Songs, Ruth, Lamentations, Ecclesiastes, Esther*. The Jewish Commentary for Bible Readers. Union of American Hebrew Congregations, 1950.

Bierhorst, John, trans. *Ballads of the Lords of New Spain: The Codex Romances de los Señores de la Nueva España*. The William & Bettye Nowlin Series in Art, History, and Culture of the Western Hemisphere. Austin: University of Texas Press, 2009.

———. *Cantares Mexicanos*. Stanford: Stanford University Press, 1985.

Black, Fiona. *The Artifice of Love: Grotesque Bodies and the Song Of Songs*. Library of the Hebrew Bible/Old Testament Studies 392. London: T&T Clark, 2009.

Bloch, Ariel, and Chana Bloch. *The Song of Songs*. Berkeley: University of California Press, 1998.

Boer, Roland. "Keeping it Literal: The Economy of the Song of Songs." *Journal of Hebrew Scriptures* 7/6 (2007) 1–14.

———. *Knockin' on Heaven's Door: The Bible and Popular Culture*. Biblical Limits. London: Routledge, 1999.

Bradley, Henry. "Ghazal." In *A New English Dictionary: On Historical Principles*, edited by James A. Murray, vol. 4: F and G, 147. Oxford: Oxford University Press, 1901.

Brenner, Athalya. "Women Poets and Authors." In *A Feminist Companion to the Song of Songs*, edited by Athalya Brenner, 87–91. Sheffield: JSOT Press, 1993.

———, ed. *A Feminist Companion to the Song of Songs*. Sheffield: JSOT Press, 1993.

Brenner, Athalya, and Carole R. Fontaine, eds. *The Song of Songs*. A Feminist Companion to the Bible (second series) 6. Sheffield: Sheffield Academic, 2000.

Breuer, Josef, and Sigmund Freud. *Studien über Hysterie*. Vienna: Franz Deuticke, 1895.
Brinton, Daniel G. *Ancient Nahuatl Poetry: Containing the Nahuatl Text of 27 poems*. Brinton's Library of Aboriginal American Literature 7 (1890).
Brown, Donald. *Human Universals*. McGraw Hill, 1991.
Burrowes, George. *A Commentary on the Song of Solomon*. Philadelphia: James S. Claxton, 1853.
Bush, Frederick. *Ruth/Esther*. Word Biblical Commentary 9. Nashville: Thomas Nelson, 1996.
Buss, David M. *The Evolution of Desire*. New York: Basic Books, 1994.
Callow, John. "Units and Flow in the Song of Songs." In *Biblical Hebrew and Discourse Linguistics*, edited by Robert D. Bergen. Summer Institute of Linguistics, 1994.
Carr, David M. *The Erotic Word: Sexuality, Spirituality, and the Bible*. Oxford: Oxford University Press, 2003.
Carr, G. Lloyd. *The Song of Solomon*. 2nd ed. Tyndale Old Testament Commentaries 19. Nottingham: Inter-Varsity Press, 2009.
Clarke, Elizabeth. *Politics, Religion and the Song of Songs in Seventeenth-Century England: Rewriting the Bride*. Basingstoke: Palgrave Macmillan, 2011.
Clines, David J. A. *I, He, We and They: A Literary Approach to Isaiah 53*. Journal for the Study of the Old Testament Supplement Series 1. Sheffield: JSOT Press, 1976.
———. "The Image of God in Man." *Tyndale Bulletin* 19 (1968) 53–103.
———. *Interested Parties: The Ideology of Writers and Readers of the Hebrew Bible*. Journal for the Study of the Old Testament Supplement Series (JSOTSS) 205: Gender, Culture, Theory 1. Sheffield: Sheffield Academic, 1995.
———. "Reading the Song of Songs as a Classic." In *A Critical Engagement: Essays on the Hebrew Bible in Honour of J. Cheryl Exum*, Hebrew Bible Monographs 38, edited by David J. A. Clines and Ellen van Wolde, 116–31. Sheffield: Sheffield Phoenix, 2011.
———. "Why Is There a Song of Songs and What Does It Do to You If You Read It?" *Jian Dao: A Journal of Bible and Theology* 1 (1994) 3–27.
Cohen, Gabriel. *Studies in the Five Scrolls: The Song of Songs*. Jerusalem: Ministry of Education and Culture, 1984.
Collins, Terrence. *Line-Forms in Hebrew Poetry: A Grammatical Approach to the Stylistic Study of the Hebrew Prophets*. Studia Pohl: Series Maior 7. Rome: Biblical Institute, 1978.
Cooper, A. M. *Biblical Poetics: A Linguistic Approach*. PhD diss., Yale University, 1976.
Dahlenberg, Jane. *The Motet c. 1580–1630: Sacred Music Based on the Song of Songs*. PhD diss., Chapel Hill: University of North Carolina, 2001.
Davidson, Richard M. *Flame of Yahweh: Sexuality in the Old Testament*. Peabody: Hendrickson, 2007.
———. "The Literary Structure of the Song of Songs Redivivus." *Journal of the Adventist Theological Society* 14 (2003) 44–65.
Dawkins, Richard. *The Selfish Gene*. Oxford: Oxford University Press, 1976.
Delitzsch, Franz. *Commentary on the Song of Songs and Ecclesiastes*. Translated by M. G. Easton. Edinburgh: T&T Clark, 1877.
———. *Das Hohelied* Leipzig: Dörffling und Franke, 1851.
———. *Hoheslied und Koheleth*. Biblischer Commentar über die poetischen Bücher des Altes Testaments, volume 4. Leipzig: Dörffling und Franke, 1875.

Denzin, Norman K. *The Research Act: A Theoretical Introduction to Sociolinguistic Methods*, New York: McGraw, 1978.
Dik, Simon C. *Functional Grammar*. North-Holland Linguistic Series 37. Amsterdam: North-Holland Publishing, 1978.
Dionysius of Halicarnassus. "On Literary Composition." In *Dionysii Halicarnasei Quae Exstant*. Volume 6. Bibliotheca Scriptorum Graecorum Et Romanorum Teubneriana, edited by Ludwig Radermacher, 1–143. Leipzig, 1904.
Dirksen, Peter B. "Song of Songs 3:6-7." *Vetus Testamentum* 39 (1989) 219–25.
Dixon, R. M. W. *Little Eva at Moonlight Creek and Other Aboriginal Song Poems*. Brisbane: University of Queensland Press, 1994.
Dooley, Robert A., and Stephen H. Levinsohn. *Analyzing Discourse*. Summer Institute of Linguistics, 2001.
Dorsey, David. *The Literary Structure of the Old Testament: A Commentary on Genesis-Malachi*. Grand Rapids: Baker, 1999.
———. "Literary Structuring in the Song of Songs." *Journal for the Study of the Old Testament* 46 (1990) 81–96.
Eco, Umberto. *Lector in fabula: La cooperazione interpretativa nei testi narrativi*. Milano: Bompiani, 1979.
———. *The Role Of The Reader: Explorations in the Semiotics of Texts*. Bloomington: Indiana University Press, 1979.
Edzard, Dietz Otto. *Sumerian Grammar*. Handbook of Oriental Studies, Part One: The Ancient Near East and Middle East [HOSANE] 71. Leiden: Brill, 2003.
Eissfeldt, Otto. *The Old Testament: An Introduction, Including the Apocrypha and Pseudepigrapha*. San Francisco: Harper, 1965.
Elliot, M. Timothea. *The Literary Unity of the Canticle*. Frankfurt: Peter Lang, 1989.
Elliott, Mark W. *The Song of Songs and Christology in the Early Church, 381–451*. Studien und Texte zu Antike und Christentum 7. Tübingen: Mohr Siebeck, 2000.
Elwin, Verrier. *The Muria and Their Ghotul*. Special reprint of 1st ed. Dehli: Oxford University Press, 1991.
Engammare, Max. *Le Cantique des Cantiques à la Renaissance: Étude et Bibliographie*. Travaux d'humanisme et Renaissance 277. Geneva: Droz, 1993.
Exum, J. Cheryl. "A Literary and Structural Analysis of the Song of Songs." *Zeitschrift für die alttestamentliche Wissenschaft* 85 (1973) 47–79.
———. *Fragmented Women*. JSOTSup 163. Sheffield: JSOT Press, 1993.
———. *Song of Songs*. Old Testament Library. Louisville: Westminster John Knox, 2005.
———. "Ten Things Every Feminist Should Know about The Song of Songs." In *The Song of Songs. A Feminist Companion to the Bible* (second series) 6, edited by Athalya Brenner and Carole R. Fontaine, 24–35. Sheffield: Sheffield Academic, 2000.
Falk, Marcia Lee. *Love Lyrics from the Bible: A Translation and Literary Study of the Song of Songs*. Bible and Literature Series 4. Sheffield: Almond, 1982.
———. *The Song of Songs: Love Lyrics from the Bible*. San Diego: Harcourt Brace Jovanovich, 1977.
Fineman, Joel. "The Structure of Allegorical Desire." *October* 12 (1980) 46–66.
Flinker, Noam. *The Song of Songs in English Renaissance Literature*. Studies in Renaissance Literature. Woodbridge: D.S. Brewer, 2000.

Fox, Michael V. *Character and Ideology in the Book of Esther*. Studies on Personalities of the Old Testament Columbia: University of South Carolina Press, 1991.

———. *The Song of Songs and the Ancient Egyptian Love Songs*. Madison, Wisconsin: University of Wisconsin Press, 1985.

French, Bryana H., et al. "Sexual Coercion Context and Psychosocial Correlates Among Diverse Males." *Psychology of Men & Masculinity* 15 (2014) 42–53.

Freud, Sigmund. "Über die weibliche Sexualität." *Internationale Zeitschrift für Psychoanalyse* 17 (1931) 317–32.

Fuchs, Esther. "Review of J. Cheryl Exum's *Song of Songs: A Commentary*." *Bible and Critical Theory* 2 (2006) 39.1–39.3.

Fulu, Emma, et al. "Why Do Some Men Use Violence against Women and How Can We Prevent It? Quantitative Findings from the UN Multi-Country Study on Men and Violence in Asia and the Pacific." Bangkok: UNDP, UNFPA, UN Women, and UNV, 2013.

Garrett, Duane and Paul R. House. *Song of Songs/Lamentations*. 2nd ed. Word Bible Commentary 23B. Nashville: Thomas Nelson, 2004.

Geller, Stephen A. *Parallelism in Early Biblical Poetry*. Harvard Semitic Monographs 20. Missoula, Montana: Scholars Press, 1979.

Geertz, Clifford. *Local Knowledge: Further Essays in Interpretative Anthropology*. New York: Basic Books, 1983.

———. *Negara: The Theatre State in Nineteenth-Century Bali*. Princeton: Princeton University Press, 1981.

Gerleman, Gillis. *Ruth/Das Hohelied*. Biblischer Kommentar: Altes Testament (BKAT) 18. Neukirchen-Vluyn: Neukirchener, 1965.

Gianto, Agustinus. *Word Order Variation in the Akkadian of Byblos*. Studia Pohl 15. Roma: Pontificium Institutum Biblicum, 1990.

Giddens, Anthony. *The Transformation of Intimacy: Sexuality, Love and Eroticism in Modern Society*. Stanford, Stanford University Press, 1992.

Ginsburg, Christian David. *The Song of Songs: Translated from the Original Hebrew, with a Commentary, Historical and Critical*. London: Longmans, Green, 1857.

Givón, Talmy. *Context as Other Minds: The Pragmatics of Sociality, Cognition, and Communication*. Amsterdam: John Benjamins, 2005.

———. *Syntax: An Introduction*. Revised edition. 2 volumes. Amsterdam: John Benjamins, 2001.

———. *Topic Continuity in Discourse*. Typological Studies in Language (TSL) 3. Amsterdam: John Benjamins, 1983.

Gleason, H. A. Jr. *Contrastive Analysis in Discourse Structure*. Monograph Series on Languages and Linguistics 21. Georgetown: Georgetown Institute of Languages and Linguistics, 1968.

Goitein, S. D. "The Song of Songs: A Female Composition." In *A Feminist Companion to the Song of Songs*. edited by Athalya Brenner, 58–66. Sheffield: JSOT Press, 1993.

Gordis, Robert. *The Song of Songs and Lamentations: A Study, Modern Translation, and Commentary*. Revised and augmented edition. New York: KTAV, 1974.

Goulder, Michael D. *The Song of Fourteen Songs*. Journal for the Study of the Old Testament Supplement Series 36. Sheffield: JSOT Press, 1986.

Grice, Herbert Paul. "Meaning." *Philosophical Review* 66 (1957) 377–88.

———. *Studies in the Way of Words*. Cambridge, MA: Harvard University Press, 1989.

Griffiths, Paul J. *Song of Songs*. Brazos Theological Commentary on the Bible. Grand Rapids: Brazos, 2011.
Grigson, Wilfred. *The Maria Gonds of Bastar*. Delhi: Oxford University Press, 1991.
Groenendael, Victoria M. Clara van. *Jaranan: The Horse Dance and Trance in East Java*. Leiden: Koninklijk Instituut voor Taal-, Land- en Volkenkunde, 2008.
Grossberg, Daniel. *Centripetal and Centrifugal Structures in Biblical Poetry*. Society of Biblical Literature Monograph Series 39. Atlanta, Georgia: Scholars Press, 1989.
Grosz, Barbara J. et al. "Discourse." In *Foundations of Cognitive Science*, edited by Michael I. Posner, 437-68 in Cambridge, MA: MIT Press, 1993.
Grosz, Barbara J. and Candace L. Sidner, "Attention, Intentions, and the Structure of Discourse." *Computational Linguistics* 12 (1986) 175-204.
Gutwinski, Waldemar. "Cohesion in Spoken and Written Discourse: Ethnic Style and the Transition to Literacy." In *Coherence in Spoken and Written Discourse*, Advances in Discourse Processes 12, edited by D. Tannen, 3-20. Norwood, New Jersey: Ablex, 1976.
Halliday, Michael A. K. "The Linguistic Study of Literary Texts." In *Proceedings of the Ninth International Congress of Linguists*, edited by H. G. Lunt, 302-7. The Hague: Mouton, 1964.
Halliday, Michael A. K. and R. Hasan. *Cohesion in English*. London: Longman, 1976.
Halliday, Michael A. K., and Christian M. I. M. Matthiessen. *An Introduction to Functional Grammar*. 3rd edition. London: Arnold, 2004.
Hasan, R. *Grammatical Cohesion in Spoken and Written English, Part One*. Programme in Linguistics and English Teaching 7. London: Longman, 1968.
Haupt, Paul. "The Book of Canticles." *American Journal of Semitic Languages and Literatures* 18 (1901-02) 193-245.
Hess, Richard S. *Song of Songs*. Baker Commentary on the Old Testament: Wisdom and Psalms. Grand Rapids: Baker, 2005.
Hobbs, Jerry R. "Abduction in Natural Language Understanding." In *Handbook of Pragmatics*, edited by L. Horn and G. Ward, 724-41. Oxford: Blackwell, 2004.
———. *Literature and Cognition*. Stanford: Center for the Study of Language, 1990.
Hobbs, Jerry R. et al. "Interpretation as Abduction." *Artificial Intelligence* 63 (1993) 69-142.
Hofstadter, Douglas. *Gödel, Escher, Bach: An Eternal Golden Braid*. New York: Basic Books, 1979.
———. "What's Gained In Translation." *New York Times* (8 December, 1996) 47-48.
Hotchkiss, Andrew K., et al. "Of Mice and Men (and Mosquitofish): Antiandrogens and Androgens in the Environment." *BioScience* 58 (2008) 1037-50.
Hug, Johann Leonhard von. *Das Hohe Lied in einer noch unversuchten Deutung*. Freyburg, 1813.
———. *Schutzschrift für seine Deutung des Hohen Liedes, und derselben weitere Erläuterungen*. Freyburg: 1816.
Huwiler, Elizabeth. "Song of Songs." In *Proverbs, Ecclesiastes, Song of Songs*. New International Biblical Commentary 12, edited by Roland Edmund Murphy and Elizabeth Huwiler, 219-90. Peabody: Hendrickson, 1999.
Jakobson, Roman. "Linguistics and Poetics." In *Style and Language*, edited by Thomas A. Sebeok, 350-77. Cambridge: MIT Press, 1960.
Jameson, Fredric. *The Political Unconscious: Narrative as a Socially Symbolic Act*. London: Methuen, 1981.

Jastrow, Morris. *The Song of Songs: Being a Collection of Love Lyrics of Ancient Palestine*. Philadelphia & London: J. B. Lippincott Company, 1921.
Jenson, Robert W. *Song of Songs*. Interpretation. Louisville: Westminster John Knox, 2005.
Johnson, Paul R. *The Song of Songs: A Gay Love Poem*. Pomona, CA: Fidelity, 1995.
Kafka, Franz. "Vor dem Gesetz." *Selbstwehr* 9/34 (1915) 2–3.
Kalidasa. *How Urvashi Was Won*. Translated by Velcheru Narayana Rao and David Dean Shulman. The Clay Sanskrit Library 48. New York University Press, 2009.
Kamp, Hans (Johan Anthony Willem). "A Theory of Truth and Semantic Representation." In *Formal Methods in the Study of Language*. Mathematical Centre Tracts 135, edited by J. A. G. Groenendijk et al., 277–322. Amsterdam: 1981.
Kamp, Hans (Johan Anthony Willem) and Uwe Reyle. *From Discourse to Logic: Introduction to Modeltheoretic Semantics of Natural Language, Formal Logic and Discourse Representation Theory*. Dordrecht: Kluwer Academic, 1993.
Keel, Othmar. *Das Hohelied*. Zürcher Bibelkommentare: Altes Testament (ZBAT) 18. Zürich: Theologischer Verlag, 1986.
———. *The Song of Songs: A Continental Commentary*. Continental Commentary Series. Philadelphia: Fortress, 1994.
Keil, Carl Friedrich and Franz Delitzsch. *Proverbs—Ecclesiastes—Song of Solomon*. Translated by James Martin. Keil and Delitzsch Commentary on the Old Testament 6. Grand Rapids: Eerdmans, 1982.
Kelefang, Bonolo. *Sexuality Education In Sweden: A Study Based on Research and Young People's Service Providers in Gothenburg*. MSc (social work) diss., Göteborgs Universtat, 2008.
Kessler, R. *Some Poetical and Structural Features of the Song of Songs*. Leeds University Oriental Society Monograph Series 8. Leeds: University of Leeds, Department of Semitic Languages and Literatures, 1957.
Keogh, Ray. *Nurulu Songs of the West Kimberlys*. PhD diss., University of Sydney, 1990.
King, J. Christopher. *Origen on the Song of Songs as the Spirit of Scripture*. Oxford: Oxford University Press, 2005.
Kleine, Michael. "Beyond Triangulation: Ethnography, Writing, and Rhetoric." *Journal of Advanced Composition* 10 (1990) 117–25.
Kline, Meredith G. "Bible Book of the Month: The Song of Songs." *Christianity Today* 3 (1959) 22–23, 39.
Koentjaraningrat. *Javanese Culture*. Singapore: Oxford University Press, 1989.
Koentjaraningrat. *Some Social-Anthropological Observations on Gotong Royong Practices in Two Villages of Central Java*. Translated by Claire Holt. Cornell Modern Indonesia Project Monograph Series. Ithaca: Cornell University Press, 1961 [1923].
Kramer, Samuel Noah. *The Sumerians: Their History, Culture, and Character*. Chicago University Press, 1963.
Krinetzki, Günter. *Das Hohe Lied: Kommentar zu Gestalt and Kerygma eines alttestamenlichen Liebeslied*. Düsseldorf: Patmos, 1964.
———. *Kommentar zum Hohenlied: Bildsprache und theologische Botschaft*. Beiträge zur biblischen Exegese und Theologie [BBET] 16. Frankfurt: Peter Lang, 1981.
Kripke, Saul. "Semantical Considerations on Modal Logic." *Acta Philosophica Fennica* 16 (1963) 83–94.
Krishna, Anand. *Kidung Agung*. Jakarta: Gramedia, 2007.

Kunst, Jaap. *Indonesian Music and Dance: Traditional Music and its Interaction with the West; A Compilation Of Articles (1934–1952)* Originally published in Dutch. Translated by Ernst Heins et al. Amsterdam: University of Amsterdam Ethnomusicology Centre, 1994.

Kurylowicz, Jerzy. *Studies in Semitic Grammar and Metrics.* Prace Jezykoznawe 67. London: Curzon, 1973.

Laclos, Pierre Choderlos de. *Les Liaisons Dangereuses.* Paris: Durand Neveu, 1782.

LaCocque, André. *Romance She Wrote.* Harrisburg: Trinity International, 1998.

Lakoff, George. *Women, Fire and Dangerous Things.* Chicago: University of Chicago Press, 1987.

Lakoff, George, and Mark Turner. *More Than Cool Reason: A Field Guide to Poetic Metaphor.* Chicago: University of Chicago Press, 1989.

Lambrecht, Knud. *Information Structure and Sentence Form: Topic, Focus, and the Mental Representations of Discourse Referents.* Cambridge Studies in Linguistics 71. Cambridge: Cambridge University Press, 1994.

Lamparter, Helmut. *Das Buch der Sehnsucht: Das Buch Ruth—Das Hohe Lied—Die Klagelieder.* Die Botschaft des Alten Testaments [BAT]: Erläuterungen alttestamentlicher Schriften 16/2. Stuttgart: Calwer, 1962.

Landsberger, Franz. "Poetic Units within the Song of Songs." Journal of Biblical Literature 73 (1954) 203-16.

Landy, Francis. *Paradoxes of Paradise: Identity And Difference in the Song of Songs.* 2nd edition. Sheffield: Sheffield Phoenix, 2011.

Legge, James, trans. *The Li Ki: Part 2.* Sacred Books of the East 29. Oxford: Clarendon, 1885.

Leick, Gwendolyn. *Sex and Eroticism in Mesopotamian Literature.* London: Routledge, 1994.

Lerner, Gerda. *The Creation of Patriarchy.* New York: Oxford University Press, 1986.

Lessing, Doris. "Political Correctness." *The New York Times.* 22 June, 1992.

Levinson, Stephen C. *Presumptive Meanings: The Theory of Generalized Conversational Implicature.* Cambridge, MA: MIT Press, 2000.

Lewis, Clive Staples. *The Allegory of Love: A Study in Medieval Tradition.* Oxford: Clarendon, 1936.

Lewis, David Kellogg. *Counterfactuals.* Oxford: Blackwell, 1973.

———. "Truth in Fiction." *American Philosophical Quarterly* 15 (1978) 37–46.

Littledale, Richard Frederick. *A Commentary on the Song of Songs.* London: Joseph Masters, 1869.

Ljungberg, Bo-Krister. "Genre and Form Criticism in Old Testament Exegesis." In *Biblical Hebrew and Discourse Linguistics*, edited by Robert D. Bergen, 415–33. Summer Institute of Linguistics, 1994.

Lane, Edward William. *Arabic-English Lexicon: Derived from the Best and the Most Copious Eastern Sources* London: Willams & Norgate, 1863.

Laclos, Pierre Choderlos de. *Les Liaisons Dangereuses.* Paris: Durand Neveu, 1782.

Longman, Tremper, III. *Song of Songs.* The New International Commentary on the Old Testament (NICOT). Grand Rapids: Eerdmans, 2001.

Loretz, Oswald. *Studien zur althebräischen Poesie.* Kevelaer: Butzon & Bercker, 1971.

Lunn, Nicholas P. *Word-Order Variation in Biblical Hebrew Poetry: Differentiating Pragmatics and Poetics.* Milton Keynes: Paternoster, 2006.

Lyons, Andrew, & Harriet Lyons. *Irregular Connections: A History of Anthropology and Sexuality*. Omaha: University of Nebraska Press, 2004.

Malinowski, Bronisław. *A Diary in the Strict Sense of the Term*. New York: Harcourt, 1967.

Mann, William C., and Sandra A. Thompson, eds. *Discourse Description: Diverse Linguistic Analyses of a Fund-Raising Text*. Pragmatics & Beyond New Series 16. Amsterdam: John Benjamins, 1992.

———. "Rhetorical Structure Theory: Towards a Functional Theory of Text Organization." *Text* 8 (1988) 243–81.

Mariaselvam, Abraham. *The Song of Songs and Ancient Tamil Love Poems: Poetry and Symbolism*. Analecta Biblica 118. Roma: Pontificium Institutum Biblicum, 1988.

Martin, J. R. "Cohesion and Texture." In *The Handbook of Discourse Analysis*, Deborah Shiffren, et al., 35–53. Oxford: Blackwell, 2001.

Matter, E. Ann. *The Voice of My Beloved: The Song of Songs in Western Medieval Christianity*. University of Pennsylvania Press Middle Ages Series. Philadelphia: University of Pennsylvania Press, 1992.

McGinnis, Mark. *Contributions of Selected Rhetorical Devices to a Biblical Theology of the Song of Songs*. Eugene, OR: Wipf & Stock, 2011.

McLuhan, Marshall. *Understanding Media: The Extensions of Man*. New York: McGraw Hill, 1964.

Meij, Dick van der. "Kakawin Sutasoma and Kakawin Nāgara Kṛtāgama." *Bijdragen tot de Taal-, Land- en Volkenkunde* 167 (2011) 322–32.

Milton, John. *The Reason of Church-Government Urg'd against Prelaty*. 2 books. London: February, 1642.

Mithun, Marianne. "Is Basic Word Order Universal?" In *Coherence and Grounding in Discourse*, Typological Studies in Language 11, edited by Russell S. Tomlin, 281–328. Amsterdam: John Benjamins, 1987.

Murphy, Roland Edmund. *The Song of Songs*. Hermeneia. Minneapolis: Fortress, 1990.

———. "The Unity of the Song of Songs." *Vetus Testamentum* 29 (1979) 436–43.

Noegel, Scott B., and Gary A. Rendsburg. *Solomon's Vineyard: Literary and Linguistic Studies in the Song of Songs*. Ancient Israel and its Literature. Atlanta: Society of Biblical Literature, 2009.

O'Brien, Kate. *Sutasoma: The Ancient Tale of a Buddha-Prince from a 14th Century Javanese Kakawin*. Bangkok: Orchid, 2009.

O'Connor, Murphy. *Hebrew Verse Structure*. Winona Lake, Indiana: Eisenbrauns, 1980.

Paavola, Sami. "Abduction through Grammar, Critic, and Methodeutic." *Transactions of the Charles S. Peirce Society* 40 (2004) 245–70.

Palestrina, Giovanni Pierluigi, da. *Motettorum quinque vocibus, liber quartus*. Rome: Alessandro Gardano, 1584.

Paul, Shalom L. "The Plural of Ecstasy in Mesopotamian Biblical Love Poetry." In *Biblical, Epigraphic, and Semitic Studies in Honor of Jonas C. Greenfield*, edited by Ziony Zevit et al., 585–97. Winona Lake, IN: Eisenbrauns, 1995.

Penner, Todd, and Caroline Vander Stichele. *Mapping Gender in Ancient Religious Discourses*. Atlanta: Society of Biblical Literature, 2010.

Pike, Kenneth L. *Linguistic Concepts: An Introduction to Tagmemics*. Lincoln: University of Nebraska Press, 1982.

Pinker, Steven. *The Blank Slate: The Modern Denial of Human Nature*. London: Alan Lane, 2002.

Plath, Sylvia. "Daddy." 12 October 1962. Published posthumously in *Ariel*. London: Faber and Faber, 1965.

Polyani, Livia. "The Linguistic Structure of Discourse." In *The Handbook of Discourse Analysis*, edited by Deborah Schiffrin et al, 265–81. Malden, MA: Blackwell, 2008.

Pope, Marvin H. *Song of Songs*. Anchor Bible. 2 volumes. Garden City: Doubleday, 1977.

Pope, Alexander. *An Essay on Man*. 4 volumes. London: 1732–1734.

———. "Preface." In *The Iliad of Homer*. Volume 1. London: W. Bowyer for Bernard Lintott, 1715–1720.

Provan, Iain W. "The Terrors of the Night: Love, Sex, and Power in Song of Songs 3." In *The Way of Wisdom: Essays in Honor of Bruce K. Waltke*. Edited by J. I. Packer and Sven K. Soderlund, 150-67. Grand Rapids: Zondervan, 2000.

Pushkin, Aleksandr Sergeevich. *Eugene Onegin: A Novel in Verse*. Translated with commentary by Vladimir Nabokov. 2nd edition. 2 volumes. Princeton: Princeton University Press, 1990.

Putnam, Linda L. "Images of the Communication–Discourse Relationship." *Discourse & Communication* 2 (2008) 339–45.

Quieroz, João, and Floyd Merrell. "Abduction: Between Subjectivity and Objectivity." *Semiotica* 153 (2005) 1–7.

Raabe, Paul R. *Psalm Structures: A Study of Psalms with Refrains*. JSOTSup 104. Sheffield: JSOT Press, 1990.

Rabin, Chaim Menachem. "The Song of Songs and Tamil Love Poetry." *Studies in Religion* 3 (1973) 205–19.

Reese, Brian, et al. *Reference Manual for the Analysis and Annotation of Rhetorical Structure (Version 1.0)*. Austin, Texas: Departments of Linguistics and Philosophy University of Texas at Austin, 2007.

Riegel, Jeffrey. "Eros, Introversion, and the Beginnings of Shijing Commentary." *Harvard Journal of Asiatic Studies* 57 (1997) 143–77.

Richards, Ivor Armstrong. *The Philosophy of Rhetoric*. Oxford: Oxford University Press, 1936.

Robert, A., and R. Tourney. *Le Cantique des Cantiques*. Paris: J. Gabalda et Cie, 1963.

Roberts, D. Phillip. *Let Me See Your Form: Seeking Poetic Structure in the Song of Songs*. Studies in Judaism. Lanham: University Press of America, 2007.

Rudolf, Wilhelm. *Das Buch Ruth—Das Hohe Lied—Die Klagelieder*. Gütersloh: G. Mohn, 1962.

Russell, D. A., ed. *Quntillian: The Orator's Education*. Books 1–12. Loeb Classical Library 124-127, 494. Cambridge, MA: Harvard University Press, 2001.

Schwab, George M. *The Song of Songs' Cautionary Message Concerning Human Love*. New York: Lang, 2002.

Scott, Craig. *Pagan Sex, Puritan Sex*. Paris: Olympia, 2013.

Searle, John Rogers. "The Logical Status of Fictional Discourse." *New Literary History* 6 (1974) 319–32.

———. *Speech Acts: An Essay in the Philosophy of Language*. Cambridge: Cambridge University Press, 1969.

Sears, Laurie Jo., ed. *Fantasizing the Feminine in Indonesia*. Durham: Duke University Press, 1996.

Segal, Benjamin J. *The Song of Songs: A Woman in Love*. Jerusalem, New York: Geffen, 2009.

Segert, Stanislav. "Die Versform des Hohenliedes." In *Charisteria orientalia praecipue ad Persiam pertinentia*, edited by Felix Tauer et al, 285-99. Prague: Nakladatelství Ceskoslovenské Akademie Věd, 1956.

Shea, William H. "The Chiastic Structure of the Song of Songs." *Zeitschrift für die alttestimentliche Wissenschaft* 92 (1980): 378.

Shelley, Percy Bysshe. "Ozymandias." *The Examiner* 524 (11 January, 1818) 24. [Autograph: Bodleian Library MS Shelley e.4, fol. 85r.]

Shimasaki, Katsuomi. *Focus Structure in Biblical Hebrew: A Study of Word Order and Information Structure*. Bethesda, MD: CDL, 2002.

Sgall, Petr, et al.. *The Meaning of the Sentence in its Semantic and Pragmatic Aspects*. Edited by Jacob L. May. Dordrecht: D. Reidel, 1986.

Skinner, Anthony David. *Gershom Scholem: A Life in Letters, 1914-1982*. Cambridge, MA: Harvard University Press, 2002.

Smith, Yancey Warren. *The Mystery of Anointing: Hippolytus' Commentary on the Song of Songs in Social and Critical Contexts*. Piscataway, NJ: Gorgias, 2013.

Snaith, John G. *The Song of Songs*. New Century Bible Commentary. Grand Rapids: Eerdmans, 1993.

Stadelmann, Luis. *Love and Politics: A New Commentary on the Song of Songs*. New York: Paulist, 1992.

Stankiewicz, E. "Centripetal and Centrifugal Structures in Poetry." *Semiotica* 38 (1982) 217-42.

Symons, Donald. *The Evolution of Human Sexuality*. Oxford: Oxford University Press, 1979.

Tanner, J. Paul. "The Message of the Song of Songs." *Bibliotecha Sacra* 154 (1997) 142-61.

Travis, Roger. *Allegory and the Tragic Chorus in Sophocles' Oedipus at Colonus*. Lanham, Maryland: Rowman & Littlefield, 1999.

Treat, Jay Curry. *Lost Keys: Text and Interpretation in Old Greek "Song of Songs" and its Earliest Manuscript Witnesses*. PhD diss., University of Pennsylvania, 1996.

Trible, Phyllis. *God and the Rhetoric of Sexuality*. Philadelphia: Fortress, 1978.

Turner, Mark. "Aspects of the Invariance Hypothesis." *Cognitive Linguistics* 1 (1990): 247-56.

Uehlinger, Christoph. "Review of Cheryl J. Exum, Song of Songs." *Review of Biblical Literature* 9 (2007) 202-11.

Urgelles-Coll, Miriam. *The Syntax and Semantics of Discourse Markers*. Continuum Studies in Theoretical Linguistics. London: Continuum, 2010.

Valladares, Hérica. "The Lover as a Model Viewer: Gendered Dynamics in Propertius 1.3." In *Gendered Dynamics in Latin Love Poetry*, edited by Ronnie Ancona and Ellen Greene, 206-42. Baltimore: John Hopkins University Press, 2005.

Valin, Robert D., van, Jr. "Semantic Macroroles in Role and Reference Grammar." In *Semantische Rollen*, edited by Rolf Kailuweit and Martin Hummel, 62-82. Tübingen: Narr, 2004.

Valin, Robert D., van, Jr. "A Synopsis of Role and Reference Grammar." *In Advances in Role and Reference Grammar*, edited by Robert D. van Valin, 1-164. Amsterdam: John Benjamins, 1993.

Valin, Robert D., van, Jr., and Randy J. LaPolla. *Syntax: Structure, Meaning and Function*. Cambridge Textbooks in Linguistics. Cambridge: Cambridge University Press, 1997.

Vern, Robyn. *The Relevance of Linguistic Evidence to the Early Dating of the Archaic Poetry of the Hebrew Bible*. Phd Diss., University Of Sydney, 2008.
Wahl, T. P. *Strophic Structure of Individual Laments in Psalms Books I and II*. PhD diss., Union Theological Seminary, 1977.
Walton, Susan Pratt. *Heavenly Nymphs and Earthly Delights: Javanese Female Singers, Their Music and Their Lives*. PhD diss., University of Michigan, 1996.
———. *Mode in Javanese Music*. Monographs in International Studies: Southeast Asia Series 67. Athens, OH: Ohio University Center for International Studies, 1987.
———. *Sindèn and Patet*. MA diss., University of Michigan, 1974.
Weintrieb, Andrew N. *Dangdut Stories: A Social and Musical History of Indonesia's Most Popular Music*. New York: Oxford University Press, 2010.
Wendland, Ernst R. "Seeking the Path through a Forest of Symbols: A Figurative and Structural Survey of the Song of Songs." *Journal of Translation and Textlinguistics* 7 (1995) 13–59.
Williams, Walter L. *Javanese Lives: Women and Men in Modern Indonesian Society*. New Jersey: Rutgers University Press, 1991.
Würthwein, Ernst. *Die fünf Megilloth: Ruth, Das Hohelied, Esther, Der Prediger, Die Klagelieder*. Handbuch zum Alten Testament, 1:18. Tübingen: Mohr, 1969.
Yamashita, Shinji. *Bali and Beyond: Explorations in the Anthropology of Tourism*. Berghahn, 2003.
Young, Ian. "Notes on the Language of 4QCantb." *Journal of Jewish Studies* 52 (2001) 122–31.
Zevit, Ziony. "Roman Jakobson, Psycholinguistics, and Biblical Poetry." *Journal of Biblical Literature* 109 (1990) 385–401.
Zoetmulder, Josephus Petrus. *Kalangwan: A Survey of Old Javanese Literature*. Koninklijk Instituut voor Taal-, Land- en Volkenkunde Translation Series 16. The Hague: Martinus Nijhoff, 1974.

www.ingramcontent.com/pod-product-compliance
Lightning Source LLC
Chambersburg PA
CBHW071233230426
43668CB00011B/1417